MUSIC IN THE MEDIEVAL AND RENAISSANCE UNIVERSITIES

Da Capo Press Music Reprint Series

GENERAL EDITOR

FREDERICK FREEDMAN

VASSAR COLLEGE

MUSIC IN THE MEDIEVAL AND RENAISSANCE UNIVERSITIES

By
NAN COOKE CARPENTER

DA CAPO PRESS • NEW YORK • 1972

Library of Congress Cataloging in Publication Data

Carpenter, Nan Cooke.
Music in the medieval and Renaissance universities.

(Da Capo Press music reprint series)
A revision of the author's thesis, Yale.
Includes bibliographical references.
1. Music in universities and colleges—Europe.
2. Music—History and criticism—Medieval. 3. Music
—History and criticism—16th century. 4. Univer-
sities and colleges—Europe. I. Title.
[ML190.C33   1972]   780.7'29'4   70-171380
ISBN 0-306-70453-6

This Da Capo Press edition of
Music in the Medieval and Renaissance Universities
is an unabridged republication of the first edition
published in Norman, Oklahoma, 1958. It is reprinted by special arrangement with the University of
Oklahoma Press.

Published by Da Capo Press, Inc.
A Subsidiary of Plenum Publishing Corporation
227 West 17th Street
New York, New York 10011

MUSIC

IN THE MEDIEVAL AND
RENAISSANCE UNIVERSITIES

MUSIC

IN THE MEDIEVAL AND
RENAISSANCE UNIVERSITIES

NAN COOKE CARPENTER

NORMAN : UNIVERSITY OF OKLAHOMA PRESS

By Nan Cooke Carpenter

Rabelais and Music (Chapel Hill, 1954)

Music in the Medieval and Renaissance Universities
(Norman, 1958)

*The publication of this book has been aided by a grant
from the* Ford Foundation.

Library of Congress Catalog Card Number: 58–11604

Copyright 1958 by the University of Oklahoma Press, Publishing Division of the
University. Composed and printed at Norman, Oklahoma, U.S.A., by the University
of Oklahoma Press. First edition.

PREFACE

THE GREAT EMPHASIS upon music in colleges and universities of our day is one of the most heartening aspects of our culture. In view of the strong interest in this subject at all levels of academic life, an understanding of the position of music in the early universities should be valuable in heightening our understanding of the present. Indeed, a backward glance at music as a field of higher learning some centuries ago shows us certain ties linking present-day musical studies with those of the earliest universities in an unbroken tradition—for example, the division of this discipline into theory and practice, with continuing development in both areas. But although many phases of the history of music have been thoroughly studied in recent years, there has been no comprehensive investigation of the study and cultivation of music as a university discipline.

Music in the Medieval and Renaissance Universities, presenting the history of music as a subject of higher learning from the founding of the universities until the end of the Renaissance (*ca.* 1600), is intended to fill this hiatus. Introductory material here includes a survey of music among the Greeks, in the Roman rhetorical schools, and as a liberal art in monastic and cathedral schools of the Middle Ages. The largest portion of the book centers upon the study of music in fourteen universities representative of the medieval period, when music held a high place among the mathematical disciplines of the quadrivium, and in nineteen universities flourishing during the fifteenth and sixteenth centuries. As a conclusion, factual information about the academic aspect of music is evaluated, and significant relationships between university studies and the development of the art of music in Italy, France, Germany, and England are pointed out.

In this book, for the first time, statutes and other rulings bearing upon music in old university records are compiled, providing a basis upon which music as a subject of higher learning may be judged. Many medieval and Renaissance musical treatises, designed for or resulting from university studies, are surveyed and related to the teaching of music. University life in general is illuminated in a number of striking and unusual ways. And, finally, the very real influence which the cultivation of music in the universities has had upon the development of the art of music in western Europe is consistently indicated.

One must not assume, however, that *Music in the Medieval and Renaissance Universities* is the last word on the subject. On the contrary, the book presents a groundwork of basic information which, one hopes, will stimulate further and more detailed studies of various kinds in the history of music, literature, philosophy, and education.

Although this book has been completely rewritten during the past few years, it was prepared originally as a doctoral dissertation at Yale University; I am indebted to Professor Leo Schrade for having suggested music in the universities as a topic for research and for having directed the original study. For unvarying kindness and courteous assistance, I should like to express my warm appreciation to members of the staffs of the Sterling Memorial Library of Yale University, the Henry E. Huntington Library, the Cambridge University Library, the Bodleian Library, and the Montana State University Library. I wish to thank the editors of the *Journal of Research in Music Education* (together with the Music Educators National Conference) and of the *Musical Quarterly* for generous permission to reprint several short sections of this book which were first published as articles in these periodicals: "The Study of Music at the University of Oxford in the Middle Ages," *Journal of Research in Music Education,* Vol. I (1953), 11–20; "The Study of Music at the University of Paris in the Middle Ages," *ibid.,* Vol. II (1954), 119–33; "The Study of Music at the University of Oxford in the Renaissance," *Musical Quarterly,* Vol. XLI (1955), 191–214. I am also most grateful to the Committee on Research, Montana State University, for providing funds, and to Miss Jeannette Fellheimer for friendly and competent assistance in checking many notes in the Yale Library.

Adequate acknowledgment of all the help and encouragement, tangible and intangible, that has come to me during more than a decade of work on this book would require many pages. It gives me great pleasure, however, to express my deepest gratitude to numerous associates from the Yale years now scattered across the country; to other more recently acquired friends in the academic world, from the Athenaeum in Pasadena to the Garden House Hotel in Cambridge; to members of my family in Virginia; to certain very dear colleagues at Montana State University; and to all others who have contributed spiritually or materially, in large ways or in small, to the making of this book.

Nan Cooke Carpenter

Missoula, Montana
May 30, 1958

ABBREVIATIONS

AfMf:	*Archiv für Musikforschung*
AfMw:	*Archiv für Musikwissenschaft*
JAMS:	*Journal of the American Musicological Society*
KmJb:	*Kirchenmusicalisches Jahrbuch*
MfMg:	*Monatshefte für Musikgeschichte*
MIGM:	*Mitteilungen der internationalen Gesellschaft für Musikwissenschaft*
PMLA:	*Publications of the Modern Language Association*
SIMG:	*Sammelbände der internationalen Musikgesellschaft*
VfMw:	*Vierteljahrsschrift für Musikwissenschaft*
ZfMw:	*Zeitschrift für Musikwissenschaft*

CONTENTS

ILLUSTRATIONS

MUSIC
IN THE MEDIEVAL AND
RENAISSANCE UNIVERSITIES

I. THE STUDY
OF MUSIC
BEFORE THE FOUNDING
OF THE MEDIEVAL
UNIVERSITIES

i. MUSICAL STUDIES AMONG THE GREEKS AND
IN THE ROMAN RHETORICAL SCHOOLS

AMONG THE GREEKS, from whom the Western world inherited the fundamental forms and substance of its instruction, the study of music followed two trends, one practical, the other speculative. Instruction in practical music—*mousiké* in its broadest sense, comprising poetry, music, and the dance—was an outgrowth, in very early times at least, of religious necessities, of the need for trained men to participate in activities connected with religious cults and agones. The great sacrificial festivals held annually by each city-state *(polis)* in honor of its own particular deity relied upon music to make these ceremonies effective, with choirs of singers praising the god, players on the kithara and aulos, and musico-gymnastic contests in which both individuals and choruses participated. The Greek drama, too, which arose in the sixth century as an outgrowth of religious practices, relied heavily upon music, for the lines of the chorus were sung throughout, sometimes with aulos accompaniment.[1] Music also had an important place in religious practices associated with military training, the aulos, lyre,

[1] Curt Sachs, *Die Musik der Antike* (Wildpark-Potsdam, 1928), 28.

3

and trumpet being used to inspire bravery.[2] Although training of the great religious choirs was a state affair relying upon oral tradition handed down from one generation to the next through actual participation, there were also individual schools for the teaching of music—Terpander, for instance, is said to have had his own school of instrumentalists and singers. Plato's *Laws* is the *locus classicus* for a discussion of education in the light of religion and the state, and in his system music everywhere predominates. Young people are to begin their education with music—the lyre to be studied for three years, along with reading, writing, and poetry—and they are to take part in annual festivals and contests supervised by professional musicians (*Laws,* VI and VII). Aristotle, too (*Politics,* VIII), believed that young people should learn music (stopping short of virtuosity) in order to be able to judge it and to use their leisure time intelligently. Two centuries after Plato, the historian Polybius speaks of musical training related to religious activities, stating that everyone studied music until his thirtieth year and that young people were required to take part in annual choral dances in the theatre, accompanied by the aulos (*Histories,* IV, 20). Still later, Cicero tells us how musicians flourished in Greece, where proof of the highest education was found in instrumental and vocal music (*Tusculan Disputations,* I, ii).

Closely connected with musical training to meet religious needs and to preserve the state religion was the cultivation of music for its ethical values—for its effects in building character and in shaping the soul harmoniously. For from early times, various attributes of music were thought to have definite effects upon the emotions. The shrill tones of the aulos (a reed instrument somewhat like the modern oboe), associated with the cult of Dionysus, could drive men to frenzy, while the soothing note of the kithara (lyre), the instrument dedicated to Apollo, calmed and moderated human passions. Simi-

---

[2] Plutarch praised highly the musical training given Grecian youths to fit them for all the serious occupations of life, especially for the perils of war; in time of war some nations, he says, used the aulos, others the lyre, and others the trumpet. See *Plutarchi De Musica* (ed. by Ricardus Volkmann) (Leipzig, 1856), 30–31. Plutarch's treatise, also available in an English translation by J. H. Brombey (Chiswick, 1822), contains much information about the cultivation of music in religion and education.

larly, such musico-poetic forms as the hymn, threnody, paean, and dithyramb each had a definite ethos, a definite emotional effect; and in religious ceremonies certain *nomoi* (fixed melodic patterns, each with its own ethos) were used for specific parts of the ritual. Most important of all, each of the *harmoniai,* the nontransposing octave scales brought into a system by the time of Aristoxenus (*ca.* 320 B.C.), was thought to have a particular ethos of its own, probably owing to the pitch of the scale: the Dorian, for example, was considered manly, energetic, and bellicose; the Phrygian, ecstatic and frenzied; the Lydian, sad and mournful. These concepts of the effects of music were basic to Plato's idea of building character and training the mind for right judgment, and of shaping the soul, making it rhythmical and harmonious—dominating themes in Plato's educational policy, which aimed at training the citizen to be of greatest service to the state.[3] Aristotle, too, believed firmly in the ethical powers of music (clearly explained in Book VIII of his *Politics*). And so it was for ethical as well as religious reasons that

[3] The great sophist Protagoras, describing the educational plan of his day, speaks of training in music, poetry, and gymnastics. See Plato, *Protagoras, The Dialogues of Plato* (tr. by Benjamin Jowett), (Oxford, 1924), I, 326:

> Then, again, the teachers of the lyre take similar care that their young disciple is temperate and gets into no mischief; and when they have taught him the use of the lyre, they introduce him to the poems of other excellent poets, who are the lyric poets; and these they set to music, and make their harmonies and rhythms quite familiar to the children's souls, in order that they may learn to be more gentle, and harmonious, and rhythmical, and so more fitted for speech and action; for the life of man in every part has need of harmony and rhythm. Then they send them to the master of gymnastic, in order that their bodies may better minister to the virtuous mind, and that they may not be compelled through bodily weakness to play the coward in war or on any other occasion.

Of the many passages in Plato's works wherein he expressed the idea that music makes for an harmonious soul, the following lines from the *Republic, Dialogues of Plato*, III, iii, 402, form a good epitome:

> And therefore, I said, Glaucon, musical training is a more potent instrument than any other, because rhythm and harmony find their way into the inward places of the soul, on which they mightily fasten, imparting grace, and making the soul of him who is rightly educated graceful, or of him who is ill-educated ungraceful; and also because he who has received this true education of the inner being will most shrewdly perceive omissions or faults in art and nature, and with a true taste while he praises and rejoices over and receives into his soul the good, and becomes noble and good, he will justly blame and hate the bad.

both great philosophers would have Grecian youth study music and eurhythmics along with poetry until they reached the late teens—*mousiké* taught by professional musicians and poets.[4]

Such training in practical music was preliminary to the second kind of musical culture which grew up among the Greek philosophers: rationalistic explanations of music as a part of mathematics, of universal harmony—indeed, the harmony of the universe in a form perceptible to man. Basic to the inclusion of music with other mathematical sciences was the Pythagorean doctrine that number is the principle of all things (a doctrine which arose, according to traditional reports, from Pythagoras' discovery of natural laws governing the relationship between the length of a string and its vibrations, and his subsequent application of these laws to the whole cosmos and to all human life),[5] that harmony resulted from simple numerical proportions, and that earthly beauty was simply the reflection of spiritual order and proportion. Following Pythagoras, the sophists included the Pythagorean *mathémata* (arithmetic, geometry, astronomy, and music) within the cycle of higher culture, adding these mathematical disciplines to the three formal arts (grammar, rhetoric, and dialectic) and thereby establishing a tradition of liberal arts which carried over into the Middle Ages.[6] The mathematical studies became the intermediate stage in Plato's system of education for the free man, after which select students began the study of philosophy proper, the science of the good (*Laws*, VII). Thus Plato led the student from actual music, through the mathematical studies, to the world of ideas, the recognition of eternal truths. Aristotle's system differed only in empha-

---

[4] Paintings on ancient Greek vases show school scenes of this type: see Joseph Clark Hoppin, *A Handbook of Attic Red-Figured Vases* (Cambridge, Mass., 1919), I, 215, and Ernst Pfuhl, *Masterpieces of Greek Drawings and Paintings* (tr. by J. D. Beazley) (London, 1926), plate 47. One such painting by Duris (*ca.* 470 B.C.) shows a youth seated before a bearded *kitharistés*, each playing a kithara, while a second youth stands before a *grammatistés* unrolling a scroll on which verses are written. Another scene depicts a youth standing before his teacher, receiving instruction in playing the double aulos, while a second pupil learns to write.

[5] Aristotle, *Metaphysics*, I, v, 1–5.

[6] For a brilliant account of the evolution of the liberal arts among the Greeks, see "The Sophists," in Werner Jaeger, *Paideia: the Ideals of Greek Culture* (tr. by Gilbert Highet) (New York, 1939–44), I, 283–328.

sis;[7] like Plato, Aristotle would lead the student (grounded in literature and practical music) from the real world to the ideal, advocating (in his *Metaphysics,* especially Book IX) the study of mathmatics, including music, before the metaphysics, the study of pure forms and ideas.

The Western world inherited from the ancient Greeks, then, a culture comprising two different traditions of musical studies: music in connection with poetry, the two inseparable and originally allied with religious practices; and music related not to literature but to mathematics, being one of the four mathematical disciplines (all having a common basis in ratio and proportion) which preceded the study of philosophy. The real musician for the Greeks was the philosopher, not the professional singer or instrumentalist.[8] In neither the practical nor the theoretical tradition, however, did the Greek philosophers establish a system for instruction in music, nor did they formulate a fixed curriculum of studies. What books they used, if any, we do not know, although some theoretical writings on music from Grecian antiquity have come down to us.[9]

[7] In his long discussion on music in Book VIII of the *Politics,* Aristotle questions the value of instruction in practical music and finds musical virtuosity degrading: "Nay," he says, "we call professional performers vulgar; no freeman would play or sing unless he were intoxicated or in jest"—an idea (closely related to the concept of the Golden Mean) which prevailed not only through the Middle Ages and the Renaissance but well into the eighteenth century. After considering the matter from many points of view, however, Aristotle concludes with regard to the study of music:

> The right measure will be attained if students of music stop short of the arts which are practised in professional contests, and do not seek to acquire those fantastic marvels of execution which are now the fashion in such contests, and from these have passed into education. Let the young pursue their studies until they are able to feel delight in noble melodies and rhythms.

Aristotle would, in fact, refer the serious student of music to the experts (VIII, vii): "But as the subject has been very well treated by many musicians of the present day, and also by philosophers who have had considerable experience of musical education, to these we would refer the more exact student of the subject."

[8] Hence Boethius' definition of a musician, often cited by medieval theorists: "*Is vero est musicus, qui ratione perpensa canendi scientiam non servitio operis sed imperio speculationis adsumpsit.*" See *Boetii De Institutione musica libri quinque* (ed. by Godofredus Friedlein) (Lipsiae, 1867), 224.

[9] For an account of these writings, see Henry S. Macran, *The Harmonics of Aristoxenos* (Oxford, 1902), 92–93; Gustave Reese, *Music in the Middle Ages* (New York, 1940), 17–19; and Curt Sachs, *The Rise of Music in the Ancient World, East and West*

But among the Greeks, there gradually arose a cycle of studies considered the minimum of liberal training for the average free man—the *artes liberales,* in contrast to the *artes illiberales* pursued for economic reasons. In the great philosophical systems, the mathematical studies were required prior to the study of supreme wisdom —*dialectica* with Plato, *metaphysica* with Aristotle. And in this group, music, as an expression of universal harmony, played a dominating role.

The Roman system of education was modeled upon that of the Greeks, with the liberal arts the basis of learning for the Roman *liber homo.* But it was the Greek rhetorical schools rather than the schools of philosophy which the practical Romans, having no tradition of their own in philosophy, used as a pattern. Rhetoric was the basis of the education of the *civis Romanus,* and music was an important part of rhetorical training. Fabius Quintilianus (*ca.* A.D. 35–100), a *professor eloquentiae* at Rome, has left in his *Institutio oratoria* a detailed description of Roman education, including a long discourse on music, which he discusses with the other encyclopedic disciplines.[10] Although Quintilian advocates a knowledge of music as necessary for effective oratory, he urges even more strongly the importance of theoretical musical knowledge—especially "the knowledge of the principles of music, which

(New York, 1943), 199. Besides the many references to music in the works of Plato and Aristotle, we find in the *Problems* attributed to Aristotle (but probably compiled later by writers under the influence of Aristotelian philosophy) a chapter (XIX) on music in which ethical and acoustical questions are discussed. The *Katatomé ķanonos* (*Sectio canonis, Division of the Monochord*) of Euclid (*fl.* 300 B.C.) is our earliest account of Pythagorean doctrine. More important as the first systematic presentation of Greek musical theory is the incomplete *Harmoniķá stoicheai* (*Elements of Harmony*) of Aristotle's pupil, Aristoxenus of Tarentum (*fl.* 320 B.C). Like the Pythagorean system, Aristoxenus' system had a mathematical basis, but it went beyond mathematics into discussions of musical judgment based on the ear as part of the concept of a musical science; that is, it attributed a new power to judgment based on the senses rather than judgment based only on abstract reason. Other works on Greek music came from a later period—the first and second centuries of the Christian era: Aristides Quintilianus' *Peri mousiķé* (*De musica*), a summary of Aristoxenian theory; Ptolomaeus' *Harmoniķá,* a simplification of Greek musical theory which became (largely through the writings of Boethius) the foundation of medieval theory; Cleonides' *Eisagogé harmoniķé,* based upon Aristoxenian ideas and long attributed to Euclid; Gaudentios' *Harmoniķé eisagogé,* drawing upon both Aristoxenian and Pythagorean theory; and Nichomachos' handbook recounting the Pythagorean theory.

   10 *Quintiliani Institutio oratoria* (ed. and tr. by H. E. Butler) (London, 1933), 160–77.

8

have power to excite or assuage the emotions of mankind." To prove his point, he cites the story of a piper accused of manslaughter "because he had played a tune in the Phrygian mode as an accompaniment to a sacrifice, with the result that the person officiating went mad and flung himself over a precipice"; and he asks, "If an orator is expected to declaim on such a theme as this, which cannot possibly be handled without some knowledge of music, how can my critics . . . fail to agree that music is a necessary element in the education of an orator?"

The fact that Quintilian pleads so eloquently for more attention to theories and principles of music is perhaps significant: for only in the great rhetorical schools at Rome were law and philosophy (including the mathematical sciences) taught; in the ordinary provincial schools throughout Italy and conquered Gaul, these studies were of secondary importance (and the schools themselves virtually disappeared in the fifth and sixth centuries).[11] It was in connection with the Roman rhetorical schools that the first writings on the liberal arts began to appear during the early centuries of our era. The neo-Platonic philosopher Macrobius (late fourth century) dealt with the sciences of the quadrivium in his commentary on Cicero's *Somnium Scipionis,* a book having considerable vogue in the Middle Ages.[12] The musical discussion here involves Pythagorean theories of numbers as applied to the harmonic

[11] See Fédor Schneider, *Rom und Romgedanke im Mittelalter* (München, 1926), 72–73, and Maurice Roger, *L'Enseignement des lettres classiques d'Ausone à Alcuin* (Paris, 1905), 36.

[12] *Ambrosii Theodosii Macrobii Commentariorum in Somnium Scipionis Libri II* (ed. by Franciscus Eyssenhardt) (Lipsiae, 1893), II, 582–99. Especially interesting is Macrobius' reason for the powerful appeal of music to men (p. 593):

Nam ideo in hac uita omnis anima musicis sonis capitur, ut non soli, qui sunt habitu cultiores, uerum uniuersae quoque barbarae nationes cantus, quibus uel ad ardorem uirtutis animentur, uel ad mollitiem uoluptatis resoluantur, exerceant, quia in corpus defert memoriam musicae, cuius in caelo fuit conscia, et ita delenimentis canticis occupatur, ut nullum sit tam inmite tam asperum pectus, quod non oblectamentorum talium teneatur affectu.

There is an English translation of Macrobius by William Harris Stahl (New York, 1952). For a recent explanation of Plato's derivation of the scale, see Jacques Handschin, "The 'Timaeus' Scale," *Musica Disciplina,* Vol. IV (1950), 3–42.

proportions of musical intervals, the soul's relation to the body compared to musical proportions (as in Plato's *Timaeus*), and the effects of music upon man. Macrobius deals at some length here with an idea important not only to music but to literature in medieval times and later—the concept of the music of the spheres, originally described by Plato in the Vision of Er (*Republic,* VIII) and incorporated by Cicero in his *Somnium Scipionis.* According to this theory, the motion of each of the planets revolving about the earth produces a definite musical tone: eight spheres revolve (in this system there are nine spheres, the stationary earth included), but only seven tones are produced, since the orbits of Mercury and Venus are alike and thus make the same sound.

It was, however, Martianus Capella, native of Carthage and neo-Platonist (first half of the fifth century), who gave definite form to the concept of seven liberal arts in his allegory *De nuptiis Philologiae et Mercurii,* probably written in connection with the Roman rhetorical schools. In this work, after two books of allegory describing wedding activities, the seven liberal arts appear as bridesmaids to Philology, the *doctissima virgo* representing encyclical learning, each attendant lady describing the art she represents. Book IX, *"De harmonia"*[13] (based largely upon the writings of Aristides Quintilianus[14]), deals briefly with Greek musical theory —tones, intervals, *genera,* modes, and poetic meters. It is interesting and significant that in establishing his cycle of arts,[15] Martianus singled out music and gave it a distinction above the other arts,

---

[13] *Martianus Capella* (ed. by Adolfus Dick) (Lipsiae, 1925), 469–535.

[14] See Hermann Deiters, *Studein zu den griechischen Musikern: Über das Verhältnis des Martianus Capella zu Aristides Quintilianus* (Posen, 1881).

[15] Martianus' treatise as a whole was modeled upon a lost work by M. Terentius Varro (a contemporary of Cicero), the *Libri novem disciplinarum,* thought to have been an encyclopedia of the chief sciences of Greece. See H. Parker, "The Seven Liberal Arts," *English Historical Review,* Vol. V (1890), 433. But Martianus chose to omit two of Varro's nine sciences—medicine and architecture—because they were not liberal studies and, although concerned with useful arts, in no way led to the study of philosophy. For Apollo's lines in the allegory referring to medicine and architecture, see the translation by Andrew F. West, *Alcuin and the Rise of the Christian Schools* (New York, 1916), 21: "Inasmuch as they are concerned with perishable earthly things, and have nothing in common with what is ethereal and divine, it will be quite fitting that they be rejected with disdain."

undoubtedly influenced by Plato's ideas concerning music's high position in philosophical studies.[16]

ii. Musical Studies in Christian Schools of the Early Middle Ages

Since Martianus' allegory *De nuptiis Philologiae et Mercurii* contained no hint of Christian doctrine, it was not as popular at first as it became after the Church, under Augustine's influence, sanctioned the reading of pagan literature as an aid in understanding the Scriptures. Following Martianus, the next names of importance in the study of music in the Middle Ages are those of two Romans who lived at the beginning of medieval times—Boethius and Cassiodorus. Boethius (481–525) made translations and adaptations of Greek scholarship in several fields, and much of his work served as textbooks and source material throughout the Middle Ages. Especially important for the study of music was his *De institutione musica libri quinque,* which, throughout medieval times and much later, was the standard text for schools and universities. Patterned after the philosophical *protreptikos* (the hortatory introduction to a science or art), this work on music is significant in carrying over into the Middle Ages the ancient Greek educational tradition which led through the study of music to philosophy proper[1]—a tradition deriving, as we have seen, from Plato and Aristotle. In content, Boethius' *Musica* follows Ptolemy. After a discussion of music in general, its effects and uses, Boethius derives the scale from Pythagorean proportions and compares the Pythagorean system with systems of other Greek theorists—chiefly Aristoxenus. In Book I of this work is found the Boethian division of music so often cited

[16] Martianus speaks of music as superior to the other heavenly muses (*Martianus Capella,* 474–75): *"postquam haec Latouis dixit, Iuppiter Harmonien uenire, quam suggestum est Mercurialium solam superesse, praecepit tuncque alias in ordinem continari"*; and again he has Jupiter praise Harmonia (p. 476): *"nunc igitur praecellentissimam feminarum Harmoniam, quae Mercurialium sola superest, audiamus."*

[1] See Leo Schrade, *"Das propädeutische Ethos in der Musikanschauung des Boethius,"* *Zeitschrift für Geschichte der Erziehung und des Unterrichts,* Vol. XX (1930), 180.

by later writers: *musica mundana,* the harmony of numbers based upon simple numerical ratios, the music of the *macrocosmos* created by rhythmical, harmonious movements among the spheres; *musica humana,* the harmony of the *microcosmos,* of the soul or of man as a whole, so often mentioned by Plato; and *musica instrumentalis,* sounding music, either vocal or instrumental.[2]

Like Boethius, Cassiodorus (480–575) came of a noble Roman family and was active for a while as a statesman under the Ostrogothic dynasty. Failing in his plan to establish with Pope Agapetus a university at Rome for the teaching of the liberal arts in connection with Christian theology, he withdrew to his monastery, Vivarium, and dedicated his life to scientific study.[3] Inspired by a love for Greek and Roman culture, Cassiodorus saved for posterity what he could of this culture by compiling ancient texts and having his monks copy these, as well as by writing his own commentaries, the *Institutiones divinarum litterarum* and the *Expositio in Psalmos.* The second book of the *Institutiones,* "*De artibus ac disciplinis liberalium litterarum,*" dealing with the seven arts which had become classic with Martianus, was heavily drawn upon by subsequent writers. The account of the arts here is short and concise, a collection of definitions rather than a full discussion. But Cassiodorus made the arts seven for all time by giving that number Scriptural support, citing as authority David's praises seven times a day and Solomon's proverb about Wisdom's house with seven pillars.[4] And *musica scientia,* the "*disciplina quae de numeris loquitur,*" was one of the seven encyclical sciences essential for the complete understanding of Christian theology.

For Cassiodorus, like Augustine a century earlier, education

---

[2] See *Boetii Musica,* 187: "*Sunt autem tria [musicae genera]. Et prima quidem mundana, secunda vero humana, tertia, quae in quibusdam constituta est instrumentis, ut in cithara vel tibiis ceterisque, quae cantilenae famulantur.*"

[3] See Max Manitius, *Geschichte der lateinischen Literatur des Mittelalters* (München, 1911–31), I, 38.

[4] *Cassiodori Senatoris Institutiones* (ed. by R. A. B. Mynors) (Oxford, 1937), 89:

Sciendum est plane quoniam frequenter, quicquid continuum atque perpetuum Scriptura sancta vult intelligi, sub isto numero comprehendit, sicut dicit David: *Septies in dei laudem dixi tibi . . . semper laus eius in ore meo,* et Salomon: *Sapientia aedificavit sibi domum; excidit columnas septem.*

was in the service of theology; and it was upon this premise that the liberal arts were accepted by Christian leaders as worthy of study. Augustine himself, before his conversion, had been greatly interested in neo-Platonic learning and had written treatises on six of the liberal arts. In his treatise *De Musica*,[5] chiefly a study of poetic meters, he showed a strong Platonic influence in dealing with musical effects and with mathematical speculation about music. It was his *De doctrina christiana,* however, written long after his conversion, in which Augustine recognized the liberal arts, including musical theory, as useful and necessary for a proper understanding of the Scriptures, in spite of their "pagan" content. *"Philosophia ancilla theologiae,"* which expresses Augustine's attitude, points to this compromise.

In accepting the curriculum of the liberal arts with Augustine's sanction, the Church placed a new emphasis upon the arts: Christians might study and teach classical literature in order to understand and interpret the Scriptures, not, as did the Greeks, as an end in themselves, nor, as did the Romans, to create the perfect orator; and Christian truth, theology, replaced the old philosophy as the ultimate goal of learning. Following this Augustinian point of view, Isidorus, Bishop of Seville (d. 636), wrote his *Etymologies,*[6] an encyclopedia containing a compilation of all learning Isidorus considered necessary for the Christian theologian. The first part of this work deals with the seven arts; and like Cassiodorus' treatment of music (upon which, in fact, Isidorus draws considerably), Isidorus' presentation of the subject is largely a series of definitions easily memorized by the student. The treatises of Augustine, Macrobius, Martianus, Boethius, Cassiodorus, and Isidorus perpetuating ancient theories of music served as instruction books in the monastic schools of the early Middle Ages and as source material for many a later writer; not until the ninth century did a different

---

[5] Jacques Migne, *Patrologiae cursus completus, series latina (Lutetiae Parisiorum,* 1844–55), XXXII, 1081–1194. For an English translation, see R. Catesby Taliaferro, *St. Augustine on Music* (Annapolis, 1939).

[6] Migne, *Patrologia latina,* LXXXII, 74–727; *"De musica,"* col. 163–69. The section on music has also been printed by Martin Gerbert, *Scriptores ecclesiastici de musica sacra potissimum* (Typis San-Blasianis, 1784), I, 19–25.

type of treatise appear, inspired by practical considerations of the ecclesiastical chant and based upon *musica practica* rather than *musica speculativa.*

In making classical studies and the copying of classical manuscripts a part of the regular pattern of life in his monastery, Cassiodorus was instrumental in establishing a monastic ideal which proved an effective weapon against ascetic monasticism, which, coming from the East, had spread in the West with the spread of Christianity and which (encouraged by the Church Fathers of the fourth century—Jerome, Ambrose, and in his early life, Augustine) favored the contemplative life (prayer, together with reading and meditation upon the Scriptures), having no place in its code for liberal studies. For it was Cassiodorus—who believed the pursuit of knowledge rather than physical labor and contemplation to be the chief duty of the monks—and not Benedict of Nursia who was the real founder of one type of institution highly important for the transmission of classical learning, including music, in the Middle Ages: the monastic school with emphasis upon the trivium and quadrivium, leading finally to the study of theology proper. Although Italian in origin, this type of school exerted its greatest influence upon the continent of Europe through the work of Celtic and Anglo-Saxon monks.[7] Christian teachers sent from Rome to Ireland in the early centuries of our era founded monasteries in which Greek and Latin studies flourished along with the study of sacred writings—a tradition maintained continuously from the fourth century, even though school systems disintegrated and culture nearly disappeared from the Western world before the inroads of the barbarians. The Irish monks, too, carried their learning into England and Scotland, and even to the continent: Columba, most notable of all the Irish monks, founded early in the seventh century in Lombardy the monastery Bobbio, famous throughout the medieval period as a seat of classical learning; and a colleague, Gallus, founded at the same time a monastery destined to be one of the

---

[7] For a very comprehensive account of the Celtic influence, see Heinrich Zimmer, *"Uber die Bedeutung des irischen Elements für die mittelalterliche Cultur,"* Preussische Jahrbücher, Vol. LIX (1887), 27–59.

great cultural centers in the north—St. Gall, especially distinguished for the cultivation of music. The monastery at Reichenau, also famous in medieval times for its contributions to the theory and practice of music, owed its classical curriculum largely to Irish influence.

More common than the monastery which emphasized classical learning, however, was the monastic school founded upon an ascetic ideal which did not include classical literature. Yet even in schools of this type, musical instruction was of primary importance—not *musica speculativa* but *musica practica,* the study of the liturgical chant. The monastery at Monte Cassino, founded by Benedict of Nursia around 529, had such a school. For the chief work of the monk, according to Benedict, was neither manual labor nor literary activities but the *Opus Dei,* the daily chanting of the canonical office;[8] and in his *Regula* he gives elaborate instructions on the psalmody proper for each office. Similar to Benedict in educational ideals was Gregory the Great (540–604), founder of several monasteries in Sicily and Italy: as Benedictine monk and afterwards pope, Gregory was a strong defender of the ascetic ideal as opposed to classical learning.[9] Yet music played a most important part in Gregory's life; and the *schola cantorum* at Rome for the study of the chant, afterwards called by his name, has made him justly famous.

Although Gregory is often credited with the founding of this school, it actually existed long before his time; for from earliest Christian times the Church had used special singers in the musical part of the liturgy. The *schola cantorum* was the practical result

---

[8] *Rule of Saint Benedict,* (tr. by Abbot Gasquet) (London, 1909), 78: "Nothing shall be put before the Divine Office."

[9] Gregory's letter berating Desiderius, Bishop of Vienne, for daring to teach grammar (obviously pagan literature) is often quoted:

A report has reached us which we cannot mention without a blush, that thou expoundest grammar to certain friends; whereat we are so offended and filled with scorn that our former opinion of thee is turned to mourning and sorrow. The same mouth singeth not the praises of Jove and the praises of Christ.

See, for example, Reginald Poole, *Illustrations in the History of Medieval Thought and Learning* (London, 1920), 7.

of the need for training such singers, analogous to the schools among the ancient Greeks for the training of singers essential to religious rituals. Gregory strengthened the *schola* and completed its organization, and it became the model for similar institutions in monasteries and cathedrals elsewhere.[10] Elementary instruction in grammar and writing (based largely upon the psalter, which every pupil had to memorize) as well as in singing was given in the Roman school and in others modeled upon it, but it is unlikely that the liberal arts were taught in these schools.

Singers trained at the papal *schola cantorum* were not only responsible for the cultivation of the chant locally but carried the Roman liturgy to other parts of Europe and taught it to people not versed in the Gregorian tradition. The Roman order was established at Canterbury, for instance, by the Benedictine Augustine, sent to England by Gregory in 596 and provided with a Gregorian antiphoner a little later; and under Augustine, as Bishop of Canterbury, a flourishing song school grew up, followed by others at Wearmouth and York.[11] In 747 the Council of Cloveshoe decided that the liturgical chant should be faithfully sung in all churches according to a songbook sent from Rome.[12] Roman singers also introduced the Roman liturgy into France during the reign of Pepin (751–768), whose plan for uniting his kingdom included the abolition of the native Gallican chant and the imposition of the Roman liturgy upon his subjects. Song schools at Metz and Rouen modeled upon the Roman *schola* and directed by men trained in the papal school became especially famous, supplying singers to all parts of the nation.[13] Like Pepin in his zeal for ecclesi-

[10] At the head of the *schola* was the *Prior scholae* or *Primicerius* and after him came the *Secundicerius*, the *Tertius*, and the *Quartus scholae*, this last official also called the *Archiparaphonista* because it was he who actually instructed the boy singers, the *Paraphonistae*. See Peter Wagner, *Einführung in die Gregorianischen Melodien* (Leipzig, 1911–21), I, 216.

[11] *Ibid.*, I, 228–29.

[12] *Ibid.*, I, 230–31.

[13] According to Wagner (*ibid.*, I, 234), the Metz song school became quite famous in Pepin's lifetime, and the chanting in Chrodegang's cathedral was considered equally as beautiful as that of the Roman *schola*. Certain liturgical melodies, moreover, were known as *metensis major, metensis minor*: see F. A. Specht, *Geschichte des Unterrichtswesen in Deutschland* (Stuttgart, 1885), 141.

astical reform, and also wishing to unite all Christians in his empire by means of the same ritual, Charles the Great carefully directed his clergy to sing the office *"sicut psallit ecclesia romana"* and established *scholae cantorum* in suitable places.[14] At Charles' own Palace School the chant was much cultivated. And although Metz remained for several centuries the most influential of all the French song schools patterned upon the Roman model, many others sprang up during Carolingian times and later—at Toul, for example, and at Dijon, Cambrai, Chartres, and Nevers.

iii. Musical Studies in the Medieval Monastic and Cathedral Schools

From the time of Charles the Great, too, the monastic schools became more and more important. Charles' great capitulary of 787 directed that "the study of letters, each to teach and learn them according to his ability and the divine assistance," be a regular part of life in the "monasteries committed by Christ's favour to our charge"; and in 789 the Emperor was even more precise in his order that schoolboys learn "psalms, notes, chants, the computus, and grammar in each monastery and bishop's house."[1] This program of studies—the same subjects taught in the Roman *schola* and in those patterned upon it—sufficed for the smaller monastic houses. But with the coming of Alcuin to France in 787, a system of higher studies was instituted, first in the Palace School where Charles himself was a pupil, and later in the large monastic schools, partly through Alcuin's influence. For after Alcuin became Abbot of St. Martin's at Tours in 796, Tours developed into a center of encyclopedic learning and young scholars came from far and near to study the liberal arts and theology with the English monk.[2] The monasteries of Ferrières, Auxerre, St.-Amand,

[14] Wagner, *Gregorianische Melodien*, I, 235.

[1] See James Bass Mullinger, *The Schools of Charles the Great* (London, 1877), 98, and Margaret Deanesly, "Medieval Schools to c. 1300," *Cambridge Medieval History* (Cambridge and New York, 1924–36), Vol. V, 774.

[2] Specht, *Geschichte des Unterrichtswesen*, 24.

St.-Germain, and Fulda all became in the tenth and eleventh centuries important centers for the study of the liberal arts as well as the cultivation of the chant, largely through the guidance of Alcuin's pupils or of those educated in the Irish tradition on the continent.

Of the monasteries established in the Irish tradition, none, perhaps, achieved such distinction in music as Reichenau and St. Gall, where music was studied both as *ars* and as *scientia*. Five antiphoners and twenty-one psalters are listed in the oldest catalogue of the St. Gall library (ninth century), testifying to the cultivation of the chant there.[3] Here the Irish monk Moengal excelled in the teaching of theology and all the liberal arts, especially music; and among his students were several who later became distinguished poet-composers and teachers of music: Ratper, Notker Balbulus, and Tuotilo. Ratper, who with Notker was in charge of the school at the time of the abbey's great flourishing under Abbot Salomo (890–920), was noted for his Latin hymns and processional litanies.[4] The *Liber Ymnorum Notkeri,* moreover, one of the oldest of the St. Gall manuscripts, attests to Notker's ability with hymns and sequences.[5] Tuotilo, gifted in many of the arts, was a skilled performer on stringed and wind instruments; and so many young noblemen came to him for instruction (according to Ekkehard in his *Casus Sancti Galli*) that a special room had to be set aside for this purpose.[6] Not only was Tuotilo known for his beautiful instrumental compositions, but also for farced Kyries

[3] J. M. Clark, *The Abbey of St. Gall as a Centre of Literature and Art* (Cambridge, 1926), 172.

[4] *Ibid.,* 92, 173.

[5] Notker's fame as a writer of sequences, indeed, was so widespread that he has often been credited with the invention of this form, although modern research has revealed that the earliest sequences were of French origin, probably from St. Martial at Limoges. See Clemens Blume and H. M. Bannister, *Analecta Hymnica Medii Aevi* (Leipzig, 1886–1922), LIII, xiv–xx. For a summary of the latest research on the origin of sequences, see Egon Wellesz, *Eastern Elements in Western Chant* (Oxford, 1947), 153ff. Wellesz is of the opinion that an exact geographical origin has not yet been established (156–60).

[6] *"Musicus sicut et socii ejus, sed in omnium genere fidium et fistularum prae omnibus; nam et filios nobilium in loco ab Abbate destinato fidibus edocuit."* Quoted by Anselm Schubiger, *Die Sängerschule St. Gallens vom achten bis zwölften Jahrhundert* (Einsiedeln und New York, 1858), 61.

and other tropes, for which form he was as famous as was Notker for the sequence. The trope *"Hodie cantandus est,"* attributed to Tuotilo, is a dialogue trope prefixed to the introit of the Mass for Christmas and thus points to Tuotilo's part in the beginnings of liturgical drama.[7]

Reichenau's claim to musical distinction came more than a century after the school at St. Gall had reached its zenith. Books in the Reichenau library in the ninth century—the works of Augustine, Isidorus, and Cassiodorus on music, along with the *Arithmetica* and *Musica* of Boethius—give evidence of instruction in speculative music, whereas ten antiphoners point to the cultivation of the liturgical chant.[8] In the eleventh century, Berno and Hermannus Contractus contributed greatly to the fame of Reichenau in the realm of music. Berno (d. 1048) compiled a *tonarium* (an arrangement of parts of the chant according to the *toni,* the ecclesiastical modes) and wrote works on psalmody.[9] And Herman the Lame (1013–54) was not only one of the most brilliant medieval theorists, attempting a new system of the church modes which reconciled ancient Greek theory with medieval theory, but he also wrote many beautiful hymns and antiphons, some of which are still in use today.[10]

The great monasteries, with their cultivation of the arts and of

---

[7] See Karl Young, *The Drama of the Medieval Church* (Oxford, 1933), I, 195.

[8] Gerhard Pietzsch, *Die Musik im Erziehungs- und Bildungsideal des ausgehenden Altertums und frühen Mittelalters* (Halle, 1932), 85–86.

[9] Berno's works may be found in Martin Gerbert, *Scriptores,* (Typis San-Blasianis, 1784), II, 62–114. These include, in addition to his highly practical *Tonarius,* a *Prologus in tonarium* (giving a rational explanation of the chant by describing the Greek system of tetrachords, intervals, and modes) and a treatise, *De varia psalmorum atque cantuum modulatione,* important because it describes in detail differences between the Roman and Gallican versions of psalmody.

[10] In his treatise *De musica* (Gerbert, *Scriptores,* II, 124–49), Hermannus expounded a theory of the modes which added a plagal mode below the Mixolydian, thus completing a symmetrical cycle of eight modes—four authentic and four plagal. See Leonard Ellinwood, *Musica Hermanni Contracti* (Rochester, 1936), 14, 31–34.

Among Hermannus' compositions are the antiphons *"Salve regina"* and *"Alma redemptoris mater,"* both of which were used frequently during the polyphonic period as *cantus firmi* for polyphonic compositions. The *"Alma redemptoris mater"* is the melody which Chaucer's "litel clergeon," hero of "The Prioress's Tale," heard the children sing "in the schole" as they "lerned hire antiphoner." As late as 1882 this melody was quoted in a larger framework—by Richard Wagner in his opera *Parsifal.*

encyclopedic learning, flourished in the tenth and eleventh centuries. In the next century a reaction set in, coincidental with the Cluniac and Cistercian reform movement and characterized by a return to the ascetic idealism of Benedict and Gregory. Although the study of the chant (*musica practica*) was continued in the monasteries, there was now less emphasis upon music as a part of the quadrivium (*musica speculativa*). Even with the return of the monastic orders to a more liberal attitude, the encyclopedic studies were pursued, from this time on, largely in the cathedral schools. With their separate divisions for song, grammar, the arts, and theology, the cathedral schools and others like them embraced a dichotomy with regard to music because they were on the one side a continuation of the Gregorian *schola cantorum* and on the other an outgrowth of the episcopal schools for the training (in arts and theology) of monks and noble laity which had been in existence for several centuries. At Canterbury, for instance, the Gregorian tradition of practical musical instruction was combined with the old Celtic tradition of secular studies; and along with the elementary grammar and song schools, the bishop's school for more advanced students kept alive the study of the liberal arts. A library catalogue from Canterbury's monastery of Christ Church (probably twelfth century) indicates that both *musica practica* and *musica speculativa* were included in these studies.[11]

York, too, was a flourishing center for liberal studies.[12] Alcuin (*ca.* 735–804), the most famous product of the school and head of

---

[11] Included in this list are the *Musica Boecii* (two copies), *Musica Osberni, Micrologus Guidonis, Musica Hogerii,* and *Expositio in Musicam Guidonis.* See James Bass Mullinger, *The University of Cambridge* (Cambridge, 1873–1911), I, 103.

[12] The Venerable Bede, whose training represented both the Celtic and the Roman tradition, had been the model for the masters of York; and Bede, like St. Augustine, favored the liberal arts as necessary to the understanding of theology. In his *De elementis philosophiae*, he wrote:

> We are to be initiated in *grammatica*, then in *dialectica*, afterward in *rhetorica*. Equipped with these arms, we should approach the study of philosophy. Here the order is first the quadrivium, and in this first *arithmetica*, second *musica*, third *geometria*, fourth *astronomia*, then holy writ, so that through knowledge of what is created we arrive at knowledge of the Creator.

See C. S. Baldwin, *Medieval Rhetoric and Poetic* (New York, 1928), 129.

it when he was called to France in 782, wrote treatises on the seven liberal arts (of which only those on the trivium have survived in complete form).[13] One small fragment on music remains,[14] important in being the earliest extant document to mention the ecclesiastical modes. In his *Poema de Pontificibus et Sancti Ecclesiae Eboracensis*, which describes educational practices at York under Alcuin's mentor, Archbishop Egbert, and lists the books in the great library at York, Alcuin refers to music several times—at one point, connecting music and poetry, and at another referring to music as a mathematical science; and still further evidence of musical study at York is seen in the works of Boethius and Cassiodorus among the books in the library.[15]

With the decline of monastic instruction after the tenth century, the continuation of the liberal arts tradition was largely left to the cathedral schools. And, as with Alcuin at York, the higher studies were usually associated with some particular man, educated in the great monastic schools and famous for his learning, who drew students to his schools—like Remigius at Paris or Fulbert at Chartres.[16] Rheims, for instance, became a center famous for the study of all branches of the trivium and quadrivium under Gerbert of Aurillac (*ca.* 940–1003), later Pope Sylvester II, who, as Abbot of Bobbio, had access to the rich classical library there. Gerbert's

[13] For a recent account of the life and accomplishments of Alcuin (of little interest, however, from the point of view of music), see Eleanor Duckett, *Alcuin, Friend of Charlemagne* (New York, 1951).

[14] Gerbert, *Scriptores*, I, 26–27.

[15] Migne, *Patrologia latina*, CI, 841 and 843. The lines concerning music and poetry and music as a sister art to astronomy (col. 841) read:

> *Illos juridica curavit cote polire,*
> *Illos Aonio docuit concinnere cantu;*
> *Castalida instituens alios resonare cicuta,*
> *Et juga Parnassi lyricis percurrere plantis.*
> *Ast alios fecit praefatus nosse magister*
> *Harmoniam coeli, solis lunaeque labores,*
> *Quinque poli zonas, errantia sidera septem,*
> *Astrorum leges, ortus, simul atque recessus.*

[16] For an account of the literary activities of many of the monks, abbots, and bishops whose musical activities caused their schools to be especially distinguished (Hucbald, Rhabanus Maurus, Gerbert of Aurillac, Fulbert of Chartres, and others) see F. J. E. Raby, *A History of Secular Latin Poetry in the Middle Ages* (Oxford, 1934).

teaching of music was based upon Boethius' *Musica*, presented as an integral part of the science of numbers, an introduction to philosophy.[17] At Chartres, to mention only one other distinguished school, the liberal arts had a place from the ninth century, and documents refer to the study of the trivium and quadrivium throughout the tenth century.[18] The great glory of Chartres, however, came in the eleventh century under the leadership of Bishop Fulbert, teacher of the liberal arts from his youth (as his pupil Sigon tells us) and especially interested in mathematics. Fulbert not only taught music to many who later became famous in this art (of Sigon, for example, it was said, *"Singularis organali regnabat in musica,"* *organali* referring, of course, to the new polyphony of the time), but he also enjoyed considerable reputation as a composer, having written several responses, an office, a farced Kyrie, a hymn, and a sequence, all of them extant.[19] The *Eptateuchon* of Thierry of Chartres (twelfth century), a *bibliotheca septem artium*,[20] mentions, significantly enough, Boethius' *De musica,* pointing to the cultivation of Boethius at Paris (where Thierry had studied) and at Chartres.

Apart from these higher studies, including music, in the cathedral schools, *scholae cantorum* of both monasteries and cathedrals provided instruction in Latin grammar, elementary arithmetic, and the elements of music; and along with this went participation in the many liturgical activities—Masses, offices, and special services—which required young voices and which actually gave the song schools their *raison d'être*. At first, training in the chant was largely a matter of oral tradition: everyone had to know the melodies by memory, for they were not noted. However, from the time of Gregory, who edited and codified the whole repertory of the chant, melodies were written in neumatic notation, and notebooks were used by choir directors as a guide for hand movements in directing the singers. The use of such books presupposes instruction in

[17] Pietzsch, *Musik im Erziehungs- und Bildungsideal,* 106–107.

[18] See L'Abbé Clerval, *Les Ecoles de Chartres au moyen-âge* (Chartres, 1895), 15, 26–28.

[19] *Ibid.,* 59–61, 6on., 128.

[20] *Ibid.,* 235.

notation in the *scholae,* and, indeed, from the ninth century onward many theorists, trained in song schools before studying the liberal arts and afterwards teaching in the monastic schools, experimented with various types of notation which would be more practicable than the staffless neumes.[21] It was one of the most zealous and successful music teachers of the entire Middle Ages, Guido d'Arezzo (*fl.* 1022), who solved the problem in a way that has lasted until our own time. Aiming always at cultivating in his students the ability to sing at sight, Guido used lines and spaces for letter names, advocated the use of red and yellow lines, and established the F and G clefs in general usage.[22] Guido also evolved a system of solmization to aid boys in reading *ignotum cantum,* and the usefulness of his *sex voces (ut, re, mi, fa, sol, la),* together with his success in teaching the scale and mutation by means of these syllables, is evidenced not only by numerous references in subsequent treatises to the Guidonian system but also by the fact that this

[21] Among these are Hucbald of St. Amand (*ca.* 840–930) with his use of Greek letters on a staff to indicate tones and semitones (*De harmonica institutione,* Gerbert, *Scriptores,* I, 103–25); the unknown author—perhaps Hucbald in his old age—of the *Musica enchiriadis* (the first work in which parallel organum is described and illustrated with musical examples, Gerbert, *Scriptores,* I, 152–73), with a system of daseian notation (the Greek *daseia* combined with parts of other letters) on a staff of as many as eight lines; Notker Labeo (d. 1022), monk of St. Gall, historically important in having left the first extant writings on music in the German language, with his *litterae significativae* as aids in singing the chant more expressively (Gerbert, *Scriptores,* I, 95–96). Concerning the last, however, see Dom Rombaut van Doren, *L'Influence musicale de l'Abbaye de Saint-Gall, VIIIe au XIe siècle* (Louvain, 1925), 94–118, who concludes that Notker quoted an anonymous treatise in his letter to Lanbertus advocating the use of *litterae significativae,* and that the treatise is more of a literary feat than a musical document of practical value. Hermannus Contractus, too, busied himself with this problem, advocating the use of certain letters to show pitch differences (*De musica,* Gerbert, *Scriptores,* II, 124–49).

[22] See Guido's *Regulae de ignoto cantu,* Gerbert, *Scriptores,* II, 34–42, and the *Epistola Guidonis Michaeli Monacho de ignoto cantu, ibid.,* II, 43–50, which recapitulates all Guido's work and doctrine. According to Dom Grégoire Suñol, *Introduction à la paléographie musicale grégorienne* (Paris, Tournai, and Rome, 1935), 58–59, Guido perfected a system already in current practice. Jos. Smits van Waesberghe, however, sees in Guidonian notation "an original invention, a stroke of genius by Guido d'Arezzo": see his description of Guido's system and methods in "The Musical Notation of Guido of Arezzo," *Musica Disciplina,* Vol. V (1951), 15–53. Especially interesting here is an account of the opposition Guido met in trying to establish his new system of notation in general usage. Smits van Waesberghe's edition of the *Micrologus* was published by the American Institute of Musicology in 1955.

system, based now on the octave instead of the hexachord, is still in use today. Musical instruction in the song schools included, too, the study of musical sounds and their relationship to mathematical numbers, consonant and dissonant intervals, the position of half steps, the formation of scales—all taught by means of the one-string instrument called the monochord (still used today in physics classes), as witness many extant treatises on the monochord.[23] The many treatises dealing with the church modes which have come down to us are, of course, significant of the emphasis upon the modes in the song schools. Many of these treatises conclude with a *tonarium,* a collection of melodic formulas used in psalmody showing the *initia* and *differentiae* of the various psalm tones (modes) and grouping parts of the chant according to mode.[24] Such vocal formulas—similar in idea to the old Greek *nomoi*—were mnemonic devices making it easy for pupils to learn the different modes, and they were used until the time of staff notation. More learned discussions of the modes, originating in the monastic schools where *musica speculativa* was taught with mathematics, treated the mathematical basis of the modes with elaborate tables and diagrams, relating these *toni* to Greek theory—as, for example, the *Musica* of Hermannus Contractus, which represents medieval speculation at its height. Rhythmical studies, moreover, undoubtedly had a place in the song schools from early times, probably in connection with poetic meters. Both Remigius of Auxerre and Guido d'Arezzo included metrical discussions in their treatises.[25]

Instruction in all these aspects of music must often have followed the favorite scholastic method of question and answer be-

---

[23] For instance, the treatises in Gerbert, *Scriptores,* I, 330–48.

[24] The *Tonarius* of Regino of Prüm (d. 915) is the first extant work of this type: see Edmond de Coussemaker, *Scriptorum de musica medii aevi nova series* (Parisiis, 1864–78), II, 1–73. Regino's purpose in assembling these chants is clear from a statement in his learned introduction to the chant, *De harmonica institutione* (Gerbert, *Scriptores,* I, 230–47), a letter to Rathbold, his bishop: there is too much variety, he says, in the chanting in his diocese.

[25] Remigius of Auxerre in his commentary *De musica* on Book IX (*"Musica"*) of Martianus Capella's *De nuptiis* (which included a section on metrics), Gerbert, *Scriptores,* I, 63–94; and Guido d'Arezzo in his *Micrologus, ibid.,* II, 2–24.

tween master and pupil, if one may judge by the treatises written in this form. The German nun Hrotswitha (tenth century) included a little dialogue on music in her play *Paphnutius*,[26] in which the hermit Paphnutius answers questions of the Discipuli, drawing upon Boethius in describing *musica mundana, humana,* and *instrumentalis,* and explaining why we cannot hear the music of the spheres—significant, again, of the great vogue of Boethius in medieval times. Among the early treatises on music, the *Scholia enchiriadis* is an arrangement in dialogue form of the material of the *Musica enchiriadis;*[27] and the *Dialogus de musica* of Odo of Cluny (d. 942), as well as the *Musica* of Wilhelm of Hirsau (d. 1091), comprise questions and answers on musical problems.[28] The student of music was undoubtedly required to memorize many musical facts and definitions, as stated in the various *compendia* on music—those of Cassiodorus and Isidorus, for instance, whose precepts were incorporated in many subsequent writings. To aid in memorization, musical information was sometimes presented in metrical form. Guido wrote one entire treatise in verse, beginning with the lines often cited by later writers:

Musicorum et cantorum magna est distantia,
Isti dicunt, illi sciunt, quae componit Musica.
Nam qui facit, quod non sapit, diffinitur bestia.[29]

[26] For the original Latin, see K. A. Barack (ed.), *Die Werke der Hrotsvitha* (Nürnberg, 1858), 241–45. For an English translation of the plays, see the edition of Christopher St. John (London, 1923).

[27] Gerbert, *Scriptores,* I, 152–212.

[28] Odo's *Dialogus de musica* (Gerbert, *Scriptores,* I, 251–64) is important in giving the first simplified form of the Pythagorean scale, copied from this time on by other writers—for example, Guido. According to Odo's division of the monochord, all whole tones were in the ratio of 8:9 and all half tones 243:256. Chromaticism, however, had no place in this scale, for the halfstep between B and Bb was larger than other halfsteps in the scale by the Pythagorean apotome (2048:2187). Besides simplifying the scale, Odo established the use of the first seven letters of the alphabet to signify the tones of the scale, repeating these in three octaves, a system in use ever since.

Wilhelm von Hirsau (1032–91) followed the doctrine of Hermannus in his *Musica* (Gerbert, *Scriptores,* II, 154–82), a dialogue between Wilhelm and a certain Othlohus, explaining the theory of the modes.

[29] The *Musicae Guidoni regulae rhythmicae* (Gerbert, *Scriptores,* II, 25–34) summarizes the information presented by Guido in his *Micrologus.* In his treatise *De sex motibus vocum ad se invicem et dimensione earum* (Coussemaker, *Scriptores,* II, 115–16), Guido

The body of musical literature written by men connected with the schools is, indeed, so indispensable in affording us insight into the study of music in medieval times, both before and after the founding of the universities, that certain other features of the treatises on music must be noticed. In general, just as musical studies from the time of the Greeks followed two trends, one theoretical, the other practical, so one sees the same dichotomy in writings about music. For each of the basic divisions of music—*musica theoretica* and *musica practica,* patterned, of course, upon the Aristotelian division of all knowledge into *philosophia theoretica* and *philosophia practica (Metaphysics,* II, i, 5–7)—produced its own literature; and so the large corpus of medieval treatises on music may roughly be divided into two categories: speculative and practical works.[30]

Speculative treatises, rationalistic studies of music as a mathematico-philosophical science, may be classified according to the purpose of the author. Designed for the student of philosophy is the hortatory introduction to music similar to the philosophical *protreptikos,*[31] pleading the necessity for the study of music by showing its benefits, divisions, and relationship to the other arts. The *Musica* of Boethius, extensive and thorough, exemplifies the predominantly hortatory introduction.[32] Briefer introductions to music as one of the seven liberal arts, patterned upon the *protreptikos,* were often incorporated by medieval writers in large philosophical works—for instance, the section on music in Al-Farabi's encyclopedia *De scientiis* (heavily drawn upon by later writers—by

deals with intervals and the modes in hexameter verse. Hermannus, too, left a set of verses, his *Versus ad discernendum cantum* (Gerbert, *Scriptores,* II, 149–50), with letters above them to show the pitch at which the text was to be sung; and in other early treatises verses appear here and there.

[30] Excerpts from many of the medieval treatises and, in some instances, entire short treatises, may be found in English translation by Oliver Strunk, *Source Readings in Music History* (New York, 1950).

[31] For a description of this type of treatise, see Wilhelm Gerhäusser, *Der Protreptikos der Poseidonios* (München, 1912), 12.

[32] For a discussion of Boethius' *Musica* in the light of Platonic and Aristotelian philosophy, see Leo Schrade, "Music in the Philosophy of Boethius," *Musical Quarterly,* Vol. XXXIII (1947), 188–200.

the Spaniard Gundissalinus, for example) giving the scope, divisions, aims, and methods of approaching the study of music as a part of philosophy, of general knowledge.[33]

For the student of music there is the more specialized *eisagogé*, a direct *introductio* to the specific field of music. Since this type of treatise was for centuries organized according to certain definite topics *(kephalaia)*, one notices a constantly recurring pattern in musical literature of this kind. The *eisagogé* invariably begins with the definition, etymology, and invention of music, describes its uses and effects, enumerates its divisions and subdivisions, and discusses its mathematical ratios. Differences, of course, appear in the varied content—for instance, inventors of music may include any collection of gods and men from Apollo and Orpheus to Tubal Cain and King David—in the different points of view expressed by various writers, and in the elaborate or abbreviated treatment of these topics. The treatise *De harmonica institutione* by Regino of Prüm is a good example of the musical *eisagogé*.[34]

Treatises dealing with *musica practica* are concerned not primarily with music as a philosophical discipline or mathematical

[33] See Henry G. Farmer, *Al-Farabi's Arabic-Latin Writings on Music* (Glasgow, 1934), 13–16, for a translation of the section on music.

[34] Regino of Prüm (d. 915), in his letter *De harmonica institutione,* and his older contemporary Aurelian of Réomé *(fl.* 850), in his *Musica disciplina* (Gerbert, *Scriptores,* I, 27–63), appear to have the distinction of being the first to explain earthly harmony as an imitation of heavenly harmony, of angelic choirs. When we sing praises to God, says Aurelian, we imitate "choros angelorum"; and he connects the eight modes of ecclesiastical plain song with the eight movements of the heavenly bodies. According to Regino, *"chordae coelesti musicae comparantur. Nam hypate meson a musicis Saturno est attributa,"* and the other Greek *chordae* are attributed to other planets, in the order of Boethius; Regino then gives their order according to Cicero in the *Somnium Scipionis* (definitely Platonic in content) and concludes (Gerbert, *Scriptores,* I, 235):

> Ecce habes in coeli motu totius musicae summam. Igitur haec pauca de coelesti musica sufficiant. Si quis autem haec plenius scire desiderat, legat secundum librum Macrobii egregii philosophi, in supra dicto somnio Scipionis. Hoc unum addimus, non solum gentilium philosophos, verum etiam Christianae fidei strenuos praedicatores in hac coelesti harmonia assentire.

Just as many philosophical ideas were reconciled with Christian beliefs by scholastic theologians, Aurelian and Regino—both of them theologians—succeeded in rationalizing the Platonic (and Boethian) music of the spheres with Christian doctrine. This was especially important for the history of *musica practica,* for polyphony now was firmly established upon a philosophical and theological basis.

science but with sounding music, vocal or instrumental. At first such treatises dealt mainly with the plain song of the Church, but with the development of polyphony in the Middle Ages, theorists turned more and more to discussions of the inevitable concomitants of polyphonic music—problems of rhythm and the notation of mensural music.[35] Practical treatises on technical aspects of the art of music fall, thus, into two large classifications: instruction books on sacred monophony, varying in points of emphasis, often including a *tonarium,* and sometimes containing important historical and critical implications; and books on sacred polyphony, involving modal and mensural rhythm, problems of notation, and the combination of voices. Many treatises of this type, as we shall see, sprang from university teaching.

Practical works on music may again be classified according to the author's source of inspiration and purpose. Treatises designed primarily for singers, like the works of Guido, are brief demonstrations of all matters of immediate use for practical purposes. If intended, however, for a learned audience of scholars and composers, these instruction books treat the subject in great detail, drawing upon speculative, mathematical theories of intervals and proportions as a background for artistic problems. The *Musica* of Hermannus Contractus illustrates the learned work of this type. Some writers, moreover, were guided by *usus*—musical techniques currently practiced in the Church or in secular groups. The early treatises on parallel organum[36] reflect the practice of this form of sing-

35 The late Guillaume de Van has explained in a somewhat unorthodox fashion the complexity of late medieval notation and the numerous treatises deriving from this subject. Beginning with the thesis that *"l'hermétisme fut, pendant tout le moyen âge, la condition essentielle de tout enseignement scientifique,"* including musical instruction, de Van explains, *"Le mécanisme essentiel de l'ésotérisme musical médiéval, fut, sans conteste, la notation";* that, in fact, *"l'objet de l'ars mensurabilis n'était pas simplement celui de communiquer une pièce musicale à l'exécutant, mais également d'entourer la science d'une protection efficace contre la curiosité illicite des non-initiés."* See his article, *"La Pedagogie musicale à la fin du moyen âge,"* Musica Disciplina, Vol. II (1948), 75–97.

36 The tenth-century *Musica enchiriadis* is the first work in which organum is described and illustrated with musical examples. The scale used is a transformation of the Greek scale and one suited to harmony in fifths; and rules are given for parallel organum at the fourth and fifth. The *Scholia enchiriadis de arte musica,* a catechism on the earlier work, emphasizes that organum at the fifth is preferred to organum at the fourth. Guido's *Micrologus* (*ca.* 1022) contains a section on *diaphonia,* with an example of three-part

ing, and several short works on English discant, obviously designed for an unlearned audience since they are actually written in the vernacular, deal with a method of improvisation indigenous to the English people.[37] Other theorists were guided in writing their treatises by musical *ars;*[38] and such works as the *Ars nova* of Philip de Vitry and the *Ars nove musice* of Jean de Muris are specialized studies dealing with specific musical problems approached intellectually, generally problems of rhythm and notation.[39]

As in the purely speculative treatises, a conventional pattern appears in the disposition of material in the practical treatises. Before problems of *musica practica* are treated—for example, the ecclesiastical modes—there will be a definition of music followed by statements of its etymology, invention, divisions, and effects, along with a discussion of intervals and mathematical proportions. For writers on practical aspects of music took over these *kephalaia* from the speculative *eisagogé,* and it was the treatment of these indispensable topics which was responsible for a strong tradition in the organization of material in the treatises,[40] a tradition, as we shall

---

organum per diatesseron and explanations of this form of polyphony (Gerbert, *Scriptores,* II, 21–23). The so-called Milan treatise, *Ad organum faciendum,* printed by E. de Coussemaker, *L'Histoire de l'harmonie au moyen-âge* (Paris, 1852), 226–43, with a parallel French translation, typifies the technical treatise deriving from musical *usus:* lacking any speculative introduction, it simply presents rules for writing parallel organum at the fourth and fifth. Many other organum treatises appeared in the twelfth century.

[37] Designed to teach improvisation at sight in parallel sixth chords upon a given tenor, these little tracts in Middle English include works by the composer Leonel Power (d. 1445?), pseudo-Chilston, Richard Cutell, John Torkesey, and certain anonymous writers. They have been printed by Manfred Bukofzer, *Geschichte des englischen Diskants und des Fauxbourdons nach den theoretischen Quellen* (Strassburg, 1936), 132–49. Power's treatise *"vpon the Gamme, for hem that wil be syngers, or makers, or techers"* and the treatise once attributed to Chilston may also be found in Thrasybulos Georgiades, *Englische Diskanttraktate aus den ersten Hälfte des 15. Jahrhunderts* (München, 1937), 12–27. See also Sanford Meech, "Three Musical Treatises in English from a Fifteenth-Century Manuscript," *Speculum,* Vol. X (1935), 235ff.

[38] I am indebted to Professor Leo Schrade of Yale University for pointing out the age-old *ars-usus* distinction and for the observation that the practice of parallel singing at the fourth and fifth was a popular technique outside the realm of *ars* and was not the model for later polyphonic compositions; descriptions of it do not occur in the really learned medieval treatises.

[39] These treatises will be discussed in connection with the University of Paris.

[40] See Leo Schrade's review of Pietzsch's *Klassifikation der Musik, ZfMw,* Vol. XIII (1931), 572–73.

see, still flourishing at the end of the medieval period and well into the Renaissance. The writings of Martianus, Boethius, Cassiodorus, and Isidorus, all coming from late antiquity and carrying over into Western philosophy speculative ideas based on ancient Greek theory, are the works most constantly used by later theorists to give a rationalistic basis to their discussions of *musica practica.*

Medieval treatises on music occasionally appear in certain other forms indigenous to scholastic philosophical or theological writings. One of these is the *scholia,* or commentary, giving explanations of the material in an original work, sometimes by means of marginal notes or glosses, sometimes by means of dialogue or conversation. The *Scholia enchiriadis de arte musica,* we recall, is an early example of this type, a dialogue between Discipulus and Magister on the doctrine of the *Musica enchiriadis.* Another form is the *diffinitorium,* the lexicon defining musical terms. Although Tinctoris is usually credited with the first musical lexicon, one such treatise exists from the eleventh century.[41] More important than these is the comprehensive musical treatise modeled upon the theological *speculum.* Voluminous works of this type comprise, in separate books, treatises dealing with the mathematical basis of music as well as treatises on all topics related to the practice of music in the field of *ars.* We shall see that such works, of which the most extensive is the *Speculum musice* of Jacques de Liège, are always the product of university learning.

If all other evidence were lacking, the musical treatises would make it abundantly clear that although instruction in music in the medieval schools followed two trends—*musica theoretica* and *musica practica*—the two were generally quite closely connected. Many of the great teachers distinguished for their work in musical speculation were also prolific in the *ars musica,* famous as singers, poets, and composers. From the time of Gregory, song schools modeled upon the papal *schola* and emphasizing the ecclesiastical chant became a regular part of the order in monasteries and cathedral

[41] This brief *Vocabularium musicum,* in alphabetical arrangement, is short and not very helpful: its unknown author (probably Italian) has drawn largely upon Isidorus in defining musical terms. For the text, see Adrien La Fage, *Essais de diphthérographie musicale* (Paris, 1864), 404–407.

churches; and, in addition, the liberal arts, music among them, were taught as higher studies in the larger cathedral schools and monasteries, generally under the bishop's personal direction. The ninth, tenth, and eleventh centuries saw a great flourishing of the monasteries famous for the cultivation of music and the other arts and sciences; but learning in these institutions declined during the next centuries, owing to monastic reform movements opposed to great display in secular culture. In general, by the end of the twelfth century the monastic schools no longer offered the scientific disciplines: until the rise of the universities, only in the schools of the great cathedrals did the encyclopedic studies find a place. As the medieval universities developed from the cathedral schools "when the intellectual enthusiasm of the Middle Age began to flow in a distinct channel from its religious enthusiasm,"[42] the cathedral schools lost their best scholars and teachers, and the higher studies ceased to be taught. With the rise of the universities in the thirteenth century, it was left to these institutions to continue the tradition of the seven liberal sciences, music among them as an integral part of the mathematical quadrivium and as a living art.

[42] Hastings Rashdall, *The Universities of Europe in the Middle Ages* (ed. by F. M. Powicke and A. B. Emden) (Oxford, 1936), I, 29.

II. THE STUDY
OF MUSIC
IN THE MEDIEVAL
UNIVERSITIES
[TO 1450]

T
i. ITALY: BOLOGNA AND PADUA
Bologna

HE GREAT AWAKENING of intellectual interests
sometimes called the Renaissance of the twelfth century brought
with it the gradual evolution of the medieval *studium generale*,
comprising various schools to which students might come from
all countries, largely an outgrowth of cathedral schools and the
immediate ancestor of the university. Originally, the latter signi-
fied a corporate body of students or teachers—the direct expression in academic life of the human need for organization similar
to that realized by the formation of the medieval trade guilds.
Eventually the terms *studium generale* and *universitas* became
synonymous. One of the oldest of these institutions was the *studium generale* at Bologna—*Bononia mater studiorum*—whose origins reach far back into the Middle Ages.[1] The *studium* developed
from the cathedral school, and throughout the medieval period
academic festivals continued to be celebrated in the cathedral[2]

[1] The *studium* at Bologna now dates officially from 1088: in 1888 the University of
Bologna celebrated its eighth centennial, dating its founding from 1088 when Irnerius
is supposed to have begun his career as a teacher of law there.

—a fact indicating the usual close connection between church and university, and having important bearing on the cultivation of music in the universities.

One cannot evaluate the place of music among studies in the early university from academic statutes, for no such documents for the arts faculty exist from the fourteenth century and no references to music appear in the statutes for the *Facultas Artistarum et Medicorum* of 1405.[3] Although the university came to be especially famous for the study of law (first taught as a part of rhetoric, later becoming an individual faculty), from earliest times Bologna was distinguished for the study of the liberal arts, among which music undoubtedly had a place. Nicolas Burtius, in a eulogistic book on Bologna (1493), stresses its culture and learning. He describes a contemporary of Guido's, Franciscus of Arezzo, philosopher, musician, and singer, who flourished *in gymnasio* in Bologna.[4] In a letter of 1308, Giovanni Bonandrea, lecturer in rhetoric and poetry in the university, included music among the other philosophical disciplines in describing a certain

professorem et doctorem in scientiis medicine et in artibus, sive gramatica, dialectica, rethorica, aritmetica, geometria, musica et astrologia de motibus et astrologia de effectibus, sive operibus que est ipsa phylosofia.[5]

---

[2] Albano Sorbelli, *Storia della Università di Bologna: Il Medioevo* (Bologna, 1944). 25–29.

[3] The latter statutes (1405) specify certain books to be read *"tam in medicina quam in phylosophya et astrologia,"* but no musical work is found in this list: see Carlo Malagola, *Statuti della università e dei collegi dello studio bolognese* (Bologna, 1888), 274. Another list of books to be read preliminary to the doctorate in medicine includes astrological and mathematical works but no specifically musical work (*ibid.*, 276). Reform statutes of 1442 for the *Universitas Artistarum et Medicorum* make no changes with regard to books (*ibid.*, 313–21).

[4] Nicolas Burtius, *Bononia Illustrata* (Bononiae, 1493). See the copy in the Huntington Library, b iii recto and verso:
Frãciscus aretinus: vir uarii īgenii. . . .
hic philosophus. hic musicus. hic cantor necnon et omniũ bonorum harmonia.
Habuit Guidonẽ musicum cõterraneũ. . . . Mõ de his: q in artibus theologiæ: philosophiæ: ac medicinæ disciplina: nostro in gymnasio floruere expediã.

[5] See Guido Zaccagnini, "Giovanni di Bonandrea," *Studi e memorie per la storia dell' Università di Bologna*, Vol. V (1920), 200.

At Bologna one could become a doctor of all the arts or, apparently, a licensed professor of a particular one[6]—a situation which, as we shall see, also prevailed in the English universities during medieval times.

If music was taught as a science of the quadrivium at Bologna, it also had an important place as a living art in academic-religious life. From 1364 there existed a Spanish College in the university: evidence of the cultivation of music there is seen in a little music notebook (now preserved in Barcelona) inscribed with the student's name, "Johannis Andree civis Bononiensis"—possibly brought back to Spain by a Catalonian student or master.[7] Statutes of the Gregorian College, moreover, established by Gregory XI in 1372, provided for six priests to carry out religious activities, including Masses *cum cantu.*[8] Regular anniversaries and festivals were to be celebrated here, some with sung Masses;[9] and vespers were to be sung each day, although students were not obliged to be present.[10]

Music was, indeed, so much a part of formal and informal student activities at Bologna that a professor in the university who lectured on astrology, Cecco d'Ascoli, in prognosticating a democratic rule for the city (*ca.* 1324), included under favorable aspects the fact that *"omnes bononienses"* were *"cantatores, tripudiatores et suppositores."*[11] One of the important manifestations of such musical interest was the embellishment of academic ceremonies.

[6] Rashdall, *Medieval Universities,* I, 242. A document from 1252, for example, decrees that not only *"domini legum"* are exempt from military duty for the city of Bologna, but also *"magistri gramatice, dialectice et fisice qui regant vel regent."* See Heinrich Denifle, *Die Universitäten des Mittelalters bis 1400* (Berlin, 1885), 205.

[7] See Heinrich Besseler, *"Neue Quellen des 14. und beginnenden 15. Jahrhunderts,"* AfMw, Vol. VII (1925), 205.

[8] According to the founder, *"perpetuo esse volumus sex sacerdotes, statuentes quod, singulis diebus, saltem due misse quarum altera sine cantu de mane ante ingressum scolarium etiam si expedierit in aurora, altera vero cum cantu ecclesie hora debita celebrentur et earum alteram quilibet scolaris audiat."* See Giuseppe Zaoli, *"Lo Studio bolognese e Papa Martino V,"* Studi e memorie, Vol. III (1912), 168–69.

[9] *Ibid.,* 169.

[10] *Ibid.,* 170: *"Insuper statuimus et volumus quod singulis diebus vespertinum officium cum nota et nihilominus subathinis Vigiliis Apostolorum Evangelistarum et quatuor doctorum Ecclesie completorium cum nota in predita capella per sacerdotes ipsius domus decantetur, sed ad interessendum hiis diebus nolumus scolares astringi."*

[11] Francesco Filippini, *"Cecco d'Ascoli a Bologna,"* Studi e memorie, Vol. X (1930), 20.

Missal from Seitenstaetten Abbey, Austria, second half of the thirteenth century, showing St. Gregory the Great within an initial "A," composing the Introit for a Mass, whose opening words appear on the book before him.

¶ Sed quoniam rurſus meſe non erat loco media: ſz ma
gis bypatis accedebat: Jccirco ſuper bypatē byp aton
addita eſt vna cozda: que dicitur proſlambanomenos a. ab
aliquibus autem pzoſmeldodos dicitur. tono intē gro di
ſtans an ea que eſt bypatē bypaton: Et ipſa quidem
idēſt pzoſlambanomenos a meſe octaua eſt reſonans cuz
ea diapaſon ſymboniam. Eadēqʒ ad lichanon bypaton

reſonas diateſſaron ad quartam ſcilicet: quʒ licanos bypa
ton ad meſon reſonat diapente ſymboniam ⁊ eſt ab ea
quinta. Rurſus meſe a param, meſe diſtat tono: quʒ eadem
meſe ad nctem diezeugmenon quintam facit diapēte cō
ſonantiam: Quʒ nete diezeugmenon ad netē byperbo
leon ſirtā facit diateſſaron ſonātiā, ⁊ proſlambanomenos
ad netē byp boleō reddit biſdiapaſon pſonātiā. boc mō.

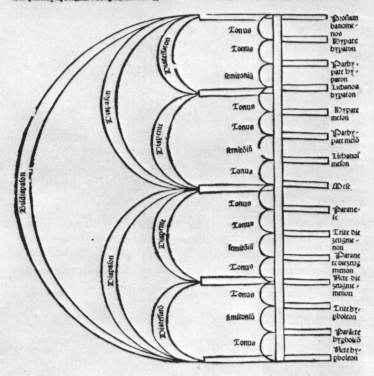

¶ De generibus cantilenarum.   Capitulum. 21.

Is igitur expediit: dicendum eſt de generib⁹
melozum. Sunt autem tria diatonum. chzo
ma. Enarmonium ⁊ diatonicum quidem ali
quanto durius ⁊ natura liue : Chzoma vero
eſt iam quaſi ab illa naturali intentione deſcendens ⁊ in
mollius occidens. Enarmonium vero oppzimeſqʒ apte
coniunctum. Cum ſint igitur quinqʒ tetracozda b ypatō
meſon ſynemmenon. diezeugmenon. byperboleon. Jn
bis omnibus ſcuundum diatonū cantileny pzcdit vox
per ſemitonium. tonum ac tonum. Jn vno tetracozdo.
Rurſus in alio per ſemitonium tonum ac tonum: ac deī

ceps. Jdeoqʒ vocatur diatonicum quaſi quod per tonum
ac per tonumpzogredia tur. Chzoma autem quod dicitur
colo: quaſi iam ab buiuſmodi intentione pzima muratō
cantatur per ſe mitonium ⁊ ſemitonium ⁊ tria ſemitonia.
Tota enim diateſſaron conſonantia eſt: quo: um tono: uʒ
ac ſemitonii: ſed non pleni. Tractum eſt autem boc vo
cabulum vt diceretur chzoma a ſuperficiebus : que cum
permutantur in alium tranſeunt colo: em: Enarmoniuʒ
vero quod eſt magis coaptatum eſt: Quod cantatur in
omnibus tetraco: dis per diſin ⁊ diſin ⁊ diatonuʒ. Die
ſis autem eſt ſe mitonii dimidium: vt ſit trium generum
deſcriptio per omnia tetraco: da diſcurrens. boc mo
de.

Page from the first edition of Boethius, *Arithmetica, Geometrica et Musica* (Venice, 1492).

Statutes for the *Universitas Juristarum,* 1317, for example, pre-scribed a sung Mass as part of the ceremonies *per doctores faci-endis.*[12] And in the statutes of 1405 for the joint *universitas* of medi-cine and arts a paragraph *"De Trombatoribus et eorum Officio et Salario"*[13] states that the university trumpeters were to be in readiness *"ad requisitionem domini Rectoris venire ad festivitates et sollempnitates"* and to appear *"diebus solempnibus in mane cum eorum instrumentis honorare dominum Rectorem."* These instru-mentalists were also to be present *"omnibus et singulis conventibus et honorare conventuandos ante et post ipsum conventum . . . per civitatem et ubidumque, pedes et eques, de die et de nocte."* The trumpeters were to be paid twice as much for their services if mounted on horseback.[14] Trumpeters participated, too, in the cele-bration of certain feasts—for instance, at the Feast of St. Mary, to which, in the words of the statutes, *"bidelli . . . debeant facere venire tubatores."*[15] This same year, 1405, university officials attempted to limit the lavish expenditures inherent in the election of a rector by including musical entertainment in their list of forbidden prac-tices[16]—significant, again, of the great emphasis upon music and dancing (with hired performers) in the lives of the students.

As in the fourteenth century, statutes of 1432 for the *Universitas*

---

[12] Malagola, *Statuti,* 40: *"Volumus autem quod, finito sermone decretiste, rectores et consciliarij ex debito iuramenti, et omnes alij scolares solum ex debito honestatis, statim conveniant apud ecclesiam Predicatorum, et ibi audiant missam de sancto spiritu cum comemoratione virginis gloriose. Fratres autem tunc in alta voce sine nota prolixa officium misse cantantes intra cancellos stare poterunt, choro superiori et inferiori dismisso scolaribus."*

[13] *Ibid.,* 292.

[14] According to the statutes *(ibid.),*

Item . . . si equitabunt cum eo per terram, habeat quilibet dictorum tromba-torum, pro suo labore et pro equo, ab ipso conventuando viginti solidos bon. Si vero non equitabunt, habeat quilibet dictorum trombatorum decem solidos bon. et ultra id ab aliquo petere non possint.

[15] *Ibid.,* 296.

[16] The statutes declare *(ibid.,* 221):

quod aliquis in Rectorem universitatis predicte electus seu eligendus, tempore sue electionis non possit vel debeat dare scolaribus . . . confectiones vel vinum, nec, infra mensem a die sue electionis usque ad completorium non computato, audeat vel presumat tripudiare aut tripudiari facere cum trombis vel sine vel cum alijs instrumentis, de nocte.

Juristarum decreed that the opening of each academic year be celebrated with a sung Mass.[17] Music was also used to heighten the elaborate degree ceremonies in this faculty, although an attempt was again made to curtail expenses. When the candidate for the doctorate rode around the city inviting his friends to the investing ceremony, he was forbidden the use of trumpets or other instruments.[18] The newly created doctor, however, might be escorted from the doctoral act at the cathedral by four trumpeters; and once more the trumpeters were to be paid a larger fee if they formed part of a mounted procession.[19] In the list of payments *"Pro expensis fiendis tam in publico quam in privato examine"* are fees for three pipers and four trumpeters.[20]

Although the most important theoretical writings from Italy's Middle Ages sprang from musical studies at the University of Padua, there is available in published form a treatise, *L'arte del biscanto misurato secondo el maestro Jacopo da Bologna,* by one of the city's most distinguished *trecento* composers.[21] Lacking any speculative introduction, the little tract goes immediately into a discussion of the notational-rhythmic elements of the *ars nova* music (figures of notation, explanations of mode, tempus, and prolation). The treatise not only reflects Bologna's interest in the

[17] *Ibid.,* 101.

[18] *Ibid.,* 116: *"Doctorandi, cum invitant ad publicam, incedere debeant sine tubis vel instrumentis quibuscunque."*

[19] According to the statutes (*ibid.*),

Adijcientes, quod tubatores nostre universitatis, qui debent esse quatuor numero, sint ista solutione contenti, scilicet, quilibet eorum pro associando doctore novello ab ecclesia sancti Petri usque ad eius domum habeat solidos decem bon. seu libram mediam. Si vero doctor novus per civitatem equitare voluerit, habeant viginti quinque solidos.

[20] *Ibid.,* 151: *"Pro piffaris tribus et quatuor tubatoribus libre due et solidi novem solvantur."*

[21] Johannes Wolf, *"L'arte del biscanto misurato secondo el maestro Jacopo da Bologna," Theodor Kroyer Festschrift* (Regensburg, 1933), 18–39, with a parallel German translation. In the fifteenth-century Florentine manuscript containing this treatise are two copies of writings on the same subject by Jean de Muris, indicative again of the widespread influence of the Sorbonne theorist. I have been unable to connect Jacopo directly with the University of Bologna.

art of music but shows the usual close association between composition and theory at this time.

Padua

The *studium* at Padua was the most notable of all the daughters of Bologna, dating its origin from 1222 when a migration of students to Padua from the mother university took place.[22] As at Bologna, this group was originally a *universitas juristarum:* not until 1399 did the *universitas artistarum* become independent of the law faculty.[23] Since there is no mention of a curriculum of studies in the only published statutes (1331),[24] the position of music in the medieval university must be evaluated from other sources. Fortunately, many of these are available, and they point conclusively to a great flourishing of music both as *ars* and as *scientia* at Padua in the fourteenth and fifteenth centuries.

As at the Bolognese *studium,* the beginning of the academic year was to be celebrated with a sung Mass in the cathedral, according to the statutes of 1331.[25] And following Bolognese custom, too, the licentiate (doctorate) was awarded in the cathedral with great magnificence,[26] to which music undoubtedly contributed. After the banquet which followed services at the cathedral, the successful candidate (according to the statutes of 1331) might be escorted through the city to the musical accompaniment of trum-

[22] This migration was the result of either political disturbances at Bologna or the fame of Paduan teachers. See Cesare Foligno, *The Story of Padua* (London, 1910), 146–47.

[23] *Acta Universitatis Patavinae Septima Saecularia Celebrantis, 1222–1922* (Padova, 1925), 2.

[24] Included here is a list of books with stationers' price for each: no music book is to be found in the list. See Heinrich Denifle (ed.), *Statuten der Juristen-Universität Padua vom Jahre 1331* (Berlin, 1892), 150–54, no. 22.

[25] *Ibid.,* 158–59, no. 1: All university personnel (*"Volumus autem quod . . . rectores et consciliarij ex debito iuramenti et omnes alij scolares"*) were to gather at the cathedral, *"et ibi audiant missam de Sancto Spiritu cum commemoracione beate virginis gloriose. . . . Sacerdos autem et clerici tunc in alta voce sine nota prolixa officium misse cantantes intra cancellos stare poterunt, choro superiori et inferiori dimissis scolaribus."* The phraseology is identical with that of Bologna's statutes of 1317.

[26] Francesco Maria Colle, *Storia scientifico-letteraria dello studio di Padova* (Padova, 1824–25), I, 104.

pets and other instruments; and candidates for the doctorate might have *in publica* whatever instruments they wished.[27]

A city ordinance of 1339, moreover, which applied to university members, forbade the making of noise *"con istromenti musicali nella città e nei borghi"* from the *"suono della campana di notte al suono di quella mattutina,"*[28] significant that music making was so general that it had become an actual nuisance. A curious and informative document is the will (1412) of Ludovico Cortusi, doctor and professor of canon law at Padua, who specified that fifty musicians, *"si reperiri poterunt,"* lead his funeral procession, performing on trumpets, various kinds of stringed instruments, organs, and drums, and singing the Gloria; and that twelve virgins also take part in the procession, singing and rejoicing.[29] Apparently it was not impossible to collect fifty instrumentalists and the twelve young ladies; for after Ludovico's death in 1418, we are told, *"la strana disposizione fu eseguita."*[30]

Other documents indicate that some students or teachers at Padua were distinguished for their musicianship. In 1309, for example, "Dominus Johannes cantor Budensis," a member of the

[27] Denifle, *Statuten*, 131, no. 20: *"Post prandium autem socient, sed non tenentur, ipsum* [the candidate] *rectores atque scolares per civitatem equitantes cum tubis et aliis instrumentis. Tantum in publica possint doctorandi habere quecumque voluerint instrumenta."*

[28] Andrea Gloria, *Monumenti della Università di Padova, 1318–1405* (Padova, 1888), I, 15, no. 42.

[29] Colle, *Storia di Padova*, III, 84 n.:
Item lego pro honoranda corporis mei sepultura illud, quod videbitur conveniens meis Commissariis, et volo, quod per meos Commissarios eligantur pulsatores, seu musici, usque ad numerum quinquaginta, si reperiri poterunt, quibus lego ducatum medium pro quoque, ut praecedant corpus meum cum tubis, zaramelis, arpis, liutis, citharis, organis, timpanis, et aliis generibus instrumentorum, pulsantes et canentes *Gloria in excelsis Deo, et in terra pax hominibus bonae voluntatis.* . . . Ego Ludovicus de Cortusiis . . . condidi meum ultimum testamentum manuscriptum, cui per praesens codicillum addo, quod pro majori honore corporis mei sepulturae, et pro majori gaudio finis omnium mearum calamitatum eligantur duodecim puellae virgines, et induantur vestibus viridis coloris, quae hinc et hinc ferre jubeantur . . . usque ad templum, ubi erit corpus meum, Sanctae Sophiae, cantantes et modulantes vocibus altis et laetantibus quaecumque voluerint, modo cantent versus honestos, et laetitiam personantes.

[30] Gloria, *Monumenti*, I, 191, no. 418.

38

Hungarian Nation, matriculated at the university.[31] And Antonio Lido, professor of medicine at Padua late in the fourteenth century, was such a skilled musician that the epithet *musicus* opens his epitaph:

> *Musicus Artista, doctorque Parisius iste*
> *Sub caeso Antonius marmore carne jacet.*[32]

Antonio is said by Savonarola to have studied the liberal arts in Paris (since they had disappeared from Padua) and to have taught them publicly at Padua—meaning as a regularly paid university lecturer *("Paduam ad eas legendas publicandasque venit")*—before turning to the study of medicine.[33] Because of his own strong musical interests, Antonio may well have included music in his public lectures on the arts in the University of Padua.

There are, in fact, many indications that mathematics and music were taught among the liberal arts at Padua. The *laurea* (doctorate in arts) was regularly given,[34] presupposing the study of all the arts. And one writer, describing the *studium* at Padua in the fourteenth century, says that practical music was taught there along with the other arts—*"religionis gratia ea Musicae pars, quae in canendis divinis laudibus adhibebatur."*[35] Another notice (*Vita*

---

[31] Andreas Veress, *Matricula et Acta Hungarorum in Universitate Patavina Studentium, 1264-1864* (Budapest, 1915–17), I, 1.

[32] *Bernardini Scardeonii De Antiquitate Vrbis Patavii et claris ciuibus Patauinis libri tres* (Basileae, 1560), 262.

[33] Savonarola is quoted by Gloria, *Monumenti*, I, 370, no. 708:

> Antonium de Lido, virum quippe divinum—Quum liberales artes nostra in urbe evanuissent, Parisiusque florerent, ad eas subtiliter capessendas, quum nimium generosi animi foret, Parisius profectus est, ubi quum artes ipsas mirum in modum adeptus esset, Paduam ad eas legendas publicandasque venit. Qui quum ingenii non mediocri subtilitate vigeret, studio medicinae se contulit, in eoque tantum profecit, ut quos medicinae scrupolosos nodos ceteri silentio pertransibant, ipse primus enodaverit. Hic plurima memoratu digna in medicina conscripsit, quibus ceteri se plurimum decorarunt.

[34] See the many *doctores artium, ibid.,* I., *passim.*

[35] *Fasti Gymnasii Patavini Jacobi Facciolati* (Patavii, 1757), quoted by Antonio Favaro, *"Intorno alla vita ed alle opere di Prosdocimo de' Beldomandi matematico padovano del secolo XV." Bullettino di bibliografia e di storia delle scienze matematiche e fisiche,* Vol. XII (1879), 18:

> Hac tamen voce [grammatica] ars & facultas omnis dicendi ac disputandi inter-

Sancti Meinwerci, 1616)[36] tells us that in the fourteenth century

> *publica floruerunt studia: quando ibi Musici fuerunt, & Dialectici enituerunt, Rhetorici, plerique Grammatici: quando Magistri Artium exercebant* Trivium, *quibus omne studium erat circa* Quadruvium: *ubi Mathematici claruerunt & Astronomici habebantur Physici, atque Geometrici.*

Especially interesting is the statement immediately following, that writers on the quadrivium were more highly regarded than those who wrote about the trivium: *"Magni olim aestimati qui* Trivium *in literis consecrant: pluris, qui* Quadrivium.*"*

The writings of Paduan *dottori* are additional evidence for the high place of the liberal arts, music always prominent among them, in the medieval university. The humanist Pietro Vergerio, student and in 1391 professor of logic in Padua, wrote (*ca.* 1404) a treatise for the son of the lord of the city, *De ingenuis moribus,* in which he advocated the study of music—both theory and practice—in true Platonic fashion "as an aid to the inner harmony of the soul" and as a liberal art.[37] Among the works of Francesca Zabarella (d. 1417), student and professor of law at both Padua and Bologna, is a treatise *De artibus liberalibus.*[38] And Pietro Donati (d. 1447), doctor of philosophy and laws (who spoke, indeed, an *Oratio in exequiis d. Francisci de Zabarellis*), left among his works an *Oratio de laudibus philosophiae.*[39]

The *Problemata* attributed to Aristotle, which contains a chapter on music, figures in several of the Paduan documents, pointing again to the inclusion of music with the mathematical sciences at

---

dum significabatur hoc est Rhetorica quoque, & Dialectica: idque *Trivium* appellabatur. Accessit postmodum Arithmetica, quam *Computatoriam* vocabant: & ad vanum quendam divinandi usum, qui mentis hominum occupaverat, etiam Astrologia tum religionis gratia ea Musicae pars, quae in canendis divinis laudibus adhibebatur.

[36] Quoted *ibid.,* 19.

[37] For an English translation of the treatise, see William Harrison Woodward, *Vittorino da Feltre and other Humanist Educators* (Cambridge, 1905), 96–118.

[38] Gloria, *Monumenti,* I, 216, no. 468.

[39] *Ibid.,* I, 510, no. 999.

Padua. Pietro d'Abano, distinguished professor of medicine, philosophy, and astrology in 1315, was the first to translate the *Problemata* into Latin; and his own great medical work, the *Conciliator* (1303), treated a problem of *musica speculativa, inter alia:* Is musical consonance found in the pulse?[40] In 1310 he wrote an *Expositio Problematum Aristotelis,* published in Mantua in 1475 with several later editions.[41] Pietro Curialti, moreover, holder of the chair of medicine in 1377, left among his works *Tabulae super problemata Aristotelis;* and among the books in the library of Antonio Cermisone, professor of medicine who died in 1431, were *"Item expositiones Petri de Abano super problemata Aristotelis . . . Item expositiones Psalterii . . . Item problemata aliqua Aristotelis cum expositione."*[42] Finally, among the mathematical works written by Biagio Pellacani (d. 1416), who taught mathematics at Padua—he had the distinction, in fact, of having taught Vittorino da Feltre—there is one which is probably a musico-mathematical treatise: *Quaestiones super tractatum de proportionibus Thomae Bernardini.*[43]

It is evident, then, that at Padua in the late Middle Ages music was taught as one of the liberal arts strongly allied to mathematics, and that both subjects were closely connected with the medical studies for which the university was especially famous. Instruction in practical music, too, had a place as always, *religionis causa.* Even more significant for evaluating the study of music at the University of Padua are certain treatises produced by men connected with the university as students or teachers or both, all of whom approached their subject from a mathematical point of view.

The first of these is Marchettus of Padua, a distinguished teacher of music in his native city. Highly praised by Scardeonius as *"doctissimus philosophus, simul et Musicus,"*[44] Marchettus wrote treat-

[40] Lynn Thorndike, "Peter of Albano," *Annual Report of the American Historical Association,* Vol. I (1919), 319, 325.

[41] Colle, *Storia di Padova,* III, 134n., 150.

[42] Gloria, *Monumenti,* I, 406, no. 772 and I, 112, no. 259 (the date 1331 is obviously a misprint for 1431).

[43] *Ibid.,* I, 416, no. 791.

[44] *De antiquitate urbis Patavii libri tres,* 262.

ises on *musica speculativa* and *musica practica,* leaning heavily upon mathematics—the learned type of music treatise generally written by university men. In his *Lucidarium in arte musicae planae* (GS, III, 64–121),[45] Marchettus aimed to teach *cantores* the philosophical as well as the artistic aspects of music, in line with the age-old desire of musical theorists to raise the unlearned singer to the level of the philosophical *musicus;* and in this work he followed the pattern of the conventional *eisagogé*—with brief discussions of the invention, division, etymology, and *genera* of music, together with a comprehensive description of mathematical proportions—relating all this to the ecclesiastical chant *(cantus planus).* In his mathematical system, Marchettus established three different sizes of half tones, eliminating the syntonic comma and using the natural third (4:5), the basis of the natural system. (In the Pythagorean system constructed of superimposed fifths, the third was altered so that the fifths would be in tune.) Owing to this use of halfsteps of different sizes, chromaticism was possible in Marchettus' system, whereas chromaticism did not fit into the Pythagorean system and modifications of it.

From monodic plain song, Marchettus, like many others in his time, turned to mensural music; and in his *Pomerium in arte musicae mensuratae* (GS, III, 121–88) he described and codified Italian notation for the first time. Following the rhythmic innovations of Petrus de Cruce, who divided the breve into varying numbers of semibreves, Marchettus used a variety of differently shaped

[45] Many of our university treatises are to be found in the two large collections of Martin Gerbert, *Scriptores ecclesiastici de musica sacra potissimum* (Typis San-Blasianis, 1784) and Edmond de Coussemaker, *Scriptorum de musica medii aevi nova series* (Parisiis, 1864–76). These will hereafter be indicated in the text as GS and CS.

The date of Marchettus' two treatises has long been in question. According to Friedrich Ludwig, *"Die Quellen der Motetten ältesten Stils," AfMw,* Vol. V (1923), 289n., the date 1273 in the explicit to the *Lucidarium* is about fifty years too early and the date 1309 (the year in which King Robert of Sicily—to whom the treatise is dedicated—ascended the throne) is several decades too early for the *Pomerium.* Quite recently, Oliver Strunk has presented cogent evidence (based upon an examination of documents relating to persons mentioned in Marchettus' dedications) for assigning the *Lucidarium* to the year 1318, the *Pomerium* to 1319. See his *"Intorno a Marchetto da Padova," Rassegna musicale,* Vol. XX (1950), 312–15. Italian *trecento* theory, Professor Strunk thus proves, was not dependent in any way upon the theory of the *ars nova,* initially formulated by Jean de Muris in 1319 and developed by Philip de Vitry.

semibreves to show their rhythmic relationship to the breve, and he used the *punctus divisionis* (also introduced by Petrus but later abandoned by French theorists in favor of Philip de Vitry's prolations) to mark off these groups.[46] As a matter of fact, Marchettus' divisions of the breve into quicker note values actually corresponded to Philip's use of tempus and prolation as explained in his *Ars nova* written a little later than Marchettus' *Pomerium*. Marchettus, moreover, not only described Italian notation: he compared it with the French system and concluded that the latter was superior. A commentary on the last part of the *Pomerium,* comparing French and Italian notation, has come down to us—the *Brevis compilatio in arte musicae mensuratae* (CS, III, 1–12), obviously pedagogical in purpose.

In addition to being the most important theorist of Italy's *trecento,* Marchettus enjoyed a high reputation as a composer—a part of the *Pomerium* deals with polyphonic composition—if we may believe contemporary reports.[47] Giovanni da Ciconia, distinguished member of the third generation of Italian *trecento* composers,[48] like Marchettus, was interested in scientific as well as artistic aspects of music; and his comprehensive speculative treatise probably owed its origin to the strong emphasis upon music as a mathematical discipline at the University of Padua, where Giovanni was

[46] See Willi Apel, *The Notation of Polyphonic Music, 900–1600* (4th rev. ed., Cambridge, Mass., 1949), 368ff.

[47] Reese, *Music in the Middle Ages,* 371, mentions a madrigal by Jacopo da Bologna which says that everyone is writing music, blossoming forth as *"Filipotti et Marchetti"*; and he also quotes lines by the poet Franco Sacchetti:

> Pieno è il mondo di chi vuol far rime . . .
> Così del canto avvien: senz alcun arte
> Mille Marchetti veggio in ogni parte.

[48] Leonard Ellinwood, "Origins of the Italian Ars Nova," *American Musicological Society Papers,* 1937, 30. For a number of compositions recently available in modern transcription, see Federico Ghisi, "Italian Ars-Nova Music," *Journal of Renaissance and Baroque Music,* Vol. I (1946–48), 173–91, and supplement. A member of the stream of foreign *maestri di cappella* which flowed into Italy after the return of the papal court from Avignon in 1377, Ciconia was mentioned in Martin le Franc's *Champion des Dames* (*ca.* 1440) along with others who were the admiration of "tout Paris" before the advent of Dufay and Binchois: see Willi Apel, *French Secular Music of the Late Fourteenth Century* (Cambridge, Mass., 1950), 1. (Ciconia is also represented in this volume.)

a canon and teacher (*ca.* 1400). Comprising five lengthy books, the entire treatise is largely a compilation of Greek musical theory which received more and more attention with the cultivation of humanistic studies.[49] Book III of this work, an arithmetical treatise *"De proportionibus,"* is known to have been written in Padua in 1411.

Vittorino da Feltre, especially famous for the humanistic school he established at the home of Gianfrancesco Gonzaga, Marquis of Mantua, was for twenty years (1396–1415) a student and teacher at the University of Padua, receiving the *laurea* and teaching mathematics there. Although Vittorino left no musical treatise himself, his interest in *musica speculativa* is seen in the treatise written by a student of his: the learned and comprehensive *Ritus canendi vetustissimus et novus* of Johannes Gallicus (d. 1473). Johannes specifically states in his *Ritus* (CS, IV, 345) that he studied Boethius' *Musica* with Vittorino: *"Sed cum ad Italiam venissem, ac sub optimo viro, Magistro Feltrensi, musicam Boetii diligenter audissem."* Vittorino, moreover, was a firm believer in Greek ideas of ethos, musical effects; and in his humanistic tutorial system of education, music had a high place—being introduced at meal time for its beneficial effects and cultivated generally by his students.[50] Among his own books was a copy of St. Augustine's *De Musica.*

Most famous of all professors in this university for the history of music, however, is Prosdocimus de Beldemandis, *"egregius Musicus, et eximinius philosophus, et clarus astrologus."*[51] A student in the university, Prosdocimus became both doctor of arts and doctor of medicine, and from 1422 until his death in 1428 he was a public professor of mathematics and astronomy.[52] A Venetian

[49] Adrien La Fage, *Essais de diphthérographie musicale* (Paris, 1864), 375–79, gives chapter headings of each book of this treatise. The five books comprised in the treatise are *"De consonantiis," "De speciebus"* (the modes), *"De proportionibus," "De accidentibus,"* and *"De tribus generibus melorum"* (diatonic, chromatic, and enharmonic *genera* demonstrated by monochord divisions).

[50] See William Harrison Woodward, *Vittorino da Feltre* (his copy of Augustine's *Musica* is referred to on pages 48 and 70), and *Studies in Education During the Age of the Renaissance* (Cambridge, 1906), 19ff.

[51] Scardeonius, *De antiquitate urbis Patavii libri tres,* 262.

[52] Favaro, *"Intorno alla vita ed alle opere di Prosdocimo," Bullettino di bibliografia e di storia delle scienze matematiche e fisiche,* Vol. XII, 18–36.

manuscript from 1413 bears his likeness with the inscription:
PROSDOCIMVS DE BELDEMANDO PAT [*avinus*] *ASTR*
[*ologiae*] *ET MVS* [*icae*] *P*[*rofessor*].[53] Prosdocimus' strong emphasis upon music in his teaching of mathematics is also evident
from the eight musical treatises he wrote, six of which are available
in print. These works deal not only with *musica speculativa,* as
one might expect, but also with contemporary problems of *musica
practica.*

Combining both aspects of musical instruction, the *Brevis sum-
mula proportionum* (CS, III, 258–61), 1409, treats of mathematical
proportions and their application in musical notation as a means
of showing rhythmic diminution and augmentation. More strictly
mathematical is the *Libellus monocordi* (CS, III, 248–58), written
in 1413 for Magister Nicolay de collo de Coneglano, which explains
three methods of deriving the scale by different divisions of the
monochord. Prosdocimus' *Tractatus musice speculative*[54] (1425),
is a mathematical work attacking Marchettus' theories of musical
proportions as posited in the fifth chapter of the *Lucidarium;* adhering to the Pythagorean scale, Prosdocimus criticizes Marchettus' "natural scale" with its pure thirds and its halfsteps of three
different sizes. Several other treatises are technical works designed
for the professional musician, but these, too, are based solidly upon
mathematics. Such a work is the *Tractatus practice de musica mensurabili* (CS, III, 200–28), 1408, a specialized discussion of rhythm
and notation, largely a commentary, as Prosdocimus says at the
beginning, *"super tractatum cantus mensurabilis Johannis de
Muris."* In addition to treating the usual divisions of mensural
music—note values in various meters, alteration, the *punctus,* metrical signs, ligatures, pauses, syncopation, diminution and augmentation—Prosdocimus gives here one of the few descriptions of *color*
and *talea* (referred to briefly in the treatise of Jean de Muris) found
in medieval treatises. And like Marchettus a century earlier, Pros-

[53] Antonio Favaro, *"Appendice a gli studi intorno alla vita ed alle opere di Prosdocimo
de' Beldomandi,"* *ibid.,* Vol. XVIII (1885), 422.

[54] Luigi Torri, *"Il 'Trattato' di Prosdocimo de' Beldomandi contro il 'Lucidario' di
Marchetto de Padova,"* *Rivista Musicale Italiana,* Vol. XX (1913), 707–62; text of treatise,
731–62.

docimus in his *Tractatus practice de musica mensurabili ad modum Italicorum* (CS, III, 228–48), 1412, compared French and Italian notation. Unlike the older theorist, however, he preferred the Italian system: both "arts," says Prosdocimus, tend toward the same end, but the Italian is clearer and therefore superior.[55] From 1412 also comes the *Tractatus de contrapuncto* (CS, III, 193–99), treating types of counterpoint and intervals to use in voice combinations; here Prosdocimus, aware of the value of judging by ear as well as by intellect, stresses the achievement of *harmonia delectabilis* to move the listener.

With Marchettus and Prosdocimus, thus, as well as others only a little less distinguished, Padua produced the most important Italian theorists of the medieval period; and the stress laid upon mathematics as the basis for music by all these theorists is certainly to be related to the great flourishing of the liberal arts, with emphasis upon mathematics and music, at the University of Padua in the late Middle Ages. The widespread fame as composers, moreover, which most of our theorists enjoyed, points to the close alignment in this university of musical theory and musical practice—a union undoubtedly responsible for the classical beauty of the Italian *ars nova.* The emphasis upon music at Padua, indeed, was brought to an academic climax in 1450 with the establishment of a chair of music in the university by Pope Nicolas V.

ii. France: Paris and Orléans
Paris

NUMEROUS MYTHS have attributed the founding of the University of Paris, most distinguished of all the medieval *studia,* to many different people. Emphasizing the part England played in spreading higher learning upon the continent, the Oxford antiquarian Anthony à Wood conferred this honor upon Charles the Great,

---

[55] CS III, 233: *"sed iste due artes Gallica scilicet et Italica sunt due artes ad eumden finem tendentes, cum finis utriusque sit mensurata cantare, et Italica est clarior . . . ergo et pulcrior et laudabilior."*

through the "persuasion" of his British mentor, Alcuin.[1] Some historians trace the origin of the Sorbonne to the time when Remigius of Auxerre taught the arts and theology there (*ca.* 900).[2] Remigius was especially distinguished for his teaching of music, and counted among his many students who later became famous as philosophers and teachers Odo of Cluny, whose vita states that he was instructed in music by Remigius, then in Paris "reading" Martianus Capella on the liberal arts.[3] Remigius' commentary *De musica* (GS, I, 63–94) upon the musical portion of Martianus' allegory *De nuptiis* was widely used in the Middle Ages.

Remigius certainly contributed to the great fame of Paris as a center for the liberal arts and theology. But the *studium* at Paris, apparently flourishing by 1170, evolved gradually from a group of schools whose origins go far back into the Middle Ages: the Cathedral School of Notre Dame, the monastic school of St. Victoire, and the schools scattered on Mont St.-Geneviève, especially famous because of Abelard's teaching. The first statutes for the university were drawn up in 1215 by the papal legate, Robert de Courçon, an Englishman who had studied at Paris: these prescribed for the *lectiones ordinariae* only Priscien's grammar and the treatises comprised in Aristotle's *Organon,* but "extraordinary" lectures (those

---

[1] *History and Antiquities of the University of Oxford* (tr. and ed. by John Gutch) (Oxford, 1792–96), I, 13:

> England flourished in the knowledge of all good arts, and was able to send of her learned men into other countries to propagate learning. . . . Alcuinus . . . was master to Charles the Great, through whose persuasion that emperor founded the University of Paris. So that England was twice schoolmistress to France, first by our Druids, and secondly by Alcuinus the Englishman.

[2] For example, James Coutts, *A History of the University of Glasgow* (Glasgow, 1909), 5.

[3] See Migne, *Patrologia latina*, CXXXIII, 45, 52: "*Deinde apud Parisium dialectica musicaque a Remigio doctissimo viro est instructus. . . . His diebus abiit Parisius, ibique dialecticam sancti Augustini Deodato filio suo missam perlegit, et Martianum in liberalibus artibus frequenter lectitavit: praeceptorem quippe in his omnibus habuit Remigium.*"

Another early work refers to Remigius' teaching of Martianus Capella: the commentary of Notker Labeo (d. 1022; Notker translated the first two books of Martianus' *De nuptiis* into German), based upon Remigius' commentary, the preface beginning, "*Remigius lêret únsih tísen auctorem in álenámen uuésen gehéizenen martianum.*" See E. H. Sehrt and Taylor Starck (eds.) *Notkers des Deutschen Werke* (Halle, 1933–35), II, 1.

given on religious holidays) included the subjects of the quadrivium.[4] *"Bachalarii examinandi in Sancta Genovefa in camera,"* ca. 1350, moreover, were required to have attended lectures on mathematics before the examination.[5] And reform statutes, promulgated in 1366, specified that before being admitted *ad licentiam,* students in the arts must have heard certain books, including *"aliquos libros mathematicos."*[6] No other statutes were given to the university until after the middle of the fifteenth century.

As in the Italian universities, then, medieval statutes for the *studium* at Paris offer little information about actual subjects taught; but there is overwhelming evidence from many other sources for the study, cultivation, and practice of music as science and art at the great French university. One especially strong bit of evidence for the regular teaching of music in the arts curriculum is the fact that many of the German universities organized directly upon the Parisian model—Prague and Vienna, for example—included music quite definitely in their courses of required studies, even specifying length of time and cost of instruction.

In early documents dealing with the university and in literary works from the pens of erstwhile students at the Sorbonne there are many references to the seven liberal arts. A certain Guy de Basoches, student at Paris and Montpellier, later canon and cantor in the cathedral at Châlons,[7] left a description of Paris ca. 1175 in which he declared, "On this island, the seven sisters, to wit, the Liberal Arts, have secured an eternal abiding place for themselves."[8]

[4] See Charles Thurot, *De l'Organisation de l'enseignement dans l'université de Paris au moyen-âge* (Paris, 1850), 71. And see Heinrich Denifle and Emile Chatelain (eds.), *Chartularium Universitatis Parisiensis* (Parisiis, 1889–97), I, 78, no. 20: *"Non legant in festivis diebus nisi philosophos et rhetoricas, et quadruvialia."*
   Certain subsequent statutes mention lists of books to be read—*"Statuta artistarum nationis anglicanae de baccalareis in artibus determinandis in Quadragesima,"* 1252; statutes of the arts faculty, 1255; and statutes of the English Nation, 1347—but no musical work is cited. See *Chartularium,* I, 227–30, no. 201; 277–79, no. 246; and II, 673, no. 1185.
   [5] *Ibid.,* II, 678, no. 1185: *"Item, quod audivistis centum lectiones de Mathematica ad minus."*
   [6] *Ibid.,* III, 145, no. 1319.
   [7] Raby, *History of Secular Latin Poetry,* II, 38.
   [8] Cited and translated by Arthur O. Norton, *Readings in the History of Education: Medieval Universities* (Cambridge, 1909), 148.

A certain Maître Gossouin, whose *Image du Monde* (1245) enjoyed great popularity in the late Middle Ages, made much of the flourishing of the seven liberal arts in France, especially in Paris, "as fortyme was in the cyte of athennes": "In lyke wyse may I saye to yow that parys Oxenford & Cambryge ben the fontayns where men may drawe out most science & more in parys than in other places & sith it is soo that clergye is somoche auaunced in ffraunce."[9]

A document from the hands of the rector (1290) mentions certain *"bacalarios in septem artibus liberalibus petentes licentiam."*[10] And the *Liber procuratorum Nationis Anglicanae (Alemanniae)* (1331–1406), refers several times to "schools of the seven liberal arts" in the university.[11]

Highly enthusiastic is the description of Parisian studies left us by Johann von Jenzenstein, student in the university, 1375 76, later Archbishop of Prague and distinguished composer of liturgical music,[12] who said that the liberal arts, music among them, were flourishing at Paris late in the fourteenth century. In a letter describing the *novitates Parisienses* in which he so delighted, Johann spoke of famous masters at Paris, some excelling in the disciplines of the trivium, others in those of the quadrivium, and others in both; a description of the various disciplines follows, and Johann's remarks about music indicate that he heard lectures on music as a mathematical science and also became acquainted with French theory and musical artistry.[13] We recall, too, that Antonio Lido,

[9] Caxton's translation (Westminster, 1481), cap. vi. This copy is owned by the Huntington Library.

[10] *Chartularium*, II, 43, no. 569.

[11] For instance, in 1342, when *"Primo quidem concordatum est per nacionem quod predictus magister Zuno scolas haberet ad septem artes"*: see Heinrich Denifle and Emile Chatelain (eds.) *Auctarium Chartularii Universitatis Parisiensis*, new ed. Henri Didier (Parisiis, 1937), I, 54.

[12] Zdeněk Nejedlý, *"Magister Záviše und seine Schule,"* SIMG, Vol. VII (1905), 63–65.

[13] J. Loserth, *"Der Codex Epistolaris des Erzbischofs von Prag Johann von Jenzenstein,"* Archiv für österreichische Geschichte, Vol. LV (1877), 385–86:

> Sunt et alii magistri septem artibus liberalibus subtiliter insigniti, quorum exemplo et doctrina universus orbis ut celum sideribus decoratur et hii tribus

musician, philosopher, and teacher at Padua late in the fourteenth century, had gone to Paris, according to Savonarola, to study the liberal arts, in the teaching of which he later became such an ornament in his native city.

A list of books to be used by Paris scholars, with stationers' prices for each (1304), includes Macrobius' commentary on Cicero's *Somnium Scipionis,* Aristotle's *Politica,* and the pseudo-Aristotelian *Problemata,* all of which contain much information about music; and another inventory here, *"Opera Fratris Richardi,"* lists two items, both of which contain sections on music: De Proprietatibus rerum and De Ortu scientiarum.[14] The first of these is the encyclopedia of Bartholomaeus Anglicus, an Oxford scholar who taught at Paris in the thirteenth century, a compendious work covering all the learning of his time and including a section on music; the second is a large encyclopedia thought to be the work of the Arab Al-Farabi, author of several music treatises especially influential upon Parisian *musici.*

In addition to this evidence for the study of music as a liberal art, there are many references to musical practices in documents relating to the medieval university. One of the most colorful of these is the account given by the chronicler Matthew Paris of the reception offered Henry III, King of England, upon his arrival in Paris in 1254: lectures were dispensed with, and students, especially those of the English-German Nation, welcomed the king with special songs and instrumental music.[15] Lists of books, too, provide

---

trivialibus, illi quatuor quadruvialibus, quidam omnibus simul sunt illustrati. . . . Alie sunt autem quadruviales, videlicet arismetrica, musica, geometria et astronomia; arismetrica considerat de numeris absolute et de variis passionibus numerorum; que subalternat sibi musicam, nam musica considerat de numero considerato ad sonum, nunc dissono, nunc semitono, nunc falseto, nunc vero bemollem cantum exornat et quomodo secundum gravitatem numerorum et mensuraciones accentuum quis decantet, quod peroptime novit *Parisiensium* turba quam plurima; igitur subalternat sibi musicam, quia arismetrica subalternat sibi tam proporciones arismetricas quam armonicas, musica vero solum armonicas.

Loserth says a word has been erased after *Parisiensium* in the manuscript, probably *musicorum* (386 n.).

[14] *Chartularium,* II, 107, 109, no. 642.

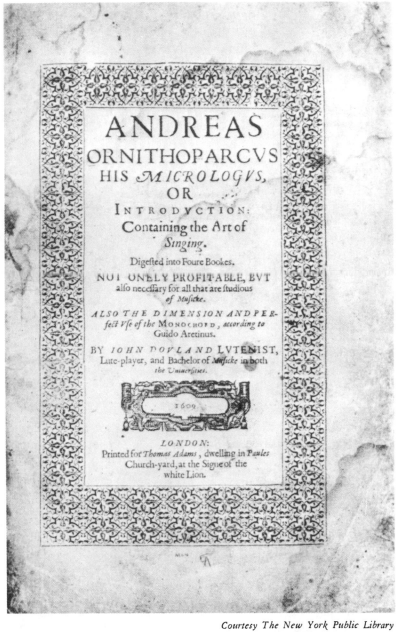

Title page from the first edition of John Dowland's translation of Ornithoparchus' *Micrologus* (London, 1609).

LES SIX

PREMIERS LIVRES

DES ELEMENTS D'EV-
CLIDE, TRADVICTS ET

COMMENTEZ PAR PIERRE
Forcadel de Bezies, Lecteur ordi-
naire du Roy és Mathema-
tiques en l'vniuerfité
de Paris.

* *
*

EN MOY, LA MORT.

EN MOY, LA VIE.

A PARIS,

Chez Hierofme de Marnef, & Guillaume Cauellat,
au mont S. Hilaire, à l'enfeigne du Pelican.

1 5 6 4.

Title page of Forcadel's translation of Euclid (Paris, 1564).

clues to musical observances among the students. An inventory of the French Nation (1339), for example, noted: *"Item quatuor libri de cantu pro capella, et duo quaterni cooperti vitulo"*; and among the goods of the Nation of Picardy (which honored Saint Nicolas as patron) in 1382 was *"Item tres parvi libri cantus in quibus continetur officium sancti Nicolai."*[16]

Musical instruction was available (if not obligatory) in some of the colleges: for instance, the Collège de Cornouailles required its members to learn plain chant, according to statutes of 1380.[17] And statutes of the various nations offer further evidence of the use of music in their religious ceremonies. A statute of the Nation of Picardy (1347) declares that *"post prandium vespere decantentur"*; and in 1370 the English-German Nation decided to employ *"aliquos bonos cantores"* to celebrate the feast of its patron saint, since either a lack of singers or the poor quality of the singing resulted in confusion and laughter.[18] Likewise in 1371 the nation decided to import professional singers to be paid *"de pecunia nacionis"* for the feast of St. Edmund; in 1372 they employed *"cantores qui divinum officium cantarent"*; and in 1374, 1375, and 1376 *"alieni cantores sub expensis nacionis"* assisted at the services.[19] This happy solution to the problem of poor singing in the English-German Nation was discontinued, however, in 1380, when the

[15] *Matthaei Parisiensis Abbreviatio Chronicorum Angliae*, in *Rerum Britannicarum Medii aevi Scriptores* (ed. by Sir Frederic Madden) (London, 1866–69), III, 342:

> Scolares autem Parisienses, maxime nationis Anglicanae, suspensis ad horam lectionibus, cereos emerunt vestesque festivas, et diversa quae gaudium poterant attestari; et, praeparatis cantantibus, florigeris, cum sertis et coronis et musicis instrumentis processerunt obviam venientibus. Sicque transegerunt totum diem illum et crastinum, civitate tota Parisius mirabiliter adornata, in gaudio et canticis, luminaribus et exultationibus.

[16] *Chartularium*, II, 491, no. 1028, and III, 310, no. 1470.

[17] André Pirro, *"L'Enseignement de la musique aux universités françaises,"* MIGM, Vol. II (1930), 30.

[18] *Chartularium*, II, 609, no. 1146; and see the proctors' account, *Auctarium Chartularii*, I, 373: *"Item proposui an expediret pro die beati Edmundi, scilicet in missa, adducere aliquos bonos cantores propter majorem solemnitatem festi sub remuneratione nationis, cum in vesperis propter defectum cantorum confusio non modica facta fuerat, et nationis vel cantantium seu ululantium derisio; quod omnibus videbatur expedire."*

[19] *Ibid.*, I, 406, 417–18, 460, 479, 508.

group decided *"quod non expediret habere cantores alienos et speciales sub expensis nacionis, sed quod quilibet voce Almanica cantaret quanto dulcius sciret."*[20]

In 1413 this nation appointed an organist for its church, St. Mathurin: *"Eciam voluit nacio habere cantores in ecclesia ad sollempnisandum, et organistam, scilicet Heinricum de Saxonia."*[21] The organist Henricus de Saxonia was one of the determinants (bachelors) in 1407; and in 1415 he became organist of Notre Dame, being a bachelor of medicine at that time.[22] In addition to Henry, various other musicians were students or teachers in the university. Names of the *cantor* and *succentor* of Paris occur in early records several times: not only were these officers closely associated with the university through their appointments at Notre Dame, but the *cantor ecclesiae Parisiensis* was in charge of many grammar schools under the jurisdiction of the university.[23] Singers and choirmasters from the royal chapel, too, were often enrolled in the university. Julianus de Muris, for instance, one of the members of the Norman Nation who petitioned for a benefice in 1349, was at that time *"doctor puerorum capelle regalis."*[24] Johannes Hollandrinus, whose verses are quoted in the *Tractatus cujusdam Carthusiensis monachi* (CS, II, 434–83), was a *magister regens* in the university in 1351; and the *cantor* Johannes Beyssel, mentioned in several records, was obviously a regent master too, for in 1369 a certain student was granted the *licentia "sub magistro Johanne Beyssel, cantore Aquensi."*[25] From 1403 we have the names of two members of the English nation, *magistri artium*, both of them engaged *"actu docenti Parisius in arte musice ex auctoritate et*

[20] *Ibid.*, I, 595.

[21] *Ibid.*, II, 159.

[22] *Ibid.*, II, 4, 4 n.; and see Pirro, *"L'Enseignement de la musique,"* MIGM, Vol. II, 32.

[23] For example, in a document of 1327 we find "Girardus de Campomuli, cantor" and "Stephanus de Novilla, succentor": *Chartularium*, II, 296, no. 860. For documents of 1357 and 1380 giving rules for teachers coming under the jurisdiction of the cantor, see *ibid.*, III, 51–53, no. 1237, and 289–91, no. 1446.

[24] *Ibid.*, II, 640, no. 1165 and Pirro, *"L'Enseignement de la musique,"* MIGM, Vol. II, 29.

[25] Jos. Smits van Waesberghe, "Some Music Treatises and Their Interrelation," *Musica Disciplina*, Vol. III (1949), 111, identifies Johannes Hollandrinus. For Beyssel, see the *Auctarium Chartularii*, I, 330.

licentia Universitatis."[26] One of these, Johannes Comitis, also held the office *"instructori puerorum chori eccl. Parisiensis,"* having twice before (1399 and 1402) held this position.[27] In 1403 the master of the children of the Sainte Chapelle, Johannes Bonne, *magister artium,* was enrolled as a student in theology; and this chapel is mentioned again in our records in 1444 when *"Magister Johannes Mortis, cantor s. Capel. palatii Paris."* appears among the doctors of law.[28] The anonymous author of a *Règles de la Seconde Rhétorique* from the fifteenth century mentions a number of poets and composers distinguished in the art of writing verse: among these is *"maistre Jehan Vaillant, lequel tenoit a Paris escolle de musique."*[29] Nicolas Grenon was one of the priests of Notre Dame in 1399 and later canon, before joining the Burgundian *maîtrise* at Cambrai; and Thomas Hoppinel was master of the children of Notre Dame before becoming chaplain to the Duke of Bedford (regent of France, 1422–35).[30] It is highly likely that Guillaume Dufay was also a student in the university: according to the epitaph on his tombstone he was both a master of arts and a bachelor of canon law.[31] In 1420, Dufay, then a priest of St.-Germain-l'Auxerrois, was involved in the robbery of a *drap d'or* from the Sainte Chapelle but was exonerated of all blame in the inquiry which followed.[32] In 1444 a remarkable event occurred which must have taxed the skill of many university musicians: Fernandus Cordubensis, who had challenged university members to a contest in

[26] *Chartularium,* IV, 110, no. 1796:

> Johanni Comitis, presb. Ebroycens. dioc. actu docenti Parisius in arte musice, ex auctoritate et licentia Universitatis ejusdem instructori puerorum chori eccl. Parisiensis.
> Guillermo Burgondi, presb. Parisiens. dioc., actu docenti in arte musice Parisius ex auctoritate et licentia Universitatis Paris. ac cantori ejusdem.

[27] *Ibid.,* IV, 110, 110 n.

[28] *Ibid.,* IV, 82, no. 1796, and 640, no. 2583; and see Pirro, *"L'Enseignement de la musique,"* MIGM, Vol. II, 31.

[29] M. Ernest Langlois, *Recueil d'arts de seconde rhétorique* (Paris, 1902), 13. Some of Vaillant's music appears in Apel, *French Secular Music of the Late Fourteenth Century.*

[30] Jacques Chailley, *Histoire musicale du moyen âge* (Paris, 1950), 269.

[31] Robert Eitner, *"Guillaume Dufay,"* MfMG, Vol. XVI (1884), 22: "His inferius jacet venerabilis vir magr. guillermus dufay, music., baccalarius in decretis."

[32] Pirro, *"L'Enseignement de la musique,"* MIGM, Vol. II, 32.

playing on instruments, singing, or "discanting," disputed with great success against more than fifty opponents in a debate held in the Collège de Navarre.[33]

The study of music as a branch of mathematics at the medieval University of Paris is reflected in numerous treatises written by alumni of that institution. Among these, several philosophical works may be mentioned. The English scholar Adelard of Bath (twelfth century), who studied and taught in France, included a brief protreptical introduction to music in his treatise *De eodem et diverso*, relating music to arithmetic and stressing the beneficial effects of music as pointed out by Plato. One sentence near the beginning of his musical discussion is especially interesting: it mentions his musical studies in France (*Gallicis studiis*, probably meaning the Sorbonne), speaks of a *magister artis una cum discipulis*, shows Adelard's ability as an instrumentalist—for he played the *cithara* before the Queen of France—and tells how "a certain little boy" was strongly moved by the music (musical effects).[34] Maitre Gossouin's *Image du monde*, an encyclopedia (1245) to which we have already referred, contains a chapter (XII) on music, relating this subject to arithmetic and emphasizing its connection with medicine.[35] And a number of Oxford theologians who

[33] *Ibid.*

[34] Hans Willner, *"Des Adelard von Bath Traktat De eodem et diverso,"* Beiträge zur Geschichte der Philosophie des Mittelalters, Vol. IV (1903), part 1, 1–34; discussion of music, 25–28. *Philosophia*, speaking to Adelard, says:

Et ne exempli postulatio longe quaesita diutius nos fatiget, tu ipse si recolligis, cum praeterito anno in eadem musica Gallicis studiis totus sudares adessetque in serotino tempore magister artis una cum discipulis, cum eorum reginaeque rogatu citharam tangeres, puerulus quidam non certe locutionis sono irretitus ex citharae sonitu tanta hilaritate affectus est, ut et manus digitosque suos simili nisu mouere aggrederetur omnibusque astantibus risum moueret.

[35] *Image du monde*, cap. xii:

The sixthe of the vij sciences is called musyque the whiche fourmeth hym of Arsmetryque/ Of this science of musyque cometh alle attemperaunce, And of this arte procedeth somme phisyque, ffor like as musyque accordeth alle thinges that dyscorde in them, & remayne them to concordaunce/ right so in lyke wyse trauaylleth phisyque to brynge Nature to poynt that disnatureth in mannes body / whan any maladye or sekenes encombreth hit.

The author proceeds to explain that medicine in not one of the seven liberal arts but

studied at Paris incorporated short sections on music in their philosophical writings—for example, Robert Grosseteste and Robert Kilwardby. Allegorical literature from the Middle Ages also reflects the study of music as a part of all philosophy, of all knowledge. One of the finest examples of this type is the *Anticlaudianus,* a long poetical allegory by a teacher at the University of Paris, Alanus de Insulis (Alain de Lille, d. 1203, whose wide learning—he may have studied at Chartres or Orléans—earned for him the epithet *doctor universalis*). The seven liberal arts (with music, of course, prominent among them) are introduced here as the daughters of Prudence, and Alanus follows Martianus Capella in having each daughter discuss the art she represents.[36] The musical discussion (chiefly lines in book III) centers around the psychological effects of music, with some information about intervals.

In view of the development of new forms of polyphony at Notre Dame in the late Middle Ages, the close connection between musical officials in the cathedral and university personnel, and the constant supply of students from the choir school to the university, it is not surprising that many treatises on artistic aspects of *musica practica* sprang, directly or indirectly, from musical studies at the University of Paris—treatises attempting to solve the problem of a clearer system of notation, attempting to evolve an unequivocal basis for rhythmic values resulting in the standard mensural system, and discussing the various forms of the new polyphony, *discantus.* Several such works are comprised in the lengthy *Tractatus de musica* (CS, I, 1–154) by Jerome of Moravia (d. after 1304), teacher at the Dominican convent in Paris—in a thirteenth-century

is a craft to keep man's body in health; the science that serves man's body deserves not the name liberal, only the science that serves man's soul:

> And this is the very reson why thise artes alle vii ben called vii sciences liberall, ffor they make the soul liberall, & delyuer it fro alle euyll/ Of this arte is musyque thus comune, that she acordeth her to euerich so well that by her the vii sciences were sette in concorde that they yet endure.

[36] For a study of Alanus, see G. Raynaud de Lage, *Alain de Lille, poète du xiie siècle* (Paris, 1951). F. J. E. Raby, *History of Christian-Latin Poetry* (Oxford, 1953), 297ff., analyzes the *Anticlaudianus.* The verses on music appear on fol. D2 recto of the Cambridge University Library copy.

document he is associated with Robertus de Sorbonne[37]—who compiled his treatise with a definitely pedagogical intent: *"ad honorem Domini nostri Jesu-Christi . . . et ad utilitatem studiosorum."* Jerome's own contribution is a learned *eisagogé* leading to the study of the ecclesiastical chant, leaning heavily upon Boethius (indeed, often quoting him verbatim), giving the definition of music, its etymology, invention, divisions, and subdivisions according to various authorities (including Alphorabius' *musica theoretica* and *musica practica*), and its effects; the "subject" of music—numbers—leads Jerome to a discussion of mathematical proportions of consonant and dissonant intervals, divisions of the monochord and derivation of the scale, and finally the ecclesiastical modes. Unique in this very conventional treatise is Jerome's chapter (XXIX) on the tuning and playing of stringed instruments—the *rubeba, viella,* and *bordunus*—played with a bow at this time.

Often in the Middle Ages a treatise on the plain song of the Church found its counterpart in one on sacred polyphony; and for his discussion of rhythmic problems connected with *discantus,* Jerome has inserted three treatises by other men. One of these, the anonymous *Discantus positio vulgaris* (CS, I, 94–97), *ca.* 1230–40, is the oldest work on the notation of the rhythmic modes, using only the *longa* and *brevis,* the *semibrevis* being considered *ultra mensuram.* Some scholars believe this little tract to have been written by Robertus de Sabilone (*fl.* 1230–60), who is known to have been *discantor* and later *praecentor* at Notre Dame,[38] where the polyphonic music described in the treatise—organum duplum, conductus, *motetus,* and *ochetus*—was developed, and who was thus a high ranking member of the university.

---

[37] E. de Coussemaker, *Traités inédits sur la musique au moyen-âge* (Lille, 1865), I, 5.

[38] See Amédée Gastoué, "Three Centuries of French Medieval Music," *Musical Quarterly,* Vol. III (1917), 178; CS, I, vii; and the remarks of Anon. IV, *ibid.,* I, 342. The *De musica libellus* of Anon. VII (CS, I, 378–83) is similar in doctrine to the *Discantus positio vulgaris* where all longs are equal to two breves; *"est recta longa que continet in se duo tempora"* (CS, I, 378). This supports Walter Odington's statement about a century later, *"Longa autem apud priores organistas duo tantum habuit tempora"* (CS, I, 235). Coussemaker has also printed the *Positio* in his *Histoire de l'harmonie au moyen-âge* (Paris, 1852), 247–53, with a parallel French version. For date of this treatise, see Ludwig, *"Die Quellen der Motteten," AfMw,* Vol. V, 289.

Next in Jerome's compilation is the *De musica mensurabili positio* (CS, I, 97–117) by another university teacher, the English grammarian, musician, mathematician, and alchemist, John of Garland. Having studied at Oxford, John went to Paris for further studies, assisted at the founding of the *studium* at Toulouse in 1229, was teaching in Paris again around 1232, and died after 1252, possibly as late as 1272.[39] His name probably deriving from the *Clos de Garlande,* in which was located one of the oldest schools of the university, John was distinguished enough to merit the praise of Philip de Vitry, who in the next century mentioned *"magistrum Johannem de Gallandia quondam in studio Parisino expertissimum atque probatissimum"* (CS, III, 23). The doctrine of rhythm and notation as explained in John's *Positio* is based upon the rhythmic modes. But John is apparently the first theorist to discuss combinations of the various modes in different voices; and his remarks on the subject of *color* appear to be the first discussion of certain melodic devices used in polyphonic composition—*sonus ordinatus, floricatio,* and *repetitio*. This latter, in fact, is an interesting attempt on the part of a scholar well versed in rhetoric to find musical analogues for certain rhetorical devices. A companion piece to John's *Positio* is his *Introductio musice*[40] (CS, I, 157–75), an introduction to the study of plain song, *cantus immesurabilis* (not included in Jerome's compilation, since he began with his own *eisagogé*). As usual, before the various elements of plain song are dealt with, there is a condensed summary of the meaning of music, etymology of the word, divisions, and uses of music. Unusual here is John's division *"in musicam planam, mensurabilem et in-*

[39] The most recent and comprehensive account of Garland's life and works is by Louis John Paetow, *Morale Scolarium of John of Garland* (Berkeley, 1927), 77–145. Paetow, however, hesitates to identify the grammarian with the musician.

[40] The section of John's *Positio* explaining rhythmic theory has been published separately by Coussemaker as *De musica mensurabili* (CS, I, 175–82), the work taken from another manuscript and showing slight variations from Jerome's copy. The *Optima introductio in contrapunctum,* attributed by Coussemaker to John of Garland (CS, III, 12–13) is now believed to have come from the fourteenth century or later. Treating of the intervals to use in *nota-contra-notam* composition, it bears a great similarity to the tracts based upon English folk practices of improvisation: see Georgiades, *Englische Diskanttraktate,* 58–60. Our survey of medieval treatises has made clear that no treatise based upon *usus* is to be associated with university learning and teaching.

strumentabilem," referring to various kinds of sounding music, quite different from the usual Boethian divisions (*mundana, humana,* and *instrumentalis*), and showing, perhaps, the influence of Al-Farabi's simple dichotomy: theoretical music and practical music.

In addition to the *Discantus positio vulgaris* and Garland's treatise on rhythmic problems and polyphony, Jerome included in his compilation the work which was, perhaps, the most important of all thirteenth-century rhythmic discussions—the *Ars cantus mensurabilis* of Franco of Cologne (CS, I, 117–35).[41] For this is the treatise which codified and standardized a system of notation eliminating ambiguities by establishing definite time values for all notes and ligatures, thereby dealing a death blow to the old modal system—in which the notes in ligature varied in time relationships according to the rhythmic modes—and laying the foundation for the system of notation still in use today. Franco was head of the cathedral school at Cologne (he is referred to in an ancient document as *scholasticus majoris ecclesiae Coloniensis*),[42] one of the schools from which the University of Cologne developed late in the fourteenth century. Chaplain to the Pope and preceptor of the order of St. John of Jerusalem in Cologne, Franco was also a practical musician of high rank: Jacobus of Liège heard a triplum of Franco's performed at Paris in the next century.[43] Franco describes the making of tripla in his treatise along with other polyphonic forms. Franconian theory was not only cited many times by sub-

---

[41] See also GS, III, 1–16, where it is attributed to Franco of Paris. Generally dated *ca.* 1260, Franconian theory is now thought to have developed *ca.* 1280 and later. See Georg Kuhlmann, *Die zweistimmigen französischen Motetten des Kodex Montpellier* (Wurzburg, 1938), I, 84n. An English translation of this important treatise appears in Strunk, *Source Readings in Music History*, 139–59.

The *Compendium discantus Magistri Franconis* (CS, I, 154–56), beginning "*Ego Franco de Colonia utilitati juvenum cupiens deservire, compendiosum tractatum de discantu, ut subsequeretur, composui,*" is a brief summary of the intervals to use in counterpoint. According to Besseler, "*Die Motette,*" *AfMw*, Vol. VIII, 157–58 and note 4, the *Ars cantus mensurabilis* is the only authentic work of Franco's; the *Compendium discantus* is a later compilation.

[42] Robert Eitner, *Biographisch-bibliographisches Quellen-Lexicon der Musiker und Musikgelehrten* (Leipzig, 1900–1904), IV, 59.

[43] CS I, 135n.; and *Speculum musicae*, CS, II, 402.

sequent theorists, but the chapter *"De discantu et ejus speciebus"* of Franco's *Ars cantus mensurabilis* was incorporated almost verbatim nearly a century later by Tunstede in the fourth section of his *Quatuor principalia* (CS, IV, 254 ff.).

The last treatise in the collection of Jerome of Moravia is a brief *Musica mensurabilis* (CS, I, 136–39) by Petrus Picardus. Petrus summarizes the mensural theory of Franco and refers several times to an *arbor* (apparently a table of note values, although the *arbor* itself is not given) of a certain Johannes de Burgundia. The latter was probably a teacher at Paris, for Jerome, introducing Franco's *Ars cantus mensurabilis,* says he heard the treatise from the lips of Johannes de Burgundia (CS, I, 117); and his *arbor* was possibly a pedagogical device aimed at clarifying rhythmic theory for his students.

But there was an older Franco than Franco of Cologne, according to the unknown Englishman immortalized by Coussemaker as Anonymus IV (CS, I, 342). Coussemaker refers to him as Franco of Paris and assigns to him the thirteenth-century treatise *De arte discantandi*,[44] a work positing pre-Franconian doctrine of notation (values of notes in the rhythmic modes) and sixteen rules for the writing of counterpoint. This work probably served as the basis for lectures by a teacher in the University of Paris, for there are three other treatises which appear to be summaries of it by students of the Parisian Franco. All three tracts begin with the classical formula, *"Gaudent brevitate moderni,"* found in the Franconian treatise just before the instruction in notation, and all contain many identical paragraphs.[45] One of the treatises, however (*Anonymi II Tractatus de discantu*), contains a great deal of material not found in the Franconian treatise, including a section on *falsa musica* (introduction of chromaticism into the scale)—perhaps the earliest statement of the origin of chromatic tones, for the sake of

---

[44] *L'Histoire de l'harmonie au moyen-âge,* 262–73, with a parallel French translation.

[45] *Anonymi II Tractatus de discantu* (CS, I, 303–19); *Anonymi III De cantu mensurabili* (*ibid.*, I, 319–27); and the *Abreviatio Magistri Franconis a Johanne dicto Balloce* (*ibid.*, I, 292–96). Nothing is known of the writer of the last tract, who, like the two anonymous writers, was probably a student of the Parisian Franco's.

necessity or of beauty.[46] In connection with the latter, there is a reference to secular music: *"Causa pulchritudinis, ut patet in Cantinellis coronatis"*—especially interesting because another member of the University of Paris, Johannes de Grocheo, also discusses the *cantus coronatus* in his famous treatise.

These three treatises are not the only ones based upon the teaching of Franco of Paris, whose influence was extensive and about whom the last word has yet to be said. In the next century an Englishman, Robert de Handlo, wrote a treatise of the *scholia* type based chiefly upon Franco's treatise: the *Regule cum maximis Magistri Franconis, cum additionibus aliorum musicorum* (CS, I, 383–403), 1326, a conversation between Handlo and a group of *musici* of former times whose doctrine is cited and commented upon. The opening remark is attributed to Franco: *"Gaudent brevitate moderni";* and his doctrine forms the main part of the work. *Alii musici* are Petrus de Cruce, who discusses the semibreve; Petrus le Viser, who speaks of three rhythmic *mores (longus, mediocer,* and *lascivus);* Johannes de Garlandia, who gives his doctrine of notation; Admetus de Aureliana, who mentions practices among the *"cantores de Navernia";* and Jacobus de Navernia, who discusses hockets.[47] Significant, too, of the Paris teacher's widespread influence is the fact that Handlo's treatise was known and copied by the later English musician John Hanboys (who properly belongs in our discussion of Oxford).

[46] CS, I, 312:

> fuit autem inventa falsa musica propter duas causas, scilicet causa necessitatis, et causa pulchritudinis cantus per se.
>
> Causa necessitatis, quia non poteramus habere diapente, diatessaron, diapason ut in locis visis in capitulo de proportionibus.
>
> Causa pulchritudinis, ut patet in Cantinellis coronatis.

[47] The rhythmic innovations for which Petrus de Cruce was famous are not mentioned in his one extant treatise (the *Tractatus de tonis,* CS, I, 282–92, an explanation of the ecclesiastical modes and their formulas); they are described by later writers. For a description of these innovations, see Apel, *The Notation of Polyphonic Music,* 318ff.

For a discussion of Petrus le Viser and the three *mores* (tempo differences), see Jacques Handschin, "The Summer Canon and Its Background," *Musica Disciplina,* Vol. III (1949), 77–78.

Unable to find out anything about *Navernia,* I venture to guess that *Nivernia* is meant —Nivernais, whose capital was Nevers, adjoining Orléanais.

From late in the thirteenth century comes a treatise already noted in connection with Franco: *De mensuris et discantu* (CS, I, 327–65) written by Coussemaker's Anonymus IV, generally thought to have been an Englishman who studied at the University of Paris in the latter half of the century. The doctrine presented here is that of the rhythmic modes; the author, indeed, refers to the work of John of Garland which explains this theory. But the treatise is unique and invaluable in giving historical information about the Notre Dame School. Composers and their works are mentioned—Leoninus, Perotinus, and Robertus de Sabilone. A certain *"Petrus notator optimus, et Johannes, dictus Primarius,"* are also included, their works being used *"usque in tempus Magistri Franconis Primi et alterius Magistri Franconis de Colonia, qui inceperunt in suis libris aliter pro parte notare"* (CS, I, 342). Not only does the enthusiastic writer cite specific composers and their works: he also describes the contents of various *volumina* of music he has examined personally, volumes of organa and conductus in two, three, and four parts. And in addition to French practices, musical matters in various nearby countries find their way into this writer's paragraphs[48]—all the result, apparently, of the writer's own observations and research as well as traditional instruction. Not only in content but in form is this treatise highly unconventional, for the author goes immediately *in medias res,* discussing notational practices of the time of Magister Leoninus and describing later practices chronologically without giving any of the usual preliminary introductory material (music's definition, invention, etymology, uses, and effects). A section on Boethian proportions, however, is inserted before the discussion of the various forms of *discantus.*

[48] He calls by name, for example, certain *"boni cantores . . . in Anglia";* he speaks of *"quidam LUMBARDI"* who do not always end their organa with perfect consonances; he mentions certain ligatures found *"in libris Hispanorum et Pompilonensium et in libris Anglicorum";* he tells the kind of staff used in music books *"apud organistas in FRANCIA, in HISPANIA et ARRAGONIA, et in partibus PAMPILONIE et ANGLIE";* he mentions the hocket *"In seculum . . . quod quidam Hispanus fecerat";* he says of major and minor thirds, which *"non sic reputantur"* with most composers, *"Tamen apud organistas optimos et prout in quibusdam terris, sicut in ANGLIA, in patria que dicitur WESTCUNTRE, optime concordantie dicuntur, quoniam apud tales magis sunt in usu."*

From the end of the thirteenth century or the first years of the fourteenth we have another highly unusual and unconventional treatise—the *Theoria*[49] of Johannes de Grocheo, unique in approaching music from a sociological point of view. Johannes' connection with the Sorbonne is clearly evident: not only is he described as *regens Parisius* but several times he speaks of music *"qua utuntur homines Parisiis."* Like Anonymus IV, Johannes bases his treatise upon his own observations, but like traditional medieval theorists he begins with a brief speculative *eisagogé* giving the meaning, etymology, and divisions of music. Possibly influenced by Arabic-Spanish sources, however, Johannes discards the reality of *musica mundana* and *humana* as ancient theories not to be believed in and tells us that his work will not deal with angelic songs, for no one can hear the music of the spheres—a view quite similar to that stated by Al-Farabi in his *Great Book on Music*[50] and similar also, as we shall see upon arrival at Oxford, to the concepts of Roger Bacon, who drew heavily upon Arabian sources. Discussing only *musica instrumentalis,* then, the one Boethian division valid for him, Johannes gives a threefold classification: *musica simplex vel civilis, mensurata,* and *ecclesiastica.*[51] In agreement with this outline, there follows the first description of secular

[49] Johannes Wolf, *"Die Musiklehre des Johannes de Grocheo," SIMG,* I (1899), 65–130; *Theoria,* 69–130, with a parallel German translation. According to Heinrich Besseler, *"Zur 'Ars Musicae' des Johannes de Grocheo," Die Musikforschung,* Vol. II (1949), 229–31, this treatise should perhaps be called *Ars Musicae.* Writing *ca.* 1300, Johannes, says Professor Besseler, belongs spiritually with the *"Pariser Naturforschern des frühen 14. Jahrhunderts."*

[50] *Al-Farabi: Grand Traité de la musique* (tr. by Baron Rodolphe d'Erlanger) (Paris, 1930). A comprehensive work on the art of music alone (outside its philosophical context), the book deals with both theory and practice of music (in line with Al-Farabi's dichotomy, *musica speculativa* and *musica activa*): Book I, intervals based upon arithmetical proportions; Book II, the lute and other stringed instruments; Book III, composition. It is in the introduction (p. 28) that Al-Farabi disagrees with the Pythagorean idea that planets in their movements cause harmonious sounds.

[51] *Theoria, SIMG,* I, 84–85:

Unum autem membrum dicimus de simplici musica vel civili, quam vulgarem musicam appellamus, aliud autem de musica composita vel regulari vel canonica, quam appellant musicam mensuratam. Sed tertium genus est, quod ex istis duobus efficitur et ad quod ista duo tamquam ad melius ordinantur. Quod ecclesiasticum dicitur et ad laudandum creatorem deputatum est.

music in medieval treatises as Johannes enumerates and describes various types of secular vocal music and instrumental dance forms, connecting them, from a sociological point of view, with old theories of the effects of music.[52] From *musica simplex vel civilis* Johannes turns to polyphonic music, the *cantus praecise mensuratus* cultivated by the "moderns" in Paris, describing the rhythmic modes, signs of notation, and such forms as *motetus,* organum, and *hoquetus,* drawing upon two theorists well known at the Sorbonne (Garland and Franco) and another (a Magister Lambert) whose doctrine connects him also with this center of learning.[53] It is in his discussion of the motet that Johannes' oft-cited words about musical connoisseurs appear: *"Cantus autem iste non debet coram vulgaribus propinari, eo quod eius subtilitatem non advertunt nec in eius auditu delectantur, sed coram litteratis et illis, qui subtilitates artium sunt quaerentes."* Johannes concludes his work with a long description of all parts of the chant, his *genus ecclesiasticum,* introducing information about the modes and comparing parts of the chant to secular forms.[54]

The *Theoria* of Johannes de Grocheo, treating one of the topics of the conventional medieval treatise, musical effects, from an unconventional point of view, had, apparently, little influence upon writers of musical treatises in the following centuries. French theorists in the fourteenth century continued to discuss both *musica theoretica* and *musica practica,* basing their speculative discussions upon Boethius and other authorities and centering their practical discussions around the inevitable problems of polyphonic music—rhythm, notation, and composition. Perhaps the greatest of all me-

[52] The *cantus gestualis,* for instance, singing of the deeds of heroes, works of patriarchs, and lives of martyrs, is valuable in holding the state together, since it makes people think their own sorrows are not so heavy as those of others; and the *cantilena stantipes* is so difficult that it requires fullest concentration and thus keeps the minds of young people from evil thoughts (*ibid.,* I, 90–93).

[53] *Tractatus de musica,* (CS, I, 251–81). Lambert has formerly been called Pseudo-Aristotle. For his identification, see Heinrich Sowa (ed.), *Ein anonymer glossierter Mensuraltraktat, 1279* (Kassel, 1930), *xvii.*

[54] He says, for example (*Theoria,* 126), that the *responsorium* and *alleluia* are sung *"ad modum stantipedis vel cantus coronati,"* implanting humility and devotion in the hearts of the listeners, whereas the *sequentia,* sung *"ad modum ductiae,"* causes the listener to rejoice.

dieval treatises on music, and certainly the most comprehensive, is the *Speculum musicae,* long attributed to Jean de Muris but now considered the work of a certain Jacques or James (Jacobus) of Liège, who studied in France near the end of the thirteenth century (*"ego puto me Parisius a quodam audivisse,"* he says in his treatise, CS, II, 281). This Jacques has been identified as *"Jacobus de Oudenarde, canonicus majoris ecclesiae Leodiensis"* who appears in a university document of 1313, and who wrote his great encyclopedia of musical knowledge when he was an old man, around 1313.[55] A true mirror of all musical learning of the time, this work is highly conservative in point of view and critically opposed to the newer musical practices of which Jean de Muris was a leading exponent; it epitomizes thirteenth-century techniques and praises especially the innovations of Franco and Petrus de Cruce. The first five books of the *Speculum* are mathematical, treating of intervals, proportions, consonance, and dissonance, with frequent reference to Boethius; the sixth and seventh deal respectively with the elements of plain song and of polyphonic music, thus together forming a treatise on *musica practica.*

If Jacques de Liège summarized the theory of the *ars antiqua,* Jean de Muris (*ca.* 1290–1350), mathematician, astronomer, and musician who taught at the Sorbonne during the first half of the fourteenth century, was an enthusiastic theorist of the *ars nova,* continuing along lines already worked out by Philip de Vitry.[56]

---

[55] Books VI and VII appear in CS, II, 193–483. Nineteen chapters of Book I are printed by Walter Grossman, *Die einleitenden Kapital des Speculum musicae* (Leipzig, 1924), 54–93. Chapter headings of the first five books are given in CS, II, xvii–xxii. For date of treatise, see Besseler, *"Neue Quellen,"* AfMw, Vol. VII, 180–81. The identification of Jacques with Jacobus de Oudenarde (*Chartularium,* II, 164) is made by Jos. Smits van Waesberghe, "Some Music Treatises and Their Interrelation," *Musica Disciplina,* Vol. III, 107–108.

[56] Deacon, canon, and finally Bishop of Meaux, active in public affairs under Charles le Bel and Jean II, friend of Petrarch (who described him as *"veri semper acutissimus et ardentissimus inquisitor, tantus etatis nostre philosophus, poeta nunc unicus Galliarum"*), poet, composer (*"Musicorum princeps egregius,"* he is called in a *partitura amorosa* in which he is arbiter), and man of letters, Philip de Vitry (1291–1361) personified the humanistic spirit *par excellence*: see Alfred Coville, *"Philippe de Vitri, notes biographiques,"* Romania, Vol. LIX (1933), 520–47, and E. Pognon, *"Du nouveau sur Philippe de Vitri et ses amis,"* Humanisme et Renaissance, Vol. VI (1939), 48–55. According to the anonymous author of *Les Règles de la seconde rhétorique* (Langlois, *Recueil d'arts de seconde*

Many musical treatises may be related to the University of Paris through the teaching and writings of this distinguished and influential son. Comprising works on both theoretical and artistic aspects of music, Jean's treatises found widespread dissemination throughout Western Europe. His mathematical *Musica speculativa* (GS, III, 249–55), a summary of Boethian proportions and derivation of the scale, is the work which superseded Boethius in the original as the musical text required of students in the arts faculty of many of the medieval (and even Renaissance) universities. Several brief tracts on musical mathematics are apparently students' notes on Jean's lectures: the *De numeris* of Ptolomaeus of Paris and a *Tractatus de proportionibus* ("*a venerandae memoriae magistro Johanne de Muris,*" GS, III, 284–91).

Jean's *Ars nove musice* combines both mathematical and practical elements of music: its first section consists of an arithmetical discussion "*De tonis*" (large and small semitones, with *dieses*) and "*De proportionibus*"; and its second section, "*De practica musica,*

rhétorique, 12), Philip was responsible for literary as well as musical innovations: "*Aprèz vint Philippe de Vitry, qui trouva la maniere des motès, et des balades, et des lais, et des simples rondeaux, et en la musique trouva les .iiij. prolacions, et les notes rouges, et la noveleté des proporcions.*" Philip was probably the inventor of the isorhythmic motet, the principal art form of the fourteenth century, and his motets are frequently quoted in treatises by other writers. The poet Gaston de la Bigne wrote of his knowledge of motets:

> *Phelippe de Vitry eust nom,*
> *Qui mieulx sceut motetz que nul hom.*

For a discussion of Philip's musical accomplishments, see Heinrich Besseler, "*Die Motette von Franko von Köln bis Phillip von Vitry,*" *AfMw,* Vol. VIII (1926), 137–258.

The *Ars nova* (CS, III, 13–22: in this treatise Philip introduced *ars nova* as a polemical term to distinguish the music of his own time from that of the preceding—Petrus de Cruce's—generation, the *ars antiqua*) of Philip de Vitry is the most important work on mensural notation from the fourteenth century. After dealing with the usual topics from the conventional *eisagogé,* it sets forth Philip's doctrine of musical rhythm and notation (recognizing duple as well as the old triple rhythm and applying both divisions to *modus,* the relation of *longa* to *brevis; tempus,* the relation of *brevis* to *semibrevis;* and *prolatio,* the relation of *semibrevis* to *semiminima*) and the use of red notes for changes in time values, chiefly in syncopation. For the latest work on Philippe and a variorum edition of his *Ars nova,* see Gilbert Reaney, André Gilles, and Jean Maillard, "The 'Ars Nova' of Philippe de Vitry," *Musica Disciplina,* Vol. X (1956), 5–33. See also André Gilles, "*Un Témoignage inédit de l'enseignement de Philippe de Vitry,*" *ibid.,* 35–53.

I have been unable to find evidence that Philip was ever a member of the University of Paris, although his friendship with Jean de Muris and possibly other *magistri* in the Sorbonne is evident.

seu de mensurabili," centers around the problems of rhythm and notation—prolation, imperfection, and alteration of notes—following the doctrine of Philip de Vitry. A remark at the end of this section relates the work to Jean's lecturing in the university: *"Alie conclusiones speciales . . . erunt manifeste studentibus."* The *Ars nove musice,* written from a mathematical point of view, shows the strong rationalistic basis upon which the music of the fourteenth century (the *ars nova*) was constructed; and as Professor Besseler has observed, it is this harmony between speculative and practical aspects of music which makes the *ars-nova* music truly classic.[57]

In his *Libellus cantus mensurabilis* (CS, III, 46–58), a work on mensural notation used as a source for many later theoretical works, Jean again shows the influence of Philip de Vitry in discussing the isorhythmic motet (probably invented by Philip) and problems of rhythm and melody (*talea* and *color*) in connection with this form. As in the *Ars nove musice,* a statement in this treatise relates it to Jean's teaching at the Sorbonne: having finished discussing the *punctus,* he says, *"Et hec de puncto sufficiant studere vobis."* The *Ars discantus* (CS, III, 68–95) again explains mensural notation, with a final section *"De compositione carminum"*—that is, ballade forms. Several tracts included by Coussemaker in this treatise (CS, III, 95–109) are probably notes of students who heard Jean lecture; and the great diversity of these is surely significant of the comprehensiveness of his teaching: the *Proportionis diffinitio,* a catechism on the mathematics of rhythmic diminution and augmentation; a tract *De octo tonis* on the ecclesiastical modes; a catechism *De diffinitionibus accidentium musicae,* giving definitions of the figures of mensural music (approaching the musical lexicon but not in alphabetical order); and *Quaedam notabilia utilia* (in the ever popular question and answer form) on mensural notation.

The great influence of Jean de Muris is seen in a number of other treatises inspired by his teaching. Interesting among these is

[57] *"Die Motette," AfMw,* Vol. VIII, 209. For the proper arrangement of parts of the *Ars nove musice,* see *ibid.,* Vol. VIII, 207–208. The short sections comprised in the treatise are found in GS, III, 308–12; 312–15; and 292–308, which includes the *"Quaedam conclusiones"* found in CS, III, 109–13.

the *Ars contrapuncti secundum Johannem de Muris* (CS, III, 59–68), a technical work on mensural notation in which the author (probably Coussemaker's Anonymus V, with whose *Ars cantus mensurabilis*—CS, III—this treatise properly belongs) draws extensively upon Jean's writings, mentioning him by name and also as *magister meus*. Among other matters, *"videns varias multorum opiniones atque diversas fallacias, dicta mei magistri nolens improbare,"* the author compares characteristic notational techniques used by Italian and French composers, referring to Guillielmus de Mastodio (Machaut), Nicolaus de Aversa, and Cechus de Florentia (the blind Francesco Landini). Highly knowledgeable about contemporary musical artistry, the writer is lavish with musical examples from both sacred and secular compositions, and he includes sections on *talea* and *color*, as does Jean de Muris.

Two Netherlanders, about whom nothing is known save for their treatises, drew upon Jean de Muris in discussing mensural notation—Christian Sadze of Flanders in his *Tractatus modi, temporis et prolationis* and the Carmelite Nicasius Weyts in his *Regule*.[58] In Italy, Jean's influence is seen in the *Dialogi de harmonia* of Georgius Anselmi of Parma (*fl.* 1440), philosopher, physician, and astrologer, whose treatise (studied later by Gafori) includes both the *Theorica musicae* and the *Libellus cantus mensurabilis* of Jean de Muris.[59] The influence of both Jean de Muris and Philip de Vitry is apparent in a treatise on notation from fourteenth-century Florence (and related to the Florentine oral rather than the university tradition), unique in being written in the Tuscan dialect.[60] Two treatises, moreover, show the influence of Jean in the city of Orvieto: the *Ars cantus figurati* (CS, IV, 421–33) by Antonius de Luca, a compilation based upon Jean's doctrine taught Antonius (as he states in the beginning) by his master, Laurentius de Urbe

[58] Both tracts deal with mensural notation. Christian's treatise (CS, III, 264–73) is in part a commentary upon Jean's *Libellus cantus mensurabilis*, ending with large tables showing the various combinations of mode, tempus, and prolation; and Nicasius' short tract (*ibid.*, III, 262–64) is based upon the same work.

[59] See Jacques Handschin, "Anselmi's Treatise on Music Annotated by Gafori," *Musica Disciplina*, Vol. II (1948), 123–40. A considerable part of the treatise is printed here.

[60] See Armen Carapetyan, "A Fourteenth-Century Florentine Treatise in the Vernacular," *Musica Disciplina*, Vol. IV (1950), 81–92.

Veteri, especially interesting for its description of white mensural notation which came into general usage around 1450; and the *Musica*[61] of Ugolino (d. 1449), a voluminous treatise of the *speculum* type, embracing all musical learning of the time. Various biographical notices mention the university studies of Ugolino of Orvieto (place of study unknown), archpriest at Ferrara; and his *Musica,* like the *Speculum musicae* of Jacques de Liège, is the comprehensive type associated with university scholarship.[62] Book III is a scholastic commentary upon the *Libellus cantus mensurabilis* of Jean de Muris.

The great fame of Jean de Muris and the unending diffusion of his doctrine at home and abroad would, alone, indicate the tremendous interest in music at the University of Paris in the Middle Ages and the great number of students who had personal contact with this *magister regens* in the Sorbonne. Added to this is evidence from the statutes, from contemporary documents, and from the numerous other treatises on music motivated directly by university studies and duties—all pointing clearly to the study of music in the university both as a mathematical discipline required of all students in the arts faculty and as a living practical art (the two never actually separated), enthusiastically cultivated by men in the university who served as professional singers, directed choirs and trained choristers, performed upon musical instruments, composed new types of polyphonic music, and evolved a body of theory to explain this new music. The fact that most of the medieval treatises on technical aspects of music are French in origin is a phenomenon directly related to France's high place in musical culture; for France was the musical capital of Europe until the mid-fifteenth century.

61 Not published; a summary and table of contents for each book are given by Utto Kornmüller, *"Die Musiklehre des Ugolino von Orvieto," KmJb,* Vol. X (1895), 19–40.

62 One of these accounts states that Ugolino was *"in pontificio jure et re philosophica magnopere versatus"* and another that he *"inter Musicos ferme supremum teneat locum et Philosophiae ac sacrarum Literarum studiis niteat"*: see Francis X. Haberl, *"Bio-bibliographische Notizen uber Ugolino von Orvieto," KmJb,* Vol. X (1895), 48–49. Haberl thinks it possible that Ugolino may have been a teacher of Dufay, who, although a progressive composer, stood firmly *"auf Grund der Theorien des 14. Jahrhunderts."* For the latest account of Ugolino's work, see Albert Seay, "Ugolino of Orvieto, Theorist and Composer," *Musica Disciplina,* Vol. IX (1955), 111–16. The treatise was published in 1956 by the American Institute of Musicology.

It was surely no accident that the Sorbonne's years *"de sérénité et de gloire universelle"*[63]—the twelfth and thirteenth centuries—coincided with the time when Paris ruled the musical world; for men who studied or taught in the university, most of them composers and theorists as well, were largely responsible for the rapid development of polyphonic forms—organum, conductus, motet—during these centuries. That students in the university were aware of these "Parisian novelties" (music of the *ars nova*) we know from the letter of Johann von Jenzenstein.[64] An anonymous poem from the late medieval period describes effectively the *clerc* who mixes his learning with musical knowledge and skill:

> *Ung clerc mixte qui scet lire et chanter,*
> *Jouer du leu, des orguez et harper,*
> *Tousjours sera partout bien venu,*
> *Plus tost congneu, de ce ne doubtez mie,*
> *Que ne sera ung maistre en theologie.*[65]

Orléans

The University of Orléans is significant for our study only in the medieval period, when the *artes liberales* reached a high development there.[66] Among these arts, music had found learned commentators during the Middle Ages. Late in the eleventh century, for example, a distinguished musical theorist, Aribo Scholasticus, was head of the cathedral school at Orléans, having formerly held the same position (*scholasticus*) at Liége. Aribo's *Musica,* an erudite and scholarly work based upon the doctrine of Hermannus of Reichenau, is largely a critical commentary on Chapter XV of Guido's *Micrologus,* on the making of symmetrical plain chant

[63] Chailley, *Histoire musicale du moyen âge,* 197.

[64] And also from the remarks criticizing these novelties made by Roger Bacon, who studied at Paris: see *Fr. Rogeri Bacon Opera quaedam hactenus inedita* (ed. by J. S. Brewer) (London, 1859), 297–98.

[65] A. Piaget, "*Les Princes de Georges Chastelain*," *Romania,* Vol. XLVII (1921), 184.

[66] Marcel Fournier, *Histoire de la science de droit en France* (Paris, 1892), III, 98.

melodies.[67] Practical musical interests also led him to incorporate a section on the making of bells—information which seems to have had considerable local circulation.[68] And perhaps Aribo's theological training was responsible for the mystical symbolism which characterizes some of his musical explanations.[69] We recall, too, that Robert de Handlo included an Admetus de Aureliana among the *alii musici* in his *Regule cum maximis Magistri Franconis, cum additionibus aliorum musicorum*.

Before the organization of a *studium generale* late in the thirteenth century, there were schools in Orléans famous for teaching the *ars dictaminis* (chiefly the writing of letters, a practical discipline which had originated in Italy) and classical Latin literature, both as a part of rhetoric.[70] Contemporary literature springing from the study of grammar and rhetoric at Orléans in medieval times emphasizes also the high position of musical studies. In 1259 a *"Programme adressé par Ponce le Provençal aux docteurs et aux écoliers d'Orléans,"* contained an allegory in which Rhetoric, the *virgo praeclarissima*, tells how to reach the city *Practica dictatoria* by passing through seven gateways, each of them representing one of the liberal arts. Music is given an honored place just before the entrance to the city:

---

[67] Wagner, *Gregorianische Melodien*, II, 15.

[68] A lengthy mathematical section at the end of the *Quaestiones in musica* by the Flemish Abbot Rudolf of St. Trond (*ca.* 1100) incorporates Aribo's theories on the making of bells. See Rudolf Steglich, *Die Quaestiones in Musica* (Leipzig, 1911).

[69] He explains, for instance, *"Quomodo tetrachordum gravium mystice pertineat ad Matthaeum & ad humanitatem Christi,"* and that the *tetrachordum finalium, superiorum,* and *excellentium* signify, respectively, Christ's passion and death, resurrection, and ascension (GS, II, 205–206).

[70] Léopold Delisle, *"Les Ecoles d'Orléans au douzième et au treizième siècle,"* *Annuaire-Bulletin de la Société de l'Histoire de France*, Vol. VII (1869), 139–40. The lines of Geoffrey de Vinsauf distinguishing Orléans for the study of *auctores*, Salerno for medicine, Bologna for law, and Paris for the arts, are often quoted:

> *In morbis sanat medici virtute Salernum*
> *Aegros. In causis Bononia legibus armat*
> *Nudos. Parisius dispensat in artibus illos*
> *Panes unde cibat robustos. Aurelianis*
> *Educat in cunis autorum lacte tenellos.*

See Louis John Paetow, *La Bataille des VII Ars of Henri d'Andeli* (Berkeley, 1927), 17n.

Et accessimus ad portam septimam, et ibi fuerunt multi lascivi juvenes, saltantes et currentes velociter, et voce consona sonum dulcissimum decantantes. Et sic intravimus civitatem.[71]

The trouvère and clerk, Henri d'Andeli, moreover, a man evidently well acquainted with both Paris and Orléans, and acquainted, too, with the art and science of music, has left a delicate and sensitive description of *"Ma dame Musique"* in his allegory *La Bataille des .VII. Ars (ca.* 1236). The poem tells of a battle between the forces of Grammar, the Lady of Orléans, and Logic, the Lady of Paris. Music and her followers are present, but significantly, *"celes ne se combatent pas"*:

Ma dame Musique aus clochetes
Et si clerc plain de chançonnetes
Portoient gigues et vieles,
Salterions et fleüteles;
De la note du premier fa
Montoient jusqu'en cc sol fa.
Li douz ton diatesaron,
Diapente, diapason,
Sont hurtez de diverses gerbes.
Par quarreüres et par trebles,
Par mi l'ost aloient chantant,
Par lor chant les vont enchantant.
Celes ne se combatent pas.[72]

[71] Delisle, *"Les Ecoles d'Orléans au douzième et au treizième siècle,"* Annuaire-Bulletin de la Société de l'Histoire de France, Vol. VII, 151, Appendix, no. V.

[72] Paetow, *Bataille des VII Ars,* 49, with a parallel translation:

Madam Music, she of the little bells
And her clerks full of songs
Carried fiddles and viols,
Psalteries and small flutes;
From the sound of the first fa
They ascended to cc sol fa.
The sweet tones diatessaron
Diapente, diapason,
Are struck in various combinations.
In groups of four and three
Through the army they went singing,
They go enchanting them with their song.
These do not engage in battle.

Henri's lines, few as they are, draw upon both speculative and practical aspects of music; and such literary allusions as these are important for insight into the teaching of music at Orléans because university statutes are deficient regarding the subjects required for study. The first statutes, drawn up between 1288 and 1296, provided for a paid staff in canon and civil law only; but in 1305 four papal bulls authorized the erection of a *litterarum studium,* and the arts apparently flourished at Orléans during the fourteenth century.[73] Absence of any reference to specific disciplines in the statutes probably presupposes the usual arts curriculum in the medieval universities, taught by *magistri regentes* who collected fees from their students—the customary procedure at this time. By the end of the Middle Ages, however, only instruction in law was given at the University of Orléans.[74]

Certain official documents are helpful in showing music's place in academic activities. A statute of 1365, for example, dealing with the celebration of the *fêtes de nations,* forbids the playing of musical instruments, along with dancing and other "vanities,"[75] implying that such diversions were a regular part of student life. Another decree (1416) specifies an anniversary Mass to be sung each year for Magister Jean de Prusse, who left property to the German Nation in the university (this Mass was still being sung in 1485).[76]

[73] See Marcel Fournier, *Les Statuts et privilèges des universités françaises* (Paris, 1890–94), I, 2, no. 2; Rashdall, *Medieval Universities,* II, 145; and John Kirkpatrick, "The Scottish Nation in the University of Orleans, 1336–1538," *Publications of the Scottish History Society,* Vol. XLIV (1904), 48. There is no reference to musical studies in the published statutes.

[74] The German Hieronimus Monetarius, visiting France in 1494/5, wrote of Orléans in his diary: "*Est item universale studium ibi, in sola tamen iuris civilis et pontificij facultate.*" See E. Ph. Goldschmidt, "*Le Voyage de Hieronimus Monetarius à travers la France,*" *Humanisme et Renaissance,* Vol. VI (1939), 210.

[75] Fournier, *Statuts et privilèges,* I, 121–22, no. 167:

Hujusmodi missam et vesperas permittimus fieri, et volumus per supposita antedicta si sue et non aliter placuerit voluntati, et tunc cum moderamine subsequente, videlicet cum quatuor cereis, quolibet de pondere unius libre cere, cessantibus tubarum, buccinarum, cymbalorum, et aliorum instrumentorum quorumcumque sollempnitatibus atque sonis ac choreis et tripudiis, ceterisque vanitatibus quibuscumque.

[76] *Ibid.,* I, 197–98, no. 265, and 250, no. 341.

Musicians, too, are sometimes mentioned in early university records. A document from the late thirteenth century tells how a candidate for the *licentia* in law was presented by a cantor, professor of law in the university.[77] And in 1332 a papal decree allowed a *"chantre de l'église de Saint-Pierre-Empont d'Orléans"* to continue his university studies for three years.[78] In 1366 the Bishop of Auxerre wrote to the *"doyen, maître-école de l'église d'Orléans et au chantre de Saint-Aignan"* concerning certain privileges of the university,[79] showing the close association of these officials. A record of 1421 tells that the usual musical officials—the *cantor* and *succentor* of the cathedral—were present when a *"décret du chapitre de l'église d'Orléans touchant l'Université"* was passed;[80] and this *congregatio* decided that a Mass be sung for certain benefactors, *"cum nota per unum concanonicorum nostrorum et pueros chori dicte ecclesie nostre."*[81] As late as 1489, a letter addressed to various university officials included *cantores* and *succentores.*[82]

The comprehensive and learned treatise *De musica* (GS, II, 287–369) by Englebert of Admont (d. 1331) is typical of the medieval university treatise—related to the teaching of music both as a mathematical science and as a practical art for use in the Church. Engelbert, sometime student at Prague and Padua, became *scholasticus Aurelianensis*—head of the cathedral school and ecclesiastical head of the university.[83] His treatise begins with the definition, "Music is the science of inquiring into harmonic proportions," and presents the usual mathematical theory before giving instruction in all aspects of music basic to the chant.

[77] *Ibid.*, I, 8, no. 13: *"Eidem igitur presentato nobis per Johannem de Busco, cantorem, Aurelianis legum venerabilem professorem, pro licentia legendi obtinenda . . . damus et concedimus licentiam legendi et regendi ordinarie in legibus."*

[78] *Ibid.*, I, 81, no. 90: *"Sur recommandation royale, Jean XXII permet à Regnaud Chauvel, chantre de l'église de Saint-Pierre-Empont d'Orléans, bachelier ès lois, de continuer ses études pendant trois ans."*

[79] *Ibid.*, I, 123, no. 168.

[80] *Ibid.*, I, 202, no. 271: *"congregatis scilicet dominis et magistris . . . Amisio Gomberti, cantore . . . Johanne de Matiscone suctentore."*

[81] *Ibid.*

[82] *Ibid.*, I, 252, no. 348.

[83] Jos. Smits van Waesberghe, *De Luiksche Muziekschool als Centrum van het Muziektheoretisch Onderricht in de Middeleeuwen* (Tilburg, 1938), 32–37.

It is highly interesting to find, moreover, that a very famous treatise on music and poetry came from the pen of a man who studied in his youth at this *studium* famous for grammar and rhetoric: *L'Art de dictier et de fere chançons*[84] by the poet Eustache Deschamps (*ca.* 1346–1406). In his youth Deschamps studied the liberal arts, astronomy, and law at the University of Orléans; and later in his life he became the pupil and friend of the poet-musician Guillaume de Machaut,[85] who, with Philip de Vitry, was the leading composer of this period. In *L'Art de dictier* Deschamps briefly describes the subjects of the trivium and devotes a short section to each of the disciplines of the quadrivium. Music he calls the medicine of the liberal arts, because of its uplifting and recreational powers.[86] And having described its effects, in approved scholastic fashion, Deschamps next gives music's divisions: *"Et est a sçavoir que nous avons deux musiques, dont l'une est artificiele et l'autre est naturele."* Although these two divisions are not new,[87] Des-

[84] Eustache Deschamps, *Oeuvres complètes* (ed. by Auguste Queux and Gaston Raynaud) (Paris, 1878–1903), VII, 266–93.

[85] *Ibid.*, XI, 11–13. And see the lines of Deschamps in the *"Balade sur lui-même et sa vieillesse,"* *ibid.*, II, 52:

> *Tous les .vii. ars oy en ma retentive*
> *Je pratiqué tant que je sceus comprandre*
> > *Le ciel et les elemens,*
> *Des estoilles les propres mouvemens . . .*
> *Je sceu les loys et les decrez entendre,*
> > *Et soutilment arguer par logique.*

[86] Deschamps, *Oeuvres complètes*, VII, 269:

> Musique est la derreniere science ainsis comme la medicine des .vii. ars; car quant le couraige et l'esperit des creatures ententives aux autres ars dessus declairez sont lassez et ennuyez de leurs labours, musique, par la doucour de sa science et la melodie de sa voix, leur chante par ses .vi. notes tierçoyées, quintes et doublées, ses chans delectables et plaisans . . . tant que par sa melodie delectable les cuers et esperis de ceuls qui auxdiz ars, par pensée, ymaginaison et labours de bras estoient traveilliez, pesans et ennuiez, sont medicinez et recreez, et plus habiles après a estudier et labourer aux autres .vi. ars dessus nommez.

> The medieval music treatises which link music and medicine are too numerous to mention, especially those written under Arabian (thus, ultimately Greek) influence—e.g., those of Gundissalinus and Roger Bacon. According to Henry G. Farmer, *Al-Farabi's Arabic-Latin Writings on Music,* 50, certain predecessors of Al-Farabi had built up "an elaborate medico-musical system . . . which was actually used in hospitals."

[87] These two divisions were mentioned by Al-Farabi as parts of *musica activa* and

champs puts a new interpretation upon them, defining *musique artificiele* as monody and polyphony and *musique naturele* as poetry.[88] Deschamps, moreover, finds music and poetry so closely dependent upon each other as to be inseparable[89]—an idea, we recall, which the Greeks also held; and in the remainder of his treatise the poet gives instruction in writing each of the verse types he has mentioned, with many examples of his own composition.

Deschamps' treatise, while somewhat unconventional compared to typical medieval treatises, is conventional in treating music as one of the usual liberal arts; and the work was undoubtedly as much the result of the poet's musical and rhetorical studies at the University of Orléans as of his private studies with Machaut. (It is a point worthy of note that Deschamps' great contemporary in England, Geoffrey Chaucer, left no musico-poetic treatise, nor did he ever, so far as is known, attend a university.) For music apparently held an honored place among the liberal arts for which Orléans was famous in the late Middle Ages. With the usual connection

by others who drew upon Al-Farabi's *De scientiis*—John of Afflighem, Juan Gil of Zamora, and Jerome of Moravia—"artificial" referring to instrumental music and "natural" to that produced by the voice: see the text of *De scientiis, ibid.*, 14.

[88] Deschamps, *Oeuvres complètes*, VII, 269–70:

> *L'artificiele* est celle dont dessus est faicte mencion; et est appellée artificiele de son art, car par ses .vi. notes, qui sont appellées, *us, ré, my, fa, sol, la,* l'en puet aprandre a chanter, acorder, doubler, quintoier, tierçoier, tenir, deschanter, par figure de notes, par clefs et par lignes . . . ou au moins tant faire, que supposé ore qu'il n'eust pas la voix habile pour chanter ou bien acorder, scaroit il et pourroit congnoistre les accors ou discors avecques tout l'art d'icelle science. . . .
> L'autre musique est appellée *naturele* pour ce qu'elle ne puet estre aprinse a nul, se son propre couraige naturelment ne s'i applique, et est une musique de bouche en proferant paroules metrifiées, aucunefoiz en *laiz,* autrefoiz en *balades,* autrefoiz en *rondeaulx cengles* et *doubles,* et en *chançons baladées* . . . et la *chançon baladée* de trois vers doubles . . . que aucuns appellent du temps present *virelays.*

[89] *Ibid.,* VII, 271–72:

> Et aussi ces deux musiques sont si consonans l'une avecques l'autre que chascune puet bien estre appellée musique, pour la douceur tant du chant comme des paroles qui toutes sont prononcées et pointoyées par douçour de voix et ouverture de bouche; et est de ces deux ainsis comme un mariage en conjunction de science. . . . Et semblablement les chançons natureles sont delectables et embellies par la melodie et les teneurs, trebles et contreteneurs du chant de la musique artificiele.

between university and cathedral found in European cities in medieval times, we may be sure that instruction in practical music was given to choristers in university foundations, many of whom, by analogy with other institutions, must have become students in the university proper. As was customary, too, *cantores* of the cathedral were important officials in the *studium,* sometimes holding the endowed professorships of law for which the university was especially renowned.

iii. ENGLAND: OXFORD AND CAMBRIDGE
Oxford

THE BEGINNINGS of the University of Oxford are veiled in myth and legend. One of the most popular of these is the account in the *Liber de Hyda,* a fourteenth-century compilation of earlier chronicles, that the university was founded in 886 during the reign of Alfred the Great, and that among the first teachers was John, monk of St. David's, who lectured on logic, music, and arithmetic.[1] Anthony à Wood identifies this John as Johannes Scotus, who, he says, "taught sometime in the Schools of Paris, and Pavia, and was with Grymbald and others desired by K. Alfred to read at Oxford."[2] Although the story that Alfred founded Oxford has long been discarded, along with other legends pointing to the great antiquity of the university, monastic schools existed at Oxford from early times, and a *studium generale* developed late in

[1] Edward Edwards (ed.), *Liber monasterii de Hyda* (Rolls Series, London, 1866), 41: *"In dialectica vero, musica, arithmetica, legente Johanne, monacho Menensis ecclesiae."*

[2] *History and Antiquities,* I, 39. Johannes Scotus Erigena (*ca.* 815–70), master of the Palace School of Charles the Bald (the successor to Alcuin, in fact, at the French court), included many references to *musica mundana* in his tremendously comprehensive philosophical work, *De divisione naturae:* Migne, *Patrologia latina,* CXXII, 439–1022. More important for the history of music is Johannes' commentary on Martianus Capella's *De nuptiis Philologiae et Mercurii,* for this *scholia* was used as the basis of the similar and widely known work by Remigius of Auxerre. Johannes' glosses on the section *"De musica"* of Martianus' allegory consist largely of definitions and identifications of musical terms and legendary characters. For a modern edition, see *Iohannis Scotti Annotationes in Marcianum* (ed. by Cora E. Lutz) (Cambridge, Mass., 1939).

THE MEDIEVAL UNIVERSITIES

the twelfth century.[3] Both the great English universities were organized along the lines of the University of Paris. With the statutes of 1431, music was assigned a definite place in the curriculum (undoubtedly having been taught along with the rest of the quadrivium for several centuries), a place it retained until the nineteenth century. According to these statutes, candidates who presented themselves *"ad incipiendum in artibus et philosophia"* (for taking the master's degree, that is) must have studied the *"septem artes liberales et tres philosophias"* for eight terms, following a specified *forma*: and this *forma* prescribed *"Musicam per terminum anni, videlicet Boecii."*[4]

It is significant that reflections of the use of Boethius' *Musica* as a standard Oxford text appear in the writings of Oxford men not primarily specialists in the field of music. The prolific Aristotelian commentator Walter Burley (1275–1345?), fellow of Oxford's Merton College who studied in Paris, returned to England as almoner for Philippa of Hainault, and became tutor to Edward the Black Prince, cites Boethius' *Musica* several times in his compilation of short lives, anecdotes, and opinions of distinguished poets and philosophers (the first work of its kind), *De vita et moribus philosophorum*.[5] The study of Boethius at Oxford and

[3] Perhaps after a migration of students from Paris in 1167: see Rashdall, *Medieval Universities*, III, 5–31. And after the terrible riots at Paris in 1228 between town and gown, another migration to England took place, with some students and masters settling at Oxford and Cambridge. Letters patent exist in which Henry III (1229) invited members of the Paris *studium "ad regnum nostrum Angl[ie] uos transferre & in eo causa studii moram facere."* See H. E. Salter, *Medieval Archives of the University of Oxford* (Oxford, 1920–21), I, 18.

[4] Strickland Gibson, *Statuta antiqua Vniversitatis Oxoniensis* (Oxford, 1931), 234. There is a tradition, indeed, that separate degrees were awarded by the medieval universities in grammar, rhetoric, and music. Wood says that the appellation of Doctor was "not known in England till the reign of Hen. II" (twelfth century), and that this degree was afterwards "common to Professors of Grammar, Music, Philosophy, Arts, &c. who being supposed to have spent a considerable time in any of those professions, and had as it were conquered them, were permitted to teach and instruct others in them" (*History and Antiquities*, 62).

The significance of early degrees in separate arts (as perhaps in the Italian and Spanish universities)—if indeed these were given—is not clear, but probably meant permission to teach them. It has recently been pointed out that a poet laureateship in the English universities actually meant a degree in rhetoric: see H. L. R. Edwards, *Skelton* (London, 1949), 34–36.

[5] See the edition published at Nuremberg, 1472 (a copy of which is owned by the

77

Cambridge is also reflected in the verse of the poet John Lydgate (1370?-1451?) who may have spent some time at the Benedictine College in Oxford (according to the antiquarian Bale, he studied in both the English universities); for in the *Courte of Sapyence* he has the lines:

> But who so lust of Musyk for to wyt
> For veray grounde of Boece I hym remyt.[6]

But other musical works besides Boethius' were known and used at Oxford too. Among the books which a constant benefactor, Humphrey, Duke of Gloucester, presented to the university at various times were *Isidorus in Etymologiis* in 1439, and *"Item, librum Augustini diversorum operum, videlicet, 'Musice,'"* in 1441.[7]

Many Oxford students, moreover, obviously had musical training either before entering the university or as choristers in Oxford foundations which carried on regular religious activities. Wood (*History and Antiquities*, III, 759) speaks of a *Schola Musicae* mentioned in a rent roll of 1440 among other schools to be lodged in a new stone building. When Robert de Eglesfield, founder of Queen's College, drew up statutes for his foundation in 1340, he specified that on the staff there should be *"duo alii Praecentores, chorum regentes in festis majoribus, ad quorum assignationem Socii aulae antedictae cantare et legere teneantur."*[8] Here, too, cer-

---

Huntington Library), cap. *xliiii*, *"De Democrito philosopho: Hic hypocrati medico tradidisse fertur que sicut corporis effectus se habet ita pulsus cordis motibus incitatur sic refert boecius libro de arte musica."*

In cap. *xvii*, *"De Pictagora philosopho,"* Burley speaks of Pythagoras' invention *"artis musice"*: *"His ut Boecius ait in primo musice. . . . Numeri disciplinam apud grecos primum pictagoram nuncupant scripsisse ac deinde a nichamaco diffusius esse dispositam. quam apud latinos primo epulegius deinde boecius transtulerunt."*

In cap. *xlviii*, *"De Empedocle philosopho"*: *"Empedocles philosophus athenis claruit tempore ciri regis persarum. Hic vt ait boecius in prologo de arte musica."*

[6] Quoted by William Edward Mead (ed.), *The Pastime of Pleasure* by Stephen Hawes (London, 1928), *lxi*. Although the *Dictionary of National Biography* ascribes the *Court of Sapience* to Lydgate, later research is somewhat doubtful.

[7] Henry Anstey, *Munimenta academica* (London, 1868), II, 761, and Henry Anstey, *Epistolae Academicae Oxoniensis* (Oxford, 1898), I, 204.

[8] *Statutes of the Colleges of Oxford* (Oxford, 1853–55), I, "Statutes of Queen's College," 29.

tain *clerici capellae,* skilled in both plain song and polyphonic music, were to instruct the *pueros pauperos* (choristers) in singing; and having become competent in plain song and polyphony, these boys were afterwards to study philosophy in the university proper.[9] New College, too, founded in 1400 by William of Wykeham, provided for sixteen choristers, *"scientes competenter legere et cantare ad ministrandum, legendum et cantandum in dicta capella."*[10] Schoolboys from this college *"in lectura, plano cantu et antiquo Donato, competenter instructi,"* were to be examined in these subjects and, if found eligible, elected to vacancies at Oxford.[11] The founder also desired to have among the members of the college certain *presbyteri et clerici* sufficiently versed in singing to lead the others in services in the chapel; from these each year one was to be elected *precentor,* in charge of musical activities.[12] Music was similarly emphasized in the statutes of 1443 drawn up by the founder of All Souls, Henry Chiceley, Archbishop of Canterbury: qualifications for admission into this foundation included a musical education, doubtless so that the younger *scholares* might act as singers in the college chapel.[13]

---

[9] *Ibid.,* I, 29, 31:

Sint etiam in eadem capella seu ecclesia duo clerici de cantu plano ac musica mensurato [sic] sufficienter instructi, qui sub praedictis capellanis ministrent, et pueros pauperes de cantu doceant. . . . Voloque quod praedicti pauperes, post solidam fundationem in grammatica ac competentem informationem in cantu plano, et insuper, quantum bono modo fieri poterit, mensurato, solum dialecticae et philosophiae intendant.

[10] *Ibid.,* I, "Statutes of New College," 78.
[11] *Ibid.,* I, 11.
[12] *Ibid.,* I, 77: The founder wished

qui quidem presbyteri et clerici vocem habeant competetem, et in cantu et lectura sint sufficienter instructi, quique presbyteri et clerici, capellam praedictam regulare, ac omnes alios scholares et Socios dicti collegii in dicta capella psallentes et legentes, quos expedit, in cantu, lectura [et] psalmodia, docere ac instruere teneantur. . . . Volentes, praeterea, quod unus de dictis presbyteris . . . annis singulis ad cantoris officium eligatur, qui canendo cantanda repetere debeat, et alias officium cantoris in choro capellae gerere ac etiam exercere.

[13] *Ibid.,* I, "Statutes of All Souls," 20: *"Statuentes, praeterea, quod nulli scholares in praedictum Collegium eligantur, nisi qui rudimentis grammaticae sufficienter, et in plano cantu competenter, prius fuerint eruditi."*

Besides these provisions for a continuous flow of competent music instructors and choristers in the college chapels, one finds many references to the performance of Masses with music on various occasions, usually memorial Masses for founders or benefactors.[14] Certain statutes governing the university in general also deal with the performance of religious ceremonies involving music. For instance, an early university statute (before 1350) decreed that regent masters[15] sing in solemn Masses and processions, that they sing *humiliter et devote* in funeral services for other masters, and that on the day of St. Edmund the Confessor they sing a Mass in memory of the king, Henry.[16] In the next century (1412) the university decided to honor Henry IV for his bounty with an annual Mass on the day of Edmund the Confessor, and *"in congregacione solenni regencium et non regencium"* further decided to sing perpetual Masses on the day of the king's death and on each anniversary of that date, with a requiem Mass on the following day.[17]

As at Paris, certain Oxford alumni evidently held high musical office. In 1274, for example, when learning and discipline were displaced by rioting among the students, certain mediators were elected to put an end to the great strife "between men of divers

---

[14] *Ibid.*, I, 47, and "Statutes of New College," 68–72.

[15] The first statutes for Oxford, 1253, contained a requirement ever since characteristic of this university: that no one should be admitted to the license in theology who had not first been a regent in the arts. See Rashdall, *Medieval Universities*, III, 49–50.

[16] See Gibson, *Statuta*, 58: *"Legant etiam magistri et cantent in solempnibus missis et processionibus secundum disposicionem procuratorum"*; 59–60: if a master die, *"communiter magistri cuiuslibet facultatis toti exequiarum servicio et etiam nocturnis vigiliis ad corpus defuncti magistri presencialiter debent interesse, et psalteria sua humiliter et deuote decantare"*; and 62: *"Et pro anima pie recordacionis Henrici regis die anniuersarii missam faciant publice decantare, scilicet die sancti Edmundi confessoris."*

[17] *Ibid.*, 210: the university decided

> quod idem illustrissimus princeps dominus noster rex, cum spiritus vitales resignauerit Altissimo, futuris ab inde temporibus habeat imperpetuum ab vniuersitate eadem in vigilia eiusdem sancti annis singulis exequias solenniter decantatas, et in crastino missam de requie solenniter decantatam.

For a recent study of fourteenth-century music composed in honor of St. Edmund (who died in 868 and for whom November 20 has been a special holy day since 1013), see Manfred Bukofzer, "Two Fourteenth-Century Motets on St. Edmund," *Studies in Medieval and Renaissance Music* (New York, 1950), 17–33. A transcription of the two motets is included.

countries that were Students therein"; among the five mediators "who were Masters also and Scholars of dignity" was "John de Wengham Chantor of St. Paules in London."[18]

If sacred music, and the training necessary for it, had a firm place in university and college life, secular music, we may be sure, was not neglected. Some of the college statutes make this clear by forbidding the playing of musical instruments and singing at unseasonable times because of the distraction such amusements offered—among them, Queen's.[19] Statutes of New College forbade *"luctationes, choræas, tripudia, saltus, cantus, clamores, tumultus et strepitus inordinatos"* in the halls and dormitories; but on feast-days when there was a fire in the hall, scholars and fellows might refresh themselves after meals *"in cantilenis et aliis solatiis honestis."*[20] This last decree appears almost verbatim in the statutes of All Souls.[21]

In Chaucer's *Canterbury Tales* we find the classic example of the "clerk of Oxenford" with his delight in books and music— "hende Nicolas," hero of "The Miller's Tale." Shelves over his bed were filled with his books and astronomical instruments,

> *And al above ther lay a gay sautrie, .*
> *On which he made a-nyghtes melodie*
> *So swetely that all the chambre rong;*
> *And Angelus ad virginem he song;*
> *And after that he song the kynges noote,*
> *Ful often blessed was his myrie throte.*

Chaucer's description of "a parish clerk, ycleped Absolon," who also figures in this tale, emphasizes the polymusical side of this Oxford alumnus:

[18] Anthony à Wood, *History and Antiquities,* I, 299–300.

[19] *College Statutes,* I, "Statutes of Queen's College," 18:

Et quoniam solet frequentia instrumentorum musicorum levitatem et insolentiam quam pluries provocare occasionemque afferre distractionis a studio et profectu, hujusmodi instrumentorum usum infra suum mansum, nisi temporibus communis solatii, scholares praedicti omnino sibi noverint interdictum.

[20] *Ibid.,* I., "Statutes of New College," 42, 100.

[21] *Ibid.,* I, "Statutes of All Souls," 36.

> *In twenty manere koude he trippe and daunce*
> *After the scole of Oxenforde tho,*
> *And with his legges casten to and fro,*
> *And pleyen songes on a smal rubible;*
> *Thereto he song som tyme a loud quynyble;*
> *And as wel koude he pleye on a giterne.*

Actual Oxford records also tell us that students owned musical instruments. An inventory of the possessions of Master Thomas Cooper, Brasenose, 1438, contained: *"Item, una antiqua cithara; Item, una 'lute' fracta";* and the appraisal of goods of another student (1448) included *"Item, unum 'Hornpipe' pretium jᵈ."*[22]

Next to Paris, the University of Oxford was the inspiration for more treatises on music than any other medieval university—and, indeed, connections between the two *studia* were always very close. As might be expected, some of these reflect the philosophical approach to music, whereas others deal with artistic problems of *musica practica.* One of the earliest of the first type is the section on music in the treatise *De artibus liberalibus*[23] of Robert Grosseteste (*ca.* 1175–1253), Bishop of Lincoln, who received the *magisterium in theologia* at Oxford and probably studied at Paris also, where he became acquainted with Arabian philosophy.[24] In discussing the arts as necessary introductory material to the study of philosophy, Grosseteste significantly placed music at the head of the quadrivium. The section on music is the hortatory introduction treating music as the ideal science of numbers, universal harmony, proportions based upon movement—*"Haec enim, ut asseruit Macrobius motuum proportionibus reperitur concordantia"*—and as such related to all phases of being. Under *speculatio musicae* Grosseteste places all kinds of harmony based upon movement;[25] he gives a very broad interpretation to the old *musica*

---

[22] Anstey, *Munimenta*, II, 515, 579.

[23] Ludwig Baur (ed.), *Die philosophischen Werke des Robert Grosseteste* (Münster, 1912), 1–7.

[24] See Ludwig Baur, *Die Philosophie des Robert Grosseteste* (Münster, 1917), 4–6.

[25] *Werke*, 3: *"non solum harmonia humanae vocis et gesticulationis, sed etiam instrumentorum et eorum, quorum delectatio in motu sive in sono consistit et cum his harmonia coelestium sive noncoelestium."*

humana;[26] and like the Arabian philosophers, he connects music quite strongly with bodily health.

An interesting commentary upon Grosseteste's own personal "delyte in Mynstrelsy" appears in lines written about him by Robert de Brunne (*fl.* fourteenth century). Characteristically, reasons for this love of music are both philosophical and theological, as the "rude rhymes" show:

> *Y shall you tell as I have herd*
> *Of the byshop Seynt Roberd,*
> *Hys toname is Grosteste*
> *Of Lyncolne, so leyth the geste,*
> *He loved moche to here the* Harpe,
> *For mans witte yt makyth sharpe.*
> *Next hys chamber, besyde his study,*
> *Hys Harper's chamber was fast the by.*
> *Many tymes, by nights and dayes,*
> *He had solace of notes and layes,*
> *One askede hem the reson why*
> *He hadde delyte in Mynstrelsy?*
> *He answerde hym on this manere*
> *Why he held the* Harpe *so dere,*
> *"The virtu of the Harpe, thurgh skyle and ryght,*
> *"Wyll destrye the fendys myght;*
> *"And to the cros by gode skeyl*
> *"Ys the* Harpe *ylykened weyl.*
> *"Thirefore, gode men, ye shall lere,*
> *"When ye any* Gleman *here,*
> *"To worshepe God at your power,*
> *"And Davyd in the Sauter.*
> *"Yn harpe and tabour and* symphan *gle*
> *"Worship God in trumpes and sautre:*
> *"In cordes, yn* organes, *and bells ringyng,*
> *"Yn all these worship the hevene Kyng."*[27]

---

[26] *Ibid.*, 4: "*Cum inquam ita sit in numeris sonantibus, protendit se musica speculatio ut harmoniam cognoscat, non solum in numeris sonantibus seu corporalibus, sed etiam in progressoribus et occursoribus, recordabilibus, sensibilibus et judicialibus.*"

[27] Charles Burney, *A General History of Music* (London, 1776), II, 356–57.

A similar but briefer introduction to music of the *protreptikos* type appears in the treatise *De ortu et divisione philosophiae*[28] by a younger contemporary of Grosseteste's, Robert Kilwardby (d. 1279), an English theologian who studied in Paris, taught theology at Oxford, and became Archbishop of Canterbury in 1272. Citing definitions from such authorities as Aristotle, Boethius, Isidorus, and Gundissalinus, Kilwardby outlines the order, subject matter (numbers), and divisions (Boethian) of music.

A more personal and less stereotyped approach to music is seen in Roger Bacon's writings on this subject. A pupil of Grosseteste's at Oxford, student at Paris, and later teacher of theology at Oxford, Bacon (*ca.* 1214–94) discussed music in his *Opus majus* and *Opus tertium*. In the former he stressed the need for understanding musical theory, if not practice, in order to interpret the Scriptures properly.[29] Chapter LIX of the *Opus tertium* treats music (and several succeeding chapters deal with music and poetry), citing numerous authorities, Arabic as well as Latin and Greek: Augustine, Cassiodorus, Martianus, Boethius, Ptolemy, Euclid, and Al-Farabi. Undoubtedly influenced by Al-Farabi, Bacon, like Grocheo a century later, turned from *musica mundana* and concentrated upon audible music: sound, he declared, is not generated *"ex radiis coelorum, et ideo nulla est musica mundana."* Typical of his overall scientific attitude, Bacon believed that the true *musicus* should not rely on authority but should prove his points by *demonstratio* (experiment), *"quia demonstratio facit scire per causam."* Like Grosseteste, Bacon connected music with the dance, with gestures; these, he said, are visible music. Farther along in the work,[30] Bacon, after describing the effects of music, with reference to Plato, criticizes certain liturgical usages: *"Sed jam per ecclesiam paulatim crevit abusus cantus."* This wrong usage, already existing in *"max-*

---

[28] Chapter XVIII, which contains the discussion of music, appears as Anhang C, Grossman, *Die einleitenden Kapitel des Speculum Musicae,* 94–96.

[29] *Opus majus* (ed.), J. H. Bridges (London, 1900), I, 236–37: *"Scriptura enim plena est vocabulis musicalibus, sicut jubilare, exultare, cantare, psallere, cythara, cymbala, et huiusmodi diversi generis."*

[30] *Fr. Rogeri Bacon Opera quaedam hactenus inedita* (ed. by J. S. Brewer) (London, 1859), 297–98.

imis ecclesiis cathedralibus, et aliis collegiis famosis," is described as a *"novarum harmoniarum curiositas, et prosarum lubrica adinventio, multipliciumque cantilenarum inepta voluptas,"* as well as the use of weak, womanly, falsetto voices. Bacon, then, viewed adversely the new polyphony cultivated at Notre Dame in Paris, which he doubtlessly heard while a student there.

Bartholomaeus Anglicus also incorporated a section on music in his encyclopedia *De proprietatibus rerum,*[31] a compendious work covering all the learning of his time, frequently drawn upon during the medieval period and later, and often included in university library lists (an example of which we have already seen at the University of Paris). Trained at Oxford, Bartholomaeus lectured on theology at Paris in 1230 and was called to teach at the *studium* of the Minorites at Magdeburg that same year, probably writing his treatise before 1250. The work was translated into English by John of Trevisa in 1398 and printed by Wynken de Worde in 1495[32]—a mark of no little distinction in itself. The section *"De musica"* begins conventionally with a scholastic introduction—definitions and divisions drawn largely from Isidorus—telling the effects, parts, and properties of music, with a lengthy discussion of voices. Quite unusual for this time, however, is the section on musical instruments which follows—identical with that found in the *Ars musica* of Juan Gil of Zamora, Spanish philosopher—beginning with the organ, which, Bartholomaeus tells us significantly, was the only instrument then permitted in the Church.[33] After the organ, fourteen instruments are described. The work concludes with some rather mystical (or mystifying) remarks on the *numerus sesquialterus,* proportions such as "twelue to eyghte, and fyftene to ten, and so of other," which the author himself confesses not to understand ("Thise wordes ben in themselfe deepe and full mystyk,

[31] Hermann Müller, *"Der Musiktraktat in dem Werke des Bartholomaeus Anglicus De proprietatibus rerum,"* *Riemann-Festschrift* (Leipzig, 1909), 241–55; text, 245–55.

[32] For easy reference, see the quotation of this text by Sir John Hawkins, *A General History of the Science and Practice of Music* (London, 1776), II, 279–88.

[33] *"Organum* is a generall name of all instrumentes of musyk, and is netheless specyally a propryte to the instrument that is made of many pipes, and blowe wyth belowes. And now holy chyrche useth oonly this instrument of musyk, in preses, sequences, and ympnes; and forsakyth for men's use of mynstralsye all other instrumentes of musyk."

derk to understondynge"). From this uneven proportion, Bartholomaeus returns to harmony in general, its connection with "heuenly thynges," and its effects on the soul.

Such treatises as these show the important place of music in philosophical and theological studies at Oxford and Paris in the Middle Ages. From fourteenth-century Oxford we have a comprehensive treatment of music of the *speculum* type: the work *De speculatione musice* (CS, I, 182–252) of Walter Odington, monk of Evesham Abbey, mathematician, musician, and astronomer, known to have been making astrological observations at Oxford in 1316 and to have been a resident of Merton College in 1330.[34] Comprising six books, the lengthy treatise combines both *musica speculativa* and *musica practica:* the first three books are purely mathematical (and interestingly enough, Odington is the earliest theorist to consider the natural third—4:5 as opposed to the Pythagorean ratio 64:81—a consonant interval,[35] stating this theory nearly two hundred years before the Spaniard Ramos and his followers at Bologna), the fourth treats of metrics, the fifth deals with the elements of *cantus planus,* and the last is a treatise on *musica mensurabilis,* containing all matters of rhythm and notation as well as directions for composing various types of polyphonic music—organum duplum and discantus (*rondelli,* conductus, *copulae,* motets, and hockets).

Another treatise of the *speculum* type, lengthy and comprehensive, sprang from musical studies at Oxford: the *Quatuor principalia musicae* (CS, IV, 200–298), written in 1351 by the theologian Simon Tunstede, a Franciscan who was then teaching at Oxford.[36] Following the pattern of the university treatise, the *Quatuor principalia* embraces *speculatio musicae* and also artistic problems of *musica practica.* The first book is a typical scholastic *eisagogé* (divisions, subdivisions, etymology, definitions, uses, and

---

[34] See article on Odington in the *Dictionary of National Biography.*

[35] See Hugo Riemann, *Geschichte der Musiktheorie im IX.–XIX. Jahrhundert* (Leipzig, 1898), 114–20.

[36] Cf. the *explicit,* CS, IV, 298: *"Illo autem anno regens erat inter Minores Oxoniae, Frater Symon de Tunstede, doctor sacrae theologiae, qui in musica pollebat, et etiam in septem liberalibus artibus."*

effects of music), the second shows the mathematical derivation of the scale, the third deals with the ecclesiastical chant, and the *"Quartum principale"*[37] is a complete treatise on mensural music—notes, ligatures, tempus and prolation, the *punctus,* the use of red notes, imperfection and alteration of notes, and the *pausa,* with a discussion of discantus and directions for composing various kinds of it. Quoting extensively from the *Ars cantus mensurabilis* of Franco of Cologne for his doctrine of the *ars antiqua* and drawing upon Philip de Vitry for *ars-nova* doctrine, Tunstede discusses *discantus cum littera,* that is, *discantus cum eadem littera* (found *"in cantilenis, rondellis et cantu aliquo ecclesiastico"*) and *discantus cum diversis litteris* (motets with their heterogeneous texts performed simultaneously). The procedure is the same in composing all these except the conductus, which must be based not upon a *cantus prius factus* but upon an original melody.

Our last treatise deriving from musical studies at medieval Oxford is one patterned upon the theological *summa:* the *Summa super musicam continuam et discretam,* subtitled *Musica Magistri Franconis cum additionibus et opinionibus diversorum* (CS, I, 403–48) by John Hanboys, called *doctor musicae* in the *explicit.* The antiquarian Bale states that Hanboys was thoroughly grounded in the liberal arts, that he made a special study of *musica speculativa,* and that after years of study at an English university he was made doctor *communi suffragio.*[38] Hawkins, too, calls Hanboys "a most celebrated musician, and a doctor in that faculty," although no record of such a degree exists.[39] Perhaps a composer as well as a scholarly *musicus*—Bale credits Hanboys with the composition of

---

[37] Published earlier by Coussemaker as *Anonymi I De musica antiqua et nova,* CS, III, 334–64. The two treatises are identical.

[38] John Bale, *Scriptorum illustrium maioris Brytannie catalogus* (Basiliae, 1557), I, 617:

> Ab adolescentia in liberalibus scientijs educatus, musicae, ut illi arti cui pre alijs fauebat semper, in finem usque ardentius adhaerebat. Vocum enim consonantias, proportionum inductiones, & quicquid est quod ad eam speculationem attinet, perfectissime uir ille officiosus ac diligens nouit. . . . Post frequentata igitur multis annis suae terrae gymnasia, ob egregie nauatam operam, in ea scientia communi suffragio fit doctor, sui temporis plane in Anglia celeberrimus.

[39] *History of Music,* II, 344–45.

Cantiones dulcissimas which are not extant—Hanboys was deeply interested in current problems of rhythm and notation, as his treatise shows. For his *Summa musicae* is a work of the *scholia* type, a commentary upon both Franco of Cologne (whom the author quotes literally in the "Proemium" and first two chapters) and Franco of Paris (excerpts from whose treatise he quotes); but Hanboys goes far beyond Franconian theory in his discussion of imperfection, diminution, and alteration of notes from longs to semiminims. The *opiniones diversorum* are those of Petrus de Cruce, John of Garland, W. of Doncastre, Robert Trowell, and Robert de Brunham. Hanboys evidently knew and drew upon the earlier *scholia* of Handlo, for there is great similarity in title and pattern, and even identity in certain passages in their works.

It is quite possible that England's earliest composer of international influence and importance was a student at either Oxford or Cambridge—John Dunstable (*ca.* 1385–1453). Dunstable probably spent much of his life as chaplain and musician in the service of the Duke of Bedford in France, and his introduction of a new "English style" to the continent was enthusiastically noticed by Martin le Franc (*Le Champion des Dames,* 1440), Tinctoris, and various others.[40] True to the tradition, however, Dunstable was also a mathematician and astronomer, and several of his mathematical tracts are still extant in libraries in Oxford and Cambridge.

At Oxford in the Middle Ages, then, both the theory and practice of music had an assured place. Boethius' *Musica* was required by statute for all masters of arts; training in plain song was provided for younger members of collegiate foundations, who actually owed their position at Oxford to their musical talents and duties; and students in Oxford's colleges were ofttimes so enthusiastic in singing, dancing, and performing on musical instruments that officials felt compelled to forbid these activities. The liberal interchange of scholars and ideas between Paris and Oxford disseminated French notational theory in England, along with knowledge

---

[40] For the latest account of Dunstable's life and works and an appraisal of his contributions to music, see Manfred Bukofzer, "John Dunstable: A Quincentenary Report," *Musical Quarterly,* Vol. XL (1954), 29–49.

of the various forms of Notre Dame polyphony and the music of the *ars nova;* at the same time, it allowed the participation of English scholars in the development of this theory in France—for instance, John of Garland.

Treatises written by Oxford scholars and teachers reflect the twofold approach to music everywhere characteristic of university studies: *musica speculativa* as a mathematical discipline, one of the encyclopedic liberal arts forming the basis of philosophy and prerequisite to the study of theology; and *musica practica* as a living art, cultivated *ad majoram gloriam Dei.* It is extremely significant, indeed, of the constant interdependency of the two sides of music's dichotomy that men distinguished for mathematical and theological knowledge—like Simon Tunstede—becoming highly skilled in the *ars musica,* were concerned in their treatises—and undoubtedly in their lectures—with artistic problems of musical techniques, problems of rhythm and notation; and that such a celebrated composer as John Dunstable was so well versed in the disciplines of the quadrivium that he could write treatises about them. By the end of the Middle Ages the great enthusiasm for music at Oxford culminated in the granting of separate degrees in music and the establishment of music as a separate faculty—the only liberal art so distinguished. From the mid-fifteenth century on, many of England's most talented musicians became bachelors or doctors of music at Oxford.

Cambridge

As at Oxford, many legends have grown up concerning the antiquity of the University of Cambridge, one assigning its foundation to a Spanish Prince Cantaber and another to King Arthur; but actually the schools of Cambridge are first heard of in the early thirteenth century, and Cambridge received formal recognition as a *studium generale* in a bull of 1318 from Pope John XXII.[41] Fol-

[41] See Rashdall, *Medieval Universities,* III, 276ff., and Mullinger, *The University of Cambridge,* I, 145. The Cambridge schools first came into notice after a *suspendium*

lowing Oxford, the Cambridge curriculum comprised the trivium, quadrivium, and three philosophies.[42] Early Cambridge documents were burned in the great Town and Gown riots of 1381, and the first extant statutes dealing with a course of studies appear to come from the late fifteenth century. One of these assigns three additional years to the study of mathematics after the bachelor's degree, the first year to be spent in arithmetic and music.

A list of books from the university library around 1424 contains two which treat musical problems—the *Problemata* attributed to Aristotle and the commentary upon this work by Peter of Albano (Peter of Padua).[43]

Like Oxford colleges, Cambridge foundations provided instruction in music for their younger members. The master of Clare Hall, according to the *"Regulae Aulae de Clare,"* 1359, was to see that choristers in this college received instruction *"in cantu, grammatica, et dialectica."*[44] In King's College, established in 1441 by Henry VI, *"sedecim pueri scientes competenter legere et cantare"* were included among the members.[45] Boys from any county in England might apply for admission, and after an examination in reading, plain song, and grammar, suitable ones would be chosen to fill vacancies in this college and in the college of Eton.[46] Of the six

---

clericorum at Oxford in 1209 and again after the Parisian migration to England in 1229. During the Wyclifite heresy in the fourteenth century, Oxford fell somewhat into disrepute with cautious parents and orthodox patrons, and it was from this time that the University of Cambridge began its rise to fame.

[42] And as at Oxford a statute of 1456 declared that *"nullus admittatur ad incipiendum in theologia, nisi prius in artibus rexerit"*; see *Documents relating to the University and Colleges of Cambridge* (London, 1852), I, 377.

[43] Henry Bradshaw, *Collected Papers* (Cambridge, 1889), 29.

[44] *Cambridge Documents*, II, 141: *"Provideat insuper dictus Magister, quod dicti pauperes in cantu, grammaticâ, et dialecticâ solicite instruantur, sumptibus dictae Domus."*

[45] *Ibid.*, II, 484.

[46] *Ibid.*, II, 491:

Quo insuper electionis et nominationis tempore chorustae Ecclesiae Collegiatae Regalis Collegii de Aetona, et chorustae Ecclesiae Collegiatae nostri Collegii Cantabrigiae, necnon alii pueri de comitatibus quibuscunque Angliae ad electionem hujusmodi confluentes, in lectura, plano cantu, et Donato competenter instructi, et infra aetatem nostris statutis limitatam constituti, per dictos examinatores et electores examinentur: et qui habiles et idonei reperti fuerint, eligantur, de quibus numerus scholarium ibidem tunc deficines impleatur.

clerks of the chapel of King's College, moreover—all of them skilled in reading, psalmody, and singing—one was to be able *"jubilare in organis in Ecclesia Collegiata."*[47]

College statutes also contain directions for the celebration of liturgical activities with music by members of the foundations. Several *Missae cum nota,* for example, are specified for members of Clare Hall, among them a *"Missa de Beatissima Maria Matre Virgine Gloriosa"* for Sundays and feastdays, at which all fellows and scholars were to be present.[48] At Trinity College, founded in 1350, Masses were to be celebrated *"cum nota vel sine nota"* each Sunday by members of the college; at King's College an *"antiphona aliqua de Beata Virgine Maria"* was to be *"communiter decantata"* each day *"post prandium,"* and statutes of this college are very specific in giving long and detailed instructions for the carrying out of musical activities by the chapel priests and choristers.[49]

Among these documents there are two references to informal music. A statute from sometime before 1430 decreed that in the customary disputes between Northerners and Southerners, students were not to ring bells, play horns or trumpets.[50] And the statutes for King's College, patterned upon those of New College, Oxford, allowed students to find recreation *"in cantilenis et aliis solatiis"* after supper when there was a fire in the hall.[51]

Although many of the English musical treatises are now preserved in the Cambridge Library, no published treatises appear to be related directly to Cambridge at this time. Degrees in grammar and rhetoric were awarded at medieval Cambridge just as at Oxford,[52] and music may well have received the same distinction.

---

[47] *Ibid.,* II, 484: *"Ac insuper sex Clerici . . . legendi et psallendi et cantandi peritiam habentes, in vocibus similiter bene dispositi, quorum capellanorum sive clericorum unus sciat jubilare in organis in Ecclesia Collegiata, ibidem in divinis quotidie deservientes."*

[48] *Ibid.,* II, 141: *"Et celebretur dicta Missa diebus Dominicis et festivis cum notâ, et tunc eidem omnes dictos Socios et pueros ad cantandum et juvandum, cessante legitimo impedimento, praecipimus interesse; aliis vero diebus profestis dicta Missa celebrari poterit sine notâ."*

[49] *Ibid.,* II, 429, 532, 564–75.

[50] *Ibid.,* I, 334: *"nec . . . campanas pulsent cornua vel tubis clangent."*

[51] *Ibid.,* II, 533.

[52] Edwards, *Skelton,* 34ff.

At any rate, degrees in music were awarded frequently from the latter part of the fifteenth century on.

iv. Spain: Salamanca

The establishment of the first *studia generalia* in Spain in the thirteenth century was backed by a long tradition of higher learning in Spanish monastic and cathedral schools. This tradition included musical instruction based upon Boethius and Guido, as in other parts of Europe,[1] which meant an academic interest in practical as well as theoretical music. According to the eleventh-century writer, Virgilius Cordubensis, organum was taught in the school of Cordova, one of Spain's most flourishing schools of music, in the eleventh century. Speaking of masters *qui legabant* each day in grammar, logic, natural science, astrology, geometry, and physics, Virgilius says, *"et duo magistri legebant de musica (de ista arte quae dicitur organum)."*[2] Cordova did not develop into a *studium generale,* but when the schools at Salamanca were organized into such a corporation, *"un maestro en órgano"* was among its first professors.

Having developed from the cathedral school at Salamanca, the university maintained a close connection with the cathedral throughout the Middle Ages: the *scholasticus* of the cathedral was also head of the schools of the university, and it was he who conferred the *licentia* in the cathedral.[3] But this university differs from other European *studia* in having been established (1215) by royal rather than papal authority[4]—a fact usually considered a mark of

---

[1] Francisco Asenjo Barbieri, *Cancionero musical español de los siglos XV y XVI* (Buenos Aires, 1945), 11.

[2] Henry George Farmer, *The Arabian Influence on Musical Theory* (London, 1925), 7. But see Higini Anglès, "Hispanic Musical Culture from the 6th to the 14th Century," *Musical Quarterly,* Vol. XXVI (1940), 516–17, for a discussion of the dubious authenticity of this document.

[3] Rashdall, *Medieval Universities,* II, 76.

[4] The University of Salamanca dates its founding from 1215, when Alfonso IX of Léon gave the schools privileges of a *studium generale* so that Spanish students need not go abroad for study: see Caro Lynn, *A College Professor of the Renaissance* (Chicago,

Spanish independence. It is also unique among other continental universities in having an endowed chair of music as early as 1254, the first such chair established in any university. According to statutes of that year promulgated under Alfonso X, there was to be on the staff *"un maestro en órgano"* with a salary of fifty *maravedis* a year.[5]

By *"maestro en órgano"* probably organum in the sense of the science of polyphonic music was meant.[6] Not only is this quite in keeping with Spanish trends and with the Arabian view of music—*musica activa* on a par with *musica theoretica*—but it is also indicative of Alfonso's deep personal interest in music. Juan Gil of Zamora, author of an important treatise on music and tutor to Alfonso's son, says in his *Vita* of the king that Alfonso was a good composer.[7] The Spanish royal chapel, moreover, had a polyphonic school at this time equal to that of St. Louis in France.[8] And it was Alfonso X who had scholars compile a great collection (more than four hundred compositions) of music, the now famous *Cantigas de Santa Maria*. Alfonso himself wrote the words and music for some of these songs.

As early as 1313 (in a bull from Clement V), we find music included among a number of subjects taught by *magistri* and *doctores* at Salamanca.[9] And later in the century (1355) a *rotulus* of

1937), 3. Alfonso's son Ferdinand renewed these privileges in a charter of 1242, the oldest extant university document. Alfonso X gave new privileges, 1254; and upon his application to Alexander IV, the *studium* received papal recognition and the privilege of granting to its graduates the *ius ubique docendi*, 1255.

5 Enrique Esperabé y Arteaga, *Historia pragmática é interna de la Universidad de Salamanca* (Salamanca, 1914–17), I, 22. It is noticeable that the music master with his fifty *maravedis* has the lowest salary on the list and that professors of law have the highest: canon law was always the most distinguished and highly paid faculty at Salamanca.

6 See Anglès, "Hispanic Musical Culture," *Musical Quarterly*, Vol. XXVI, 518.

7 Marqués de Valmar (ed.), *Cantigas de Santa Maria de Don Alfonso el Sabio* (Madrid, 1889), I, 126: *"Multas et perpulchras composuit cantilenas, sonis convenientibus et proportionibus musicis modulatas."*

8 Anglès, "Hispanic Musical Culture," *Musical Quarterly*, Vol. XXVI, 523.

9 D. Vicente de la Fuente, *Historia de las universidades en Espana* (Madrid, 1884–89), I, 313, no. 17: *"Magistrorum, et Doctorum, quos in Decretis, Decretalibus, Legibus, Medicina, Logicalibus, et Gramaticalibus, et Musica, regere, ac docere pro tempore in dicta civitate contigerit."*

the university sent to Innocent VI contained two *"magistri in musica dicti studii."*[10] The term *magister in musica* probably referred to the academic position rather than to a degree in music; if separate disciplines were singled out for distinction,[11] these awards very likely amounted to permission to teach the subjects (as in the Italian and English universities). Under the authority of Benedict XIII, who reformed and enlarged the *studium* (1411), the number of endowed chairs (called *cátedras de propriedad,* with permanent tenure for their incumbents) was increased to twenty-five, one of which was a chair of music; according to a statute of Eugenius IV (1423), professors holding these chairs had to be either doctors or masters, except for teachers of astrology, music, rhetoric, and languages, who might be bachelors.[12]

The one available treatise from the medieval period probably related to musical studies at the University of Salamanca is the thirteenth-century *Ars musica* (GS, II, 369–93) of Juan Gil of Zamora (Aegidius Zamorensis) in Castile. The tutor of Sancho IV, Juan Gil was a *lector* and *doctor* (who compiled his writings from the philosophers in typical scholastic fashion) and also a composer of hymns and sequences, some of which are still extant.[13] This highly learned work—definitely of the type generally springing from university studies—opens with the usual speculative topics (invention, effects, definitions, divisions, and subdivisions of music), followed by a mathematical discussion based upon the monochord leading to more practical aspects of the chant (notation, the modes), with great stress always upon effects. Juan concludes with a lengthy section describing fourteen musical instruments—possibly a reflection of Spanish liturgical practices—a section practically

[10] Denifle, *Universitäten des Mittelalters,* 494.

[11] Rashdall, *Medieval Universities,* II, 81: "The University of Salamanca appears to be the first which gave both degrees and practical instruction in music. A master of music was always included among its professors."

[12] Pedro Chacon, *"Historia de la Universidad de Salamanca,"* 1569, *Semanario erudito,* Vol. XVIII (Madrid, 1789), 30, 47.

[13] He says at the beginning of his treatise, *"Musicam absque demonstrationibus, quas melius novistis, iuxta mandatum vestrum brevius & puerilius, ut potui, ex dictis philosophorum praesentibus scribo vobis."* We do not know that Juan Gil was enrolled in the university, but this seems likely in view of the proximity of Zamora to Salamanca.

identical with that in Bartholomaeus Anglicus' *De proprietatibus rerum*.[14]

This treatise, conventional except for the great emphasis upon musical instruments, is important for the history of musical studies in Spain, for not only is it the only available medieval treatise, but few treatises from Spain's Middle Ages exist even in manuscript.[15] The high position of music at Salamanca, with emphasis upon theoretical and artistic aspects of music, including the composition of polyphonic music, seems to be related to a long tradition of musical instruction in Spanish schools, to royal interest in and patronage of music, and to the great flourishing of instrumental and vocal music in medieval Spain.

V. BOHEMIA: PRAGUE

IN 1348 CHARLES IV established at Prague, with the sanction of Pope Clement, a *studium generale*: modeled upon the archetype at Paris, this *universitas magistrorum et scholarium* was the first university to be erected in Central Europe and the model for subsequent German foundations.[1] From the early days of the Prague *studium*, music had a regular place among the "ordinary" lectures in the arts faculty. A statute of 1367 included musical works among the "ordinary" books to be distributed to the regent masters and read—that is, lectured upon—completely.[2] Another statute empha-

[14] According to Müller, *"Der Musiktraktat in dem Werke des Bartholomaeus Anglicus De proprietatibus rerum,"* *Riemann-Festschrift*, 241–44, both treatises may derive from a common source. The Englishman's treatise was written *ca.* 1250 and the Spaniard's *ca.* 1270.

[15] Anglès, "Hispanic Musical Culture," *Musical Quarterly*, Vol. XXVI, 519.

[1] Clement's bull of 1348 granted *"privilegia, immunitates et libertates omnes, quibus tam in Parisiensi, quam Bononiensi studiis doctores et scolares auctoritate regia uti et gaudere sunt soliti"*: see the charter of foundation, Jan Krcmar, *The Prague Universities* (Prague, 1934), 4. Owing to Charles' position as head of the Holy Roman Empire, the University of Prague has often been called the first German university. Actually the emperor chartered this *studium* by virtue of his authority as King of Bohemia, and its foundation was approved by the Bohemian nobility (*ibid.*, 3–12).

[2] *Monumenta Universitatis Pragensis*, I, *Liber Decanorum Facultatis Philosophicae, pars i* (Pragae, 1830), 15, 68–69 (where the rule is repeated):

debent quoque omnes libri Aristotelis una cum geometricalibus, arithmeticalibus, astronomicalibus & musicalibus secundum deliberationem magistrorum regentium,

sized the fact that disciplines of the quadrivium were a part of the *lectiones ordinariae* and were not to be read on holidays.[3] A statute *"de maximo et minimo tempore pro legendi libris requisito"* mentioned the musical textbook to be used—the *Musica* of Jean de Muris, with a maximum of one month, a minimum of three weeks to be spent on this book; in 1389 it was again decreed that Muris' *Musica* be taught among the "ordinary" disciplines.[4] A statute of 1390 specified that no candidate be admitted *ad gradum magisterii* without having heard *aliquid in Musica*.[5] These statutes were all written down in 1390 and were in effect at that time.

Such emphasis placed upon music by the statutes is underlined by other university documents. The *Registrum librorum Collegii Carolini,* for instance, compiled around 1370, contains books regularly used in the study of *musica speculativa,* some of which we have noticed in other libraries: *Libri Richardi de sancto Victore &c, Isidorus ethymologiarum, Liber de nupcijs philologie cum alijs, Macrobius de Sompno Cipionis, Liber de proprietatibus rerum,* and *Quadrivium Boecij.*[6] The last of these is a manuscript from the tenth or eleventh century containing the *Arithmetica, Geometria, Euclidis Geometria a Boethio translata, Musica,* and *Astronomia,* significant again of the vogue of Boethius in pre-university schools; and Truhlar's enormous catalogue of library holdings includes

---

seu pro illo anno regere volentium inter illos distribui 1ᵐᵃ die Septembris taliter, quod omnes ordinarie, prout sequitur, finiantur, & quicumque magistrorum eadem die distributioni non interfuerit, vel caruerit habitu, locum amittat secundum senium ordinarium eligendi.

[3] *Ibid.,* I, i, 75: *"Item in plena congregatione conclusum & statutum fuit, quod nullus baccalarius, licentiatus, aut magister deberet legere diebus celebribus aliquem librum in logica . . . nec aliquem librum in quadruvio, qui requiritur pro ordinario secundum dictamen facultatis."*

[4] *Ibid.,* I, i, 82–83: *"pro de sensu et sensato unus mensis ad maximum, minimum, infra quod non, tres septimanae. . . . similiter pro musica Muri."* And in 1389, *"In quadruvio sex libri Euclidis, arithmetica, musica Muri . . . non debent legi diebus festivis"* (p. 92).

[5] *Ibid.,* I, i, 56: *"nullus magistrorum de facultate nostra, qui pro examinatore magistrandorum fuerit deputatus, aliquem ad tentamen admittat, nisi complete audiverit libros infra scriptos, videlicet . . . aliquid in musica et arithmetica."*

[6] Pietzsch, *"Musik an den Universitäten im Osten,"* AfMf, Vol. I, 274–75.

copies of Alanus' *Anticlaudianus,* Aristotle's *Problemata,* and other treatises with musical information.[7]

There are extant, too, several musical treatises written by students in the university during this period—the oldest, a *Tractatus de cantu perfecto et imperfecto* by Henricus de Zelandia, found in a Prague manuscript (CS, III, 113–15). The writer is probably Nicolaus Hinrici de Selandia, whose name appears on the matriculation roll of 1390.[8] From the opening sentence of the little work we may assume that it was designed for students of music: *"Gaudent musicorum discipuli, quod Henricus de Zeelandia aliqua brevia tractat de musica,"* and at least one set of lecture notes which it seems to have provoked is extant.[9] In two sections, the treatise deals with intervals used in plain song and the six *voces* of solmization; in the manuscript there follows a copy of the *Libellus cantus mensurabilis* of Jean de Muris, a technical discussion of the elements of the *ars-nova* music.

An *"Oratio inedita ut videtur M. Johannis Huss,"* 1409, a *Recommendatio artium liberalium,* picturing the liberal arts as seven virgins, daughters of philosophy, contains a section on music—the *"sexta virgo . . . cujus vero manus baiulat citharam, altera vero manus cordas continue sollicitat";* both theoretical and practical music are represented symbolically on music's gown.[10] And a commentary on the *Musica speculativa* of Jean de Muris from the early part of the fifteenth century reflects musical studies in the university based upon the text required in the statutes: a set of notes by the Prague student, medical doctor, and professor, Wenceslaus de

[7] Josepho Truhlář, *Catalogus Codicum Manu Scriptorum Latinorum* (Pragae, 1905–1906), II, 13 and *passim.*

[8] *Monumenta Universitatis Pragensis,* II, *Album seu Matricula Facultatis Juridicae,* 143.

[9] Truhlář, *Catalogus,* II, 158.

[10] E. Höfler, *Geschichtschreiber der Husitischen Bewegung in Böhmen* (Wien, 1865), Theil II, 112–28. One side of her robe shows pictures *"cur non una vox omne melos dulcisque cantus sonorum pertineat, sed potius unio vocum dissimilis. . . . Sic haec virgo in sua parte tunicae insignia defert artis musicae. At vero pars altera vestis hujus gaudet in se habere suos depictos artifices"* (p. 118). Among the *artifices* are Orpheus, Millesius, Micalus and *noster Gregorius.* The rest of the oration is a plea for the study of the arts and of Wyclif's works.

Prachatitz.[11] Since Muris' *Musica* was required for the *magisterium*, Wenceslaus may have written his commentary just before attaining that degree, but whether it is original or lecture notes cannot be determined. Following the usual medieval pattern, Wenceslaus begins with the question *"Quis sit musica?"* and gives definitions, etymology, divisions, inventors of music, and a statement of music's place in philosophy; he then outlines and quotes Muris' treatise and concludes with a discussion of musical effects.

Some of the material of this commentary is incorporated in another Prague treatise, the *Tractatus de simplici cantu* compiled by Stanislaus de Gnezna (bachelor, 1442, master, 1445, licentiate, 1446, and active in the arts faculty until 1458), but according to the explicit *"actum et datum in studio alme univ Cor——[?] sub a.d.1402."*[12] Designed *ad utilitatem puerorum*, the treatise is highly practical in purpose, but it contains speculative sections, *"Quid sit musica"* and *"De divisione musice"* similar to those in the Muris commentary, indicating that both may have sprung from the same source. Both certainly reflect the study of Muris' *Musica*.

Some of the men who taught the music required at Prague in the late Middle Ages are known to us. Hermannus de Winterswijk and Johannes Westfali, *"magistri artium artes in studio Pragensi actu legentes"* in 1355, later became choirmasters[13]—pointing to musical interests probably exploited in their university teaching. Magister Petrus de Stupna, student in arts and law at Prague

---

[11] Bachelor and master of arts, 1415 and 1430; *licentiatus in artibus*, 1430; official in arts faculty, 1434, 1436; doctor of medicine, 1443; rector, 1454; see the *Liber Decanorum*, I, i, 435 and ii, 8ff. See also Wenzel Tomek, *Geschichte der Präger Universität* (Prag, 1849), 357–58. Truhlář, *Catalogus*, I, 382, describes the treatise. For the text of the treatise, see Gerhard Pietzsch, *"Die Pflege der Musik an den Universitäten bis zur Mitte des 16. Jahrhunderts: I. Die Universität Prag und ihre Vorbilder,"* *Mitteilungen des Vereines für Geschichte der Deutschen in Böhmen*, Vol. LXXIII (1935), 112–18.

Wenceslaus figured later (1447) in a case with surprisingly modern overtones, when a "Mag. Paulus" (who had spoken out of turn against the medical profession, saying *"quod omnis medicus est homicida"*) was *"accusatus per venerabilem Mag. Wenceslaum de Prachaticz Medicinae Doctorem, et testibus coram Universitate idoneis convictus verba sua taliter retractavit."* See Antonius Dittrich and Antonius Spirk (eds.), *Statuta Universitatis Pragensis* (Pragae, n.d.), 35–36.

[12] Truhlář, *Catalogus*, I, 382; and see the *Liber Decanorum*, I, ii, 16ff., for references to Stanislaus.

[13] Pietzsch, *"Musik an den Universitäten im Osten, AfMf*, Vol. I, 265.

and author of several theological tracts, was praised along with other professors in a sermon of Johannes Hus as a *musicus dulcissimus*.[14] He may well have begun his regency with the teaching of music, as was often the case in the German universities. A number of men who studied in the university later became *cantores*—either singers or masters of choirs—in various places: Zacharias de Premislavia, bachelor of arts, 1370, later doctor of medicine, obtained the *cantoriam* in Magdeburg in 1391; Joannes de Lindau, bachelor of arts, 1382, and licentiate in 1384, later became *cantor* in Mainz; Conradus de Fulda, bachelor of arts, 1386, later matriculated at Heidelberg and Erfurt as *"cantor eccles. S. Severi Erfordensis"*; and Thomas Mas, bachelor of arts, 1396, became *cantor* of the Breslau cathedral in 1429, after holding other positions in that diocese.[15]

Canutus Boecij was already *"cantor ecclesiae Lyncopens"* when he matriculated in 1381; and Nicolaus de nova civitate, admitted to the bachelor's examination in 1392,[16] is probably identical with Nicolaus von Neustadt, who taught music at the University of Vienna in 1393. One man who studied and taught at Prague became a composer of great distinction: a Magister Záviš, bachelor in 1379, master of arts in 1382, and professor in the university for most of his later life.[17] Záviš is said to be the first representative of a truly Bohemian school of composition in which native folk elements were reconciled with French and German influences: five of his compositions exist (all monophonic and influenced by the Gregorian chant), one of them—a *Liebeslied*—having been written while he was a student at the University of Prague.[18] We have already pointed out the importance of Jan of Jenštejn (Johann von Jenzenstein), who studied at the University of Paris (1375–76), where he became familiar with the *ars-nova* music, became Arch-

---

[14] Tomek, *Geschichte der Präger Universität*, 44.

[15] Pietzsch, *"Musik an den Universitäten im Osten," AfMf*, Vol. I, 276, 277, 279, 281.

[16] *Album seu Matricula Facultatis Juridicae, i,* 129, and *Liber Decanorum,* I, *i,* 275.

[17] Z. Nejedlý, *"Magister Záviše und seine Schule," SIMG,* Vol. VII (1905), 56.

[18] *Ibid.,* Vol. VII, 56–57; and see Rita Petschek Kafka, "Music in Bohemia," in Gustave Reese, *Music in the Renaissance* (New York, 1954), 730.

bishop of Prague (1380–96), and gained distinction as a composer of mensural music.

The position of music at the medieval University of Prague is, thus, especially clear, for music was found among the "ordinary" lectures in the arts faculty and was required of all bachelors seeking the *magisterium*. The *Musica speculativa* of Jean de Muris appears for the first time in any university statutes in early Prague statutes (*ca.* 1370), indicative of the close connection between this university and the Sorbonne. Commentaries of Henricus de Zelandia and other Prague students show that Muris' work on the *ars nova* (*Libellus cantus mensurabilis*) was also known and used at Prague; and the fact that musical studies inspired Bohemia's earliest composers of music known by name (Záviš for monophonic and Jenštejn for polyphonic music) points again to the traditional combination of theory with practical artistry in the teaching of music. Prague documents are also important in clarifying the place of music at the University of Paris, about whose early curriculum not much is known. In view of the Prague requirements, one may conclude that the textbook of Muris was also the basis of musical instruction at the Sorbonne and at the various German universities modeled upon the *studium* at Prague.

vi. GERMANY: VIENNA, HEIDELBERG, COLOGNE, AND LEIPZIG

Vienna

LESS THAN two decades after the founding of the University of Prague, the Archduke Rudolf IV of the House of Habsburg established a university in Vienna (1365), authorized by Pope Urban V, modeled upon the University of Paris, and providing for the study of the liberal arts, theology, law, and medicine.[1] As at Prague, music apparently had a well defined place in the arts curriculum

---

[1] Rudolf Kink, *Geschichte der kaiserlichen Universität zu Wien* (Wien, 1854), II ("*Statutenbuch*"), 4, no. 1.

from the beginning. Statutes of the arts faculty (1389), specified *"aliquem librum de Musica et, aliquem in Arithmetica"* among books to be heard by bachelors seeking the licentiate, in addition to books heard before the baccalaureate; and in a ruling *"circa tempus et horas legendi,"* from 1449, *"musica per 4 ebdomadas, 16 lecciones"* was listed along with other mathematical disciplines.[2]

Several late medieval documents record the names of men who lectured on music and the books they "read." The earliest of these is Nicolaus von Neustadt, who lectured on music in 1393, having finished his studies, we recall, at the University of Prague; and in 1397 Georg von Horb began his regency with lectures on music.[3] In 1401 the faculty met to decide upon promoting certain bachelors to the licentiate: one of these was *"Thomas de Muschna Septem-castrensis, qui deficit in quarto Euclidis ... et musica et non legit."*[4] In 1421 Johann Geuss lectured on the *Musica* of Jean de Muris; and in 1431 when books to be "read" were distributed to the regent masters, *"M. Paulus Troppauer [recepit] Musicam Muris."*[5] When Johannes de Gmunden, mathematician and astronomer, left his books and instruments to the arts faculty in 1435, he included both the *Musica* and the *Arithmetica* of Boethius in the bequest.[6] In 1445, finally, Johannes de Werdea, beginning his regency, lectured on the *Musica* of Muris.[7]

Although from these records Jean de Muris appears to have been the standard author for the music lectures, Euclid may have been used also as a musical textbook, and lectures on music may have been required in the medical faculty. A book in the Wiener Staatsbibliothek—presented to the *Rosenburse* of the university at the owner's death in 1480—contains a list of books required *"ad gradum*

---

[2] *Ibid.*, II, 199, no. 15, and I, *"Urkundliche Beilagen,"* 111, no. 28.

[3] Joseph Aschbach, *Geschichte der Wiener Universität* (Wien, 1865–88), I, 145, 162, 602.

[4] Pietzsch, *"Musik an den Universitäten im Osten,"* AfMf, Vol. I, 283.

[5] Kink, *Universität Wien*, I, *"Urkundliche Beilagen,* 11, no. 7.

[6] *Ibid.*, I, 110, no. 27: *"Item liber in pergameno continens musicam Boecij cathenetur. Idem fiat de libro continente arithmeticam Boecij."*

[7] P. Ludwig Glückert, *"Hieronymus von Mondsee (Magister Johannes de Werdea),"* *Studien und Mitteilungen zur Geschichte des Benediktiner-Ordens und seiner Zweige,* Vol. XVII (Neue Folge, 1930), 103.

doctoratus medicinis," including the item, *"Musica Euclidis 3 gr., 4 septim., 16 lectionis."*[8]

Two musical treatises written by men who studied and taught at Vienna give us further insight into the study of music in the university. One of these is the *Introductorium musicae* (GS, III, 319–29) of Johannes Keckius, *"artium ac sacrae theologiae professor,"* as he says in his treatise, who lectured on mathematics, philosophy, and theology at Vienna (1429–31).[9] His treatise is speculative and mathematical, dealing largely with arithmetical proportions; and his theological background was probably responsible for his emphasis upon musical effects, especially those related to the Scriptures. The encyclopedia of Paulus Paulirinus of Prague, written after the mid-century in Pilsen, also sprang from Viennese studies, for Paulus attained the *magisterium* and began his regency there in 1442.[10] Comprising twenty books on the arts, the encyclopedia contains a section on music, drawing upon both speculative and artistic divisions of the art.

Students of St. Stephen's school who furnished music for the cathedral services received regular musical training under the direction of the cathedral *cantor,* generally a graduate of the university in philosophy and theology. The school, in fact, was supervised by the university, and its staff was chosen with the approval of the rector of the university.[11] Frequently the same men taught in both institutions. Singers from the cathedral choir were used in academic ceremonies, and many of the poor students living in the various *bursae* of the university (boarding houses in charge of *magistri*) earned money by singing in the services in convents and churches in Vienna.[12]

Religious celebrations with music were, too, a regular part of university life. In the year of its founding, Rudolf gave explicit instructions for the observance of certain religious festivals in the university at which *"soll der Schuell Maister der grossen Schuell*

[8] Pietzsch, *"Musik an den Universitäten im Osten," AfMf,* Vol. I, 283.
[9] *Ibid.,* I, 287.
[10] Aschbach, *Geschichte der Wiener Universität,* I, 619.
[11] Kink, *Universität Wien,* I, 26–27.
[12] *Ibid.,* I, 36n.

mit ganzer Vniuersitet der Maister, Studenten vnd Schueller bey sein vnd helffen zusingen."[13] Statutes of the arts faculty (1389) also gave directions for the performance of religious services with music, in which all student members of the university were required to participate. Payments made by the arts faculty in 1412 to persons who had assisted in the observance of St. Katherine's Day included several items for musical services: *"duobus cantoribus 4 gr., organistae 2 gr., campanatori 1 gr."*[14] Throughout the fourteenth century and until the mid-fifteenth, the medical faculty, too, celebrated its patrons' day—*In die sanctorum Cosme et Damiani*—with musical embellishments, as records of payments made to choirmaster, soloist, and organist show.[15]

Like university students everywhere, Viennese students were given to music making, so much so that the university eventually legislated against the use of musical instruments. In 1385 *"noctiuagi cum instrumentis musicis"* were among those liable for punishment; and in 1389 all who wished to be promoted to any degree in the university were warned not to frequent *loca suspecta* and not to wander around at night playing on musical instruments and singing.[16] A statute similar to those regulating the English colleges was passed in 1413, forbidding singing and dancing *indecenter* in the various *bursae*.[17]

The medieval University of Vienna, then, was quite definite in its musical requirements and quite strict in enforcing them. Music was regularly required by statute of bachelors seeking the *magisterium,* and failure to complete successfully the course in music meant failure in attaining the status of *magister* and the coveted license to teach. An explanation of this probably lies in the fact

[13] *Ibid.,* II, 25, no. 2.

[14] *Ibid.,* I, 95n.

[15] Pietzsch, "*Musik an den Universitäten im Osten,*" *AfMf,* Vol. I, 283.

[16] Kink, *Universität Wien,* II, 76, no. 12, and 187, no. 15: "*Item non visitent Scolas dimicatorum nec Tabernas publicas nec alia Loca suspecta, nec sint noctiuagi cum Instrumentis musicis et cantibus in Plateis et precipue illi qui in nostra Facultate voluerint ad aliquem gradum promoueri.*"

[17] *Ibid.,* II, 250, no. 21: "*Item nullus Bursalium Instrumentis musicalibus indecenter canat in commodo suo Vel alias in Bursa, nec Clamores ac strepitus indecentes et merito perturbatores sui Vel suorum socij, Vel sociorum et praesertim Vicini Vel Vicinorum exerceat.*"

that lectures in music were given by graduates of the philosophical faculty, *magistri regentes,* who alternated their teaching of music with other subjects—usually mathematics and Aristotelian philosophy; and from extant documents it seems to have been customary for a master to begin his regency with lectures on music. The very strong medical faculty at the Viennese *studium,* moreover, apparently had its own musical requirements in addition to those of the arts faculty. Boethius and Euclid were read by some if not all students; and the use of Muris' *Musica* at Vienna testifies again to the widespread dependence of university studies upon this book.

Heidelberg

Like the Viennese *studium,* the University of Heidelberg was founded during the time of papal schism when many German students and masters left the Sorbonne and returned to their native land.[18] Authorized by Urban VI, whose bull of 1385 granted the erection of a *"studium generale ad instar Parisiensis,"* this university was established in 1386 by Ruprecht I, Elector of Bavaria; and not only was it patterned upon the Paris *studium* but its first rector, Marsilius, private chaplain to the elector, was a *magister artium* from Paris.[19] Oldest statutes of the arts faculty (undated but drawn up before 1402) ruled that applicants for the licentiate hear, in addition to books already heard in preparation for the baccalaureate, *"aliquos distinctos libros totales mathematice et non solum plures parciales eiusdem"*[20]—*totales* probably referring to the comprehensive study of the mathematical disciplines, which would certainly include music. Supporting this view is the fact that Conrad von Zabern, bachelor of arts, 1428, and master of arts, 1430, lectured on music in Heidelberg in 1430[21]—significant again of the tendency to begin one's regency with lectures on music.

[18] Gerhard Ritter, *Die Heidelberger Universität* (Heidelberg, 1936), I, 42–60.
[19] See the papal bull, Eduard Winkelmann, *Urkundenbuch der Universität Heidelberg* (Heidelberg, 1886), I, 3, no. 2.
[20] *Ibid.,* I, 38, no. 23.
[21] Gerhard Pietzsch, *"Zur Pflege der Musik an den deutschen Universitäten bis zur Mitte des 16. Jahrhunderts: Heidelberg und Köln," AfMf,* Vol. V (1940), 70.

Evidence for the study of music is seen, too, in the acquisition of musical works by Heidelberg's library from time to time.[22] Among these are three presented to the university in 1390 by Conradus de Geylnhusen: *Item Ysidorus ethymologiarum, Item Hugo de numeris, ponderibus et mensuris,* and *Item liber de proprietatibus rerum cum tabula.* "*Item musica Gwidonis*" was left the library in 1392 by a certain Conradus de Wormacia, and an *ars cantandi* by a Magister Gerhardus around 1396. Between 1396 and 1432 the university acquired: *Item musicam siue carmina beati Jeronimi, Item scriptum super Macrobium de sompnio Cypionis, Item anticlaudianum, Item musicam,* and *Item Alanum in anteclaudiano in papiro sine asseribus.*

The same close connection between local church and university existed in Heidelberg as in other cities having a *studium generale,* and many documents in the *Urkundenbuch* refer to the Marienkirche and the Heilige-Geistkirche, afterwards the cathedral. In 1398, Boniface IX established twelve canonical prebendaries in the latter church to be held by teachers in the university.[23] And, of course, members of the university participated in services in the church, often in sung Masses. When Marsilius, the first rector, died in 1422, all members of the university were urged to be present at a *missa decantanda* held "*in ecclesia sancti spiritus*" as part of the funeral obsequies.[24] As in other German towns, too, students from the Neckarschule, Heidelberg's *Stadtschule,* furnished music for the city churches, and these choristers, some of whom later entered the university, received training in practical music under the supervision of the *precentor* of the Heilige-Geistkirche, an official high in the university hierarchy. Between 1421 and 1438 the library of this church acquired a copy of Augustine's treatise *De musica.*[25]

Besides musical activities under ecclesiastical auspices in the university, since Heidelberg was the seat of the Elector of Bavaria,

22 *Ibid.,* Vol. V, 67, from Thorbecke, *Statuten und Reformationen der Universität Heidelberg.*

23 Winkelmann, *Urkundenbuch,* I, 65–69, no. 46.

24 *Ibid.,* I, 122, no. 86.

25 Pietzsch, "*Zur Pflege der Musik: Heidelberg,*" *AfMf,* Vol. V, 67.

there was yet another source of musical inspiration with academic connections—the *Burgkapelle* established by Ruprecht I in 1346 for the cultivation of music at the electoral court. Said to be the first *Hofkapelle* in Germany, this choir drew upon students in the university who often supported themselves during their time of study by singing in the electoral chapel.[26] The matriculation rolls of the university supply the names of some of these young men in the elector's *Sängerei:* in 1406 Nycolaus Beabronner from Munich was entered as *Cantor domini regis;* in 1416 four *chorales* matriculated; in 1434 Nicolaus Wanebach, *cantor ducis,* enrolled, taking the bachelor's degree in 1436.[27] Connections between ducal chapel and university are further seen in the position of the choir in the *Calendarium academicum,* 1414, when its members furnished music for the festivities, academic and civic, welcoming King Sigismund to Heidelberg.[28]

If extra-curricular musical activities of the medieval student oftentimes became violent and disturbing, those of the Heidelberg student seem to have been especially vigorous, as appears from records of an investigation held in 1430 to determine whether a student, Stephan von Rotweil, died because of negligence on the part of the attending physician or because of his own actions after his skull was fractured. During the trial one witness testified that the student *"cantavit et clamavit cum sociis";* another witness *"deposuit de cantu et quomodo audivit, quod eciam visitavit mulieres";* and a third witness *"dixit hoc, quod vidit oculum strabosum et audivit eum sepe cantantem."*[29] One is glad to report that the medical attendant was acquitted.

There are apparently no published treatises to be related to the early years of Heidelberg. But strong mathematical requirements for the licentiate with evidence for the inclusion of music, the usual close connection between university and cathedral with musical personnel and celebrations common to both institutions, and the

---

[26] Fritz Stein, *Zur Geschichte der Musik in Heidelberg* (Heidelberg, 1912), 3–6.

[27] *Ibid.,* 5–6.

[28] *Ibid.,* 6–7.

[29] Winkelmann, *Urkundenbuch,* I, 127, no. 91.

additional inspiration of a princely chapel whose singing members were regularly enrolled in the university—all these show the important place of music among the liberal arts at the medieval University of Heidelberg.

Cologne

The *studium generale* established at Cologne in 1388 *"ad instar studii Parisiensis"*—at the instigation of Cologne's Town Council and under the authority of Pope Urban VI—was actually organized from schools long in existence, monastic and cathedral schools for which the city was famous during the Middle Ages.[30] It was here that the Dominicans had the chief school of their order in Germany, and in this school Thomas Aquinas studied with Albertus Magnus (who wrote on all subjects of knowledge, including music); and here in the Franciscan convent Duns Scotus taught.[31] We recall, too, that one of the most important of all medieval musical theorists held the position of *scholasticus Coloniensis* in the thirteenth century—Franco. According to the Jesuit Harzheim (1752), a music school was actually among the educational institutions from which the University of Cologne developed.[32]

[30] See the foundation bull, Franz Joseph von Bianco, *Die alte Universität Köln und die spätern Gelehrten-Schulen dieser Stadt* (Koln, 1856), 2, Anlagen, no. 1. Several factors made the establishment of a *studium* at this time especially propitious. The great schism in the Church caused many German masters and students to leave Paris for seats of learning in their native land. Cologne drew numbers of these, as Heidelberg had done a few years previously. The disastrous effects of a great pestilence at Heidelberg in 1388, moreover, caused many scholars to leave that university for the new *studium* at Cologne. See Hermann Keussen, *"Die alte Universität Köln, 1388–1798," Universität Köln, 1919–1929* (Köln, 1929), 11–12.

[31] Bianco, *Universität Köln*, and A. G. Little, "Chronological Notes on the Life of Duns Scotus," *English Historical Review*, Vol. XLVII (1932), 582.

[32] *Harzheim in praefat. Catalogi historici critici codicum Mss. Bibliothecae ecclesiae Metropolitanae Coloniensis.* Col. 1752, cited by Bianco, *Universität Köln*, 11, note 1:

> Erant etiam ante Universitas Studiorum quam Coloniae a Pontifice et Augusto Caesare conderetur anno 1388, apud Ecclesias praesertim Cathedrales, praeter Scholas Grammaticae Latinae, Arithmeticae, Philosophiae, Schola Cantorum, Schola Lectorum, qui Latinae linguae notitiam, intelligendae Scripturae divinae (haec non nisi latine in his partibus legebatur) et Ss. Patrum libris explicandis necessariam praebebant.

In the list of men who formed the original professorial body of the new university, it is significant that most of the masters came from Paris and a few from Prague,[33] both *studia* strong in their emphasis of music. The earliest statutes (1392) do not mention subjects for study. But the *"Statuta Facultatis Artium,"* 1398, specify *aliquem in musica* among the books required of bachelors seeking the licentiate.[34] These statutes also give the length of time and the master's fee for these "ordinary" lectures: *"Musica quoad duas partes—einen Monat für 2 Albus,"*[35] the *duae partes* undoubtedly referring to theoretical music and applied music.

The same formal and informal musical activities cultivated generally in the medieval universities characterized the University of Cologne. In the very elaborate doctoral celebrations, the mounted procession of candidates and doctors was preceded by trumpets and drums.[36] And the *Doktorats-Festessen* which ended the doctoral exercises was embellished by musical entertainment, at great expense to the new doctors.[37] Religious celebrations, too, regularly took place with music. In a university expense account, 1408, we read of payment to *sex cantoribus* for a celebration of Mass in honor of St. Thomas Aquinas.[38] And like medieval students everywhere, Cologne students owned stringed instruments, which they were fond of playing in their nightly wandering.[39]

In 1420 the town council built the *Schola artium* with a lecture hall seating six hundred listeners where the liberal arts, philology, and philosophy were taught, music having a regular place along

---

[33] See the list of the first masters, Bianco, *Universität Köln,* 87–88.

[34] *Ibid.,* 68, Anlagen, VII:

Item statuimus quod Bacalarius temptandus debet audivisse libros infrascriptos: primo, libros spectantes ad gradum Bacalariatus in artibus. Item talis debet audivisse ultra illos in aliquibus Scolis publicis alicujus Universitatis in qua protunc fuerunt quinque Regentes magistri in artibus libros infrascriptos: . . . aliquem in musica.

[35] *Ibid.,* 129–30, no. 75.

[36] Keussen, *"Die alte Universität,"* *"Universität Köln,* 43.

[37] Bianco, *Universität Köln,* 144.

[38] Pietzsch, *"Zur Pflege der Musik: Köln,"* AfMf, Vol. V, 77.

[39] Keussen, *"Die alte Universität,"* *Universität Köln,* 22, 33.

with the other arts.[40] It was in the great hall of this building that the arts faculty held their elaborate *disputatio de quolibet* each year, a series of orations on various subjects, humorous as well as serious, led by the *quodlibetarius,* and concluded by a magnificent banquet.[41] The statutes of 1398 setting up this academic festival mentioned specifically the use of material *"de singulis septem artibus liberalibus"* in the disputations.[42] There are several interesting records from later times showing the very important place of music in *quodlibet* orations. And we may assume that this art had its place in earlier disputations, judging by Cologne's stress upon music by statutory requirements from its early years, and by its emphasis upon all the liberal arts in the medieval period of the university.

Leipzig

Differing markedly from Cologne's *studium generale* (which was, in effect, the acquisition of papal privileges and the right to award the coveted *ius ubique docendi* by schools long flourishing), the University of Leipzig resulted spontaneously from a secession of German scholars from the University of Prague during the dissension over ecclesiastical reform between Bohemian Hussites and Germans early in the fifteenth century. Migrating to Leipzig in 1409, a group of these seceding masters, bachelors, and students accepted the invitation of the Landgraves of Thuringia to found a university in that city, under the authority of Nicholas V.[43] Musical requirements at this new university were identical with those

---

[40] Bianco, *Universität Köln,* 169.

[41] Hermann Keussen, *Die alte Universität Köln* (Köln, 1934), 338–43.

[42] Bianco, *Universität Köln,* 62, Anlagen, VII:

Item de disputatione de quolibet statuimus et ordinamus, quod omni anno semel regulariter circa festum beate Lucie Virginis disputatio de quolibet solemniter habeatur. In qua proponi volumus materias de singulis septem artibus liberalibus, et alias philosophicas prout spectat ad artistam disputare.

[43] See the bull of Nicolas V allowing Friedrich and Wilhelm, *Land-* and *Markgrafen,* to establish a *studium generale* at Leipzig, 1409: Georg Erler, *Die Matrikel der Universität Leipzig* (Leipzig, 1895–1902), I, 3–4.

of the University of Prague: the oldest statutes of the arts faculty (1410) mention the *Musica* of Muris to be read by candidates for the master's degree.[44] A maximum of one month, minimum of three weeks was specified as the length of time to be spent attending lectures on music; the regent master was to receive two *Groschen* for his lectures.[45] These same *libri ad gradum magisterii,* including the *musica Muris,* appear again in statutes of 1437, with identical requirements of time and fee; and *"Statuta legibilia,"* probably drawn up around 1440, once more require Muris' *Musica* for the *magisterium.*[46]

Of students who matriculated at Leipzig early in the fifteenth century, several were musicians before entering the university and others followed musical careers after leaving the *studium,* probably influenced in their choice of a profession by musical studies in the university. Sigismund Lemchen, who matriculated in 1411, studied later at Cracow and became *precentor* in Breslau; and Johannes Stephani, whose name appears on the register for 1413, became *cantor* of the Thomas Kloster in Leipzig, 1435.[47] In 1414 *"dns. Otto de Hayn cantor ecclesie Merseburgensis"* matriculated.[48] Nicolas Kauffmann, who enrolled in 1417, became *cantor* of the cathedral at Meissen in 1431; Clemens Heseler de Brega, who registered at Leipzig in 1422, later lectured on the *Musica* of Muris at Cracow; and Nicolas Tronitz, bachelor and master of arts, 1434 and 1440, held several clerical positions, among them that of *cantor* of the *Hochstift* at Meissen.[49] In 1442 a different kind of musician matriculated, *"Engelbertus Orgelmacher de Hamburg."*[50]

Thus from its early years, the University of Leipzig attracted students with varying musical interests—singing, choir directing,

---

[44] Friedrich Zarncke, *Die Statutenbücher der Universität Leipzig* (Leipzig, 1861), 311, no. 13: *"Ad gradum magisterii sunt libri isti: ... musica (Muris)."*

[45] *Ibid.,* 312, no. 21: *"Pro de sensu et sensato maximum i mensis; minimum 3 septimanae ... similiter pro musica Muris; pro quolibet illorum 2 gr."*

[46] *Ibid.,* 326–27, no. 21, and 352, no. 2.

[47] Gerhard Pietzsch, *"Zur Pflege der Musik an den deutschen Universitäten bis zur Mitte des 16. Jahrhunderts: Leipzig,"* *AfMf,* Vol. III (1938), 321, 327–28.

[48] Erler, *Matrikel,* I, 45.

[49] Pietzsch, *"Zur Pflege der Musik: Leipzig,"* *AfMf,* Vol. III, 312, 319, 328.

[50] Erler, *Matrikel,* I, 139.

even organ building—to matriculate for higher studies. This tradition carried over into the Renaissance, as we shall see, along with the same emphasis upon music as a requirement for the master of arts degree.

vii. Poland: Cracow

Although the University of Cracow was created by Casimir the Great in 1364 as a possible rival to the flourishing *studium* at Prague, it seems to have had a doubtful existence until its reorganization in 1400 by King Ladislaus, who modeled it upon the German universities, especially Prague and Leipzig; subsequently this *studium* became noted for mathematics and astronomy, with a special chair in these disciplines established in 1400.[1] With emphasis upon mathematics, the course of studies would, of course, include music. Statutes of 1406 declared that certain books must be read before attaining the master's degree, among them the *musica Muris;* students were to spend one month attending lectures on music and to pay the regent master *duos grossos.*[2]

Many records reflect the study of music based upon the Muris text at the University of Cracow. Johannes de Szydlow, bachelor of arts, 1414, left several tracts on astronomy, arithmetic, and music (now in the Berlin Library); among them is a copy of Muris' *Musica speculativa,* possibly lecture notes gathered by Johannes while a student in the university.[3] Clemens de Heseler de Brega

---

[1] Casimir Morawski, *Histoire de l'Université de Cracovie* (tr. by P. Rongier) (Paris, 1900–1905), I, 9–17, 110. See also Rashdall, *Medieval Universities,* II, 289–92.

[2] *Statuta necnon Liber promotionum philosophorum ordinis in universitate studiorum jagellonica ab anno 1402 ad annum 1849* (ed. by Josephus Muczkowski) (Cracoviae, 1849), *xii–xv:*

> Item. Placuit omnibus magistris, quod hy libri audiantur ante gradum baccalariatus: [*no music*]. Subscripti autem: . . . musica muris . . . ante magisterium audiantur.
>
> Per quantum tempus debent legi libri predicti: . . . musica per mensem.
>
> Quantum autem unusquisque pro laboribus magistrorum tenebitur soluere: . . . a musica duos grossos.

[3] Pietzsch, *AfMf,* Vol. I, 437.

(formerly of Leipzig), bachelor of arts in 1425, lectured on the *Musica* of Muris, according to the testimony of a student, Nicolaus de Monsterberg (bachelor of arts, 1431), who listed the lectures he had heard before receiving the master's degree; and Johannes de Elkusz, graduating in the arts and medicine around the middle of the century, left a set of notes on the Muris text.[4]

Among those who matriculated at Cracow in the first half of the fifteenth century were some who registered as *cantores*: Petrus de Wolfram, enrolling as *"lic. in decretis, cantor eccl. S. Mariae Wisliciensis,"* and *"Andreas Petri cantor de Sigeth,"* registering in 1445.[5] In 1441 six *cantores* of the Bishop of Cracow matriculated, students who earned their living by singing in the episcopal chapel.[6] Others who studied at the university registered as *precentores* or directed choirs after leaving. *"Mathias Johannis Precentor de Magna Glogouia"* enrolled in 1400.[7] Sigismund Lemchen, formerly a Leipzig student, became a master of arts at Cracow, 1418, and *precentor* of the Holy Cross Church in Breslau in 1436; two years later Nikolaus Spitzmer, graduate in arts and law at Cracow, became *cantor* in Breslau; Johannes Stock, matricuating in 1411, was head of the Holy Cross School in Breslau in 1419 and *cantor* of that church, 1449–64; and Nicolas Stock enrolled at Cracow in 1412, studied at Vienna, and held the position of *precentor* in Gross-Glogau, 1418–27.[8] Near the mid-century occurs one of the most interesting of all

---

[4] *Liber promotionum, cxliii, "Scheda pro magisterii gradu," 1431*:

Item a Mgro Clemente de Brega audiuit Arithmeticam communem in lectorio Theologorum. Item ab eodem musicam muris in eodem lectorio per eandem commutacionem, qui incepit ante caniculares et finiuit secundum statuta.

For Clemens' degree, 1425, see 17; for Johannes' (de Ilkus), 1444, see 36. Pietzsch, *AfMf*, Vol. I, 436, quotes the explicit to Johannes' notes: *"Explicit Musica mgri Johannis de Muris, concordans cum Musica Bohecij, per manus Johannis baccalarij de Eljusz . . . 1445."*

[5] *Codex Diplomaticus Universitatis Studii Generalia Cracoviensis* (Cracoviae, 1870–1900), I, 111, and B. Ulanowski and A. Chmiel (eds.), *Album studiosorum Universitatis Cracoviensis* (Cracoviae, 1887–1904), I, 110.

[6] *Album studiosorum*, I, 97: Nicolaus de albo Castro, Othmarus Opilionis de Jawor, Nikasius Opilionis de Jawor, Bartholomeus Nicolai de Auris, Johannes Andree de Auris, and Mathias Andree de Auris, all of whom enrolled as *Cantores Reuerendissimi patris domini Sbignei Cracouiensis Episcopi.*

[7] *Ibid.*, I, 13.

[8] Pietzsch, *"Musik an den Universitäten im Osten," AfMf*, Vol, I, 438, 444, 446.

records in Cracow's *Album studiosorum*—the matriculation of Magister Marcus Bonifily, *precentor* of Barcelona's cathedral and royal professor of sacred theology in Spain.[9]

Wislocki's famous *Catalogus codicorum* (manuscript holdings in the university library) lists a number of musical treatises in addition to the student notes on Muris' *Musica* already mentioned.[10] From the fifteenth century there are anonymous works dealing with speculative and practical aspects of music: *Explicationes Antiphonarij et aliorum canticorum ecclesie,* at the end of which the scribe has made the challenging remark, *"finivi librum, scribsi sine manibus ipsum"; Notae musicae cum regulis,* 1421; *De musica* (beginning *"Musica secundum Bohecium sic diffinitur"*); and a treatise *De musica* which begins by referring to Aristotle's *Politica.* Found here also in a fifteenth-century manuscript are Boethius' *De musica libri V,* the section on music from Isidorus' *Etymologiae,* and several copies of the *Musica* of Jean de Muris.

All these reflect the emphasis on music during the medieval period at the University of Cracow, which offered music as one of the liberal arts and consistently required the *Musica speculativa* of Jean de Muris of all bachelors studying for the *magisterium.*

viii. Scotland: St. Andrews

Like some of the German universities, the University of St. Andrews was organized early in the fifteenth century, an outgrowth of the ever increasing nationalistic spirit and an attempt to fill a definite need not felt so long as the continental universities were international in character and open to all students.[1] Bishop Ward-

---

[9] *Album studiosorum,* I, 112: *"Magister Marcus Bonifilÿ precentor Barsolensis Sacree theologie professor de Cathalonia domini Regis Aragonum de villa Castillionis, diocesis Gerundensis."*

[10] Pietzsch, *"Musik an den Universitäten im Osten," AfMf,* Vol. I, 425–27, has compiled a list of these from Wislocki's *Catalogus codicorum manuscriptorum bibliothecae universitatis Jagellonicae Cracoviensis* (1877–81).

[1] Scottish students had long gone to Paris for higher studies. But with the papal schism of 1378—in which France, Spain, and Scotland supported the Avignon popes whereas Italy, Germany, and England upheld the Roman claims to the papacy—these scholars

law was the leading spirit in organizing the university, using the Paris *studium* as model. In 1411–12 he granted a charter and privileges to a society of scholars who had begun teaching at St. Andrews some years earlier; and in 1413 a series of bulls from Benedict XIII made the school of St. Andrews a *studium generale* comprising the usual faculties.[2] The oldest statutes (1416) declare that books for the "ordinary" lectures, according to Parisian usage, should be read, which would, of course, include musical works; and an old and undated statute from the arts faculty required *aliquos libros mathematicos* of all candidates before admittance *ad licenciam,* which would again, in all probability, include music.[3]

The university was closely connected with the cathedral, and many of the St. Andrews foundations were established to support poor scholars and choristers.[4] It is especially interesting, in fact, to note that one of the great collections of Notre Dame polyphony (Wolfenbüttel 677) is inscribed *Liber monasterii s. Andree in Scocia;* once the property of the Priory of St. Andrews, the manuscript later belonged to the Collegiate Church of St. Salvator, founded in 1450.[5] The location of this manuscript in Scotland points to the very close associations between the St. Andrews *studium* and the Sorbonne; and the performance of this music at St. Andrews in the fourteenth century presupposes high musical standards in the cathedral and university foundations. As a matter of fact, the Scottish historian Hector Boece wrote in his famous *Lives* (1522) that there had always been many *excellentes et clari* performers of music at St. Andrews.[6] When the *Acta Facultatis*

left the English universities; and when later France abandoned the Avignon papacy, only distant Spain was left for the Scots, still loyal to Benedict XIII. See R. G. Cant, *The University of St. Andrews* (Edinburgh, 1946), 1–3.

[2] *Ibid.,* 4.

[3] Robert Kerr Hannay, *The Statutes of the Faculty of Arts and the Faculty of Theology at the Period of the Reformation* (St. Andrews University Publications, No. 7, 1910), 7 n.: *"More Parisiensi libri consueti legantur ordinarie."* For the mathematical requirement, see James H. Baxter, *Copiale Prioratus Sanctiandree* (Oxford, 1930), 456.

[4] Cant, *University of St. Andrews,* 25.

[5] James H. Baxter, *An Old St. Andrews Music Book* (London and Paris, 1931), v–vii.

[6] *Hectoris Boetii Murthlacensium et Aberdonensium Episcoporum Vitae* (ed. and tr. by James Moir) (Aberdeen, 1894), 87.

Arcium are published we shall know more about musical studies and activities in this university.[7]

ix. Music in the Medieval Universities

WHEN THE MEDIEVAL UNIVERSITIES assumed the leadership in intellectual life and the propagation of higher learning, these academic corporations carried on in the faculty of arts or philosophy traditions of higher studies well established by cathedral and monastic schools from which the universities in many instances developed—the seven liberal arts and Aristotelian philosophy. Although the lowest faculty in the medieval *studium generale,* the faculty of arts was by far the most important. All students began their university career in the arts faculty, and many did not proceed beyond this faculty. Several years' study in the arts faculty, moreover, and the successful completion of various public exercises (determination) leading to the baccalaureate in arts (with, perhaps, additional years of study leading to the *magisterium in artibus*) were everywhere prerequisite to study in any of the higher faculties of law, medicine, and theology. Thus, everyone who went to the universities for higher learning studied the liberal arts, and everyone who got beyond the trivium studied music along with the other subjects of the quadrivium.

Music as a regular subject for study among the liberal arts was supplemented by musical activities of many different kinds under university auspices; for since the medieval universities were, in effect, scholastic guilds very much under the rule of Mother Church, religious observances formed a never-ending part of university life. Among these was the opening of each academic year with a Mass sung in the cathedral or university church; and statutes drawn up under papal authority generally required the celebration of other Masses at specific times during the year, with university personnel in attendance. The four nations forming the *universitas* at Paris

---

[7] According to James Robb, "Student Life in St. Andrews before 1450," *Scottish Historical Review,* Vol. IX (1912), 348, these were still unpublished in 1912.

(and others modeled upon this archetype) relied upon music for effective celebration of the feastdays of their patron saints and for other ceremonies indigenous to the various nations. When musical talent was lacking among the members of the English-German Nation at the Sorbonne, for instance, these men imported *alienos cantores* so that their celebrations might proceed in a dignified manner with the usual musical accompaniment; and this nation also supported an organist at its own expense. Other academic ceremonies beloved of the medieval man of learning depended heavily upon music not only for religious overtones but for aural pageantry. Thus, city trumpeters heralded the procession of successful candidate and doctors to the cathedral for the elaborate doctoral act, accompanying them afterwards to the banquet which followed this important degree ceremony; and singing by the cathedral choir was a part of the ceremony of investiture. More informal musical pastimes—dancing, singing, playing on instruments—were also the inevitable concomitants of medieval student life. These musical pursuits were cultivated so strenuously, indeed, that universities and collegiate foundations often drew up rules prohibiting all such practices as nuisances distracting from study.

As aids in understanding the specifically academic aspects of music's cultivation in the universities, definite regulations on the statute books, where such regulations exist, are most illuminating; these will generally be found in the universities organized spontaneously and modeled upon some archetype. It is somewhat more difficult to judge the position of music in those universities which evolved gradually from schools long in existence, with their traditions of higher studies so well established that a set curriculum did not have to be written down, at least not for years and sometimes even centuries after the institution's consecration, under papal authority and with papal privileges, as a *studium generale*. Generally available, fortunately, are documents of various kinds which define the place of music in those universities having no course of studies set down in the statutes. Documents of various sorts indicate that instruction in music in the medieval universities varied somewhat according to the needs, interests, and traditions of the particular country and *studium*.

In the Italian universities musical studies must be evaluated from other sources than university statutes, for with their long years of evolution behind them, the *studia* at neither Bologna nor Padua recognized any need for listing individual subjects to be studied. There is evidence in abundance, however, for a great flourishing of the liberal arts at both Bologna and Padua, and we know that many Italians as well as ultramontanes studied the arts in first one university and then the other. In both centers of learning, mathematical studies appear to have been strongly emphasized in medieval times, taught often by professors distinguished for their musical knowledge. The *Musica* of Boethius and the condensation of this work by Jean de Muris were both studied at Padua in the fourteenth century. Vittorino da Feltre, responsible through his pupils for the transmission of humanistic learning throughout much of Italy, included Boethius' *Musica* with his teaching of mathematics during his years at Padua, as we know from the words of his admiring pupil from the north, Johannes Gallicus; and Proscodimus de Beldemandis, public professor in the University of Padua, lectured upon and wrote about *musica speculativa* along with mathematics and astronomy. There are many indications, too, that musical problems were investigated in medical courses, and occasionally we find men teaching music along with medicine. Indeed, it is significant of the strong connection between these two fields that the first translation of an important musical source, the *Problemata* attributed to Aristotle, was made by a Paduan philosopher and astronomer famous for his medical writings, Pietro d'Abano, who also left a personal commentary on this pseudo-Aristotelian work.

But music as a mathematical science among the liberal arts was obviously only one part of the dichotomy of musical studies: within the framework of university studies, music was also cultivated as a living art. Prosdocimus de Beldemandis, distinguished mathematician and astronomer, went far beyond *musica speculativa* into the realm of artistic problems of *musica practica*. Such theorists as

Marchettus of Padua and Jacopo of Bologna were also high-ranking composers; and such famous composers as Giovanni da Ciconia were highly skilled in mathematics and quite competent to produce a bulky work on musical mathematics.

Since the *studium* at Paris developed chiefly from the Cathedral School of Notre Dame, and since in medieval times it remained closely integrated with the cathedral, the center of progressive musical culture for all Europe, one is not surprised to find indications of strong emphasis upon musical studies at Paris. Requirements by university statute, it is true, are vague, not only for music but for other disciplines as well; undoubtedly such regulations were unnecessary in the early years of the university, backed by its own traditions of study. By the fourteenth century, however, there were mathematical requirements for both bachelors and masters. Even without other evidence, one would assume that these included music, and a glance at statutes of universities patterned upon the Sorbonne reveals the truth of this assumption. Both the Prague and Viennese statutes, for instance, setting up a well defined course of studies based upon the Paris curriculum, specified music along with other mathematical disciplines required of bachelors studying for the licentiate, and carefully noted that four music lectures a week be given for four weeks. The Sorbonne, indeed, owed not a little of its glory during the Middle Ages to distinguished mathematicians who illumined its lecture rooms with musical dialectics, accounts of which have come down to us in students' notebooks and other sources. Overshadowing all others here is Jean de Muris, whose mathematical interests not only made him an expert on *musica speculativa* but led him to write a summary of Boethius' lengthy treatise which superseded Boethius in the original as the textbook to be used in many of the medieval universities. Through the writings and teaching of Muris alone, the influence of musical studies at the University of Paris in the fourteenth and fifteenth centuries reached from Poland to Bohemia to Italy, not only dominating university studies but also penetrating into tutorial humanistic schools, especially in Italy.

Along with *musica theoretica* allied with mathematics, musical studies at Paris comprised the enthusiastic cultivation of musical artistry, under the leadership of distinguished composers and musicians who lectured in the university and also under the inspiration of such active musical groups as the Notre Dame choir and the king's personal chapel. A close connection between both these groups and the university was inevitable, for musical officials in the cathedral were at the same time university officials, and many singers in the royal choir or masters of the children of the king's private chapel were enrolled in the university either as students or teachers. Notre Dame's choir school actually served as a preparatory school for the university, constantly sending students to the Sorbonne for higher studies, many of these choristers on scholarships. All evidence points to the fact that instruction in *musica activa* was required of members of some colleges in the university—at least, knowledge of plain song—and was always available; for distinguished French composers—many of them, like Franco, theorists as well—were constantly associated with the Sorbonne and undoubtedly offered instruction to university students. Indeed, the two greatest musical figures associated with Notre Dame in the twelfth and thirteenth centuries—Léonin and Pérotin, whose innovations in organum duplum and triplum and various forms of discantus laid the foundations for all that has developed since—probably gave private musical instruction under university auspices along with other Paris *musici* known to us through their writings. And of those who built up a body of practical theory to explain the new polyphony and to attempt a solution of some of its ineluctable rhythmic-notational problems, Franco of Cologne in the thirteenth century and Jean de Muris in the fourteenth achieved the most widespread influence and found the greatest following. The more one investigates the cultivation of music in the university, in fact, the clearer it becomes that Paris' leadership in the medieval musical world derived very largely from the remarkable achievements of theorists and composers associated directly or indirectly with the University of Paris.

The English universities were established *ad instar studii Parisiensis,* and lively intercourse between Paris and Oxford not only transmitted Notre Dame doctrine to England but also permitted the participation of English scholars in the development of this theory in France—for example, John of Garland. Connections between St. Andrews and the Sorbonne were, in some respects, even closer than those of Oxford and Cambridge; and it may have been some enterprising and musically astute scholar who brought from Paris one of the four existing manuscript collections of Notre Dame polyphony—perhaps one of the very *volumina* of music described in such glowing terms by Anonymus IV—which for many years belonged to a collegiate foundation in the Scottish university. The English universities early inaugurated a system of colleges endowed by royal patrons or wealthy ecclesiasts, generally for the support of theology students; and practical musical instruction was an integral part of life in these foundations, with their many Masses and other observances depending upon music. Many of the colleges supported a *precentor,* master of the choirboys, and varying numbers of clerics who could bear a part in song, while the wealthier colleges even kept an organist among their members. Choirboys in collegiate foundations *competenter* instructed in plain song and "pricksonge" regularly enrolled later in the university proper; in fact, they were often given preference when vacancies in university scholarship lists occurred. With such a solid core of musico-religious activities at the center of academic life and the need for musical instructors to fill positions in the colleges, it is not surprising that music was singled out from among the other members of the quadrivium for especial distinction, and that degrees in music were awarded at least from the fifteenth century and probably much earlier. During the Renaissance, the graduate in music was granted permission "to lecture in any of the books of Boethius," and this may well have been true during the medieval period too, for Boethius' *Musica* was a regular part of the mathematical requirement at Oxford—and by analogy at Cambridge— for bachelors proceeding to the *magisterium.* Mathematicians who lectured on music, however, were concerned as much with problems of practical artistry as with problems of numerical proportions; and treatises written by Oxford scholars reflect the usual twofold approach in musical studies—the mathematical and the practical.

In awarding separate degrees in music, the University of Salamanca perhaps resembled the English universities; at any rate, in Spain and Italy as well as in England, licenses to teach the separate arts seem to have been granted in very early times, although the practice was given up sometime during the medieval period everywhere except in England. More remarkable for Salamanca's role in the history of musical studies is its distinction of being the first European university to establish a chair of music among its endowed professorships. Founded at the mid-thirteenth century, this lectureship stressed musical *ars* as well as *scientia* by specifying the teaching of composition (organum). The chair of music was maintained continuously throughout the medieval period and became even more firmly fixed in the fifteenth century when it acquired permanent tenure for its incumbent. The strong position of music at Salamanca, with definite emphasis upon practical music, was related, in part at least, to the great love of music, patronage of that art, and occasional personal talent on the part of Spain's medieval rulers, who showed continual interest in university affairs. It was directly in line, too, with the Spanish (Arabic) tradition which kept *musica activa* on a par with *musica theoretica* (as in the treatises of Al-Farabi and many Paris and Oxford *musici* who cited his divisions), a tradition which partially explains the small number of treatises on music from Spain's Middle Ages.

In very early statutes of the universities of central and northern Europe—most of them organized more or less spontaneously and patterned upon pre-existing models—exact requirements for graduates in the arts faculty were specified. Of six distinguished universities originating in medieval times and still in existence today, five required music quite plainly in the statutes and the sixth (Heidelberg) had a mathematical requirement which undoubtedly included music. Both Prague and Cologne cited music among "ordinary" lectures. From its first years, Prague specified as textbook the *Musica* of Jean Muris, as did Leipzig, whereas Vienna and Cologne made the regulation more flexible by simply requiring *aliquem in musica* as the basis for the music lectures. Reflecting a love of careful precision and minute detail characteristic of the German temperament, most of these statutes were explicit in giving details regarding the length of time to be spent hearing music lectures (generally three weeks to one month, although Vienna required sixteen lectures during a period of four weeks) and the fee due the regent master. Prague appears to have required music for both the baccalaureate and the *magisterium,* although Muris' condensation of Boethius was required only for the latter. The musical regulation at Vienna, Cologne, and Leipzig applied to bachelors seeking the licentiate (consecration of the master's degree with the license to teach), as did Heidelberg's mathematical requirement; and Cracow, too, listed the Muris text among books to be "heard" *ante gradum magisterii.* Such detailed specifications as these in the statute books tell us a great deal about musical studies at Paris, the archetype from which all these *studia* ultimately derived, with the possible exception of Cologne, which evolved gradually from schools long in existence in the city.

One of these schools from which the University of Cologne developed was a music school—a fact which may explain why *musica quoad duas partes* is carefully noted in the Cologne statutes, underlining the twofold study of music. And even where not specifically noted, musical studies in the northern universities appear to have combined the practical with the mathematical. Each of these *studia* was closely allied with a large church or cathedral whose priests, canons, *precentor,* and singers were also students and teachers in the university and whose choir school was supervised by the university. Instruction in technical aspects of musical art, then, would always be available from professional musicians under university auspices; that many students availed themselves of this instruction we know from notebooks and other documents. Treatises written by *magistri* actively teaching in the universities deal more often with the elements of practical music, both plain song and mensural music, than with purely mathematical theory, whereas notes and commentaries that have come down to us reflect both aspects of music, based generally upon the writings of Jean de Muris.

Musical studies in the universities of Europe, thus, actually continue a trend noticeable with the ancient Greeks, continued in the Roman rhetorical schools, and cultivated in the monastic and cathedral schools of the Middle Ages—*musica speculativa* allied with mathematics and *musica practica* allied with religious needs and uses. For from one point of view, far from being an independent subject worthy of study, music owed its existence to its membership in the mathematical quadrivium of the liberal arts, to its position among the encyclopedic disciplines, all of them, since the time of Augustine, considered essential for a proper understanding of the Scriptures. This tradition accounts for the general lack of references to individual subjects of study in early university statute books; and it explains, too, why a vague mathematical requirement among other university regulations would automatically presuppose the study of *musica speculativa*. Like the rest of the arts, music as a mathematical discipline was generally taught by *magistri regentes* who tutored their students through the whole cycle of the quadrivium and ultimately presented successful ones as candidates for the coveted *ius ubique docendi,* the right to teach anywhere in all Christendom. There is evidence that failure in music (at the German universities, at least) meant failure to obtain the much sought after license. Such strictness in enforcing musical regulations finds a cogent explanation, however, not only in the encyclopedic ideal of competence in all fields of knowledge but also in the custom generally prevailing in Germany and perhaps elsewhere by which a newly created *magister* began his regency with lectures on music, a parallel to the fact that many of the medieval philosophers began their writings with a treatise on music. Sometimes *musica speculativa* advanced from the arts faculty, moreover, to one of the higher faculties. In universities having strong traditions in medical studies, such as Padua and Vienna, one finds much documentary evidence for musical studies allied with medicine, a parallel to which is seen in the close connection between music and bodily health in philosophical writings from the time of Plato onward.

There are many indications, however, that instruction in music was often given by specialists in the field, either as public lecturers on university stipends or as tutors on a fee basis; and doubtless some *magistri* required to teach music became specialists through years of dealing with this discipline. Nonetheless, the position of music among the other arts of the quadrivium never varied, and many of our most important musical theorists were at the same time astronomers and mathematicians—Prosdocimus at Padua, Jean de Muris at Paris, and Odington at Oxford. But it is especially significant for the history of musical studies that each of these men—and many other university teachers as well—proceeded from musical mathematics to artistic problems of *musica practica,* as witness innumerable writings on technical problems of rhythm and notation by university teachers, student notebooks containing this doctrine, and the widespread dissemination of ever developing theory explaining new developments in polyphony, chiefly Franconian doctrine in the thirteenth century and *ars-nova* theory (Philip de Vitry, Jean de Muris) for the more complicated music of the fourteenth. It seems obvious, then, that whether required by university ruling or not, mathematicians who became highly skilled in the artistic side of music included this aspect in their lecturing, public or private. Instruction in singing, instruments, and composition was regularly available to, and sometimes even required of, younger members of university communities, who oftentimes owed their scholarly careers to their position as choristers; and others enrolled in the universities could receive instruction of this type from professional musicians incorporated in the universities *actu docendi in arte musice.* It follows, of course, that university studies apparently influenced many to follow musical careers; and the matriculation rolls show that the universities also attracted many who had already become professional singers or choirmasters. University towns having a princely chapel (Paris, Heidelberg) found even more incentive for the cultivation of *musica practica* than those whose musical activities were chiefly *religionis causa,* both in university and cathedral; for singers and choirmasters from these chapels who matriculated in the universities brought additional musical interests to their university studies and undoubtedly gave of their own talents in teaching others.

Treatises springing from university studies or used in connection with university teaching amply illustrate these varied aspects of music in the medieval universities. Reflecting the age-old study of music as one of the seven encyclopedic disciplines, writers of philosophical encyclopedias—for instance Johannes Scotus, Kilwardby, and Grosseteste—included discussions of music with the other liberal arts, generally drawing their material from the usual standard authorities—Boethius, Isidorus, Martianus Capella. Many of the medieval allegories also introduce the seven liberal arts with a brief account of each. Most often these discussions are short hortatory introductions to music designed for the student of philosophy, presenting only enough information properly to establish music's place in the sum total of knowledge—generally the definition, divisions, and statement of music's uses and effects. More numerous are treatises on the science of music, which usually begin with the same scholastic formula but proceed to a detailed discussion of musical mathematics—chiefly the numerical proportions basic to intervals and the derivation of the scale from numerical proportions. Even in pre-university days, this type of *eisagogé* was often followed by a discussion of the ecclesiastical modes, a section on practical music, that is, following the mathematical discussion; and in university treatises devoted to the art of music alone, prevalent from the thirteenth century onward, this same unity between speculative and practical aspects of music is consistently maintained. It was thirteenth-century learning, indeed, a century characterized by great comprehensiveness as well as unity in all branches of knowledge, that inspired the first great musical *Speculum,* the work of Jacques de Liège, who translated the philosophical and theological *speculum* into the field of one art and combined into one art both speculative and practical sides of music. In the fourteenth and fifteenth centuries other treatises of the comprehensive *speculum* type appeared, representing all the musical knowledge of the time—the works of Odington, Ugolino, Tunstede, and Johannes Gallicus; and there is not one of them unrelated to university studies.

As polyphony developed in the thirteenth century, bringing

with it special problems of rhythm and notation unfelt as long as music was monophonic, a good many of our university men wrote specialized treatises on artistic aspects of *musica practica,* always in harmonious relation to *musica speculativa* and generally preceded by a discussion of the latter. These works, in fact, fall into a more or less definite pattern in which the usual scholastic *eisagogé* (definition, divisions, effects, and explanation of musical proportions) is introductory to matters of rhythm, notation, and composition. The compilation of Jerome of Moravia and the *Ars nove musice* of Jean de Muris are typical examples. So very stereotyped is this pattern that one may use it as a criterion for judging as university writings certain treatises about whose authors little is known. The *Lucidarium* and *Pomerium* of Marchettus of Padua, for instance, together form a unified discussion of both aspects of music's dichotomy, similar to other university treatises, although Marchettus cannot be definitely related to the University of Padua. To this group would also belong such works as the fourteenth-century *Liber de musica* (CS, III, 129–77) of Johannes Verulus de Anagnia, about whom virtually nothing is known (Johannes is called *magister* and *musice doctor* by Theodoricus of Campo, CS, III, 193): for the author not only begins with a speculative introduction and presents his doctrine of rhythm and notation upon a strong mathematical basis but also finds many symbolical relationships between music and the Scriptures, probably deriving from the writer's theological studies.

Throughout the Middle Ages, then, we find music in the universities closely integrated with philosophy, both originally in the service of theology, and becoming an independent art with its own dichotomy of theory and practice—both studies originally pursued *ad majoram gloriam Dei.* The authoritative method generally prevails; the *ipse dixit* approach, with scholastic divisions and subdivisions, is generally followed. But occasionally there appears a different type of treatise, sometimes quite iconoclastic, which takes as point of departure a premise other than, say, the standard Boethian divisions (*musica mundana, humana, instrumentalis*), or which describes secular musical forms (largely unheard of in scholarly writings until Johannes de Grocheo considered them worth discussing for their ethical effects). The most obviously unconventional of these—the treatise of Anonymus IV, certain discussions of Roger Bacon, the *Theoria* of Johannes de Grocheo—were not only the result of university studies but of Arabic influence at the medieval University of Paris and Oxford. Musical studies at Orléans, famous for its emphasis upon rhetoric, were at least partly responsible for the poet Deschamps' very interesting and unconventional treatise relating music to poetry. It is remarkable, too, that although certain postulations of rhythmic-notational doctrine became firmly entrenched, there were always theorists who did not agree with this established authority. Jacques de Liège, for example, in his *Speculum musicae* thoroughly disapproved of the innovations of Jean de Muris and Philip de Vitry, and infinitely preferred the older doctrine of Franco and Petrus de Cruce. All such unorthodoxy leads to the inevitable conclusion that musical studies in the universities were characterized by a far greater flexibility and freedom of thought than one might suppose, considering music's perennial position under the shadow of scholastic philosophy and theology.

And although during the medieval period, music, on the one hand, never lost its theological and philosophical connotations, on the other, it was beginning to emerge as a separate art by the end of the Middle Ages, always maintaining a traditional balance between theory and practice, supported by its own corpus of technical theory, and allowing secular influences to become prominent among forms of discantus largely ecclesiastical up to now. This new attitude toward music was underlined in the universities in many different ways: by the awarding of degrees in music (Italy, Spain, and England); by careful attention to musical requirements in the northern universities; by the occasional establishment of a chair of music (Padua) at the close of the Middle Ages; by the strengthening of a musical endowment already long in existence (Salamanca); and by the translation of music from a single art among seven to an independent faculty with its own regulations and privileges in the English universities.

III. THE STUDY
OF MUSIC IN
THE RENAISSANCE
UNIVERSITIES
[1450-1600]

i. ITALY: BOLOGNA AND PADUA

Bologna

IN MEDIEVAL TIMES the liberal arts were strongly emphasized at the University of Bologna, music among them. As in other universities, instruction in music was apparently given by private masters who collected their fees directly from their students. At the beginning of our period (1450), however, Nicolas V, aiming at a reform of the *studium,* issued a bull setting up certain endowed professorships in various academic subjects with definite salaries specified. The Pope singled out music for distinction here and included a public lecturer in music in the faculty of arts and medicine.[1]

Legal studies continued to hold a place of primary importance at Bologna, as in medieval times; but the sixteenth century saw a great flourishing of mathematics as well. Statutes of 1545 required the various mathematical disciplines for students in the faculty of philosophy (arts),[2] and there are indications that the teaching of

[1] Guido Zaccagnini, *Storia dello studio di Bologna durante il Rinascimento* (Genève, 1930), 49–50, 148.

[2] *Ibid.,* 148. Music was not specifically mentioned, nor do we find any musicians listed

mathematics included music at this time. In 1547, for example, Ludovico Ferrari, who studied in Milan with the mathematician Cardano (both Cardano and Ferrari later held professorial chairs at Bologna, Cardano in medicine and Ferrari in mathematics[3]), offered to debate with the mathematician Niccolò Tartaglia (who had maligned his master) on any mathematical discipline, including music.[4] Cardano, too, combined music with mathematical interests and studies: he even undertook to write a treatise on music, unfinished according to his *testamentum* of 1571.[5] And Tartaglia, according to Zarlino, experimented with musical proportions, attempting to divide the tone into equal semitones.[6] In the seventeenth century the strong connection between music and mathematics was maintained. Bonaventura Cavalieri, pupil of Galileo and professor of mathematics at Bologna (1629), left among his published works a *Centuria di vari problemi per dimostrare l'uso e la facilità de logaritmi nella gnomonica, astronomia, geografia, etc., toccandosi anche qualche cosa della mechanica, arte militaire e musica* (1639).[7]

Although the medieval tradition keeping music and mathematics closely associated seems to have held at Bologna throughout the period of the Renaissance, the endowed lectureship in music among the chairs established by Nicolas V was apparently quickly abolished, and actually there may never have been a public pro-

among the professors of mathematics in the sixteenth century; see Luigi Simeoni, *Storia della università di Bologna*, II, *L'Età moderna* (Bologna, 1940), 239–64.

[3] Serafino Mazzetti, *Repertorio di tutti professori antichi, e moderni della famosa università, e del celebre istituto delle scienza di Bologna* (Bologna, 1848), 84, 125.

[4] Ettore Bortolotti, "*I Cartelli di Matematica Disfida,*" *Studi e memorie per la storia dell' Università di Bologna*, Vol. XII (1935), 13–14:

> Mi offerisco in Geometria, Arithmetica et in tutte le discipline che da esse dipendono, come è Astrologia, Musica, Cosmographia, Prospettiva, Architettura et altre, a disputar in luogo egualmente commodo, dinanzi a giudici idonei, pubblicamente con voi.

[5] Enrico Rivari, "*Un Testamento inedito del Cardano,*" *Studi e memorie*, Vol. IV (1920), 18: "*Libri autem a me scripti non editi nunc sunt hi . . . Musice libri quinque sed non perfecti.*"

[6] Hawkins, *History of Music*, III, 118–19.

[7] François Joseph Fétis, *Biographie universelle des musiciens et bibliographie générale de la musique* (2nd ed., Paris, 1873–83), II, 226.

fessorship in music.[8] Nonetheless, the Spanish musician Bartholomé Ramos, coming from Salamanca to Bologna around 1482 or perhaps earlier (Spataro said that Ramos worked ten years on his *Musica practica,* published in 1482, and that he wrote it in Italy under the influence of Italian theorists[9]), certainly taught music in the university, either in a public or private capacity, or perhaps both. The *explicit* of each of the two editions of the *Musica practica* (both published in 1482) mentions Ramos' public lecturing.[10] And Gafori said of his archenemy Ramos, *"dum illiteratus tamen, publice legeret."*[11] But Spataro, pupil of Ramos, wrote Pietro Aron in 1532 that Ramos was unable to complete the treatise, as he wanted it printed at Bologna in the hope of receiving a public professorship, which he did not receive.[12]

Ramos' *Musica practica*—to be treated at greater length in our discussion of the University of Salamanca—had far-reaching effects among musical theorists in Italy. One of the chief tenets set forth in this treatise was an attack upon Guido d'Arezzo and the formulation of a scale system based not upon Guido's hexachord but upon the octave. This aroused Nicolas Burtius to publish a

---

[8] In the list of lecturers, 1451–52, the name of the professor *ad lecturam musice* has been carefully erased: see Luigi Torri, *"Il Trattato di Prosdocimo de' Beldomandi contro il Lucidario di Marchetto da Padova,"* *Rivista Musicale Italiana,* Vol. XX (1913), 712.

[9] *Musica practica Bartolomei Rami de Pareia* (ed. by Johannes Wolf) (Leipzig, 1901), *xiii.*

[10] *Ibid.,* 104:

> *Explicit musica practica Bartolomei Rami de Pareia Hispani . . .*
> *almae urbis Bononiae, dum eam ibidem publice legeret. . . .*
> *Explicit feliciter prima pars musicae egregii et famosi musici*
> *Bartholomei Parea Hispani, dum publice musicam Bononiae legeret.*

[11] *Ibid., xiii.*

[12] *Ibid., xiv:*

In quanto a lopera del mio preceptore, la quale desiderati de haver tuta et complecta, Ve dico certamente che lui ma non dete complemento a tale opera, et quella che se trova non e complecta, perche lui fece stampare a Bologna tale particole, perche el se credeva de legerla con stipendio in publico. Ma in quello tempo acade che per certe cause lui non hebe la lectura publica, et lui quasi sdegnato ando a Roma et porto con lui tute quelle particule impresse con intentione de fornirle a Roma. Ma lui non la fornite mai, ma lui attendeva a certo suo modo de vivere lascivo, el quale fu causa della sua morte.

defense of Guido in a scathing attack upon Ramos: *Nicolai Burtii Parmensis musices Professoris, ac juris Pontifici studiosissimi Musices opusculum incipit, cum defensione Guidonis Aretini adversus quemdam Hyspanum veritatis prevaricatorem (Bononiae, 1487).*[13] Burtius, born around 1450, had studied canon law at Bologna in 1472[14] and had studied music at Mantua before that. It is, indeed, Burtius' copy of the compendious *Ritus canendi* of Johannes Gallicus of Mantua which Coussemaker published, and in the *explicit* of this work (CS, IV, 421) Nicolas says he was a pupil of Gallicus who died in 1473. In the controversy between Ramos and Burtius, thus, the old conservative musical outlook deriving from the teaching of Vittorino da Feltre (with whom, we recall, Gallicus studied the *Musica* of Boethius) was challenged—and eventually superseded—by new musico-mathematical theories brought from Spain to Italy by Ramos.

Four years after the publication of Burtius' *Musices opusculum,* Giovanni Spataro published a defense of his teacher, Ramos: *M. Joannis Spatari in Musica humillimi professoris ejusdem praeceptoris honesta defensio; in Nicolai Burtii Parmensis opusculum* (1491). Spataro, born around 1460, studied music with Ramos at Bologna and succeeded the latter as lecturer on music in the university. He also held the position of *maestro di capella* at St. Petronius', 1512–41.[15] In the treatise against Burtius, Spataro followed Ramos' tenets in treating of temperament, including alteration of thirds in order to make perfect fourths and fifths.

At this point Burtius dropped out of the controversy, but Franchino Gafori (Gafurius), *magister biscantandi* at the cathedral in Milan, carried on the attack against the new theorists. First he annotated a copy of Ramos' *Musica practica,* pointing out errors in it, and sent this to Spataro; the latter replied with a treatise, *Utile e breve regule di Canto composte per Maestro Zoanne di Spadari da Bologna* (1510, unpublished), in which he described the

---

[13] Bononiae, 1487.

[14] Fétis, *Biographie universelle,* II, 113. There is a copy of the *Musices opusculum* in the Huntington Library.

[15] *Ibid.,* VIII, 76.

errors of Gafori.[16] After the appearance of Gafori's treatise *De harmonia musicorum instrumentorum*, which again criticized Ramos' division of the monochord, Spataro pointed out his mistakes to him in eighteen letters.[17] Gafori then published (1520) his critique against the whole Bolognese school: *Apologia adversus Joannem Spatarium et complices musicos Bononienses*, a work which, according to Wolf, really proved Ramos to be in error with his acoustical divisions.[18] Spataro published two more tracts refuting Gafori, the titles again indicative of the vehemence of feeling between the two men: *Errori di Franchino Gafurio da Lodi ... subtilimente demonstrati* and *Dilucide et probatissime Demonstratione de Maestro Zoanne Spatario Musico Bolognese contra certe friuole et uane excusatione da Franchino (Maestro de li errori) in luce aducte* (both 1521). In the latter treatise Spataro berated Gafori for his mistakes in Latin grammar before criticizing his mathematical divisions.[19] Spataro's last work was his *Tractato di musica ... nel quale si tracta de la perfectione de la sesquialtera producta in la musica mensurata* (Vinegia, 1531). This deals with certain difficulties of proportional notation, much of it again directed against Gafori.[20]

Judging by these treatises, all springing directly or indirectly from the study of music in the University of Bologna, one may assume that such study was a lively business indeed, and that instruction in music followed progressive lines as opposed to the more conservative approach of the musicians in Milan and Parma. It is especially significant, too, that both Ramos and Spataro were interested in the artistic as well as the scientific side of music, that both were composers of music, and that Spataro held for many years an important musical position in one of the city's churches. Their work, then, embraced both *musica speculativa* and *musica practica*, generally with the former put to the use of the latter;

16 *Dilucide et probatissime demonstratione de Maestro Zoanne Spatario Musico Bolognese* (facsimile ed. and tr. into German by Johannes Wolf) (Berlin, 1925), 7.
17 *Ibid.*
18 *Ibid.*
19 *Ibid.*, fol. a^ii verso and recto.
20 Fétis, *Biographie universelle*, VIII, 77.

and we may be reasonably certain that this was reflected in their teaching.

Padua

During the period of the Renaissance the University of Padua was especially noted for its mathematical and medical studies. The liberal arts, always of primary importance at Padua, continued to be cultivated during this time, and the *laurea* continued to be awarded. As late as 1600 we hear of a public lecture on the liberal arts given before the German Nation of the *universitas artistarum et medicorum;* and again in 1606 an *"oratio ad liberalium artium ac disciplinarum culturam adhortatoria fuit habita."*[21] Music apparently continued to hold its own with the other arts at Padua, and the fact that it is not singled out for special notice in university documents is in no way unusual. As in medieval times, moreover, music was used to embellish academic ceremonies. It was still customary that the successful candidate for the doctorate be escorted home from the elaborate degree ceremonies to the accompaniment of trumpets and drums.[22] The trumpet was used, too, to proclaim public meetings.[23]

According to a notice from 1450, a *cantor ecclesiae* took part, along with other *venerabiles et egregii viri domini,* in the doctoral examination of a student in canon law.[24] And two notices in Scar-

[21] Antonio Favaro, *Atti della nazione Germanica artista nello studio di Padova* (Venezia, 1911–12), II, 180 ("2. d. Novembris pro felici studiorum auspicio, in Templo Cathedrali, praesente utroque Urbis Rectore Clarissimo, de more iam antiquitus recepto, oratio ad liberalium artium culturam exhortatoria habita est ab adolescente quodam Nobili Patavino"); see also page 261.

[22] *Ibid.,* II, 101: "*Cerimoniis omnibus finitis, cum de more cum tympanis et tubis domum reducendus esset.*"

[23] *Ibid.,* II, 114–15: a notice from 1598, for example, speaks of a *"sequestratio publice ad vocem tubae proclamata."*

[24] Andreas Veress, *Matricula et Acta Hungarorum in Universitate Patavina Studentium, 1264–1864* (Budapest, 1915), I, 9–10:

Paduae in episcopali palatio. Licentia privati examinis et publica doctoratus in iure canonico domini Nicolai Barii praepositi et canonici ecclesiae Agriensis . . . praesentibus Venerabilibus et egregiis viris dominis Antonio cantore ecclesiae Transilvaniensi.

deonius' description of Padua probably apply to teachers of music in the university. Scardeonius (d. 1574) states that there were at that time in Padua many men *Musicae artis studijs peritissimi,* one of them Antonius Martorellus, highly thought of for his madrigals, published in Italy and France, and highly successful as a teacher.[25] Another Paduan teacher of music, he says, was Antonio Rota, almost without an equal as a performer on the lute and especially distinguished as a *praeceptor* also.[26] The musical interests of Galileo Galilei, furthermore, are well known. Professor of mathematics and astronomy at the University of Padua, 1592–1608, Galileo collected in his personal library many musical works—publications of music and theoretical works ranging from relics of Grecian antiquity (Aristoxenos, Ptolemy, and Aristotle) to the writings of Mersennes, and including, of course, many publications of his distinguished father Vincenzo Galilei, composer and theorist.[27]

[25] Bernardinus Scardeonius, *De antiquitate vrbis Patavii de claris ciuibus Patavinis Libri tres* (Basiliae, 1560), 263: *"Composuit is Mandrialia, quae impressa per totam Italiam, & Galliam, & ubique a cantoribus plurimi existimantur. Atqui is admodum iuuenis Ariminum accitus ad docendam Musicam, cum impense omnib. placeret."*

[26] *Ibid.*: *"qui in pulsando liutum in Italia eruditorum iudicio, uix parem habuit: necque artem hanc sciuit solum, sed quod maius est, unus praecæteris eximinus praeceptor extitit."*

[27] See Antonio Favoro, *La Libreria di Galileo Galilei* (Roma, 1887), 72–74:

Aristoxeni musici antiquissimi, Harmonicorum elementorum libri IIII. Cl. Ptolemaei de Musica libri itidem III. Aristotelis fragmenta super eadem re: omnia nunc primum latine conscripta et edita ab Ant. Gogavino Graviensi. *Venetiis.* . . . 1562.

Discorso di M. Francesco Bocchi sopra la musica. *In Fiorenza.* . . . MDLXXX.

La Sambuca Lincea, ovvero dell' istrumento musico perfetto Lib. III di Fabio Colonna. Ne' quali oltre la descrizione e construttione dell' istrumento si tratta della divisione del Monocordo: della proporzione dei tuoni, semituoni e lor minute parti. Della differenza di tre Generi di Musica, de' Gradi enarmonici et Chromatici, et in che differiscano da quelli degli antichi osservati et descritti alla Santità di N. S. Papa Paolo V Borghese. Così l'organo Hidraulico di Herone Alessandrino dichiarato dall' istesso Autore . . . *in Napoli* . . . MDCXVIII.

Annotazioni sopra il compendio del genere e de' modi della musica, di Gio. Battista Doni patrizio fiorentino, con due trattati, uno sopra i tuoni e modi veri, l'altro sopra i tuoni o armonie degli antichi, e sette discorsi sopra le materie più principali della Musica, o concernenti alcuni strumenti nuovi praticati dall' Autore. *In Roma* . . . 1635.

Fronimo. Dialogo di Vincentio Galilei fiorentino, nel quale si contengono le vere e necessarie regole dell' intavolare la musica del liuto. *Venezia* . . . 1568.

Galileo undoubtedly included music in his teaching of mathematics and physics at Padua, although he left no original treatise on the subject. Indeed, it is said that Galileo was the first to point out the mathematical errors in Boethius' account—copied verbatim in many of the medieval music treatises—of Pythagoras and the hammers, and that he was the first to emphasize frequency (rate of vibrations) as the important factor in determining the pitch of a tone.[28]

Dialogo di Vincenzio Galilei nobile fiorentino della Musica antica e moderna. *Firenze* . . . 1581.

Canto de' Contrappunti a due voci di Vincentio Galilei nobile fiorentino. in *Fiorenza*, MDLXXIIII.

Fronimo. Dialogo di Vincentio Galilei nobile fiorentino sopra l'arte di bene intavolare e rettamente suonare la musica negli strumenti artificiali sì di corde come di fiato et in particolare del Liuto, nuovamente ristampato et dall' autore istesso arricchito et ornato di novità di concetti et d'esempi. *Venetia* . . . 1584.

Discorso di Vincentio Galilei nobile fiorentino intorno all' opere de Messer Gioseffe Zarlino da Chioggia, et altri importanti particolari attinenti alla Musica. *In Fiorenza* . . . 1589.

Discorso sopra l'antica e moderna musica di M. Girolamo Mei cittadino fiorentino. *In Venetia* M. DC. II.

Marini Mersenni. Harmonicorum libri XII, in quibus agitur de sonorum natura, causis et effectibus, de consonantis et dissonantis rationibus, generibus, modis, cantibus, compositione, orbisque totius harmonicis instrumentis. *Parisiis*, 1636.

Il compendio della Musica, nel quale brevemente si tratta del contrappunto. Libri III del M. R. Orazio Tigrini Canonico Aretino. *In Venezia* . . . MDLXXXVIII.

Vincenzo Galilei, the father of Galileo, was a famous composer and theorist who upheld the Pythagorean system against the "just intonation" based on Ptolemy's mathematical divisions advocated by Vincenzo's former teacher, Zarlino. I can find no evidence to connect Vincenzo with the University of Padua or with any other university. Rather, he seems to have been privately tutored, as was generally the case with Italian musicians. For an account of his life and works, see Fabio Fano, *Vincenzo Galilei* (*La Camerata Fiorentino*, Milano, 1934).

[28] See C. F. Abdy Williams, *A Short Historical Account of the Degrees in Music at Oxford and Cambridge* (London and New York, 1894), 23:

So unquestioned was the authority of Boethius all through the Middle Ages, and so averse were students to anything like practical experiments, that Galileo was perhaps the first to point out, that the notes would vary according to the size of the anvil, not that of the hammer, and that, in addition to this, Boethius gives the proportions of the sizes of the intervals wrongly.

For an account of Galileo's experiments in musical pitch, see A. Wolf, *A History of Science, Technology, and Philosophy in the 16th and 17th Centuries* (ed. by Douglas McKie) (London, 1950), 281–82.

If private teachers of music were available to students in the university, various libraries in university foundations contained certain musical works from which we may gain further insight into the status of music in the university. The library of the convent of St. Giustina contained in the late fifteenth century the encyclopedia of Isidorus and the allegory of Martianus Capella,[29] both traditional for the study of music. Records of the German Nation, moreover, contain lists of books presented to the library of that nation from time to time. Although the greater part of these gifts dealt with medicine, works relating to music, both theoretical and practical, were donated occasionally. In 1597, for example, and again in 1603 the library received the *Ethica et politica Aristotelis*— the latter, we recall, particularly important in presenting Aristotle's views on musical studies—and in 1604 it received *Platonis operibus in 16, tomis V.*[30] From the late sixteenth century this library was the recipient of many books of musical compositions for instruments or voices, some by northerners, some by Italians, and some by anonymous composers. In 1599 a copy of the *Teutsch Lauttenbuch Melchior Newsidlers* was given the library by the nation's

[29] Biagio Brugi, *"La Scuola Padovana di Diritto Romano nel secolo XVI," Studi editi della università di Padova,* Vol. III (1888), 39.

[30] For these and subsequent donations, see Favaro, *Atti della nazione Germanica,* II, under appropriate years. From 1601 the complete musical list is as follows:

> 1601: Cantiones Orlandi di Lusso [*sic*], 3 vocum.
> Cantiones And. Gabrielis, 3 vocum.
> 1603: Aristotelis ethica, politica et economica.
> 1604: Platonis operibus in 16, tomis V.
> Canzonette di Giulio Cesare Barbetta.
> Canzonette di Giulio Belli.
> Madrigali a 2 voci di Mattheo Asola.
> Canzonette di Giulio Cesare Barbetta.
> Canzonette di Gio. Francesco Pelaia.
> 1605: Canzonette a 3 di Ruggiero Giovanelli, in 8°.
> Libro secundo della Rondinella a 5 di Gabriele Farrotini, in 4°.
> Canzoni francese a 4 d'Orfeo Vecchi, in 4°.
> Capricci o Madrigali a 2 di Paolo Tonghetti, in 4°.
> 1613: Canzonette amorose di Giulio Caesare Barbetta.
> Dominus Andreas Crucius [dedit] Cantilenas varias a tribus et quatuor vocibus.
> 1614: Cantionibus quibusdam, ut Mascharatis Giovanni Croce. Item eiusdem: Madrigal. Item Madrigal. Petri Mariae Matreoli, in 4°.

German *procurator, Dn. Conradus Hofmann Friburg. Brisgo.* Two years later, *"Dominus Ernestus Soner Norimbergensis dedit . . . Cantiones aliquot, in 4°."* And accessions in the early seventeenth century included songs and madrigals by Lasso, Gabrieli, Vecchi, and others.

The interest in instrumental and vocal music among Paduan students is reflected in certain other records also. A list of the possessions of a Hungarian student, 1552, contained the item, *"1 klavikordiomot vettem uramnak."*[31] And from 1576 there is the notice of a student who died of the plague, Valentinus Grevius Transylvanus. This obituary emphasizes Valentine's skill and fame as a musician and praises highly his compositions for the lute (*pro pulsandis chordis*) published with the sanction of the King of Poland, in whose service the young man had been for some time.[32] Our final notice relating to musical instruments is the record of a gift presented to the library of the German Nation in 1605: *"Chely praeterea, quam vocant vulgo una violina."*[33]

Treatises springing from Paduan studies indicate, too, that music had a regular place in the university during the Renaissance. First of these is the *Ritus canendi vetustissimus et novus* (CS, IV, 298–421) of Johannes Gallicus or John of Mantua (d. 1473). A Frenchman and a singer (*"Gallia namque me genuit et fecit cantorem"*), Johannes came to study privately with Vittorino da Feltre at Mantua (*"Sed cum ad Italiam venissem, ac sub optimo viro, Magistro Feltrensi, musicam Boetii diligenter audissem"*). Reflecting this study is the *Ritus canendi,* a comprehensive, learned mathematical treatise designed chiefly for teachers of singing *in ecclesiis* and, like the older treatises which sought to bridge the gap between *cantor* and *musicus,* explaining matters of *musica practica* upon

[31] Veress, *Matricula et Acta,* I, 165.

[32] *Ibid.,* I, 213 (*"qui cum ob insignem artis Musicae peritiam et psallendi suavitatem nominis sui famam apud omnes maximam fecerit"*); and 214:

Testari poterit quomodocunque de illius eminentia volumen illud cantionum musicis numeris pro pulsandis chordis adaptatum, et aliquando sub nomine Serenissimi regis Poloniae Sigismundi Augusti (in cuius aula diu servivit) publicatum.

[33] Favaro, *Atti della nazione Germanica,* II, 233.

speculative grounds. Although this work typifies the medieval treatise—comprising, as it does, the usual scholastic introduction, a book on plain chant, and a third on polyphonic music—it looks to the future in arguing against the Guidonian system of solmization based upon the hexachord; for Johannes advocated a simplification of this based upon the tetrachord (Book II, *"Facilis ad cantandum atque brevis introductio"*). Like Prosdocimus in his attack upon Marchettus, Johannes opposed the use of halfsteps of three different sizes—a speculative aspect of music closely related to practice in *musica ficta* (the use of chromatic halftones of varying ratios) which came to be of primary interest to theorists in the late fifteenth and sixteenth centuries. Written during the reign of Pius II (1458–62), as Johannes says in his opening paragraph, the treatise was copied by Johannes' pupil, Nicolas Burtius, who, with the publication of his own *Musices opusculum* in 1487 at Bologna, entered the controversy between "ancient" and "modern" theorists in Bologna, Nicolas adhering to the Guidonian system and opposing the new octave system posited by Ramos in his *Musica practica*.

A treatise of an entirely different nature reflects the study of the liberal arts, music among them, at Bologna: the section *"De musica"* in the *Lucubratiunculae bonarum septem artium liberalium* of Theodoricus Gresemundus, published at Mainz, 1494. Gresemundus (1472–1512) studied at Padua, Bologna, and Ferrara before going to the University of Heidelberg, where he matriculated *legum doctor* in 1498.[34] His *Lucubratiunculae* consists of a dialogue between Aristobolus (Jewish philosopher of the second century, B.C.), opponent of the arts, and Chiron (Achilles' wise tutor), upholder of the liberal arts, with Theodoricus as adjudicator. The entire tract is an *apologia* for music, useful and worthwhile in private life, since it heals the sick and cheers the melancholy, as well as *in negotiis publicis,* especially in warfare. Chiron ends by citing the legend of Arion (a favorite with literary men of the Renaissance—Rabelais, Du Bartas, and many others), who was saved from death by music as he charmed a dolphin with the

[34] Gerhard Pietzsch, *"Zur Pflege der Musik an den deutschen Universitäten bis zur Mitte des 16. Jahrhunderts: Heidelberg, Köln,"* AfMf, Vol. V (1940), 72.

strains of his lyre and was carried ashore to safety. But Aristobolus is not persuaded that there is any good in music, and so Theodoricus gives his judgment, very much on the side of music.[35] The little debate is perhaps representative of the struggle between the old liberal arts and the new humanistic learning:[36] Gresemundus, with his Italian background, wished to see music and the other liberal arts kept in the academic curriculum. It is also indicative of a usage in music treatises which came to be general during the Renaissance—the use of one (or several) of the old *kephalaia* of the musical *protreptikos* as the basis for an entire work, usually, like this, a discussion of the uses and effects of music.

A musical work no longer extant by Johannes Taisnier apparently derived from musical studies at the University of Padua. In the preface to his *Opus mathematicum* (1562), Taisnier states that he had taught mathematics at Padua as well as at other Italian universities during the course of his life.[37] Among his many mathematical and astrological works there was a treatise on music *(nostrum librum Musicae),* of which only a description has survived; but this description indicates a strong interest in musical mathematics as affecting chromaticism. And finally, among men who combined music and mathematics at Renaissance Padua is Johannes Paduanus, philosopher and mathematician.[38] His work on counterpoint, *Institutiones ad diversas ex plurimum vocum harmonia cantilenas* (1578), indicates his interest in the artistic as well as the philosophical and mathematical side of music.

Exactly this interest, in fact, appears to characterize the study of music in the University of Padua during our period. Although evidence from the statutes is nonexistent—probably because written statutes were unnecessary, as the old medieval curriculum con-

[35] Peter Wagner, *"Aus der Musikgeschichte des deutschen Humanismus,"* Z*f*M*w,* Vol. III (1921), 27: *"Musica vero (quam detestatus es, Aristobole) haud parum habet momenti, cum in rebus humanis . . . tum in rebus bellicis."* The treatise is given with a parallel German translation, 22–27.

[36] Suggested by Wagner, *ibid.,* III, 27.

[37] Lynn Thorndike, *History of Magic and Experimental Science* (New York, 1929–41), V, 581. Taisnier's treatise more properly belongs in our discussion of the University of Cologne, where he established himself at the end of his life.

[38] Fétis, *Biographie universelle,* VI, 401–402.

tinued in effect—we have seen that the liberal arts continued to be the basis for the doctorate and preparatory to the higher faculties, with a strong emphasis upon mathematics, including music. And although the history of the chair of music established by Nicolas V is equally vague, we know that distinguished teachers of music were available in the university and that professors of mathematics, physics, and astronomy included music within the framework of their teaching.

ii. France: Paris

Two sets of statutes were given the University of Paris during the Renaissance. The first of these, drawn up by Guillaume d'Estouteville, cardinal legate, 1452, specified that no one was to be admitted *ad licentiam* unless he had heard certain books, including *"aliquos libros mathematicales,"* which very likely included music; and further, *"ut predicti libri audiantur non cursim et transcurrendo, sed studiose et graviter."*[1] At the end of our period during the reign of Henri IV (1598), a humanistic course of studies was outlined for the university by new statutes designed to emphasize classical writings in the original rather than commentaries, and empirical rather than scholastic methods. The course in arts was to conclude with two years of Aristotelian philosophy; and the curriculum for the second year comprised physics, metaphysics, and geometry.[2]

Renaissance statutes, thus, tell us very little more about the various university disciplines than medieval statutes, and nothing about music, which was probably taught as a part of mathematics until the end of the century, when it became a part of physics. At

---

[1] Heinrich Denifle, *Chartularium Universitatis Parisiensis* (Parisiis, 1889–97), IV, 729.

[2] *Réformation de l'Vniversité de Paris* (Paris, 1667), *"Statuta Facultatis Artium,"* 34-35:

Secundo anno Aristotelis Physica manè interpretentur: post meridiem Metaphysica; si fieri potest, integra, saltem horum primum, quartum & vndecim libros, magna cura & diligentia explicent: hora sexta matutina Sphaeram, cum aliquot Euclidis libris praelegant.

the beginning of the Renaissance, Parisian instruction in the seven arts was especially good: *Een schoone Historie van Mariken van Nimwegen,* 1465, speaks of the superiority of the *clercs* of Paris in all sciences, especially music.[3] And there are numerous indications of the close connection between music and mathematics in the university. Jacques Lefèvre d'Etaples (Jacobus Faber Stapulensis), for example, a *magister artium* of the university and professor in the Collège de Cardinal Lemoine (around 1494), was a great advocate of mathematical studies;[4] and his writings include many works on mathematics, one of them a musical treatise—*Musica libris demonstrata quatuor,* first published in 1496. Lefèvre was the teacher of many men later distinguished for their humanistic learning, among them the Swiss humanist and *musicus* Glareanus.[5] Oronce Finé, first professor of mathematics in the Collège de France established by Francis I in 1530 and incumbent until his death in 1555, left among his mathematical writings an *Epithoma musice instrumentalis,* published in 1530; and two other professors in this college have left evidence of their interest in music as a part of mathematics: Jean Pena, who published in 1557 *Euclidis optica et catoptrica et musica, graece et latine,* and Pierre Forcadel, who translated Euclid's book on music, 1565.[6]

Petrus Ramus (Pierre de la Ramée), professor of philosophy who was widely known for his efforts to replace Aristotelian scholasticism with empirical thinking (and was thus the forerunner of Descartes in the next century) left many mathematical works among his numerous *opera,* one of which was a treatise on music, no longer extant.[7] Even more significant of Ramus' interest in music as a part of mathematics was the provision in his will for the establishment of a professorship in mathematics in the univer-

---

[3] Cited by Pirro, *"L'Enseignement de la musique," MIGM,* Vol. II, 46.

[4] Karl Heinrich Graf, *"Jacobus Faber Stapulensis," Zeitschrift für die historische Theologie,* Vol. XXII (1852), 7–12.

[5] Stephen d'Irsay, *Histoire des universités, françaises et étrangères* (Paris, 1933–35), I, 266.

[6] Abel Lefranc, *Histoire du Collège de France* (Paris, 1893), 120; and Pirro, *"L'Enseignement de la musique," MIGM,* Vol. II, 49–50.

[7] See Charles Waddington, *Ramus, sa vie, ses écrits et ses opinions* (Paris, 1855), 473.

sity (1568), with music clearly specified.[8] Ramus appointed his pupil Frederic Reisner to this position for the first three years, at the end of which time examinations were to be held to choose the most worthy candidate as his successor; but owing to machinations of Jacques Charpentier, royal professor of mathematics (a doctor of medicine who admitted to knowing neither Greek nor mathematics) and great adversary of Ramus, the chair was adjudged superfluous and in 1573 its stipend was put to other uses.[9] All this time, however, a student of Ramus taught mathematics gratuitously, and after the death of Charpentier the chair of Ramus was occupied successively by distinguished mathematicians.[10]

Along with the study of music as a part of mathematics there was an even greater flourishing of music in the various divisions of the university, perhaps, than in medieval times. The German Nation continued to heighten its religious observances with music. Payments to an organist in 1461 and 1465 are recorded in accounts of this nation; payments *cantoribus ecclesiae parisiensis* are noted in 1465; and in 1475 it was specified that the organ be used at Mass and vespers.[11] As in earlier times, the *mors solitus* of this nation was to import qualified singers to assist on special occasions: a record of 1486 refers to this custom and also to plans for inviting *doctores nostre nationis* to assist at services in honor of the nation's patron saint (Edmund).[12] In 1489, Johannes Lantman and singers

---

8 *Ibid.*, 326: according to the terms of the will, certain rents were to be paid

pour le traitement d'un professeur de mathématiques qui, dans l'espace de trois ans, enseignera au collège royal l'arithmétique, la musique, la géométrie, l'optique, la méchanique, la géographie et l'astronomie, non selon l'opinion des hommes, mais selon la raison et la vérité.

9 *Ibid.*, 175, 326–27; and see Charles Jourdain, *Index chronologicus Chartarum pertinentium ad Historiam Universitatis Parisiensis* (Parisiis, 1862), 392, which tells that in 1573, according to a parliamentary order, the money left *"par Pierre de la Ramée pour la fondation d'une nouvelle chaire de mathématiques, est attribuée provisoirement à Me Jacques Gohorry, advocat, pour continuer en latin l'histoire de France de Paul Emile."*

10 Bressieu (1577–1608), Martin and Roberval in the seventeenth century: see Waddington, *Ramus*, 337–38.

11 Pirro, *"L'Enseignement de la musique,"* *MIGM*, Vol. II, 47.

12 Charles Samaran and E. A. von Moé (eds.) *Auctarium Chartularii Universitatis Parisiensis* (Parisiis, 1935–38), III, 620: *"placuit natione quod festum [Alemanorum]*

from the Burgundian College were invited to participate; and in 1491 this master of theology, proctor, and later rector of the nation celebrated *festum nationis* by singing Mass and vespers with the Notre Dame choir.[13] Payments made to singers and organist are also recorded in documents of this nation, 1494–1530.[14] Late in the Renaissance (1575), Claude Mignault mentions the custom of scholars celebrating with feasts and music the day upon which they paid their masters.[15]

The *Libri procuratorum* of the various nations, in fact, tell much about the use of music on festive occasions within the university. In 1468, for example, members of the university convened to hear news that *pax eterna* had been concluded between the king and the Duke of Burgundy, and celebrated with a *Te Deum* at St. Mathurin's and solemn processions to Notre Dame.[16] In 1478 the Nation of Picardy, wishing to celebrate the feast of St. Nicolas *"cantando videlicet vesperas in nocte festi et missam de mane,"* decided to make a payment of two *denarii* to any *magistri* who could sing at vespers, four *denarii* to any who could sing at Mass.[17] According to a notice of 1482, this nation decided to celebrate its feast day in a less expensive and more dignified way by concentrating upon hymns and doing without *"mimis seu instrumentis musi-*

celebriter festivaretur more solito, invitando scilicet cantores aliquos bonos et etiam invitando doctores nostre nationis et eis distributiones solitas contribuendo."

[13] *Ibid.*, III, 718: *"placuit nacioni more solito festum [Alemanorum] celebrare; voluit tamen ut magister Jo. Lantman una cum collegii Burgundie cantoribus missam et vesperas peragerent [i.e. cantarent]";* and III, 778: *"placuit prefate nationi celebrare festum nationis ut consuetum est fieri; voluit ut magister Johannes Lantsman cantaret vesperas et missam cum cantoribus de Nostra Domina."* See *ibid.*, III, 863 (Index), for biographical data.

[14] Pirro, *L'Enseignement de la musique," MIGM*, Vol. II, 47. These documents apparently are unpublished.

[15] *Ibid.*, II, 51n.: *"Adjiciuntur auloedi, cantores, citharoedi, tibicines, interdum tympana, quasi ad urbis obsidionem,"* from *De liberali adolescentum institutione in academia parisiensi,* 1575.

[16] *Auctarium Chartularii,* III, 98: *"Deinceps placuit decantare ympnum illum videlicet Te Deum laudamus, finita congregatione, in ecclesia Sancti Maturini. Denique placuit quod fierent processiones ad Nostram Dominam die Mercurii sequenti."*

[17] *Ibid.*, IV, 163: *"Natio etiam considerans quod in illa die vix sunt magistri qui decantare habeant servicium, volens festivitatem nationis peramplius decorari, ordinat quod cuilibet magistro comparenti in vesperis distribuantur duo denarii, et in missa quatuor denarii."*

calibus."[18] In 1487 the French Nation had an organ placed in the chapel of the Collège de Navarre; and in 1552 this organ was repaired or replaced.[19] One organist whose name we know was a *magister artium* (1509) in the university—Pierre Mouton, canon of the Cathedral of Notre Dame: in 1502 he was organist at St. Merry, later organist to the king and organist at Notre Dame.[20]

Two of the *magistri* in the Nation of Picardy were musicians, if we may judge by their names: Dionysius and Johannes Citharedi (Le Harpeur).[21] A blind musician whom Tinctoris admired in Brussels for his skill in playing the violin, Charles Fernand, had taught in *celeberrimo gymnasio parisiensi,* and his name appears among the musicians of Charles VIII in 1488 and 1490.[22] Priest, musician, composer, member of Louis XII's private choir, Antoine de Févin (died 1512?) probably studied at the University of Paris; a native of Arras, in all likelihood he stayed at the Collège de Dainville, one of three maintained by the city of Arras for its students in the university.[23]

As in medieval times, many of the students in the university received musical training in choir schools before entering the arts faculty of the university proper. Notre Dame's *psallette* continually sent choristers to the university. We know, for example, that in 1456 one of the Notre Dame choirboys asked permission *"ire ad studium pro addiscendo artes";* this permission was granted in 1460.[24] In 1475, two Notre Dame choristers received scholarships

[18] *Ibid.,* IV, 384: *"Deliberavit et conclusit natio . . . quod ista festa non amplius celebrentur cum mimis seu instrumentis musicalibus, sed tantum, si qui fuerint qui illa continuare voluerint in suis collegiis, cum cantilenis et dictaminibus seu Sanctorum ymnis."*

[19] Jourdain, *Index chronologicus,* 305: *"Charta qua magistri, provisores, capellanus et bursarii collegii Navarrae profitentur, organa quae in ejusdem collegii capella reponuntur, pertinere ad magistros Nationis Gallicanae, quorum expensis confecta fuerunt;* and 363: *Quittance par laquelle Josse Lebel, maître faiseur d'orgues et autres instruments de musique . . . confesse avoir reçu . . . de la Nation de France en l'Université de Paris la somme de deux cent trente livres tournois pour la façon des orgues par lui faites et livrées à l'église du collége de Navarre, pour ladite Nation de France."*

[20] Pirro, *"L'Enseignement de la musique," MIGM,* Vol. II, 48.

[21] Their names occur in several documents: see, for example, *Auctarium Chartularii,* III, 363, 391.

[22] Pirro, *"L'Enseignement de la musique," MIGM,* Vol. II, 46.

[23] B. Kahlmann, *"Antoine de Févin," Musica Disciplina,* Vol. IV (1950), 154–56.

[24] Pirro, *"L'Enseignement de la musique," MIGM,* Vol. II, 45.

in the Collège de Navarre; and in 1484 Jean Boucard established a foundation for two choristers from Rouen in the Collège de Justice.[25] Many singers from the Sainte Chapelle, too, were later sent to the university: records of 1537 and 1538, for instance, tell us that Jacques Colombeau, Jean Devaulx, and Guillaume Dufresne, *chantres de la chambre du roi,* were given funds for study in the university.[26] Records of two other colleges in the university, Harcourt (1513) and Plessis (1519), show the maintenance of scholarships for choirboys in these foundations.[27]

Known by name, moreover, are certain musicians who taught music in the university. Lefèvre quite significantly dedicated his musical treatise (1496) to two musicians who had formerly been his teachers: *"Iacobo Labinio et Iacobo Turbelino Musicis: suis charissimis praeceptoribus."*[28] The dedication in Wollick's *Enchiridion musices* (1512) indicates that he had taught students in Paris; and while at the Sorbonne for the study of law, the composer Adrian Willaert studied composition under the tutelage of Jean Mouton, and Glareanus also came in contact with Mouton in Paris.[29] Jean Dorat, professor of Greek literature at the Collège de Coqueret, was an enthusiastic musician. In the words of a modern critic, *"Au collège de Coqueret, où la musique est souveraine, Jean Dorat fait grand accueil aux lutistes.... Son logis résonne du matin au soir d'un frémissement de lyres."*[30]

One highly important aspect of musical studies during the Renaissance, indeed, was the investigation of ancient musical theories in connection with Greek poetry, nowhere pursued with more enthusiasm than in certain of the Paris colleges. The famous Pléiade actually originated in Dorat's lecture room; and it was Dorat, with his enthusiasm for music and ancient lyrical poetry, who was at least indirectly responsible for Baïf's Academy of Poetry and Music. For Baïf, a private pupil of Dorat's, followed the latter to

[25] *Ibid.,* II, 48f.
[26] *Ibid.,* II, 49.
[27] Jourdain, *Index chronologicus,* pp. 321 and 326.
[28] *Musica libris quatuor demonstrata* (Parisiis, 1552), fol. A^{ij} verso.
[29] Pirro, *"L'Enseignement de la musique,"* MIGM, Vol. II, 46f.
[30] Constantin Photiades, *Ronsard et son luth* (Paris, 1925), 20.

the Collège de Coqueret when Dorat became head of that institution in 1547.[31] In 1570 Charles IX granted Baïf and the composer Joachim Thibault permission to open an *Académie de poésie et de musique* to give instruction in and performance of *musique mesurée à l'antique*—a true union of words and music, with musical settings related rhythmically to the poetic meter of the text and with many implications of ethos in the old Greek sense.[32] Both Parliament and the Sorbonne opposed the plan of the academy to open a school of music and poetry, the university feeling that this would be a breach of privilege; and the academy, supported only by royal authority, came to an end with the death of King Charles in 1574.[33] The full complement of musicians connected with this institution cannot be determined. Known to have contributed to the productions of the academy, however, are Jacques du Faur (bachelor of law and student at the university in 1568), Thibault de Courville, Eustache du Courroy (*maître de musique de la Chambre*), Claude Le Jeune, and Jacques Mauduit[34] —distinguished composers whose musical output was greatly influenced by their classical studies and who aimed at a revival of musical ethos (effects) through a very close relationship between words and music.

Another member of the Academy of Poetry and Music and of the Pléiade was Pierre de Ronsard, who had studied with Dorat

[31] Mathieu Augé-Chiquet, *La Vie, les idées et l'œuvre de Jean-Antoine Baïf* (Paris et Toulouse, 1909), 30–31.

[32] See *ibid.*, 436–40, note 1, *"Lettres patentes,"* and see the aims as set forth in the opening words of the statutes of the *Académie*, 434: *"Afin de remettre en usage la Musique selon sa perfection, qui est de representer la parole en chant accomply de son harmonie et melodie, qui consistent au choix, regle des voix, sons et accords bien accomodez pour faire l'effet selon que le sens de la lettre le requiert, ou resserrant ou desserrant, ou accroississant l'esprit, renouvellant aussi l'ancienne façon de composer Vers mesurez pour y accommoder le chant pareillement mesuré selon l'Art Metrique."*

For a discussion of the aims, ideas, and activities of the Academy, see D. P. Walker, "Musical Humanism in the 16th and Early 17th Centuries," *The Music Review*, Vol. II (1941), 1–13, 111–21, 220–26, 288–308; Vol. II (1942), 55–71; D. P. Walker, "The Aims of Baïf's *Académie de Poésie et de Musique*," *Journal of Renaissance and Baroque Music*, Vol. I (1945–47), 91–100; Frances A. Yates, *The French Academies of the Sixteenth Century* (London, 1947). The letters patent appear also in Yates, 319–22.

[33] Augé-Chiquet, *Baïf*, 436–56.

[34] *Ibid.*, 402n.; Photiades, *Ronsard*, 95.

at the Collège de Coqueret and who was himself a capable performer on the lute. Ronsard's famous *Préface,* addressed successively to Francis II and Charles IX, and printed at the beginning of
two collections of songs published in 1560 and 1572 by LeRoy and
Ballard, reflects his own musical training and ideas.[35] Carrying on
the *protreptikos* tradition from medieval literature, the *Préface*
is an exhortation praising music. It is significant, however, of the
changed aspects under which this type of treatise appeared in the
Renaissance, for it is primarily an appeal for royal patronage of
music; it is equally significant of the great emphasis placed upon
Greek ideas by Renaissance humanists. Like Shakespeare, Ronsard
finds that man most worthy who has music in his soul; he briefly
outlines the elements of the art of music, discussing the three ancient *genera* (enharmonic, chromatic, and diatonic) and the effects
of the various modes upon man; he cites legends to show how
kings have always encouraged the cultivation of music and he begs
the present king's protection and support, naming a number of
deserving contemporary composers, with Josquin des Prés at the
head of the list. The fact that Ronsard refers the reader for more
information to Boethius and Plutarch shows once again the great
influence and authority of the former and the new interest in
Plutarch characteristic of French humanists—an interest which
culminated in a French translation (1575) of certain works of
Plutarch, including his treatise *De musica,* by Jacques Amyot,
student of mathematics with Finé, later professor of Greek and
Latin in the university.

Earlier in the century another humanist, François Rabelais,
sometime student at the University of Paris and several other French
universities, published his novel *Gargantua et Pantagruel,* drawing heavily upon his musical knowledge for both ideas and im-
agery.[36] Among his most striking musical references in a passage
unique in Renaissance literature—a list of fifty-nine of the most

[35] This *Préface* has been reprinted by Julien Tiersot, *Ronsard et la musique de son
temps* (Leipzig and New York, 1903), 16–18. For an English translation, see Oliver
Strunk, *Source Readings in Music History* (New York, 1950), 286–89.

[36] For an analysis of Rabelais' musical ideas and rhetoric, see Nan Cooke Carpenter,
Rabelais and Music (Chapel Hill, 1954).

famous musicians of two centuries, largely Flemish and French composers. Dividing his men into two groups, Rabelais begins with "Josquin des Prez, Olkegan, Hobrethz" and others, and places in his second group "Adrian Villart, Gombert, Janequin, Arcadelt, Claudin ... *et autres joyeulx musiciens*" (Nouveau Prologue, *Quart Livre*). Although these lists are not strictly chronological, in general they represent three successive generations of composers in the Netherlandish tradition; and it is interesting to note that Rabelais places the leading composer of two of the three generations at the head of each list. Music figures largely, moreover, in Rabelais' ideas on education. A product of encyclopedic learning himself, Rabelais has Gargantua taught not only arithmetic, "*mais des aultres sciences mathematicques, comme geometrie, astronomie et musicque*" (*Gargantua, xxiii*); and to supplement this theoretical training, "*Au reguard des instrumens de musicque, il aprint jouer de luc, de l'espinette, de la harpe, de la flutte de Alemant et à neuf trouz, de la viole et de la sacquebutte.*" Gargantua's education was characteristic of the tutorial aspect of humanistic pedagogy, but his son Pantagruel enrolled in various universities—including the University of Paris—and here again Rabelais emphasizes music. Gargantua, in a famous letter (thought by most critics to refer to Francis I's endowment of the royal professorships in 1530, which we have seen had important implications for the study of music) outlines a course of studies completely humanistic, not omitting music. Rejoicing in the restitution of light and letters after dark Gothic times, the giant advises his son to learn Greek, Hebrew, Chaldean, and Latin, and to read the works of Plutarch, Plato, Pausanias, and Athenaeus—all of which have some bearing on music. Further, "*Des ars liberaux, Geometrie, Arismeticque et Musicque, je t'en donnay quelque goust quand tu estois encores petit ... poursuys la reste*" (*Pantagruel, viii*).

In this same letter, Gargantua, advising his son to take advantage of opportunities for study in Paris, says, "*Tout le monde est plein de gens sçavans, de precepteurs très doctes, de librairies très amples.*" A glance at the list of books published in the fifteenth and sixteenth centuries owned by the University of Paris (acquired from various colleges and monasteries in the seventeenth century) shows that both ancient and contemporary works on music were accessible to students in the university at the time Rabelais was writing (1532 onwards) and later.[37] Among the fifteenth-century incunabula we find *De proprietatibus rerum* of Bartholomaeus Anglicus, with a French translation from 1495; the *Elementa musicalia* of Lefèvre d'Etaples; the *Musica* of Cleonides, printed at Venice in 1498; and several editions of Quintilian's *Institutiones.* Of books printed between 1501 and 1540 in the university library are Martianus Capella's *De nuptiis,* Cassiodorus' *De quatuor Mathematicis disciplinis Compendium* and his *Psalterij dauidici expositio.* A *Chronicon* containing *opvs ervditissimorvm avtorum* includes writings of Cassiodorus and Hermannus Contractus, published as late as 1529 at Basel; and these two appear *inter alios* in a later *Chronicon* (1536). Several editions of Quintilian's *Institutiones oratoriae* attest again to the perennial popularity of that writer. Rabanus Maurus' work *De clericorum institutione,* published at Cologne in 1532, also appears in the library catalogue. Among all these theoretical works on music one practical work is listed: *Manuale seu agenda ad vsum Remensem,* with *musique notée* and three Masses at the end. Books printed in the next decade (1541–50) in the library collection include, again, several editions of Quintilian. And here we find several "modern" works: the treatise *In Ptolemaeum,* 1541, by Georgius Peurbachius (mathematician active at the University of Vienna), a work *"svper propositiones Ptolemaei de Sinubus & Chordis";* the *Res musicae* of Johannes Froschius, 1535; and the *Dodecachordon* of Glareanus, 1547.

Treatises written by members of the university, some of which have already been mentioned, continued to spring from the dichotomy noticeable throughout the medieval period—that is, they dealt with music as a mathematical discipline or as a living art with its own technical problems. Lefèvre's *Musica demonstrata,* reflect-

---

[37] See Emile Chatelain, "*Catalogue des incunables de la Bibliothèque de l'Université de Paris*," *Revue des Bibliothèques,* Vol. XII (1902), and Charles Beaulieux, *Catalogue de la réserve XVIe siècle . . . de la Bibliothèque de l'Université de Paris* (Paris, 1910–23), under appropriate years.

ing his own mathematical interests, is largely mathematical, its four books dealing with proportions of intervals and division of the monochord. This work had considerable vogue in various European countries as well as in Paris. In Spain, for example, Pedro Ciruelo —professor of music for a while at the University of Paris and later professor of mathematics at Alcalá—published the whole of Lefèvre's *Musica* in his *Cursus quatuor mathematicarum artium liberalium;* Thomas Morley in his *Plaine and Easie Introduction* (published nearly a hundred years later) referred to it; and Ornithoparcus in his *Micrologus* (translated by John Dowland in 1609) included Faber Stapulensis among the "speciall Patrons" drawn upon.

Nicolas Wollick, whose *Opus aureum musices castigatissimum* appeared first in 1501 at Cologne while Wollick was teaching in the university there, was more concerned with problems of *musica practica*. His treatise is a handbook on the Gregorian chant and on the elements and composition of *musica figurata* (polyphony), as he states in the title and explicit.[38] It is significant for insight into the study of music at Paris that this book was expanded and published under the title *Enchiridion musices* in 1512 while Wollick was lecturing at the University of Paris and that it is dedicated to Wollick's students at Paris. The treatises of Wollick (who underlined the fact that he was French by signing a letter—at the end of his book—to a former teacher in the University of Cologne as Nicolas *Gallus*) were known and drawn upon by subsequent theorists as late as the eighteenth century; and parts of his writings were incorporated in the *Margarita philosophica* (edition of 1512 and later), famous humanistic encyclopedia compiled by a Heidelberg professor of philosophy, Gregorius Reisch.[39]

The *Utilissime musicales regule* of Guillaume Guerson (1513) presented both speculative and practical aspects of music, its three books embracing the elements of music, figures of notation, and

[38] See the edition of 1508 in the Munich Library.

[39] Ernest T. Ferand, " 'Sodaine and Unexpected' Music in the Renaissance," *Musical Quarterly,* Vol. XXXVII (1951), 10–27; here are traced *sortisatio* (improvisation, music "by chance") and other aspects of composition from Wollick's *Opus aureum* and *Enchiridion* until the mid-seventeenth century.

plain song and polyphonic music, as did the anonymous *L'art, science et practique de plaine musique,* which appeared early in the sixteenth century.[40] In 1552 there was published at Paris a mathematical treatise involving music—the *Tabulae in astronomiam, in arithmeticam theoricam et in musicam theoricam* by Guillaume Postell, professor of mathematics at Paris in 1551 and lecturer in classical languages and mathematics at Vienna in 1554.[41] Oronce Finé, professor of mathematics for many years in the Collège de France, treated music in two of his mathematical works: the *Protomathesis, seu opera mathematica* (Paris, 1552) and the *De rebus mathematicis hactenus desideratis libri IV* (Paris, 1556); in addition, he wrote the first practical instruction book on the lute—he was himself a performer on this instrument—published by Attaingnant in 1529, translated into Latin and published in 1530 as *Epithoma musice instrumentalis ad omnimodam Hemispherii seu luthina et theoreticam et practicam.*[42] We have already mentioned other musical works among publications by professors of mathematics in the university—Pena's *Euclidis optica et catoptrica et musica* (1557) and Forcadel's translation of Euclid's *Musica* (1565).

These translations of Euclid's book on music indicate the great interest in ancient Greek theory paramount in some of the Paris colleges. A musical humanist connected with the Pléiade was the poet and philosopher Pontus de Tyard, who studied at the University of Paris and whose *Solitaire second ou Discours de la Musique* (Lyons, 1555) was a complementary volume to his *ars poetica* called *Solitaire premier ou Discours des Muses et de la fureur Poëtique* (1552). The treatise on music is largely a discussion of musical effects, with copious information about the modes (based upon Glarean's system) and many stories illustrating the power of music.[43] Like Tyard, Marin Mersenne (whose great importance to

[40] Fétis, *Biographie universelle,* IV, 136, and Pirro, "L'Enseignement de la musique," *MIGM,* Vol. II, 47.

[41] Joseph Aschbach, *Geschichte der Wiener Universität* (Wien, 1865–88), III, 243–47, 251n.

[42] Fétis, *Biographie universelle,* III, 251, and Pirro, *loc. cit.*

[43] Both treatises are found in Pontus de Tyard, *Discours philosophiques* (Paris, 1587). For the influence of the *Solitaire second* upon literature, see Nan Cooke Carpenter, "Spenser and Timotheus: A Musical Gloss on E. K.'s Gloss," *PMLA,* Vol. LXXI (1956), 1141–51.

music is properly a part of the history of the Baroque) believed in the tremendous power possessed by music in ancient times and the possibility of reviving this power for ethical purposes in modern times: Mersenne's *Quaestiones* (written half a century after the foundation of Baïf's Academy) discuss the ideals of the Academy retrospectively as he had learned them from one of the group's leading musicians, Jacques Mauduit.[44] And Amyot's translation of Plutarch's *Moralia* included the essay *De Musica* (1575). Amyot's remarks at the beginning of the essay calling attention to the fact that the music referred to is not modern polyphony but an ancient style of music in which the melody is related "to the sense and measure of the words" (the Greek ideal, that is) undoubtedly contributed to the vogue of *musique mesurée*.[45]

It appears, then, that music was very much a part of higher learning in the University of Paris during the sixteenth century, continuing on the one hand along medieval lines and assuming on the other certain new characteristics typical of the Renaissance. The continued output of musico-mathematical treatises (Lefévre's dedicated to his former music teachers in the university) and the fact that mathematicians known for their musical interest regularly taught in the university show a continuation of the medieval tradition which allied music inevitably with mathematics; but the probable implication of music as a part of physics in statutes at the end of the century, the greater emphasis upon instrumental (especially lute) music and composition, and above all, the close association of music and classical studies (poetry)—all these denote the changed aspects of musical studies in the Renaissance which prevailed not only at the Sorbonne but in most of the Renaissance universities. The investigation of musical ideas as an intrinsic part of Greek poetry in Paris colleges and the attempt to apply these ideas in contemporary music and literature was responsible, indeed, for a new type of polyphonic music—*musique mesurée*, musical settings of *vers mesuré à l'antique* in which the quantities of the verse are reflected identically in the musical time

[44] John C. Lapp (ed.), *The Universe of Pontus de Tyard* (Ithaca, 1950), 41.
[45] *Ibid.*, 37–38.

values—which forms a considerable part of the total musical output of the French Renaissance.

iii. ENGLAND: OXFORD AND CAMBRIDGE

Oxford

FROM 1431, when the *forma* for the *magisterium in artibus* required Boethius' *Musica,* no new statutes were promulgated for the University of Oxford until the period of the Reformation. According to the code established in 1549 during King Edward's Visitation of Oxford, candidates for the bachelor's degree were to concentrate on disciplines of the quadrivium the first year; and music may have been understood here with arithmetic, although it is not specifically mentioned.[1] Statutes given in 1556 during the reign of Mary and the chancellorship of Reginald Pole dealt chiefly with administrative affairs and did not touch upon the curriculum. But the Elizabethan Statutes, the *Nova Statuta* of 1564–65, "set out afresh the rules for reading, disputations and degrees . . . reverting apparently to the old ideas which the Edwardian Statutes had varied."[2] The *forma* to be fulfilled before attaining the baccalaureate (based upon the liberal arts and the three philosophies) specified four years (sixteen terms) in grammar, rhetoric, dialectic, arithmetic, and *"in musica Boetium,"* giving the length of time to be spent in each, including *"duos (terminos) demum musicae."*[3] Not only were undergraduates to hear lectures in music, but so were bachelors studying for the master's degree; for during the three additional years leading to the *magisterium, "Vetera statuta,*

---

[1] Strickland Gibson (ed.), *Statuta antiqua Vniversitatis Oxoniensis* (Oxford, 1931), 344: *"Recenter venientem a ludo literario primum excipiant mathematica. Illa toto eo anno discet, arithmeticen nimirum, geometriam, et astronomiae cosmographiaeque quantum poterit."* Candidates for the *magisterium* were required to spend three more years in the study of philosophy, astronomy, perspective, and Greek, but again no music was specified.

[2] Sir Charles Mallet, *History of the University of Oxford* (London, 1924), II, 120.

[3] Gibson, *Statuta,* 390.

quae ab artium magistris obseruari solebant, obseruabunt."[4] The Caroline Code established by Archbishop Laud under the authority of King Charles I (1636) named no books to be read, but it did make attendance at public lectures obligatory for both bachelors and masters—of interest to us because by this time the Music Lecture had been in existence for ten years; and the Laudian Statutes further decreed that students below the grade of master take the lectures down in writing.[5] As in present-day Oxford, moreover, each student was to be instructed by his own tutor until he had obtained his first degree[6]—of interest to us, too, because the musical careers of some students were undoubtedly shaped by their having capable musicians for tutors, as was the case with Richard Edwards, whose tutor was the distinguished Greek scholar and *musicus* George Etheridge.

The sixteenth century saw the foundation of public lectureships (beginning with Lady Margaret's Lecture in Divinity, 1502) in law, medicine, and theology; but in the arts faculty the *magistri regentes* continued to carry out the ordinary lectures. With the increase in the number of regents, however, there was a tendency to deputize certain *magistri* as *publici praelectores* and to exempt others from the duty of lecturing.[7] A *lectorum ordinarium designatio* of 1563 gives the names of three men lecturing on music: Robert Leche, John Reve, and John Foux.[8] In 1592 when the queen

---

[4] *Ibid.*, 378.

[5] John Griffiths, *Statutes of the University of Oxford Codified in the Year 1636 under the Authority of Archbishop Laud* (London, 1888), 45: "*Statutum est, quod Scholares in Facultate Artium, antequam Gradum Baccalaureatus suscipiant, quatuor annos integros sive sedecim Terminos, numerandos a die Matriculationis, in Studio Artium, et in publicis Lectoribus, prout Statuta requirunt, diligenter audiendis, in Academia . . . ponere teneantur.*" And for masters, 50: "*A Tempore admissionis ad Gradum Baccalaurei, tenentur singuli in audiendis publicis Lecturis sibi destinatis, et in Disputationibus iuxta Statuta requisitis, tum habendis, tum frequentandis, duodecim Terminos ponere; nec ante completum illud tempus Gratiam suam petere cuiquam fas esto.*" P. 43: "*Et quotquot infra Gradum Magistralem sunt, scriptis excipiant ea quae leguntur.*"

[6] *Ibid.*, 31. Much light will be thrown on this aspect of university music when Mr. James Osborn publishes the recently discovered autobiography of Thomas Whythorne (1528–92?), a professional musician, for six years at Magdalen College School and from 1559 tutor at one of the Cambridge colleges. See the abstract, *JAMS*, Vol. IX (1956), 60.

[7] Andrew Clark, *Register of the University of Oxford* (Oxford, 1885–89), II, part 1, 95.

visited Oxford, it was decided that ordinary lectures in the three philosophies and seven liberal arts would be read as usual during Her Majesty's stay: Mr. Pelling was the lecturer in music.[9]

The fact that occasional dispensations were granted in connection with the music lecture shows that ordinarily these lectures were regularly given, even during the Edwardian period when music was not specifically mentioned in the statutes as a part of the formal curriculum. In 1562, for instance, the lecture was omitted.[10] In 1564/5 the lecture was again dispensed with: *"numerus scholarium non patitur, et ejusdem lectio prae caeteris minus necessaria est."* In several subsequent years there were no students, or not enough students to warrant the lecture: Robert Benbow was allowed to discontinue the lecture (1567) because *"non idoneos habet auditores";* John Wickham, 1569/70, *"auditores non habet";* Robert Brooke, 1585, *"nulli solent interesse auditores";* William Redden, 1586, *"propter paucitatem auditorum";* Thomas King, 1594, *"non habet auditores";* Edmund Chaundler, 1595, *"auditores in eadem facultate non est habiturus";* and Samuel Hanmer, 1596/7, *"auditores interesse non solent."* In 1579/80, Johannes Lant, *publicus musicae praelector,* asked for release from lecturing and requested that his students be transferred to arithmetic because of the greater

---

[8] *Ibid.,* II, part 1, 97. According to Clark (*ibid.,* I, 217–18, 228), these men were bachelors of arts (all three) and masters of arts (Leche and Reve).

[9] *Ibid.,* II, part 1, 229.

[10] All instances cited are found *ibid.,* II, part 1, 100. Neglect of academic duties was by no means confined to the music lecturers, if we may believe contemporary documents. Wood, for example, quotes a letter of 1582 from the then chancellor, the Earl of Leicester, berating the university for various disorders, chiefly neglect of all duties (*History and Antiquities,* II, 212–14):

> The Q. Readers of Greek and Hebrue are plainlye said to read seldome or never. The Physick, Law, and Divinity Readers few times, and very negligently when they do read. The Lady Margaret's Lecture is read in like sort. The Schoole Lectures worse, and almost only pro forma to no purpose. The hearers at most Lectures few, at some none.

Two years later the chancellor again complained in a letter to the university (*ibid.,* II, 219), "That neither Lectures nor Disputations, nor any other kind of Exercises of Learning are almost in any tolerable sort observed." And in 1590 the new chancellor, Christopher Hatton, wrote at length about abuses in the university—looseness of dress, neglect of lecturing, failure to speak Latin, and the like (*ibid.,* II, 241ff.).

usefulness of the latter—a dispensation which was granted.[11] In 1582–83, Matthew Gwin was allowed to dispense with lecturing in music, not only because *"libri ad eam lectionem idonei difficulter inveniuntur"* but also because *"praxis ejus scientiae si non inutilis at inusitata reputatur."* And in 1599 when two students who had not attended the music lectures were summoned before the convocation, their excuse for nonattendance was unanswerable: "They said the Praelector had not lectured, as he had been dispensed from that duty."[12] William Harrison, onetime student at both Oxford and Cambridge, stated in his *Description of England (ca.* 1577) that the universities allowed "competent stipends" to those lecturing in philosophy and the arts, although the "quadrivials" were "smallie regarded" at that time.[13]

In 1596, by terms of the will of Sir Thomas Gresham, a series of lectures was established for the city of London—"divers Lectures in sundry Faculties to bee professed and publiquely red . . . namely of Divinitie, Law, Phisick, Geometrie, Astronomie, Rhetorique and Musick"; and both Oxford and Cambridge were invited to nominate candidates for the positions, with fifty pounds a year "in perpetuitie" for each professor.[14] Mr. Gifford and Mr. Newton were Oxford's candidates for the position.[15] Dr. John Bull of Cambridge, however, was appointed "upon the special recom-

[11] Clark, *Register,* II, part 1, 100:

> Supplicat Johannes Lant, publicus musicae praelector, ut a munere legendi liberetur et scholares illi qui teneantur interesse musicae lectioni ad arithmeticam transferantur. Causa est quod illius lectionis utilitas modica sit auditoribus, et ideo ex more haec dispensatio concedi solet.

[12] *Ibid.,* II, part, 1, 10.

[13] William Harrison, *Description of England in Shakespeare's Youth* (ed. by F. J. Furnivall) (London, 1877), Part I, Book 2, 78:

> Moreouer, in the publike schooles of both the vniuersities, there are found at the princes charge . . . fiue professors and readers, that is to saie, of diunitie, of the ciuill law, physicke, the Hebrue, and the Greeke toongs. And for the other lectures, as of philosophie, logike, rhetorike, and the quadriuials, although the latter (I meane arethmetike, musike, geometrie, and astronomie, and with them all skill in the perspectiues, are now smallie regarded in either of them) the vniuersities themselves doo allow competent stipends to such as reade the same.

[14] Wood, *History and Antiquities,* II, 262.

[15] *Ibid.,* II, 263: "And lastly for Music ——— Gifford, ——— of ——— and ——— Newton." I cannot find that these men were musicians.

mendation of queen Elizabeth"; and although Bull was a skillful musician,

> it seems that he was not able to read his lectures in Latin; and therefore, by a special provision in the ordinances respecting the Gresham professors, made anno 1597, it is declared, that because Dr. Bull is recommended to the place of music professor by the queen's most excellent majesty, being not able to speak Latin, his lectures are permitted to be altogether English, so long as he shall continue music professor there.[16]

A public lectureship with musical implications was founded at Oxford in 1619 when Henry Savile, *"cernens studia mathematica nostris hominibus neglecta iacere,"* established *"duas lecturas sive professiones publicas in scienciis mathematicis, vnam in geometria alteram in astronomia";* a part of the duty of the geometry lecturer was to teach and explain *"arithmetcam [sic], tam speculativam quam practicam, omnis generis, geodoesiam sive geometriam practicam, canonicam, sive musicam, et mechanicam."*[17] According to the wishes of the founder, all students were to attend these lectures from the end of their second year to the first year of their baccalaureate.[18] By the terms of the Laudian Code (1636), the Savillian Professor of Geometry was to lecture twice a week.[19]

Less than a decade after the establishment of the mathematics lectureship, William Heather founded at Oxford a professorship in music (1626) embracing both aspects of music's dichotomy traditional since medieval times: that is, the endowment specifically

[16] Sir John Hawkins, *A General History of the Science and Practice of Music* (London, 1776), III, 318–19. The erudite Hawkins continues:

> In this instance it seems that the queen's affection for Bull got the better of her judgment, for not being able to speak Latin, it may be presumed that he was unable to read it; and if so, he must have been ignorant of the very principles of the science, and consequently but very indifferently qualified to lecture on it even in English."

[17] Gibson, *Statuta*, 528–29.

[18] *Ibid.*, 530: *"omnes scholares post annum secundum completum ab aduentu ad vniuersitatem vsque ad annum primum baccalaureatus completum assignentur audiendo professori geometriae."*

[19] Griffiths, *Laudian Code*, 36.

provided for both the practice and the theory of music. Regarding the first of these, Heather's statutes, confirmed by the university in convocation, are quite definite:

Inprimis, that the exercise of Musicke bee constantly keept every weeke on Thursday in the afternoone: Afternoones in Lent excepted.

Secondly I appoint Mr Nicholson the nowe Organist of Mag: Colledge to bee the Master of the Musicke, and to take charge of the Instrumentes. . . .

Thirdlie I doe ordaine that the said Master bring with him two boyes weekely at the day and time aforesaid, and there to receaue such Company as will practise Musicke and to play Lessons of Three partes if none other come.

Lastlie I ordaine that once every yeare the Instrumentes bee viewed and the bookes: And that neyther of these bee lent abroade vppon any pretence whatsoever, nor removed out of the Schoole and place appointed.[20]

Heather's interest in the care of books and instruments was quite natural, for besides endowing the professorship he himself "gave an Harpsycon, Chest of Viols, divers Music books, both printed and written" to the music school.[21] In addition to his annuity for maintaining at Oxford "one able and fitt man, who shalbee called the Musick Master, to plaie and exercise Musick with twoe boyes in his Companie," Heather included in his endowment three pounds annually "for and towards the maintenance within the said Vniversitie of Oxon of one able and fitt man who shall lecture and read the Theorie of Musick once euery tearme or oftner."[22] The stipend was later increased by forty-five shillings, and it was decided to give the lectures in English.[23] The Laudian Code placed the Music Lecture among the public lectures, but made no

[20] Gibson, *Statuta*, 556.
[21] Wood, *History and Antiquities*, II, 887.
[22] Gibson, *Statuta*, 558.
[23] *Ibid.*, 557: "*tempore comitiorum publicorum in vniversitate hae lectiones Anglice legantur vt a peregrinis et advenis linguam Latinam non satis bene intelligentibus, quae lecta sunt, intelligantur.*" Wood's interpretation of this is a bit different, recalling Dr. Bull's ignorance of the Latin language (*History and Antiquities*, II, 359): "whereas this Lecture in the University is usually read in Lattin; at the Act time especially the Reader may ex-

requirement about attendance beyond the general requirement already noted. According to these statutes, the speech at Vesperies during Act time was to be delivered in English with interpolated instrumental music.[24]

The theoretical part of the music professorship, in fact, eventually became a part of the Music Act at commencement. Wood tells us that the first and last lecturer "for the said Theory part" was John Allibond of Magdalen, "who read it for a year or thereabouts"; afterwards, none undertook it, and "the said small sum" which went with the office was allotted "to him that should speech it at the Act time in the Musick School."[25] It is significant that Dr. Heather chose John Allibond, a *magister artium* rather than a musician, as the first lecturer in music, thus maintaining the traditional connection between mathematics and music. Subsequent speakers on music at Act time continued to be chosen from among candidates proceeding to the master's degree.[26]

One unique circumstance connected with the study of music in the English universities was the award of the baccalaureate and doctorate in music by Oxford and Cambridge, traditional, apparently, since the fifteenth century. Admission to the bachelor of music degree gave the candidate the right to lecture in "any of the Musical Books of *Boethius*,"[27] probably because of the place of Boethius in the statute books and the fact that graduates in music should be qualified to lecture on this authoritative work. Although the earliest record of the granting of such an award comes from 1502, when Henry Parker, "eminent in these times for his Compo-

pound the principall points of this Lecture in English, because divers skilful Musitians are not so well acquainted with the Lattin Tongue as University men."

24 Griffiths, *Laudian Code,* 36.

Praelector Musicae, a Gulielmo Heyther Musices Doctore institutus, semel vel saepius quolibet anni Termino, in Schola Musica, illius Artis Theoriam, inter horas octavam et nonam antemeridianas, legat. In Vesperiis autem Comitiorum quotannis, inter horas nonam et decimam antemeridianas, (interposita musicorum instrumentorum modulatione,) vernacula lingua solennem etiam ibidem habeat lectionem.

25 Wood, *History and Antiquities,* II, 358.

26 Williams, *Degrees in Music,* 30–31.

27 Anthony à Wood, *Fasti* in the *Athenae Oxonienses* (London, 1691), I, 639.

sitions in Vocal and Instrumental Musick," was made bachelor of music, Oxford probably awarded the degree before that time, for in 1502 Robert Wydow was incorporated at Cambridge as a bachelor of music from Oxford, where he must have taken his degree sometime earlier.[28] There is no indication that candidates for the music degree had to be first a bachelor of arts, although some candidates held the latter degree—for instance, Robert Porret.[29] Throughout the sixteenth century some were admitted to the degree unconditionally, most of them described by Wood as already eminent in the musical profession, and others supplicated for the degree, but it is not known whether or not they obtained it. Wood tells us that the records around 1550 are very imperfect, and he complains of the neglect of the public register by the scribe "who was afterwards deservedly turn'd out of his place."[30]

Supplications for the musical degree generally emphasize the traditional dichotomy with regard to musical studies by requiring the composition of polyphonic music as well as a certain length of time to be spent in learning the theory of music. The first known instance of the award of the baccalaureate in music upon the fulfillment of certain conditions dates from February 16, 1506/7, when the supplication of Richard Ede, *"canonicus regularis et scolaris musice,"* who had spent ten years studying music *extra universitatem,* was passed on condition that he compose a Mass and antiphon to be sung on the day of admission to the degree.[31] John Charde, 1518/9, having studied music for sixteen years, was re-

---

[28] *Ibid.;* and see, for the incorporation, *Grace Book* Γ (ed. by William George Searle) (Cambridge, 1908), 8.

[29] C. W. Boase and Andrew Clark (eds.), *Register of the University of Oxford* (Oxford, 1885–89), I, 60, 98.

[30] *Fasti,* I, 704. For a convenient listing of all Oxford graduates in music with biographical data about each, see Williams, *Degrees in Music,* 64ff. (the list is compiled largely from Wood's *Fasti*).

[31] Gibson, *Statuta, xciii:*

Eodem die supplicat Dominus Ricardus Ede, canonicus regularis et scolaris musice, quatenus studium 10 annorum extra vniuersitatem in musica sibi sufficiat ut admittatur ad lecturam alicuius libri musices Boecii, non obstante quocunque statuto in oppositum. Hic est concessa, conditionata quod componat missam vnam cum antiphona ante diem admissionis que eodem die admissionis sue solenniter cantetur.

quired to compose a five-part Mass for his bachelor's degree, the first requirement in so many parts.[32] Robert Stephenson (1587), however, holds the record for length of time spent in the study of music prior to attaining the baccalaureate—thirty-three years; he was admitted to the bachelor of arts degree at the same time.[33]

Many of the Oxford bachelors of music in the sixteenth and early seventeenth century held, either at the time of the baccalaureate or later, important posts as organists: for example, Nathaniel Giles (1585) was organist of St. George's Chapel, Windsor, and later at the Chapel Royal; John Bull (1586), at Hereford Cathedral in 1582 and at the Chapel Royal in 1591; John Munday (1586), Merbecke's successor at Windsor in 1585; George Waterhouse (1592), at Lincoln's Cathedral; Edward Gibbons (1592), at Bristol Cathedral; Arthur Cocke (1593), at Exeter Cathedral; Thomas Weelkes (1602), at Winchester College; and others later in the seventeenth century. Further, at Oxford the "first Professor of the Musical Praxis was Richard Nicholson, Bachelaur of Music, and Organist of Magdalen College"; and apparently Nicholson was Master of the Music until his death, because his successor, Arthur Philipps, Wood tells us, was "elected on the death of Mr. Nicholson Nov. 18, an. 1639, and the next year Jul. 9, was admitted Bachelaur of Music."[34] Wood tells us that Mr. Heather, founder of the Music Lecture, was organist of the Chapel Royal. In addition to these organists—most of them composers as well—many other men responsible for the great flowering of music in Renaissance England held the Oxford bachelor's degree in music: Thomas Morley (1588), John Dowland (1588), Giles Farnaby (1592), Francis Pilkington (1595), Robert Jones (1597), Thomas Tomkins (1607), and Richard Deering (1612).

The first record of an Oxford doctorate in music comes from 1511 when Robert Fairfax was incorporated doctor of music from Cambridge.[35] A few years later (1515),

---

[32] Williams, *Degrees in Music*, 67.

[33] Wood, *Fasti*, I, 758.

[34] *History and Antiquities*, II, 893.

[35] Wood, *Fasti*, I, 652. For the facts of Fairfax' life, together with a catalogue and

Robert Perrot Bach. of Musick, and about this time Organist of *Magd.* College, supplicated that he might be licensed to proceed in the said Faculty. —His request was granted conditionally that he compose a Mass and one Song, before he really proceed, or stand in the *Comitia.* . . . .This *Robert Perrot* . . . was an eminent Musitian of his time, and did compose several Church Services and other Matters, which have been since antiquated.[36]

Before the end of the century, four others had become inceptors or doctors of music—John Gwyneth (1531), John Merbecke (1550), John Shepeard (1554), and Robert Stevenson (1596); and in the early years of the next century, three others received the coveted Oxford doctorate: Orlando Gibbons and Nathaniel Giles (1622) and John Munday (1624). Of these, Giles, Munday, and Stevenson had previously been made bachelors of music at Oxford, whereas Robert Porret (as his name usually appears) and Orlando Gibbons had received the bachelor's degree at Cambridge. In addition to Robert Fairfax, Christopher Tye (1548) and John Bull (1592) were incorporated at Oxford as doctors of music from Cambridge, both having previously graduated bachelor of music, Tye at Cambridge (1536) and Bull at Oxford (1586).

William Heather, who later founded the Music Lectureship, was the first to accumulate both degrees—bachelor and doctor—at one time (1622). Heather was a professional musician and a Gentleman of the Chapel Royal, and it is probable that these degrees (honorary) were awarded him because of his activities with William Camden in founding the History Lectureship.[37] Heather's commencement composition is said to have been written by Orlando Gibbons, possibly the anthem, "O clap your hands"; and according to a reliable source, Gibbons' doctorate was also honorary to accompany Dr. Heather.[38] In 1629, Mathew White accumulated

---

description of his works, see Dom Anselm Hughes, "An Introduction to Fayrfax," *"Musica Disciplina,* Vol. VI (1952), 83–104.

[36] Wood, *Fasti,* I, 656.

[37] See the letter from Piers to Camden: Hawkins, *History of Music,* IV, 31n.

[38] Wood, *Fasti,* I, 842: "However the Song of 6 parts or more, which was performed in the *Act.* for *Will. Heather,* was composed by him [Orlando Gibbons], as one or more

the two degrees, having been organist at Christ Church, Oxford, and a Gentleman of the Chapel Royal.

It is significant for the scholarly background of English musicians that several men who followed musical careers studied the arts or one of the higher faculties at Oxford without taking a degree in music, especially in the early part of the sixteenth century. One of these was the composer Hugh Ashton, bachelor and master of arts, 1505 and 1507, bachelor of canon law (Cambridge), 1507, and possibly a supplicant for the bachelor of music degree at Oxford in 1510.[39] Ashton, whose "Hornpipe" is perhaps his best known piece, is especially important in the history of instrumental music for the invention of a florid type of keyboard music particularly suited to the instrument for which it was written (as opposed to the transference of vocal music to a keyboard instrument)—an innovation which laid the foundation for the brilliant fantasias and variations of Byrd, Bull, and others later in the century. Thomas Tallis, whose motets, *Service,* and other sacred works are among the century's best cathedral music, is probably identical with the "Thomas Talley" who attained the baccalaureate in arts in 1528 and the *magisterium* in 1531.[40] Richard Edwards, talented Master of the Children of the Chapel Royal from 1563, especially gifted in the writing of plays for performance at court and elsewhere, proceeded to the master of arts degree at Oxford in 1547.[41]

During the Renaissance the taking of a university degree continued to involve elaborate and expensive ceremonies as in medieval times. Statutes of 1601/2 contain a list of fees imposed upon candidates for graduation, and many items refer to musical degrees, placed quite definitely with degrees in the three usual higher faculties. The bachelor of music, for instance, paid the same fee for his grace (twelve pence) as the bachelor of theology, law,

eminent Musitians then living have several times told me." According to Piers' letter to Camden (Hawkins, *History of Music,* IV, 31n.), "We have made Mr. Heather a doctor in music; so that now he is no more Master, but Doctor Heather; the like honour for your sake we have conferred upon Mr. Orlando Gibbons, and made him a doctor too, to accompany Dr. Heather."

[39] Joseph Foster, *Alumni Oxonienses, 1500–1714* (Oxford and London, 1892), I, 39.
[40] *Ibid.,* IV, 1455.
[41] Wood, *Athenae Oxonienses,* I, 118.

or medicine.[42] And "Fees to be payde vnto the Beedle of Divinitye by the Esquyer Beedle of Artes" include specified amounts from doctors and bachelors of music as well as candidates in this faculty incorporating from another university.[43] In addition, each *baccalaureus in musica* owed certain amounts for various commencement requirements and to various university officials, the largest item being *pro vino, "Si beneficiatus vel patrimoniatus fuerit."*[44] The same set of fees owed by the *doctor in musica* were much greater; in addition to these he had to give a banquet for the vice-chancellor, *regius professor,* proctors, registrar, and beadles of his faculty, and he was required to present gloves or the sum of three shillings to the beadles.[45] Fees for the *baccalaureus in musica in-*

[42] Gibson, *Statuta,* 459: "*Pro gracia bacchalaureorum in sacra theologia, iurisprudentia, medicina, et musica pro quolibet eorum xij^d.*"

[43] *Ibid.,* 467:

Item, he is to receve of everie Docter of musicke ij^s yf he be a compounder xvij^s iiij^d.
Item, he is to receve of everie Bachelor of musicke iij^d yf he b[e] a compounder viij^s x^d.
Item, of everie Docter of Musicke incorporated xij^d.
Item of everie Batchelor of Musicke incorporated iij^d.

[44] *Ibid.,* 475: *Baccalaureus in musica solvet:*

Inprimis pro cumulatione presentantis	vj^s viij^d.
Pro communiis	vj^d.
Pro scriba vniversitatis	xij^d.
Pro circuitu	xij^d.
Pro camera	iiij^d.
Pro cumulatione sex annorum	ij^s.
Pro anno instante	xij^d.
Pro horologio	ij^d.
Pro clerico vniversitatis	ij^d.
Pro inferiore bedello artium	vj^d.
Summa	xiij^s iiij^d.
Si beneficiatus vel patrimoniatus fuerit solvet pro vino	vij^s iiij^d.
Si non praebeat convivia solvet bedellis facultatis suae pro prandio	ix^d.

[45] *Ibid.,* 475–76: *Doctor in musica solvet:*

Inprimis pro cumulatione presentantis	vj^s viij^d.
Pro communiis	xij^d.
Pro cumulatione sex annorum	vj^s viij^d.
Pro scriba	xviij^d.
Pro anno instante	vj^s viij^d.
Pro circuitu	ij^s.
Pro vino	vij^s iiij^d.

corporandus and *doctor in musica incorporandus* are similar to those in these same lists.[46] We know, however, that occasionally a musical candidate was allowed a dispensation from some part of the expense of the commencement exercises: in 1595 Francis Pilkington, graduating bachelor of music, was dispensed *pro circuitu*.[47]

The Laudian Statutes of 1636 are equally exact with regard to other aspects of the musical degrees. According to this code, a candidate for the baccalaureate in music had to swear that he had spent seven years in the study and practice of music, and had to compose and produce a five-part composition.[48] And to become an inceptor or doctor of music, the candidate must have spent five years in the study or practice of music after the baccalaureate and had to present a composition in six or eight parts.[49] The Laudian

Pro scribo regii professoris	iiij[d].
Pro clerico vniversitatis	iiij[d].
Pro actu	xxv[s].
Pro presentacione	v[s].
Summa	iij[l] ij[s] vj[d].

Faciet convivia pro domino vicecancellario, regio professore, magistris procuratoribus, registrario et bedellis facultatis suae; dabit bedellis suae facultatis chirothecas vel tres solidos.

[46] *Ibid.*, 479.

[47] Clark, *Register*, II, part 1, 46. The *circuitus*, according to Clark (p. 42), "consisted in asking the Vice-Chancellor and proctors to summon a Congregation in which the student might be admitted to his degree." And on the afternoon before this Congregation, "the student (preceded by one or both of the bedells of his faculty and accompanied by the person who was to present him in Congregation), attired in his academical dress but *bareheaded*, went round the Schools" and also called on the Vice-Chancellor and both proctors.

[48] Griffiths, *Laudian Code*, 59:

Statutum est, quod qui Musicae dat operam, antequam Gradum Baccalaurei in illa Facultate consequatur, septem annos in studio vel praxi Musices ponat, et id ipsum sub Chirographis hominum fide dignorum testatum afferat.

Statutum est, quod qui ad Baccalaureatum in Musica promoveri cupit, priusquam pro Gratia sua supplicet, unum Canticum quinque Partium componat, quod in Schola Musicae . . . publice, tam vocibus quam instrumentis Musicis, exhibeat.

[49] *Ibid.*, 59–60:

Statutum est, quod Baccalaureus Musicae, priusquam ad Doctoratum promoveatur, quinque Annos, post susceptum Gradum, in studio vel praxi Musices ponat; et id ipsum sub Chirographis hominum fide dignorum testatum afferat.

Statutum est, quod Baccalaureus Musicae, priusquam ad Incipiendum in eadem Facultate admittatur, unum Canticum sex vel octo Partium componat, quod in Schola Musicae, tam vocibus quam instrumentis etiam Musicis . . . publice exhibeat.

Code also gives the form by which a grace might be requested, passage of which continued to allow the bachelor *"ad Lectionem cuiuslibet libri Boethii"* and the doctor *"ad Incipiendum in eadem Facultate."*[50] When the bachelor was ready for inception, his grace was to be proposed by the Heather lecturer; and when the grace was granted, he was to be presented for the degree by one of the Savillian professors or by their deputy, a master of arts.[51] At the Act, the candidate's composition was to be performed. And the candidate was to be created doctor by one of the Savillian professors if one of them were a doctor; if not, one of them might assume doctoral dress for the occasion.[52]

In addition to the strictly formal and academic aspects, all completely regularized by the seventeenth century, musical pre-

[50] *Ibid.*, 96:

Pro Gradu Baccalaurei in Musica.

Supplicat &c. A. B. Scolaris in Musica e Coll. L. quatenus 7 annos in studio vel praxi Musices posuerit, et unum Canticum 5 Partium in Schola Musices ediderit; et reliqua praestiterit quae per Statuta requiruntur (nisi quatenus cum eo dispensatum fuerit); ut haec sibi sufficiant, quo admittatur ad Lectionem cuiuslibet libri Boethii.

Pro Gradu Inceptoris in Musica.

Supplicat &c. A. B. Baccalaureus Musicae, quatenus, a tempore suscepti Gradus Baccalaureatus sui, 5 annos in studio vel praxi Musices posuerit; unum Canticum 6 vel 8 Partium in Schola Musices ediderit; et caetera praestiterit omnia quae per Statuta requiruntur (nisi quatenus cum eo dispensatum fuerit); ut haec sibi sufficiant, quo admittatur ad Incipiendum in eadem Facultate.

[51] *Ibid.*, 60:

Quibus Exercitiis per eundem praestitis, per publicum eiusdem Facultatis Praelectorem Heytherianum, aut alium quemvis per eundem assignatum, Gratis ipsius in Venerabili Domo Congregationis proponatur; qua concessa, per alterutrum Professorum Savil. (qui ad hoc alternis praestandum tenentur), vel per alium quemvis in Artibus Magistrum ab iis deputatum, ad Gradum praesentetur.

[52] *Ibid.*, 73:

Post Exercitia Artistarum in Comitiis finita, si quis sit qui in Musica Gradum suscipiet, eius erit unam vel alteram Cantilenam sex vel octo Partium, una cum Vocum et Instrumentorum musicorum harmonia, exhibere; Qua finita, a Savilianus Professoribus Creationis suae Solennia recipiet; qui hoc alternis praestare tenentur, sive uterque Doctor in aliqua Facultate fuerit, sive neuter; sed tunc impetrata prius venia a Domo Congregationis, ut liceat sibi ad tempus Habitum Doctoralem assumere; Quod si alter solummodo Professorum Doctor fuerit, ei soli Creandi munus incumbit.

occupations of the various colleges in the university add to our understanding of musical studies at Oxford. As in medieval Oxford, statutes of some colleges during the Renaissance show a great emphasis upon musical activities, especially Masses for the souls of the founders. A document of November 20, 1504, describes in great detail how an annual celebration "be holden and kept" for the "good and prosperous estate of the said kyng oure soverayne duryng his lif," for the souls of his wife, children, father, mother, "and all Christen soules." Decreeing that "the Chaunceler, maisters and scolers graduat . . . with the hoole congregacion of regentes and non regentes of the said vniuersite, shall in the evyn next before the day of euery suche anniuersarie solempnely with note syng Placebo and Dirige with nyne lessons and laudes," this document gives details of procedure. Further, it declares, the requiem Mass is to be "songen or saied" at each anniversary, and the bells of the uni versity are to be "solempnely rongen."[53] In 1535/6, as a memorial to the establishment by Parliament of "Kyng Henry the eight his lecture" at Oxford, it was decreed that two Masses annually "be there solempnelye songe," one "of the Holye Trynyte" and the other "of tholye Gooste," with a requiem Mass after the king's decease.[54] Although the custom of singing perpetual Masses for the souls of founders and benefactors disappeared with the Reformation,[55] many of the colleges maintained choir schools throughout the century. Choristers supported by these foundations received a thorough grounding in *cantus planus* and in prick song, and later these youths were preferred when vacancies occurred in the university scholarship lists. Wood tells us that "one John Atkins who became Fellow of Merton College an. 1467 is stiled in the Album of the Fellows of that House 'Nobilis Musicus,' having been accounted in his time very famous for that Faculty, and especially for the public Exercises he performed therein in the University."[56]

[53] Gibson, *Statuta*, 310–20.
[54] *Ibid.*, 338.
[55] *Ibid.*, 385 statutes of 1564/5: "*Illa statuta, quae pertinent ad missas, exequias, processiones, precationes pro mortuis, prorsus abscindimus et amputamus, nec amplius robur aliquod aut momentum habere volumus.*"
[56] *History and Antiquities*, II, 722.

Statutes given to Magdalen College (1479) by the founder, William Waynflete, Bishop of Winchester, provided for four priests, eight chaplains, and sixteen choristers to celebrate divine service, the priests and clerics to be *"in cantu et in lectura sufficienter aut saltem competenter instructi."*[57] One of these was to be appointed *cantor* by the president, a man *"in cantu eruditus ad instruendum choristas in plano cantu et in alio cantu";* but the president might call in an outsider if no one so qualified could be found in the college.[58] Magdalen was also to include among its members thirty indigent students called *Demyes "in lectura et plano cantu competenter instructi."*[59] Magdalen's choir school, indeed, has an especially honorable history in the production of distinguished musicians. Of those who received degrees in music at Oxford during our period, Nathaniel Giles and Thomas Tomkins were trained as choristers in the Magdalen chapel, and John Mason, Robert Porret, and John Shepherd held the position of *instructor choristarum* in this college.[60] Years later (1579), Simon Perot (alias Parret) left money to be distributed among Magdalen's fellows at the annual commencement, five shillings fourpence to the choristers and one shilling fourpence "to be given to the Organist or Master of the said Choristers, because Robert Perot, alias Parret, father of the said Simon, did sometime undergo that office."[61]

Statutes drawn up by Richard Fox, founder of Corpus Christi College (1517), provided for four ministers in the chapel, one of them to be *chori praecentor* and to have charge of all matters *"quae ad Praecentoris officium attinent."*[62] There were also to be two choristers trained in music, studying grammar and *bonos auctores* either at Corpus Christi or at Magdalen.[63]

[57] *Statutes of the Colleges of Oxford* (Oxford, 1853–55), II, 23.
[58] *Ibid.*, II, 24: *"si autem nullus capellanorum praedictorum aut clericorum voluerit praedictam super se assumere, tunc Praesidens alium extraneum ad hujusmodi informationem aptum et idoneum praedicto modo conducat."*
[59] *Ibid.*, II, 15.
[60] For information about these and other Oxford musicians, see Williams, *Degrees in Music, passim.*
[61] Wood, *History and Antiquities*, III, 314.
[62] *Oxford College Statutes*, II, 37.

Cardinal Wolsey's elaborate foundation, Cardinal College (1525: statutes revised by Wolsey in 1527), had among its membership sixty senior and forty petty canons, the former *"in plano cantu competenter eruditi";* other musical members included thirteen priests and twelve clerics, as well as sixteen choirboys with their instructor.[64] These *chorustae,* chosen for their musical talents, were to become minor canons when their voices changed.[65] Wood, in fact, credits Wolsey with having inspired new interest in music: "at the coming of the noble generous Wolsey . . . Musick flourished, and Degrees were also oftner taken in it than before."[66] But the prelate's lavish establishment lasted only five years (until 1530): "for when the Cardinall, by the Law of Praemunire, fell into the King's danger, his Colledge alsoe fell with him, as beeing loose, and not by Law setled and established."[67] Cardinal College was superseded by Henry VIII's College, 1532 (afterwards Christ Church), a strictly ecclesiastical foundation which had on its staff a vicar to be *precentor* in charge of all the singing; and another vicar, *"in grammatica et cantu tradendo doctior"* than the rest, was to be the choristers' instructor.[68] Foundation statutes required of the members of the college a knowledge of instruments as well as plain song: no one was to be admitted as vicar, clerk, or chorister

[63] *Ibid.,* II, 38: "*Duo vero choristae, quos volumus per Praesidentem nominari et assumi, erunt in omni genere cantus, ad minus plano et intorto (pricked appellant) edocti antequam assumantur, ut ita statim aut in Collegio, impensis amicorum, aut ludo Magdalenensi, grammaticam discant et bonos auctores.*"

[64] *Ibid.,* II, 13, 20: "*tredecim presbyteri conductitii, et duodecim alii clerici conductitii, omnes musices periti, necnon sexdecim pueri chorustae, et unus aliquis musices peritissimus qui eosdem instruat et musicam artem commode doceat.*"

[65] *Ibid.,* II, 49:

Statuimus . . . nec ullos pueros in chorustas assumant nisi quos et voce et ingenii indole morumque, maxime aptos idoneosque ad artem musicam putaverint; utque dictis chorustis hujusmodi de tali informatore provideant, qui artis musices peritus fuerit, et eos artem musicam diligenter docere et velit et possit.

And p. 51: "qui si bene se gesserint et, permutata voce, grammaticis literis sic fuerint provecti ut idonei videantur qui in secundi ordinis canonicos assumantur, volumus ut caeteris omnibus praeferantur."

[66] *History and Antiquities,* II, 79.
[67] Leonard Hutten (1557?–1632), "Antiquities of Oxford," in *Elizabethan Oxford: Reprints of Rare Tracts* (ed. by Charles Plummer) (Oxford, 1887), 59.
[68] *Oxford College Statutes,* II, 192–94.

"nisi modulandi competens habeat instrumentum et cantus scientiam competentem"[69]—possibly a reflection of the king's own well-known musical interests and talents.

St. John's College, too, founded in 1555 by Sir Thomas White, provided for scholars and clerics *"in cantu saltem plano competenter instructi,"* one of them to act as *precentor,* and for six choristers.[70] As in other foundations, the choristers here were to be instructed in both plain song and prick song, and they were to remain in the college until their voices changed.[71] They were also to be preferred for scholarships in the college when vacancies occurred, *"si bene se gerant."*[72]

We have many more records of organists maintained by various Oxford colleges during the Renaissance than in the Middle Ages. For example, Cardinal Wolsey specifically ordained that one of the twelve *clerici* in his college be *"scitum et peritum organorum pulsatorem."*[73] Nor was this an empty wish: the cardinal actually chose a man truly *scitum et peritum* when he made John Taverner organist of his college. Moreover, when "John Taverner the Organist" was accused of participating in a Lutheran controversy at Oxford in 1528, "the Cardinal pleaded for him, saying that he was but a Musitian, and thought that no great harm might be done by him."[74] St. John's statutes, too, called for various ministers, one of whom was to be *organorum pulsator;* John Frith held this position at St. John's when he became bachelor of music in 1626.[75] Trinity College, in 1556, ruled that one scholar *ludendi organis peritus* be admitted *("ne quando dictum Collegium organorum pulsatore sit destitutum")* to play the organ *"diebus festis aliasque in officiis*

[69] *Ibid.,* II, 193.

[70] *Ibid.,* III, 27, 41.

[71] *Ibid.,* III, 42: *"Erunt omnes et singuli omni genere cantus, ad minus plano et intorto, pricked appellant, edocti, antequam assumantur, ut ita statim grammaticam discant et bonos auctores: quos permittimus in collegio permanere usque ad primam vocis permutationem."*

[72] *Ibid.*

[73] *Ibid.,* II, "Cardinal College," 51.

[74] Wood, *History and Antiquities,* II, 31.

[75] *Oxford College Statutes,* III, "St. John's College," 41, and Williams, *Degrees in Music,* 79.

divinis, more in ecclesiis consueto."[76] And we know that All Souls had an organist as early as 1458, for a document of that year tells how the All Souls organist was convicted of adultery, spent three hours in jail, and was freed when the warden of the college spoke a good word for him.[77] William Stonard was organist of Christ Church when he graduated bachelor of music, 1608; and he appears to have been university organist later, for a document of 1624, *"De organista et eius stipendio,"* mentions a *magister* Stonard as holding that position.[78] Mathew White, who accumulated the baccalaureate and doctorate in music in 1629, was organist of Christ Church from 1611 until 1613.[79] Robert Porret, we recall, was organist of Magdalen College when he took the doctorate of music degree in 1515, and Richard Nicholson held this position when he was appointed Heather Lecturer in Music, 1626.

Music instruction was thus given to a large corps of junior members of the university—and undoubtedly to others who availed themselves of it privately—by musicians who held positions as organist and choirmaster in the colleges; and occasionally other members of the university also taught music privately. Richard Edwards, for instance, admitted to Corpus Christi in 1540 under the tutelage of George Etheridge, professor of Greek at Oxford, is said to have studied music with Etheridge, "a noted Mathematician, well skill'd in vocal and instrumental Musick, an eminent He-

[76] *Oxford College Statutes,* IV, "Trinity College," 26.

[77] Henry Anstey, *Munimenta academica* (London, 1868), II, 674–75:

Thomas Bentlee, *alias* Deneley, *"organpleyer"* de Collegio Animarum, convictus est publice et in judicio confessus, quod erat solus cum sola in camera cum uxore Johannis Gwasmere . . . igitur Magister . . . Keele, custos Collegii Animarum, bonam spem habens quod dictus Thomas bene se gereret in futurum, fidejussit pro eodem; dictus igitur Thomas per tres horas incarceratus liberatur.

[78] Wood, *Fasti,* I, 801, and Gibson, *Statuta,* 555:

Delegati . . . organistam voluerunt magistrum Stonard, et huic stipendium decem librarum legalis monetae Anglie allocarunt. . . . Huius erit in initio cuiusque termini in academia, cum preces publicae habeantur, cum dictis instrumentis divinis officiis inservire, necnon diebus Dominicis et festivis ante et post conciones habitas.

[79] Williams, *Degrees in Music,* 80.

brician, Grecian, and Poet, and above all an excellent Physician."[80] And Lord Edward Herbert, writing in 1598/9, says of his life at Oxford:

> During this time of living in the University . . . I attained also to sing my part at first sight in music, and to play on the lute with very little or almost no teaching . . . and my learning of music was for this end, that I might entertain myself at home, and together refresh my mind after my studies, to which I was exceedingly inclined, and that I might not need the company of young men, in whom I obserbed [*sic*] in those times much ill example and debauchery.[81]

There are numerous indications that other Oxford students besides Lord Herbert cultivated music for its recreational powers— first of all, prohibitions of one kind or another. Statutes of Corpus Christi (1517) legislated against dancing, singing, and playing musical instruments at times of study or sleep; and Brasenose statutes (1521) similarly prohibited noises—song and musical instruments included—which might impede study or sleep.[82] A unique item in All Souls' Ordinances of the Royal Visitors (1549) allowed *rusticam musicam* as a warning that the town was on fire,[83] *rustica musica* being about as euphonious as Bottom's well-known tongs and bones.

Such prohibitions imply that it was not unusual for Oxford students to own and play musical instruments, and other documents confirm this fact. Oxford had its own harp maker (that is,

[80] Wood, *Athenae Oxonienses*, I, 117, 191.

[81] Lord Edward Herbert of Cherbury, *Autobiography* (ed. by Sidney Lee) (London and New York, 1906), 23.

[82] *Oxford College Statutes*, II, "Corpus Christi College," 80: "*Statuimus . . . ut . . . nullum quovis tempore a somno quiete aut studio impediat per immoderatos clamores, risus, cantica, strepitus saltationes, musicorum instrumentorum pulsationes.*" And *ibid.*, II, "Brasenose College," 27: "*Nec etiam cantu, clamore, vociferatione, instrumento musico, aut quovis genere tumultus, Socium aut scholarem quemcunque dicti Collegii, quo minus studere aut dormire valeat, quoquo modo impediat.*"

[83] *Ibid.*, I, "All Soul's College," 88: "*Rusticam vero musicam illam, ac velut conviciantium aut insanientium inter se voces, non ferimus, nisi tum cum flamma aut incendia urbi excidium minantur.*"

one who made stringed instruments), for Robert "Harpemaker" figures in certain records of 1452: Robert promises that *"non vexabit Magistrum Johannem Van, nec aliquem alium servientem Universitatis occasione incarcerationis suae"*; and *"idem Robertus Harper"* is warned against going to the home of Joan Fytz-John at unseasonable times.[84] Apparently the harpmaker did not heed the warnings, for records dated a few weeks later remind us of the unfortunate All Souls organist, saying that "Robertus Smyth, *alias* Harpmaker, *de 'Candich,' suspectus de adulterio commisso cum Johanna Fytz-John, tapsetricem . . . abjuravit societatem ejusdem Johannae."*[85] An inventory of the goods of Sir John Lydbery (1462) includes *"Item, a lewt, pretium vj^d,"* and the inventory of the goods of John Hosear (1463) contains *"Item, an harpe, iv^d"*[86]—both records showing that musical instruments were considered valuable enough to merit formal appraisal. In 1486 there was an organ maker named Edward Wotton active in Oxford, for Wood tells us that an Oxford priest involved in a treasonable plot to restore the House of York to the throne confessed "that he by flattery had seduced the son of a certain Organ Maker of the University of Oxford, and had caused him to be sent into Ireland. . . . And who that should be but one Edward Wotton I cannot tell, knowing very well from various obscure Scripts, that such an one and nobody else professed that art at this time in Oxford."[87] In 1595 a committee to investigate carriers *(de tabellariis)* decided that carriers might charge for transporting goods between Oxford and London the same "for lutes and virginalls as in former years"[88]— indicating that the importation of these instruments from London was quite customary.

One important aspect of the cultivation of music at Oxford was its use in plays presented in various colleges, plays which not only employed collegiate choristers but were often embellished by music composed for the occasion by members of the university. Mag-

[84] Anstey, *Munimenta academica,* II, 626–27.
[85] *Ibid.,* II, 633.
[86] *Ibid.,* II, 698, 705.
[87] Wood, *History and Antiquities,* I, 643.
[88] Clark, *Register,* II, part 1, 319.

dalen College, perennially distinguished for its musical contributions, appears to have been especially active in producing these entertainments, and several records of payments to choristers and musicians who helped in the production of liturgical drama in the late fifteenth and sixteenth centuries are significant of the importance of music in these performances.[89] An item from 1509/10 notes the payment in food and other things to boys who performed in an Easter play *("Sol. pane, cibo et aliis datis pueris ludentibus in die Paschae")*; in 1512/3 payments were made *"Petro Pyper pro pypyng in interludio nocte Sancti Iohannis"* and *"Iohanni Tabourner pro lusione in interludio Octavis Epiphanie"*—probably the same John Taverner who became organist of Cardinal College in 1525; and in 1538 payments were recorded for fuel consumed *"in sacrario, per custodes sepulchri, et per pueros in festis hiemalibus."* Payments were made in 1518/9 "To Perrot, the Master of the choristers," for dyeing a robe to be worn by the actor who played the part of Christ, and for wigs to adorn the women, showing the multifold duties which went with the office held by Porret.[90]

Of university men who furnished music for academic drama, John Burgess, B.A., was paid five shillings for music to embellish a miracle play on Mary Magdalene and eightpence was given a man who brought some songs from Edward Martyn, M.A. Especially interesting for our study is the record of the performance at Oxford *(ca.* 1540) of a play by Nicolas Grimald, *De puerorum in musicis institutione,* unfortunately no longer extant, which, in spite of its Latin title, was one of the first academic plays written in English.[91] Richard Edwards, in his plays performed at Christ Church *(Palamon and Arcyte,* 1566, and *Damon and Pythias,* 1567/8), was perhaps the first playwright to use music dramatically, to heighten tragic climaxes with music.[92] William Gager also

[89] Cited by Frederick S. Boas, *University Drama in the Tudor Age* (Oxford, 1914), 3. See also Nan Cooke Carpenter, "Musicians in Early University Drama," *Notes and Queries,* Vol. CXCV (1950), 470–72

[90] "To Perrot, the Master of the choristers, *pro tinctura et facture tunice ejus qui ageret partem Christi, et pro crinibus mulieribus."*

[91] Boas, *University Drama,* 32. Alfred Harbage, *Annals of English Drama* (Philadelphia, 1940), 30, gives 1547 as the date of this play.

introduced music in his plays produced at Christ Church later in the century—*Dido,* 1583, and *Ulysses redux,* 1591/2; in fact, the part of the minstrel Phemius in 'the latter play was taken by "the Master of owre Choristers."[93] Gager, unlike Edwards, apparently did not compose his own music.

Edwards' *Palamon and Arcyte* received far more attention than its author could ever have anticipated, for it was performed in two parts before Queen Elizabeth on the occasion of a royal progress to Oxford in 1566, during the first night of which a well and stairway collapsed, killing three men. In accounts of the queen's visit, there are descriptions of other musical activities in honor of her majesty. When the queen arrived in town, psalms were sung to the accompaniment of various musical instruments in the chapel.[94] Later on, "with a canopy over her, carryed by four Senior Doctors, she entred into the church, and there abode while the quyer sang and play'd with cornetts, *Te Deum.*"[95] When the queen saw Oxford for the second and last time some decades later (1592), Matthew Gwin, *praelector* in music in 1582, took part in a disputation before the royal party; and on the seventh day of the queen's visit, "There was also . . . a Lecture in Musick, with the practice thereof by instrument, in the Common Schooles."[96] We recall, too, that during this visit ordinary lectures in the arts and philosophy were read as usual, with Mr. Pelling lecturing in music. During this visit, moreover, Henry Saville—later founder of the professorship in mathematics made an oration before Elizabeth, praising music as one of the "leisurely arts"—"*otia liberalia (ut*

[92] G. E. P. Arkwright, "Elizabethan Choirboy Plays and their Music," *Proceedings of the Musical Association,* Vol. XL (1914), 127–28.

[93] Boas, *University Drama,* 186n., 215–16, 236.

[94] Nicholas Robinson, "Of the Actes Done at Oxford When the Queen's Majesty Was There," in Plummer, *Elizabethan Oxford Reprints,* 178: "*Ad preces recta in Sacellum quam primum itur, variis musicis instrumentis Psalmi canuntur, et oratione Latine absolvuntur per Decanum.*"

[95] Richard Stephens, "A Brief Rehearsall of all such Things as were done in the University of Oxford During the Queen Majesty's Abode There," *ibid.,* 199.

[96] Philip Stringer, "The Grand Reception and Entertainment of Queen Elizabeth at Oxford at 1592," *ibid.,* 252, 259.

gymnastica), musica, & haec ipsa mater artium Philosophia"—
which flourish in time of peace.[97]

During the third year of his reign (1605), James and his court
visited the university, where as part of their reception they heard
a service "mixt with instrumental and vocal musick" in the cathedral church; on the third day of this visit "they went to New
College, where they were entertained with a royal feast and incom-
parable musick."[98] At times the town waits (instrumentalists) lent
their music to university ceremonies—for instance in 1583, when
a "noble and learned Polonian named Albertus Alaskie or Laskie"
paid a visit to Oxford, he was met by Oxford officials, welcomed
with a Latin oration, and presented with gloves, "which being
done a consort of musicians, that stood over the East Gate, played
on their wind-music till they were gone into the City."[99] In 1613,
just after the death of Sir Thomas Bodley, the cornerstone was laid
for a new quadrangle, of which the west end was to be the Bodleian Library: "There was Music with voices," Wood tells us, "and
other instruments."[100] Wood's description of the laying of the cornerstone for the new library (1634) not only shows the dependence
of academic ceremonies upon music but also points out the occasional dangers of university life:

> On the thirteenth of May, being Tuesday, 1634, the Vice-
> chancellor, Doctors, Heads of Houses and Proctors, met at St.
> Mary's Church about 8 of the clock in the morning; from thence
> each having his respective formalities on, came to this place, and
> took their seats that were then erected on the brim of the foun-
> dation. Over against them was built a scaffold where the two
> Proctors with divers Masters stood. After they were all settled,
> the University Musicians who stood upon the leads at the west
> end of the Library sounded a lesson on their wind music. Which
> being done the singing men of Christ Church, with others, sang

[97] *Ibid.*, Appendix A, 263–64: *"Otium pacemque nactae vel pro gloriâ tantùm dimi-
cantis civitatis, alumna est Philosophia."*

[98] Wood, *History and Antiquities*, II, 285–86.

[99] *Ibid.*, II, 215.

[100] *Ibid.*, II, 790.

a lesson, after which the Senior Proctor Mr. Herbert Pelham of Magdalen College made an eloquent Oration: that being ended also the music sounded again,.and continued playing till the Vicechancellor went to the bottom of the foundation to lay the first stone in one of the south angles. But no sooner he had deposited a piece of gold on the said stone, according to the usual manner in such ceremonies, but the earth fell in from one side of the foundation, and the scaffold that was thereon broke and fell with it, so that all those that were thereon to the number of an hundred at least, namely the Proctors, Principals of Halls, Masters, and some Bachelaurs fell down all together one upon another into the foundation.[101]

With the elevation of music to a separate faculty having its own academic regulations, with the maintenance of musical studies (Boethius) within the traditional framework of mathematics, with the numerous religio-academic musical activities constantly going on at Oxford, and with the widespread cultivation of music informally, it is no wonder that most of the treatises on music which appeared in England during the Renaissance can be related, directly or indirectly, to this university. As one might expect, the earliest of these (three brief tracts and one long work by John Hothby) continue along lines characteristic of medieval treatises. In the latter part of the fifteenth century, Hothby, a Carmelite, doctor of theology, and teacher at Oxford in 1435, traveled to Italy where he held various teaching posts, including that of *magister scholae* and *precentor* at the cathedral school in Lucca (1467–83).[102] Three brief works by Hothby (CS, III, 328–34) together make up a little treatise on *musica speculativa* and *musica practica*: the *Regulae super proportionem,* a discussion of proportions similar to that usually found in the conventional medieval treatise; a set of note values, meter signs, and the like, *De cantu figurato,* designating as *croma* and *semicroma* the next lowest notes after the semiminima; and the *Regulae super contrapunctum,* which gives directions for singing *discantus visibilis*—the typical English practice of singing

---

[101] *Ibid.,* II, 939–40.
[102] See Utto Kornmüller, "Johann Hothby," *KmJb,* Vol. VIII (1893), 3.

at sight in sixth chords upon a given tenor. A much longer work, written in the Italian language, is Hothby's *Caliopea legale,* designed for his students at Lucca and dealing with such practical matters as solmization, note values, metrical proportions, and the singing of plain song.[103] Like many of his contemporaries, Hothby was concerned with problems of *musica ficta* (Book I); using the hexachordal system of Guido, he applied a new system of mutation by which he was able to alter any note chromatically.[104] Among his unpublished works are a letter against Ramos de Pareia and a treatise, *Excitatio quaedem musicae artis per refutationem,* which also upheld the mathematical divisions of Marchettus and the six-tone system of Guido against the octave system of solmization postulated by Ramos.[105] Thus Hothby had a part in the theoretical controversy carried on so vehemently later by Gafori and Spataro; in fact, Hothby's treatise *De cantu figurato* was copied in 1474 by Johannes Bonadies, teacher of Gafori—and so Oxford was at least partly responsible for the conservative attitude of Gafori. But, like many another Renaissance theorist, Hothby did not stop with treatises on music: he also wrote a number of three-part compositions.[106] In 1486 he was recalled to England by royal command, probably owing to his fame as a musician, and he died in England the following year.

After the time of Hothby, no original works on musical theory appeared in England for about one hundred years.[107] The first

[103] E. de Coussemaker, *Histoire de l'harmonie au moyen âge* (Paris, 1852), 295–349.

[104] See Johannes Wolf, "Early English Musical Theorists," *Musical Quarterly,* Vol. XXV (1939), 423.

[105] See Kornmüller, "Johann Hothby," *KmJb,* Vol. VIII (1893), 16, and Anton Wilhelm Schmidt, *Die Calliopea Legale des Johannes Hothby* (Leipzig, 1897), 9. See also Albert Seay, "The *Dialogus Johannis Ottobi Anglici in arte musica,*" *JAMS,* Vol. VIII (1955), 86–100, for a short treatise in a collection made by a student ("doubtless from one of Hothby's own classes"). The treatise refutes Ramos' views on the derivation of the scale, tuning, and other matters.

[106] For easy reference, see the *Dictionary of National Biography.*

[107] Hawkins, following Bishop Tanner, credits William Chelle (bachelor of music, Oxford, 1524, later *precentor* of Hereford Cathedral) with two tracts, *Musicae practicae compendium* and *De proportionibus musicis* (*History of Music,* II, 522). According to Henry Davey, *History of English Music* (second ed., London, 1921), 92, Tucke of New College made a collection of theoretical works in 1500 and Chelle copied these in 1526, adding nothing new. Chelle's treatises are probably copies of the works of Tunstede and

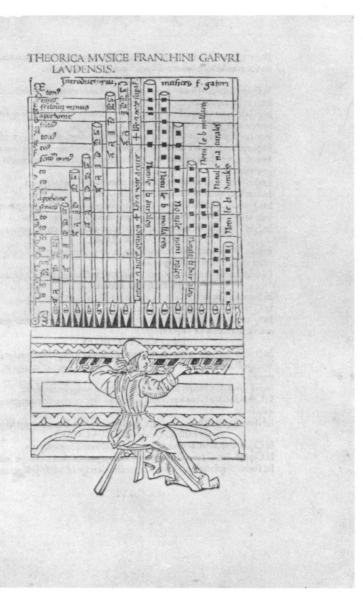

Title page of volume I of the second edition of Gafori's *Theorica musica* (Milan, 1492).

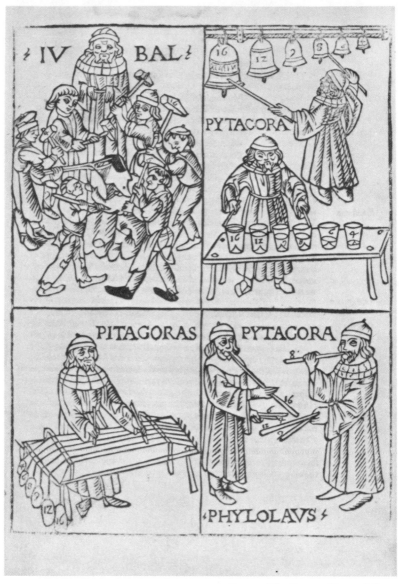

Title page of volume II of the second edition of Gafori's *Theorica musica* (Milan, 1492).

book on musical theory published in England was an instruction book in the elements of sight singing by an Oxford student: *A Briefe Introduction to the True Art of Musicke* (1584) by William Bathe. In 1600, Bathe published a new edition called *A Briefe Introduction to the skill of Song,* in which he attempted to postulate a new system of sight singing, based upon the octave instead of the hexachordal system and approaching the movable *do* system.[108] Strictly practical (lacking any theoretical introduction), this curious treatise was pedagogical in purpose, designed to teach the elements of music to schoolboys. With four "ante rules of Song" *(naming, quantitie, time* and *tune)* and four "post rules of Song" (more details about the same), Bathe discussed nomenclature, note values, mutation, and other aspects of music. For *Time* (post rules), he gave a very strange set of directions (B vii recto and verso):

> Take a stick of a certaine length, and a stone of a certaine weight, hold the stick standing vpon an end of some table: See you haue vpon the stick diuers marks: hold the stone vp by the side of the stick: then as you let fall the stone, instantly begin to sing one Note, and iust with the noyse that it maketh vpon the table, beegin another Note, and as long as thou holdest the first Note, so long hold the rest, and let that note thy Crachet or thy Minim, &c. as thou seest cause, and thus maist thou measure the very Time it selfe that thou keepest, and know whether thou hast altered it, or not.

Bathe also included a curious *Gladius musicus,* a sword-diagram for determining concords and discords (C ii verso); and he ends with musical examples—"Sundry waies of 2. parts in one vpon the plain song."

Hothby. (Williams, *Degrees in Music,* 67, says these treatises were copied from John Dunstable and John Otteby: the treatise once thought to be Dunstable's is the *Quatuor principalia* of Simon Tunstede.) The fact that Chelle copied these works shows his interest in the mathematical side of music as well as in practical aspects—all with an eye, doubtlessly, to the pedagogical duties contingent upon the office of *precentor.*

[108] A copy of the second treatise is in the Bodleian Library, Oxford. For easy reference, see Morrison Comegys Boyd, *Elizabethan Music and Musical Criticism* (Philadelphia, 1940), 250–51, for a summary of the solmization system.

Bathe himself was a musician of some note, having pleased the queen by his skill in playing various instruments, according to a letter of Lord Burghley's, and having made "a late device of a new harp, which he presented to her Majesty."[109] The first of his musical treatises was written while he was a student at Oxford, and his subsequent activities, like Hothby's, show the widespread influence of musical affairs at Oxford. For after leaving Oxford, Bathe studied theology at Louvain and Padua; and early in the seventeenth century he began teaching in the Irish College—the Real Colegio de Nobles Irlandeses, founded by Philip II, 1592—incorporated in the University of Salamanca. Statutes of this college, probably drawn up the year Bathe joined the staff (1604), provided that each student spend some time each day in the study of music and of Greek literature: the musical requirement may have been owing to Bathe's personal interest in the subject.

In 1586 appeared *The Praise of Musicke.*[110] Although published anonymously, this has generally been attributed to John Case, once a chorister at Christ Church, doctor of medicine, and fellow of St. John's College, Oxford. Unlike Bathe's very practical treatises, this work is an *apologia* for music—indeed, it is a thorough elaboration of the uses and effects of music, one of the topics invariably found in the medieval treatises—discussing music's antiquity, its cultivation by "Emperours, Kings and Captaines" from time immemorial, its powers and medicinal effects upon man, and its many uses in civil, military, and ecclesiastical matters. The book simply abounds in legends and anecdotes having to do with the power of music. Moreover, the author gives a brief history of church music from the time of David, showing that music has always been sanctioned by the Church; and he concludes with "A refutation of objections against the lawful use of Musicke in the Church," answering and refuting specific objections of the Puritans to music. Two years after the publication of *The Praise of Musicke,* Case published in Latin a work covering much of the same material: the *Apologia*

109 For this and subsequent biographical data on Bathe, see Timothy Corcoran, *Studies in the History of Classical Teaching* (London, 1911), 6ff.

110 A copy of this treatise is owned by the Huntington Library. Ample citations from it appear in Boyd, *Elizabethan Music,* Appendix C, 292ff.

musices tam vocalis quam instrumentalis et mixtae (Oxoniae, 1588). The fact that this was specifically designed for an academic audience is seen in the use of the Latin language instead of English and also in the inclusion of a section "Problemata" following the text, a catechism on the material of the treatise. Of special interest here (and unique in such a treatise) is a list of the leading musicians of the century: in discussing the great power and influence of music, Case points out that just as kings of antiquity had their honored musicians, so the English should take pride in theirs —Taverner, Blithman, Tallis, More (?), Bird, Munday, Bull, Morley, Dowland, and Johnson.[111] Case had earlier shown his interest

[111] See the Huntington Library copy, 43–44:

binc olim imperatores, reges, gentes ac nationes summos honores peritis musicorum instrumentorum tribuerunt. Quid opus est exemplis? Periander Rex Corinthiorum Arionem, Hieron Rex Siciliæ Symonidem, Alexander ille magnus Timotheum, Agamemnon Demonicū, Iulius Cæsar Hermoglnem, Vespasianus Diodorum; Intergentes Ægyptij Mercurium, Lacedæmonij Terpandrum, Græci Ismeniam, Angli non ita pridem Tauernerum, Blithmanū, Tallesium, Morum aliosqʒ insignes magnis præmijs affecerūt: & quæ causa nunc est cur hos superstites adhue viros Birdū, Mūdanum, Bullum, Morleum, Doulandum, Ionsonum aliosqʒ hodie permultos instrumentorū peritissimos iustis suis laudibus non persequamur?

Mr. William Clary has called my attention to the fact that neither Anthony à Wood nor Falconer Madan believed John Case to be the author of *The Praise of Musicke*: see Wood, *Athenae Oxonienses*, I, 686, and Madan, *Oxford Books* (Oxford, 1895–1931), I, 279–80. Madan's final judgment against Case rests on Wood's statement that Case's inclination to Catholicism caused him to resign his fellowship in 1574: Madan finds several remarks against popery and popish church music in the *Praise*, none in the *Apologia*. The *Praise* has been ascribed to Case largely because of a poem by Thomas Watson: "A gratification vnto Mr. John Case, for his learned Booke, lately made in the prayes of Musick." The poem certainly appears to describe both the English and the Latin treatises (as even Madan admits). See the article by Haslewood in Sir Egerton Brydges and Joseph Haslewood, *The British Bibliographer* (London, 1810–14), where Case is upheld as the author of both treatises.

Lack of space precludes a lengthy comparison of the works here. The Latin work is certainly more in line with Case's Latin philosophical writings (see a list of his Aristotelian commentaries in the *D. N. B.*), scholastic in approach and drawing chiefly upon older authorities (Aristotle, Cicero, Augustine, Aquinas) than is the *Praise*, which draws more generally upon later writers (Polydore Vergil, Castiglione, Sir Thomas Elyot). Although many *exempla* are common to both books, marginal notes almost invariably cite different sources; e.g., the Timotheus story in the *Praise* has a reference to Gyraldus, *De Poetis*, whereas the same story in the *Apologia* is taken from Suidas. Actually, the episode as described in the *Praise* follows Suidas; I am unable to find any mention of Timotheus in Gyraldus. See Nan Cooke Carpenter, "Spenser and Timotheus," *PMLA*, Vol. LXXI (1956), 1141n.

in the arts by defending the performance of academic plays against Puritan objections in his *Speculum Moralium Quaestionum in Vniversam Ethicen Aristotelis,* 1585; and the Latin poem by "I. C." prefacing the 1592 edition of Gager's *Meleager* probably came from his pen.[112]

In 1596, William Barley printed *The Pathway to Music,* by an unknown writer who apparently compiled his book on mensural music and discantus from various German treatises, as we know from the words of Thomas Morley, who criticizes it unmercifully.[113] *The Pathway to Music,* however, indicated the mounting interest in problems of practical music to which Morley's own *Plaine and Easie Introduction to Practicall Musicke* (1597), the first comprehensive work on musical theory in the English language, was a really satisfactory answer. The opening sentences here, indeed, are often cited to show the high regard in which music was held in Elizabethan England: the cultivated gentleman must be able to bear his part in a madrigal at sight or to sustain some point of view in a debate on music. Philomathes (the name is indicative of Morley's classical background), the unfortunate *discipulus* in Morley's dialogue, had attended a "banket" the night before, at which "all the propose which then was discoursed vpon, was Musicke." When asked to be arbiter in a musical argument, Philomathes refused, pretending ignorance; and then, he says,

[112] Boas, *University Drama,* 177–78, 227–29. Wood praises highly "that eminent Philosopher Dr. John Case" (*History and Antiquities,* II, 269) and tells us earlier that Case, who had been industrious "in training up Students after the old fashion in Townsmens houses," had been promised by Chancellor Leicester the headship of a hall when there was a vacancy; "but it never came to pass, being reserved for those of this beloved party, the Puritans" (*ibid.,* II, 233).

[113] Thomas Morley, *A Plaine and Easie Introduction to Practicall Musicke,* 1597 (facsimile ed. Shakespeare Society, Oxford, 1937), "Annotations," unpaged:

> And as for him of whom he haue spoken so much, one part of his booke he stole out of *Beurhusius,* another out of *Lossius,* peruerting the sence of *Lossius* his wordes, and giuing examples flatte to the contrary, of that which *Lossius* saith. And the last part of his booke treating of *Descant,* he took *verbatim* out of an old written booke which I haue. But it should seeme, that whatsoeuer or whosoeuer he was, that gaue it to the presse, was not the Author of it himselfe, else would he haue set his name to it, or then hee was ashamed of his labour.

the whole companie condemned mee of discurtesie, being fully perswaded, that I had beene as skilfull in that art, as they tooke mee to be learned in others. But supper being ended, and Musicke bookes, according to the custome being brought to the table: the mistress of the house presented mee with a part, earnestly requesting mee to sing. But when after manie excuses, I protested vnfainedly that I could not: euerie one began to wonder. Yea, some whispered to others, demaunding how I was brought vp: so that vpon shame of mine ignorance I go nowe to seeke out mine olde frinde master *Gnorimus,* to make my selfe his scholler.[114]

And Master Gnorimus proceeds to instruct Philomathes in the art of music. The first part of the *Introduction,* "teaching to sing," deals with the solmization scales, notes and ligatures, and metrical proportions, with many musical examples and references to continental theorists and composers; the second part, "treating of Descant," teaches the rules for counterpoint; and the third part, "treating of composing or setting of Songes," teaches how to write music in two to six parts, with a discussion of various musical forms.

Morley's treatise is significant of one trend with regard to musical studies at Oxford: that one who wished to follow a musical career or to cultivate music as an amateur studied privately with a qualified musician, whether in an academic community or not. Morley himself had been a pupil of William Byrd, to whom the book is dedicated, before he became bachelor of music at Oxford in 1588. But although the book is highly practical in purpose and its style charming and whimsical, Morley's personal scholarship is everywhere apparent in his many references to ancient theorists and contemporary writers on music—Jacobus Faber Stapulensis, Gafori, Lossius, Listenius, Beurhusius, Calvisius, Rasselius, and others. His classical background, furthermore, which must surely be a product of his Oxford studies, is seen not only in the names of his characters but in his choice of the dialogue form (especially favored by the humanists following the plan of the Platonic dialogues), the introduction of many Greek words, the reference to

114 *Ibid.,* 1.

his Greek lexicon, and most of all in the "Annotations necessary for the vnderstanding of the Booke," placed significantly at the end of the work, in which Morley discusses Greek musical theory, citing critically ancient and medieval authorities. So popular was the work that several editions were published, as well as a German translation called *Musica practica* by J. C. Trost.

The same year in which Morley was awarded the coveted Oxford degree (1588), John Dowland also became a bachelor of music at Oxford. Famous as a lutenist at the Jacobean Court and at various royal courts on the continent, Dowland was a distinguished example of the Renaissance *musicus*—theorist, composer, and performer all in one. He wrote no original treatise, but he translated into English the *Micrologus* of Andreas Ornithoparchus, written nearly a century earlier, and published this book in 1609.[115] When Dowland's son Robert published in 1610 his *Varietie of Lute-Lessons,* moreover, he "annexed" a short treatise by his father, "Other Necessary Obseruations belonging to the Lute." Although these are predominantly practical directions for stringing, fretting, and tuning the lute, Dowland constantly maintains a strong connection with the old *musica speculativa* (as does Ornithoparchus in his treatise), with definitions from ancient authorities, a discussion of intervals according to Pythagoras and Boethius, and constant exhortation for an understanding of musical theory:

> Wherefore I exhort all Practitioners on this Instrument to the learning of their Pricke-song, also to vnderstand the Elements and Principles of that knowledge . . . for which purpose I did lately set forth the Worke of that most learned *Andreas Ornithoparcus* his *Micrologus,* in the English tongue.[116]

If Dowland's work thus maintains the old connection between *musica speculativa* and *musica practica,* a musical treatise by Robert Fludd (1618) may best be described as metaphysical. A medical mystic and Rosicrucian who had received the baccalaureate and

---

[115] A copy of this book is owned by the Huntington Library.
[116] Folio E recto (copy in the Huntington Library).

doctorate in arts and medicine at Oxford, Fludd attempted to investigate every aspect of man's knowledge in an effort to understand universal science, believing that man, the microcosm, is the image of God, the macrocosm. Ideas of universal harmony played a large part in Fludd's philosophy, in which he agreed with and differed from Kepler.[117] One tract, indeed, written in refutation to Kepler, the *Monochordum Mundi Symphoniacum* (Frankfurt, 1623), contains a great diagram in which the universe is represented as a monochord, played by a motor *extra mundanem*.[118] The treatise on music, *"De Templo Musicae"* in the *Utriusque cosmi historia*,[119] is headed by a large symbolical picture of the temple of music; and in his discussion of the elements of music Fludd carries out this symbolism: scales are columns of the temple, notes are bricks, intervals are windows. Although Fludd, like Kepler, properly belongs to the history of the Baroque, his treatise is for the most part medieval in form and content, with a conventional scholastic introduction followed by a description of the elements of music. Descriptions and pictures of many stringed instruments with their tablature, several wind instruments, and one percussion instrument follow. The climax of the book appears in the section *"De instrumento nostro Magno"*—Fludd's invention of a great instrument worked by a handle (a kind of hurdy-gurdy), with diagrams and music for the instrument.

Our last musical treatise written by an Oxford man is Charles Butler's *Principles of Musik, in Singing and Setting* (London, 1636). Chorister in Magdalen College's choir school, bachelor of arts, music master at the Magdalen school, and later schoolmaster in the country, Butler drew upon the medieval *protreptikos* as well as the practical handbook in compiling his treatise. The first part of this work deals with the modes, elements of music, and composition, with constant quotation from ancient, medieval, and contemporary authorities; the second part resembles Case's *Praise of*

---

117 See J. B. Craven, *Doctor Robert Fludd* (Kirkwall, 1902), 149–52.

118 See *ibid.*, 153, for this diagram. And see Hawkins, *History of Music*, IV, 168–72, for a description of the treatise and diagram.

119 *Utriusque cosmi majoris scilicet et minoris metaphysica, physica atqve technia historia, tractatus secundus* (In nobili Oppenheimio, 1618).

Musicke in elaborating upon music's effects and uses in civil and ecclesiastical life, with specific refutation of many Puritan objections. In addition to its importance musically, the work is interesting from a literary point of view, for in it Butler quotes Du Bartas at great length and makes a very derogatory remark about Christopher Marlowe;[120] and Butler's interest in problems of philology (he was a grammarian and beekeeper, and he wrote treatises on these subjects also) is seen in the printing of this book according to his own system of phonetics.

Although none of these treatises was written specifically *ad utilitatem studiosorum* or *ad pueros instruendos,* as is the case with many contemporary German treatises, they all appear to reflect some aspect of the many musical activities constantly going on at Oxford. And the study of music at Renaissance Oxford presents a very unusual picture. On the statute books we find Boethius' *Musica* a requirement for the baccalaureate in arts and music as a mathematical discipline—possibly required for the *magisterium* also, as in medieval times. The lecturer in music had a regular place among the *magistri regentes* each year. The retention of music within the frame of mathematical studies appears, too, in the first endowed professorship in mathematics, which called quite specifically for lectures on music along with other branches of mathematics; and the chair of music endowed by Heather embraced both theory and practice. Sometime during the fifteenth century, moreover, the single art of music had become a separate faculty on a par with the faculties of theology, law, and medicine—the only member of the liberal arts to be so distinguished—privileged to award its own degrees. Arrival at this new status involved for music the standardizing of certain academic matters—such as regulations for academic dress, applications for degrees, fees, and other details connected

---

[120] See Nan Cooke Carpenter, "A Note on Marlowe in Charles Butler's *Principles of Musik* (1636)," *Notes and Queries,* Vol. CXCVIII (1953), 16–18, "Charles Butler and Du Bartas," *ibid.,* Vol. I (n.s., 1954), 2–7, and "Charles Butler and the Bees' Madrigal," *ibid.,* Vol. II (1955), 103–106. The Huntington Library owns a copy of *The Principles of Musik, in Singing and Setting: with the two-fold Use thereof* [*Ecclesiasticall and Civil*] (London, 1636), as well as several of Butler's other treatises (on bees, grammar, rhetoric, and other subjects).

with graduation: these features were carefully worked out in statutes of 1601 and 1636.

According to the very uneven records, however—largely Wood's *Fasti*—there were no standardized requirements for music degrees at Oxford in the sixteenth century: degrees were generally granted after the candidate had spent years in the study of music and had shown some proficiency as a composer, but each supplication for a degree was dealt with individually. Determinations and disputations appear not to have been generally required of music candidates, although students in the arts still participated in these exercises. The performance of the candidate's musical composition at the Act probably substituted for this. Judged by those supplications still extant, most candidates for musical degrees studied music (and practiced it too) privately, either within or away from the university. Bull, for example, was a pupil of the royal organist William Blitheman, and both Thomas Tompkins and Thomas Morley were pupils of William Byrd, himself a pupil of Thomas Tallis, who may have graduated in the arts at Oxford. None of the great English musicians, moreover, ever held a public teaching position at Oxford, for, as we have noted, music in the university proper was taught by *magistri regentes* who lectured on all the arts. But it is highly significant that many distinguished Renaissance musicians were choirmasters and organists in collegiate foundations there, where valuable training in theory, singing, playing of instruments, and composition was obtainable; and some musically gifted private tutors also provided musical instruction for interested students.

The Caroline (Laudian) Code of 1636 pulled together all loose ends from the preceding century and established quite definite requirements for musical degrees, making the bachelor's degree a prerequisite for the doctorate. These statutes, specifying a certain length of time to be spent in theory and practice, maintained the traditional close connection between these two aspects of music; they pointed up music's traditional alignment with mathematics, too, by allowing the successful candidate to lecture on any book of Boethius and to have the bachelor created doctor or *inceptor* by the Savilian professor of mathematics. The Renaissance conception of *musicus*—theorist, composer, performer—carried over, thus, well into the Baroque.

Although Wood does not mention in the *Fasti* any musical degrees under his heading "Creations"—honorary degrees, most of them doctor of laws or divinity—it seems that many of the Oxford degrees, especially the doctorate, were, like those granted Heather and Gibbons, of an honorary nature. In awarding these degrees, Oxford honored musicians who had already achieved fame in the field and at the same time embellished its commencement exercises with excellent musical compositions written and produced by these men. Never awarded lightly, the Oxford baccalaureate and doctorate in music were hallmarks of distinction, proudly advertised by those who obtained the coveted awards. In 1553, for instance, there appeared *The Actes of the Apostles, translated into Englysh Metre . . . by Christofer Tye, Doctor in Musyke;* Ornithoparchus' *Micrologus* was translated by "J. D. Lutenist, Lute-player, and Bachelor of Musicke in both the Universities"; and the most important treatise of the century was written by "Thomas Morley, Batcheler of musicke."

Cambridge

The oldest statutes for the University of Cambridge, the *"Statuta antiqua in ordinem redacta,"* compiled in the Senior Proctor's Book around 1498, contain an item *"De incipientibus in artibus"* which specifies that bachelors must spend three years studying in the arts faculty before inception (attaining the *magisterium*), and that these years must be spent in the study of philosophy and mathematics.[121] Although not mentioned specifically, music is

[121] *Documents relating to the University and Colleges of Cambridge* (London, 1852), I, 360:

Item statuimus quod nullus admittatur ad incipiendum in artibus nisi prius determinaverit; et ultra hoc ad minus per triennium hic vel alibi in universitate in eadem facultate continue studuerit; quod etiam per triennium in scholis libros Aristotelis in philosophia, quos eo tempore a magistro suo ordinarie legi

probably to be understood in accordance with the traditional teaching of mathematics. Indeed, a later statute from the same collection does include music with the other mathematical sciences upon which a skilled teacher will lecture to bachelors and scholars; according to this decree, bachelors seeking the master's degree must spend the first of three years in the study of arithmetic and music.[122] The first *lector* in mathematics whose name we know is Roger Collingwood, who began to receive his stipend *pro lectura in mathematicalibus* in 1501 and received it for several years afterwards.[123]

In the next century (1535) music is again specified as a subject for study in the arts faculty by the Royal Injunctions of Henry VIII, issued by Henry's Royal Visitor to the university, Chancellor Cromwell. These injunctions contained the following notice:

> That students in arts should be instructed in the elements of logic, rhetoric, arithmetic, geography, music, and philosophy, and should read Aristotle, Rodolphus Agricola, Philip Melanchthon, Trapezuntius, &c. and not the frivolous questions and obscure glosses of Scotus, Burleus, Anthony Trombet, Bricot, Bruliferius, &c.[124]

A few years after the accession of a new monarch, the Edwardian Statutes of 1549 named mathematics as the first subject for study by would-be bachelors of arts (exactly as at Oxford under the same regulations); and the phrasing of the regulation—specifying that the student study at least arithmetic, geometry, astronomy,

contigerit, audierit; necnon per triennium mathematicalia quae tunc in scholis lecta fuerint audierit.

122 *Ibid.*, I, 382:

Statuimus quod annis singulis . . . peritus in his artibus magister quispiam majoris partis regentium sententia delegatus . . . legat baccalaureis atque scholaribus, (quos omnes baccalaureos hoc eodem decreto adesse coarctamus) per annum primum annorum trium arithmeticam et musicam, alterum geometriam et perspectivam, tertium astronomiam.

123 *Grace Book B* (ed. by Mary Bateson) (Cambridge, 1903), I, *xviii*, 171. The *"Statuta antiqua in ordinem non redacta,"* from the early years of the sixteenth century, contain no reference to a curriculum of studies (*Cambridge Documents*, I, 417–53).

124 Charles Henry Cooper, *Annals of Cambridge* (Cambridge, 1842–56), I, 375.

cosmography, and as much else as possible—leaves room for the inclusion of music, not specifically mentioned.[125] Two sets of Elizabethan *Statutes* (given in the first and twelfth years of Elizabeth's reign, with a course of studies identical in both) substituted rhetoric for the mathematics required earlier of first-year students, but retained the mathematical requirements for candidates for the *magisterium*.[126]

If the musical requirements in the Cambridge statutes are somewhat vague, they are quite clear in the statutes of certain individual colleges. Dr. John Caius, for instance, who refounded Gonville Hall (1557), calling it Gonville and Caius College, decreed that his students learn *artem numerorum et modorum*—arithmetic and music—along with Greek, Latin, and other liberal sciences.[127] And in the Elizabethan Statutes given to Trinity College in 1560, it is stated that the *lector mathematicus* teach music along with the other mathematical disciplines, and that all bachelors attend the lectures.[128] Students desiring election to this college, moreover,

[125] John Lamb, *A Collection of Letters, Statutes, and other Documents* (London, 1838), 125: *"Recens venientem a ludo literario primum escipiant mathematica. Illa toto eo anno discet arithmeticen nimirum geometriam et astronomiae cosmographiaeque quantum poterit. Sequens annus dialecticam docebit. Tertius et quartus adjunget philosophiam."* As to bachelors seeking the *magisterium*, *"Hi auditores assidui philosophicae lectionis astronomiae perspectivae et graecae linguae sint idque quod inchoatum antea erat suo industria perficiant."* Since the *"Ordinationes Reginaldi Poli pro regimine Universitatis,"* 1557, fail to mention the curriculum, one may assume that these requirements held during Mary's reign (*ibid.*, 237–69).

[126] *Cambridge Documents*, I, 459, Cap. VI: *"Primus annus rhetoricam docebit: secundus et tertius dialecticam. Quartus adjungat philosophiam."* And Cap. VII, dealing with requirements for the *magisterium*: *"Hi auditores assidui philosophicae lectionis, astronomiae, perspectivae et Graecae linguae sint, idque quod inchoatum antea erat sua industria perficiant."* George Peacock, *Observations on the Statutes of the University of Cambridge* (London, 1841), 10, says that bachelors of arts were required to study, in the three years before they became masters, Aristotelian philosophy, "astronomy, cosmography, music, and the Greek language," citing Caput VII of the Elizabethan Statutes.

[127] *Cambridge Documents*, II, 251–52:

Dent [scholastici] operam linguae Graecae et Latinae, scientiis liberalibus ea lingua qua quaeque scripta sunt, praecipue Logicae et Rhetoricae, dein utrique philosophiae naturali et morali. . . . Volumus etiam et teneant artem numerorum et modorum, hoc est Arithmeticam et Musicam.

[128] James Bass Mullinger, *The University of Cambridge* (Cambridge, 1873–1911),

are to be examined in grammar, literature, and song; and those *qui cantare norunt* are to be preferred.[129]

College statutes make definite, too, certain other requirements—for musical practices in religious exercises or for the college choristers. From 1446, Queen's College statutes specify that in the convocation of its members to elect a president, *"Hymnus, 'Veni Creator Spiritus,' ab omnibus Sociis praesentibus in Capella . . . solemniter decantetur"*; and after the election, *"Psalmum, 'Te Deum laudamus,' omnes Socii praesentes solemniter cantent."*[130] This foundation included among its members eight choristers whose duty it was *"diebus festivis legere, cantare, et juvare in Choro"*; and the statutes mention other musical requirements in connection with memorial Masses to be celebrated annually for benefactors of the college.[101]

Jesus College (1497) also provided for eight scholars *in cantu competenter instructos* who were to perform religious exercises in the chapel during their years of study for the baccalaureate.[132] And we know that King's College with its beautiful chapel supported a *precentor*, organist, and master of the choristers, for in the report of King Henry's commissioner who visited the university in 1545

II, 509, Appendix A, Stat. 9: *"Lector autem mathematicus doceat primum arithmeticam, deinde geometriam, tum cognitionem sphaerae et cosmographiam, deinde astronomiam, postremo musicam. Huic lectioni intersint omnes baccalaurei."*

[129] *Ibid.*, II, 609, Stat. 13. *"Omnes qui discipulatum in collegio petunt, ab electoribus . . . diligenter quid in grammatica et litteris humanioribus, quid etiam in cantu possunt, examinentur. Et qui cantare norunt, modo ceteris qui petunt virtute et doctrina pares sint, praeferantur."*

[130] *Cambridge Documents*, III, 20–21.

[131] *Ibid.*, III, 30, 38.

[132] *Ibid.*, III, 104, Caput Nonum:

Item statuimus, ordinamus et volumus, quod in nostro Collegio sint octo scholares, quos in grāmatica, rhetorica, logica, mathematica, vel philosophia continue studere volumus; et quod magis grāmaticae, rhetoricae, mathematicae, logicae vel philosophiae illos operam dare cupimus, ideo eos in cantu ante eorum admissionem, competenter instructos fore decernimus et ordinamus, ita quod in divinis cum sociis psallere, et Deo servire, ac caetera in choro officia, per scholares exequi consueta, adimplere possint et debeant.

there are records of payments to all these officials.[133] The report on Trinity College mentions annual payment for college trumpeters.[134] There is, in fact, great emphasis upon music in the Elizabethan Statutes given to Trinity in 1559, which must have been owing, in part at least, to the musical interests of Henry Harvey, who became Master of Trinity in 1558 and who had been *precentor* of St. Paul's in London before that.[135] Trinity's statutes of 1559 provided for ten choristers, an organist, and a teacher of the choirboys; and an item in these statutes also set aside a certain sum for the choirmaster's expense account. We know that the composer John Tomkins, bachelor of music, 1608, was organist in this distinguished college in 1606.[136]

Dr. John Caius, whose statutes, we recall, specified that scholars of Gonville and Caius College learn arithmetic and music, left additional musical provisions in his statutes (1557). Included in the membership of this college were to be three London organists; and the three-day examination preliminary to the election of fellows to the college was to test each candidate's knowledge of music —even to playing the organ—along with proficiency in writing, grammar, Greek, and the composition of poetry.[137] Caius was likewise very definite in desiring all members of his college to "worship God with song and organs," and he laid down a rigid requirement

---

[133] *Ibid.*, I, 241–42:

Stipend uni' ex pd psbit voc pcentor p am	iiij li. vj s. viij d.
Stipend jubilator in organis p annu	c s.
Stipend informator chorsataz p annu	iiij li. vj s viij d.

[134] *Ibid.*, I, 158: "*Regard dat tubicinibus p annu xx d.*"

[135] Edmund Carter, *History of the University of Cambridge* (London, 1753), 105.

[136] *Cambridge Documents*, III, 415, Caput I: "*Sint . . . decem pueri Symphoniaci qui Choristae nominentur, et unus qui Organa pulset Choristasque doceat. Sit item unus qui Choristas in bonis literis instituat.*" And *ibid.*, III, 465, Caput XLIII: "*Magister Choristarum pro musica habeat pro commeatu 1 s 8 d.*"

[137] *Ibid.*, II, 250:

Volo etiam ex Londino tres, sed Organistas. . . . Secernantur omnes per Custodes ubi venerint, aut per praesidentem si absit custos, sed consentiente prius eo, et proponantur eligendi sociis hi, quos custos approbaverit, diligenter prius examinati ad dies tres in sacello publice, primo die per Scholasticos, per insequentes duos dies per decanum et socios omnes praesentes, quam eligantur, an scribant scite, an canant musice, an grammaticen calleant perfecte, an organistae sint, an graece sciant, et an carmen componant.

that all musical people, whether scholars or fellows, be present at services on each religious day throughout the year unless excused for a serious reason by the warden or president.[138]

Some accounts of special religious celebrations with music have come down to us. John Mere's *Diary,* for example, which describes Queen Mary's Visitation of Cambridge in 1556, mentions several Masses sung during this event. Visiting Trinity College, "they all went towards the chapell with summ. trinitati in picksonge and so to masse of the holy Ghost solempnly songe."[139] Later, all members of the university took part in a procession through the town, "and so to S. Maryes synginge *salva festa dies* all the waye. Then masse songe by the Vic. with deacon and subdeacon in piksonge and organs."[140]

Music, of course, formed a very important part of the religious ceremonies held when Elizabeth made a royal progress to Cambridge in 1564. To greet the queen upon her arrival, the Provost said a psalm and a collect for her. "Which done," Matthew Stokys relates,

> the whole quire began to sing, in English, a song of gladness; and so went orderly into their stalls in the quire. . . . This song ended, the Provost began the 'Te Deum' in English, in his cope: which was solemnly sung in prick-song, and the organs playing. After that, he began even-song, which also was solemnly sung: every man standing in his cope.[141]

At morning prayer the next day, "the quire sung, in prick-song, a song"; and at evening prayer,

[138] *Ibid.,* II, 271, 276:

Volumus etiam ut divinis officiis festivis diebus omnes socii, scholares et pensionarii cantu, lectione canora et organis (qui hoc possunt) laudent Deum. . . . Volumus etiam et ordinamus ut socii musici et organistae, ut et scholares musici et organistae, non absint festis majoribus et solennioribus per omnem annum, imo neque aliis diebus festis, nisi gravi de causa per custodem aut eo absente praesidentem approbanda.

[139] Lamb, *Documents,* 212.
[140] *Ibid.,* 218.
[141] Cooper, *Annals of Cambridge,* II, 191, quoting the narrative of Matthew Stokys.

the company of King's College, being informed that the Queens Majestie would not come unto the same, began and did sing. And then, being advertised that her Grace was coming, staid. And when she was come unto her travis by the secret way, they of new did begin the even-song.[142]

But the use of music to embellish religious ceremonies was only one side of the cultivation of music at Renaissance Cambridge; many records deal with a more informal type of music, both vocal and instrumental, among university students. Like their fellows at Oxford, Cambridge students apparently kept musical instruments in their rooms—to the great annoyance, sometimes, of nonmusical neighbors. Foxe, for instance, tells (1531) how Thomas Bilney was much upset by a scholar who constantly played the recorder in the room below.[143] The inventory of goods of one Leonard Metcalfe, scholar of St. John's who had the misfortune to be convicted and executed for the murder of a townsman (1540/1), contained "Item, an old Lute."[144] Thomas Mace, who in the next century produced a unique treatise on the lute, mentions "our University of *Cambridge*" as being the home of "eminent *Performances*" upon the lute by "divers very *Worthy Persons*."[145] The colleges, too, seem to have had their own musical instruments, as we know from the bursar's book of Trinity College (1595/6), which records payments for buying and repairing stringed instruments.[146] And the

---

[142] *Ibid.,* II, 192–93.

[143] John Foxe, *Book of Martyrs* (ed. by Stephen Cattley) (London, 1837), IV, 621:

> He could abide no swearing or singing. Coming from the church where singing was, he would lament to his scholars the curiosity of their dainty singing, which he called rather a mockery with God, than otherwise. And when Dr. Thurlby, afterwards bishop, then a scholar living in the chamber underneath him, would play upon his recorder (as he would often do), he would resort strait to his prayer.

[144] Cooper, *Annals of Cambridge,* I, 399.

[145] Thomas Mace, *Musick's Monument* (London, 1676), 45, speaking of the ease with which one may learn to play the lute:

> As by many years *Experience* I can *Justifie,* and by eminent *Performances* upon that *Instrument* by divers very *Worthy Persons;* several such at this present remaining in our University of *Cambridge,* who have not been at *It* from their first undertaking yet a full *Year;* and in *one Quarter of a Year* could play extremely well, even to *Admiration.*

iuncta dicuntur & funt potentia,quia ad duas circūferentias à fub-
endente duodecimam circuli partem recta linea, factas,ipfe cir cu-

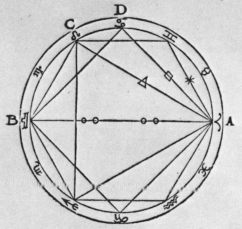

Diapafon feu dupla ratio tripliciter ⌠Totius circuli ad dimidium
respondet : Vel⟨ A B C ad A C, nępe 8 ad 4.
⌊A C B ad A D, fex ad tria.

Diapente feu fefquialtera, item tri- ⌠Totius circuli, feu 1 2. 8
pliciter : Vel⟨ D A B, ideſt, 9 ad 6
⌊A B, ideſt, 6 ad A C, ideſt 4.

Diateſſaron feu fefquitertia , item ⌠Totius circuli ad A B C D,
tripliciter : Vel⟨ feu 1 2 ad 4 in A B D.
⟨ A B C ad A B, ideſt 8 ad 6.
⌊A C ad A D, 4 ad 3.

Diapafon & Diapente, item tripliciter, Bifdiapafon uero dupliciter
Tonus femel .

Ius facit rationes,quæ funt duodecim ad unū,uel 1 1 quę alienæ funt
à confonantibus, non tamen à canoris: ad factas uero duas circūferentias

Page from Claudii Ptolemae, *Harmonicorum,* sive de musica libri III
(Venice, 1562).

LE ISTITVTIONI
HARMONICHE

DI M. GIOSEFFO ZARLINO DA CHIOGGIA;

Nelle quali ; oltra le materie appartenenti

ALLA MVSICA;

Si trouano dichiarati molti luoghi

di Poeti, d'Historici, & di Filosofi;

Si come nel leggerle si potrà chiaramente vedere.

Θεῦ διδόντος, οὐδὲν ἰσχύει φθόνος.
Καὶ μὴ διδόντος, οὐδὲν ἰσχύει πόνος.

Con Priuilegio dell'Illustriss. Signoria di Venetia,
per anni X.

IN VENETIA   M D LVIII.

Title page and illustration from the first edition of G. Zarlino, *Le Institutioni harmoniche* (Venice, 1558).

Elizabethan Statutes for St. John's College (1576), like statutes of Oxford and of continental universities, forbade the playing of musical instruments at times of quiet and study.[147]

The trumpeters employed by Trinity College at the time of Henry VIII, already mentioned, were probably regular employees of the college. At any rate, we find them embellishing a play performed during the Visitation of the University in Mary's reign (1556): "It. a show in trinite college in ther courte of the wynninge of an holde and takinge of prisoners, with waytes, trumpettes, gonnes, and squybbes."[148] And university trumpeters added pageantry to the visit of Queen Elizabeth to Cambridge in 1564: "Then came the Trumpetters and by solemn blast, declared her Majestie to approach."[149] There are many references, too, to the town waits of Cambridge in Cooper's *Annals* and occasional records of payments to visiting minstrels.[150] The performance of Thomas Legge's *Ricardus Tertius,* acted in St. John's College at commencement, 1579/80, contained a three-part song by no less a figure than William Byrd, founder of the great English madrigal school, written especially for this first of the many plays about the unfortunate hero of Bosworth Field.[151] Another university custom made pleasant by music—the celebration of John Port Latin Day—is described by Sir Symonds d'Ewes, a student of St. John's, in his diary, 1618:

And after the feast in hall was ended, all the fellow-commoners

[146] Robert Willis and John Willis Clark, *Architectural History of the University of Cambridge* (Cambridge, 1886), III, 358n.:

Inprimis, for a sette of newe vialls, viij il.
Item, for viall strings and mending the Colledge Instruments, xij s.
Item, for a sackbutt and the Carriage, iiij li xj s.

[147] *Cambridge Documents*, III, 299:

Statuimus igitur ut unusquisque dicti Collegii in suo cubiculo se honeste gerat et modeste cum vicinis suis, ut nullum quovis tempore a somno, quiete aut studio impediat per immoderatos clamores, risus, cantica, strepitus, saltationes aut musicorum instrumentorum pulsationes.

[148] Lamb, *Documents*, 196.
[149] Cooper, *Annals of Cambridge*, II, 188, quoting Stokys' narrative.
[150] See, for example, *ibid.*, I, 250.
[151] Edmund H. Fellowes, *William Byrd* (Oxford, 1936), 174. See Cooper, *Annals*, II, 372, for an account of the play.

and bachelors of the house, according to their annuary custom, went down the river to a pretty green near Chesterton, accompanied by a band of loud music; and having busied ourselves awhile with honest recreations, we returned to supper.[152]

From the sixteenth century onward, the Music Act sometimes formed a part of the commencement exercises, but no record of this occurs until 1574 when Matthew Stokys, former fellow of King's College, Esquire Bedell, and Registrar of the University, included a brief remark in his diary: "The masse don, after the Actes in Grammar, Arte, Musyke, and Physyke be fynyshyde, than shall begyn the Acte in Cyvill, iff there be any Commensers in Civill; iff none, then shall begynne the Acte in Canon."[153] As described in the diary of Sir Symonds d'Ewes, the participants in the Music Act performed instrumentally and also debated on music theory; indeed, we may assume from d'Ewes' description that musical disputation certainly occurred at times, although perhaps somewhat rarely.[154]

Musical works among the books owned by the university library in the late fifteenth century reflect certain interests and studies. Several of these appear in a list of books owned by the university in 1473, writers much in vogue during the Middle Ages—Isidorus, Aristotle, Richard of St. Victor, Rhabanus Maurus—as well as a tonale and a volume of hymns.[155] Among the cautions deposited

[152] Quoted by John H. Marsden, *College Life in the Time of James the First* (London, 1851), 62.

[153] Excerpts from *Stokys' Book* appear as Appendix A, Peacock, *Observations on the Statutes*. This remark, p. 11, is the only reference to music in the excerpts published.

[154] Marsden, *College Life*, 104–105, gives an epitome of d'Ewes' account:

> After making the remark that our University, like Africa, *semper aliquid producit novi*, Symonds proceeds to give an account of an Act in Music. A Sophister 'came up' in the schools bringing with him a viol; and he commenced his proceedings by playing upon ·his viol an original 'lesson' or exercise. After this he entered upon his position 'of sol, fa, mi, la,' which he defended against three opponents. When the opponents had left him master of the field he played another piece, probably in a triumphant strain; which gave the Moderator occasion to observe that *ubi desinit philosophus, ibi incipit musicus*. This Symonds has recorded 'a very pretty jest.'

by students, 1454–1511, are many service books which possibly include music, and one *antiphonarius notulatus*.[156]

Like its sister university, Cambridge granted degrees in music during the time of the Renaissance and perhaps earlier. And since one often encounters the statement that the early English degrees in music were on a par with the degrees in grammar (that is, permission to teach grammar), it is worth pointing out that in Cambridge documents bachelors of music rank above bachelors of arts —many of the early candidates for musical degrees, indeed, were already masters of arts—and are named along with bachelors in the three higher faculties—law, medicine, and theology. By the end of the Middle Ages (*ca.* 1450), music had become a separate faculty at Cambridge with its own personnel. There is a reference to bachelors of music in the *"Statuta antiqua,"* possibly from 1456, in a paragraph *"De cautionibus bacculaureorum"*: the caution deposited by the candidate for a musical degree must be valued at thirteen shillings, fourpence.[157] Money owed at commencement by bachelors of music—and these, significantly, appear in the lists

---

[155] Henry Bradshaw, *Collected Papers* (Cambridge, 1889), 37–42:

> *Ysiderus in ethimologiis,*
> *Problemata Aristotelis,*
> *Tabula politicorum,*
> *Tonale musicale,*
> *Ric^{us} de sancto victore,*
> *Rabanus de 2^a parte psalterij,*
> *Liber ympnorum.*

John Caius, listing the books in the library in 1574, has a section called "Cosmographia, Musica," which contains the item, *Quadripartitum Tholomei*: see his *Historiae Cantabrigiensis Academiae Libri duo* (Londini, 1574) in his *Works* (ed. by E. S. Roberts) (Cambridge, 1912), 69. This work, however, is one of Ptolemy's astronomical writings and not his book on music.

[156] See *Grace Book A* (ed. by Stanley M. Leathes) (Cambridge, 1897), *xiv–xv,* and *Grace Book B,* II, *xii.* According to Mr. Leathes (*Grace Book A, viii*), "On admission to a degree students were bound to deposit a 'caution' or pledge that they would proceed to perform the requisite acts: questionists, that they would 'determine': inceptors that they would actually commence, and incept within a fixed period."

[157] *Cambridge Documents*: I, 373:

> Item statuimus quod quilibet, admittendus ad gradum baccalaureatus in quacunque facultate, antequam admittatur cautionem realem exponat in manibus procuratorum, sub modo tamen et forma quae sequuntur, viz . . . in musica xiii. solidorum et iv. denariorum.

after masters of grammar, bachelors of arts, and masters of arts—according to the Elizabethan Statutes of 1559, include such customary items as fees to the vice-chancellor, the official who presented the candidate, proctors, registrar, bell ringer, and beadles, as well as fees for banquets, gloves, and various academic ceremonies contingent upon the taking of a degree.[158] The list of fees owed by the *baccalaureus in musica,* in fact, is used as a model in these statutes for listing fees owed by the bachelor of medicine and of civil law.[159] The doctor of music, along with the *inceptor* in medicine and civil law, had to pay almost identical sums to the same university officials, fees for certain commencement acts (responsions, for example), and higher fees for gloves and banquets.[160] One item in this list (*"pro duabus responsionibus xiii^s iiii^d"*) indicates that the *inceptor* in music would ordinarily perform two responsions,[161] although there are no rules regarding disputation for candidates in music as there are for students in the other faculties. An identical statute for *inceptores* in music appeared in the Elizabethan Statutes of 1570, which set forth a list of fees owed by bachelors of music similar to those of 1559.[162]

[158] Lamb, *Documents,* 297:

Baccalaureus in musica solvet vice-chancellario ii^s praesentatori ii^s procuratoribus ii^s pro communa xx^d registro iiii^d pulsatori xii^d bedellis pro collectis iiii^s viii^d pro prandiis xviii^d pro chirothecis xviii^d pro introitu vi^s viii^d pro visitatione vi^s viii^d. Summa xxx^s.

[159] *Ibid.*: "*Baccalaureus in medicina et in jure civili solvent quemadmodum dictum est de baccalaureo in musica.*"

[160] *Ibid.*:

Inceptor in musica medicina vel jure civili vice-cancellario ii^s praesentatori ii^s procuratoribus ii^s pro communa xx^d registro viii^d pulsatori xii^d bedellis pro collectis ii^s viii^d pro duabus responsionibus xiii^s iiii^d pro introitu vi^s viii^d pro prandiis et chirothecis iii^s crastino comitiorum xiii^s iiii^d pro calendario iii^s iiii^d. Summa li^s viii^d.

[161] According to *Grace Book A,* xxiv, "responding" was one of the acts "forming part of the general exercise of disputation," the exact character of which is not known.

[162] *Cambridge Documents,* I, 487:

Baccalaureus in musica solvet cancellario ii^s, presentatori xii^d, procuratoribus ii^s, pro communa i^s viii^d, registro iiii^d, pulsatori xii^d, bedellis pro collectis iiii^s viii^d, pro prandiis i^s vi^d, pro chirothecis i^s vi^d, pro introitu vi^s viii^d, pro visitatione vi^s viii^d. Summa xxx^s.

In these statutes of 1570 bachelors of music are twice classed above bachelors of arts and placed with masters of arts and bachelors in the higher faculties. One statute requiring strict attendance at public lectures, with deans acting as monitors, excepts *"artium magistros, legum, musicae et medicinae baccalaureos."*[163] Another ruling excuses these same persons from certain restrictions with regard to dining in town.[164] Bachelors of music are named again in a curious decree of 1571, forbidding bathing in the waters of Cambridge County and making this offense punishable by whipping if the offender is below the grade of bachelor of arts, and by expulsion for a second offense; bachelors of arts who broke this law were to be put in the stocks for one day and fined, and bachelors of law, medicine, and music were to be severely punished.[165] Bachelors of music are also mentioned several times in a decree of 1585 giving "minute regulations respecting the apparel of the Scholars"—for instance, for the "facing of gownes for Bachelors

---

[163] *Ibid.*, I, 457–58:

Nullus scholaris . . . ullam publicam lectionem ejus professionis cui destinatus est omittat. . . . Statuimus ut Decani cujusque collegii aut, si nullus ibi sit decanus, tunc primarii lectores monitores singulis septimanis pro qualibet dictorum auditorum classe (artium magistros, legum, musicae et medicinae baccalaureos et superiores gradus excipimus) constituant.

[164] *Ibid.*, I, 485:

Baccalaurei tamen legum, medicinae et musicae, artium magistri et superiores gradus, pupilli etiam tutores comitantes, vel ad parentes et amicos in oppidum tanquam hospites adventantes, accersiti solummodo, ad prandium et coenam impune recipi possunt.

[165] George Dyer, *Privileges of the University of Cambridge* (London, 1824), I, 303–305:

Si quis Scholarium hujus Universitatis . . . infra Gradum Bac. Artium rivum, stagnum, aut aliam aquam quamcunq. intro Comitatum Cantabrigiae, natandi seu lavandi causa, diurno seu nocturno tempore ingrediatur . . . delinquens . . . verberibus castigetur et puniatur palam et publice. . . . Quod si sit in Artibus Magister, aut Bac. in Jure, Medicina, aut Musicâ, aut superioris Gradus aut ordinis, tunc eum severe puniendum et castigandum judicio et arbitrio Praepositi Collegii, in quo idem delinquens inhabitat.

According to Peacock (*Observations on the Statutes,* 53n.), the severity of this decree reflects the "harsh and domineering temper and conduct" of the then vice-chancellor, Dr. Whitgift.

of musick, phisick and law, and for Masters of Art and upward, at the onely half a yard downe ward by the brest, and a quarter of a yard at the handes of a streight sleeve, and no where else."[166] Offenders against this ruling were fined, with certain exceptions: among them, "All doctors of Law Phisick and musicke, whiles they shal be abroade out of the Universitie and in going and coming to and fro."[167] In line with this dispensation for less somber dress on certain occasions, bachelors and doctors of music were excepted from other regulations specifying solid, unrelieved black for academic gowns.[168]

The earliest existing record of a degree in music awarded by the University of Cambridge antedates the earliest Oxford record of such a degree by about forty years, for in 1463/4, according to *Grace Book A,* Henry Abyngton was made a bachelor of music; and later in the same year he was created doctor of music on condition that he remain in Cambridge a year.[169] In 1470/1 a certain Lessy of the Duchess of York's private chapel was awarded the baccalaureate in music, having had both theory and practice in music; and that same year John Baudwyn was awarded the degree under the same specifications.[170] Several notices refer to a certain

[166] Cooper, *Annals of Cambridge,* II, 411.

[167] *Ibid.,* II, 413.

[168] *Ibid.*:

Finally, if hereafter any new forme or excesse in apparell, either other colour then blacke or such like sad colour, except that the doublett being close worne and not seene may be of other colour. Saving that it may be lawfull to Bachelers of law phisicke and musick, Masters of arte and other of highe degree, to have two playne stitches or one small lace of silke of the colour of the garment about the edges thereof, and at the gorgett, and in the length of the doublett sleeves. . . . Nor to weare anye slop but the playne small slop . . . of none other colour but blacke, or of like sad colour, except Masters of Arte, Bachelers and Doctors of law, phisicke and musicke.

[169] *Grace Book A,* 41, 45:

Item admissus fuit Henricus Abyngton in musica bachalaureus xxij° die Febr. cuius communa xx d. . . . Concessa est gracia henrico habyngton quod post admissionem ad gradum bachalarii in Musica possit admitti ad incipiendum in eadem sic quod continuet hic ante admissionem per annum.

[170] *Ibid.,* 86, 88:

Concessa est gracia lessy de capella ducisse Eboracensis vt cum studio et specu-

Sothey or Suthey who became a bachelor of music in 1489, probably the same man whose name occurs in a list of expenses connected with the performance of plays at King's College some years earlier (1482).[171] In 1493, Magister Robert Cowper deposited a caution against becoming a bachelor of music and was allowed to be away from the university on condition that he "commence within the year."[172] Two more degrees in music were granted in the fifteenth century—to Humphrey Frevill, 1496, after two years' study of music at Cambridge and five years' practice elsewhere in England; and to a certain Pypis, whose admission was allowed to stand *pro completa forma* upon payment of five shillings.[173]

No definite generalization on the awarding of musical degrees at Cambridge in the fifteenth century can be drawn from these graces, as almost every petition appears to have been treated differently. With two candidates, *musica speculativa et practica was re-* quired. One candidate had studied music at Cambridge and practiced it in England. Abyngton, who had been appointed Succentor of Wells Cathedral in 1447 and who subsequently (1465) became Master of the Song at the Chapel Royal, received the doctorate in music *per saltem*—without the customary interval between the baccalaureate and doctorate. Cowper, who later took the doctor of music degree, was apparently a *magister artium* before taking

lacione in musica et cum practica eiusdem possit intrare in musica. . . . Concessa est gracia domino Johanni Baudwyn vt cum forma habita possit intrare in musica vt supra.

171 *Grace Book B*, I, 15, 20f.; "*Caucio Suthey bachalaurii in musica et est vna murra cum rosa in fundo. . . . Communia Suthey bachalaurei in musica.*" And among the bachelors of 1489 is Sothey, *in Musica.* See also Frederick S. Boas, *University Drama in the Tudor Age* (Oxford, 1914), 2, for the reference to Suthey in an account of expenses for plays performed at King's: "*Item sol. Goldyng & Suthey pro expensis circa ludos in festo Natalis domini vii*[s] *ij*[d]." See also Nan Cooke Carpenter, "Musicians in Early University Drama," *Notes and Queries*, Vol. 195 (1950), 470–72.

172 *Grace Book B*, I, 59, 65: "*Caucio Roberti Cowper admissi ad intrandum in musica die quo supra et est vnum regale et ij*[s] *iiij*[d]. . . . *Conceditur magistro Cowper quod absentet se post admissionem sic quod commenset infra annum.*"

173 *Ibid.*, I, 100, 107:

Conceditur humfrido fryvel ut studium duorum annorum in musica in ista vniuersitate cum practica quinque annorum in eadem in patria sufficiat sibi ad intrandum in eadem. . . . Conceditur domino pypis admisso ad intrandum in musica ut sua admissio stet pro completa forma sic quod soluat quinque solidos.

his degree in music; Humphrey Frevill, too, became a doctor of music eventually, and the grace conceding this refers to him as *magister*. About the academic background of the other candidates there is no evidence.

Robert Fairfax, one of England's leading composers in the first quarter of the sixteenth century and head of the royal singers with Henry VIII at the Field of the Cloth of Gold, was the first man to receive the doctorate in music in the sixteenth century. A notice from 1500/1 concedes him the baccalaureate on the basis of ten years' study *"in musica speculatiua simul et in practica"*; and a grace given the next year (1501/2) permits him to become an *inceptor in musica*, his own *erudicio* standing *pro forma*.[174] Fairfax apparently did not actually become a doctor of music until 1503/4, however; for the *"Caucio Roberti fayerfaxe sex nobilia"* was deposited that year, and "doctor ffarefax" is listed among the *Inceptores in musica* of that year.[175]

Robert Cowper, who, like Fairfax, was one of England's foremost composers in the early sixteenth century, was required to spend five years in the study and practice of music from the time of his baccalaureate before receiving the doctor's degree, according to his grace of 1501/2; in 1504/5 his *forma habita* was allowed to stand *pro completa forma* with the understanding that he "incept" within two years; and in 1506/7 "doctor Cowper" incepted in music.[176] Humphrey Frevill's grace for the doctorate

[174] *Ibid.*, I, 161, and *Grace Book* Γ, 4:

Item habet Robertus fayrfax ut studium in musica speculatiua simul et in practica decem annos sufficiat ad intrandum in eadem.

Item conceditur magistro ffayerfax erudito in musica quod post gradum baccalariatus sua erudicio potest stare pro forma ad incipiendum in musica.

[175] *Grace Book B*, I, 190, 192.
[176] *Grace Book* Γ, 4, 38:

Item conceditur magistro Roberto Cowper vt studium quinque annorum cum practica totidem annorum citra introitum suum in eadem sufficiat sibi ad incipiendum in musica. . . . Item conceditur magistro Cowpar bacallario in musica vt forma habita possit stare pro completa forma ad incipiendum in eadem sic quod incipiat infra biennium.

See *Grace Book B*, I, 223 for his inception in 1506/7.

was also passed in 1504/5, allowing three years' study of music at Cambridge and in England to stand *pro completa forma*.[177]

The first record of the incorporation of an Oxford graduate in music comes from 1501/2, when Magister Wydow, dressed in a robe of any color he liked (because the faculty of music had no standards of its own for academic dress) was granted the Cambridge degree.[178] The next year John Parker, after three and one-half years of study at the university, was granted the bachelor's degree.[179] In 1507/8, Robert Porret deposited a cup as his caution and received the bachelor's degree later that same year.[180] In 1515/6, John Watkins deposited his caution, and later that same year his grace for the baccalaureate in music was passed on the condition that he compose a Mass and antiphon.[181] A similar requirement appears in the grace of John Firtun, passed also in 1515/6; a vicar of St. Stephens College, Westminster, Firtun's eight years of study in that college together with a like number of years in the chapel of the Duke of Norfolk were thought sufficient for granting him the baccalaureate in music, provided he compose a Mass and antiphon.[182] *Intrantes in musica*, 1516/7, were *Dominus Borow, Dominus plummer;* both had studied music *in hac vniuersitate* and practiced it for seven years, and both

[177] *Grace Book* Γ, 37: *Item conceditur magistro Humfrido ffrevill baccallario in musica vt studium trium annorum in hac vniuersitate et in patria sibi stent pro completa forma ad incipiendum in musica.*"

[178] *Ibid.*, 8: *"Item conceditur magistro Qydow bacallario in musica Oxonie quod possit stare eodem [gradu] et incorporari hic et vti habitu suo gradui competente cuiuscunque coloris velit."*

[179] *Ibid.*, 16: *"Item conceditur Johanni Parker vt studium trium annorum et dimidii in hac vniuersitate in arte musica sufficiat sibi pro completa forma ad intrandum in eadem arte."*

[180] *Grace Book* B, I, 229 *("Caucio domini Porret musici vna mirra in linthio cum nomine suprascripto"),* 233.

[181] *Ibid.*, II, 42 *("Caucio Magistri watkyns Intrantis in musica admissi eodem die"),* and *Grace Book* Γ, 132: *"Item conceditur Johanni Watkyns vt studium septem annorum in musica hic et alibi sufficiant [sic] sibi ad intrandum in sciencia musicali sic quod missam et antiphonam pro forma componat."*

[182] *Ibid.*:

Item conceditur domino Johanni Firtun sacerdoti vni vicariorum de collegio regali sancti Stephen Westmonasterii ut studium octo annorum in eodem collegio et totidem in capella domine Norff' sit sibi sufficiens ad intrandum in sciencia musicali sic quod faciat missam et antiphonam de sancta Maria.

were required to compose a Mass *pro forma*.[183] In 1519/20, Benjamin Beryderyke was granted the bachelor's degree in music, having studied *musica speculativa* at Cambridge for a year and having practiced and taught music in England; in addition, he had to compose a Mass or antiphon.[184]

More than a decade elapsed before another degree in music was recorded. In 1533/4, the grace of a Dominus Henry Corsse, student of music for seven years, was passed on condition that he compose a Mass.[185] A few years later (1536/7), Christopher Tye, one of the most distinguished teachers and composers of the reign of Henry VIII, received the bachelor's degree in music at Cambridge. According to his grace, ten years spent in the study of music *cum practica multa* both in composing and in teaching were considered sufficient *ad intrandum* in music, provided that Tye show some very obvious evidence of his erudition at commencement and compose a Mass to be sung at this time or on the birthday of the prince (Edward VI).[186] In 1544/5, Tye's grace for the doctorate in music was passed. Since there was no doctor in the music faculty,

---

[183] *Ibid.*, 140.

> Item conceditur Thome Burrow vt studium in hac vniuersitate et septem anni in patria in practica sciencie musicalis sufficiant sibi ad intrandum in eadem facultate sic quod componat missam pro forma. . . . Item eadem gracia conceditur domino Plumer presbitero de verbo in verbum.

See *Grace Book B*, II, 55, for *Intrantes in musica*, 1516/7.

[184] *Grace Book* Γ, 176:

> Item conceditur domino Beniamin Beryderyke vt studium vnius anni in speculatione musice hic in akademia (sic) et quinque in quibus practicauit et docuit in patria sufficiant sibi ad intrandum in eadem facultate sic quod componat missam vel antiphonam.

[185] *Ibid.*, 277: *"Item conceditur Henrico Crosse presbitero vt studium septem annorum in musica sufficiant [sic] ei ad intrandum in eadem sic quod componat missam."* See *Graec Book B*, II, 187, for an item from 1533/4, *"Intrans in musica: Dominus Crosse."*

[186] *Grace Book* Γ, 312:

> In primis conceditur Christofero Tye vt studium decem annorum in arte musica cum practica multa in eadem tum componendo tum pueros erudiendo sufficiat ei ad intrandum in eadem sic vt componat vnam missam vel paulo post commitia canendam vel eo ipso die quo serenissimi principis obseruabitur aduentus saltem saltem (sic) vt manifestum ac euidens aliquod specimen eius eruditionis hic ostendat in commitiis.

Tye was to be presented by one of the proctors, and he was allowed to use the robes of a doctor of medicine at the commencement exercises; according to this grace, study and practice of music for ten years after the baccalaureate were considered sufficient *pro completo gradu doctoratus* on condition that he compose a Mass to be sung at the commencement exercises.[187] One other degree is recorded from the sixteenth century, that of the composer Robert White, 1560/1, whose ten years of study in music sufficed *ad intrandum in eadem,* with the provision that he compose a communion service (the word Mass is no longer used) to be sung in the university's St. Mary's Church at commencement.[188] Others created bachelor of music at Cambridge in this century were Richard Carleton (1577), William Blitheman (1586), and Edward Johnson (1594).[189]

Graces awarding musical degrees to Orlando Gibbons and Robert Ramsey were passed early in the next century (1606 and 1616). Seven years spent in the study of music were thought adequate for awarding Gibbons, royal organist, the baccalaureate, provided that he compose a song to be performed at Act time; he was to be presented for his degree by a regent master and was to wear the

[187]*Grace Book* Δ (ed. by John Venn) (Cambridge, 1910), 28:

> Item conceditur Christofero Tye hic apud vos in musica bacchalaureus (sic) vt studium et practica decem annorum post gradum bacchalaureatus susceptum sufficiat ei pro completo gradu doctoratus in eadem facultate ita tamen vt componat missam in die commitiorum canendam coram vobis conviuet et satisfaciat officiariis et quoniam non reperitur doctor in eadem facultate presentetur in habitu non regentis per vnum procuratorum.

> Item conceditur eidem nuper admisso ad incipiendum in musica vt possit vti commitiorum tempore habitu doctorum in medicina.

[188] *Ibid.,* 148:

> Conceditur 13 Decembris Roberto Wight vt studium 10 annorum in musica sufficiat ei ad intrandum in eadem sic tamen vt componat communionem cantandam in ecclesia beate Marie coram vniuersitate in die comitiorum sub pena quadraginta solidorum.

[189] Williams, *Degrees in Music,* 119–51, gives biographical notices of Cambridge graduates in music, omitting, however, several whose names appear in the early *Grace Books.*

dress of a bachelor of arts.[190] Ramsey's grace was couched in virtually the same terms, although his composition was to be sung in St. Mary's on commencement day.[191] Thomas Bangcroft, Thomas Ravenscroft, and John Tomkins were also made bachelors of music at Cambridge early in the seventeenth century—in 1605, 1607, and 1608 respectively.[192]

From the existing graces awarding the baccalaureate and doctorate in music at Cambridge in the sixteenth century it appears that there were no rigid requirements. Many of the early musical candidates held degrees in arts: Fairfax, Frevill, Cowper, Wydow, Watkins, and perhaps Plummer[193] were masters of arts, and Firtun and Beryderyke were bachelors of arts when they received their degrees in music. From 1516, when Magister Watkins was admitted to the bachelor's degree in music, the requirements seem to have become rather more strict: Watkins and subsequent candidates had to show that they had studied music at Cambridge or elsewhere for a certain number of years, and they were required to prove their proficiency *in eadem arte* by the composition of a Mass or antiphon or both, usually to be performed at St. Mary's during commencement. These requirements, in fact, may have been in force much earlier; and it was probably the usual custom for the university to draw upon gifted *musici* in preparing for commencement festivities. There is no record in the Cambridge documents showing that

---

[190] *Grace Book E* (unpublished). I am indebted to Mrs. C. P. Hall, assistant archivist, Cambridge, for help in deciphering these graces.

1606. Bacchalaureus in musica.

Conceditur Orlando Gibbins (sic) regius organista (sic) vt studium septem annorum in musica sufficiat ei ad intrandum in eadem: sic tamen vt canticum componat cantandum hora et loco per vicecancellarium designandis coram vniuersitate in die commitiorum et vt presentetur per magistrum regentem in habitu baccalarei in artibus.

[191] *Ibid.*:

1616. Practicantes in Musica. Conceditur 10 Junij 1616. Supplicat reverentijs vestris Robertus Ramsey vt studium septem annorum in Musica sufficiat ei ad intrandum in eadem, sic tamen vt canticum componat cantandum in ecclesia Beate Marie coram uniuersitate in die Commitiorum, et vt presentetur per Magistrum in habitu baccalarei in Artibus.

[192] See note 189.

[193] A *dominus Plummer* became master of arts in 1510/1: see *Grace Book* Γ, 84.

Robert Fairfax had to compose a Mass for either of his degrees, and yet the Lambeth Manuscript at Cambridge contains, among several Fairfax Masses, one which is superscribed, "Doctor Fayrfax for his forme in proceeding to his degree."[194]

Of the four men awarded the doctorate in music at Cambridge in the sixteenth century, each fulfilled different requirements. Fairfax, *eruditus in musica,* may have been required to compose a Mass; according to his grace, *"erudicio sua potest stare pro forma ad incipiendum in musica."* Cowper was required to spend five additional years in the study of music after attaining the baccalaureate, *"cum practica totidem annorum."* Frevill had to show that he had studied three years, after receiving the bachelor's degree, *"in hac universitate et in patria."* And Tye had to study for ten more years after the baccalaureate[195] and to compose a Mass as well. The graces of some of these candidates specified the person to present the aspirant, since there was no professor of music on the faculty. Others told the robe the *inceptor* must use: Wydow, from Oxford, a robe of any color he wished; Tye, the robe of a doctor of medicine; Ramsey, the robe of a bachelor of arts—all this signifying the lack of set academic dress for graduates in music.[196]

Some of the men honored by Cambridge in the fifteenth and sixteenth centuries were at the time or became later leading composers of sacred and secular music in England—especially Fairfax, Cowper, Tye, Robert White, Gibbons, and Ramsey. Some became famous as organists or choir directors in the great cathedrals and in

---

[194] Henry Davey, *History of English Music* (2nd revised edition, London, 1921), 85. Davey assumes (p. 92) that the Mass was written as the commencement exercise for the doctorate, 1504. Williams, however, says that this Mass was performed when Fairfax was incorporated at Oxford, 1511 (*Degrees in Music,* 120). More recently, Don Anselm Hughes (*Musica Disciplina,* VI, 88) states that the five-part Mass *O quam glorifica* was Fairfax' doctoral exercise for the Cambridge investiture.

[195] According to the records, about nine years elapsed between the two degrees. Tye was incorporated doctor at Oxford in 1548.

[196] One is not surprised at this absence of set rules for graduates in music, for the number of men who received degrees in music is small compared with lists of graduates in arts, law, medicine, and divinity. To cite only one example, in the decade 1501-11, two degrees in music were awarded; in 1507, there was one doctor of music among a total of ninety-six degrees; and in 1508, there was one bachelor of music among sixty-eight degrees. See *Grace Book* Γ.

the Chapel Royal—Abington, Wydow, Firtun, Porret, Tye, Blithe-man, and Gibbons. Although Hugh Ashton, England's first great instrumental composer, did not receive a degree in music from either university, he, too, had a university background. An Oxford graduate in the arts, he was a scholar of St. John's, Cambridge, a *magister artium* who paid a fee *pro non legendo* in 1507/8, and a bachelor in canon law that same year; and in 1511/12 he was still in the university, for that year he again paid a fee *pro non legendo*.[197]

Several music treatises which appeared late in the sixteenth and early in the seventeenth centuries are also related to the study of music at Cambridge, both *musica speculativa* and *musica prac-tica*. In 1568, John Alford's translation of Adrien Le Roy's famous treatise on lute playing was published, the *Instruction de partir toute musique des huit tons divers en tablature de luth,* 1557.[198] Alford matriculated as a member of Pembroke College, Cambridge, in 1545,[199] and his interest in lute playing may have been stimulated by informal musical activities as an undergraduate in the university. Two other Cambridge men also published an instrumental instruction book: *The Cittharne Schoole,* 1597, by Anthony Holborne, to which were added "sixe short Aers . . . done by his brother, William Holborne."[200] Anthony Holborne, composer and member of the Chapel Royal, matriculated at Cambridge in 1562 and his brother William in 1578/9.[201] The instrumentalist Thomas Robinson was probably a Cambridge man.[202] His *Schoole of Mu-sicke* (1603) gives instruction in lute playing and compositions for that instrument, and his *New Citharen Lessons* (1609) provided music for the cittern. And John Dowland, in his translation of Ornithoparcus' *Micrologus* (1609), was pleased to sign himself, "Lute-player, and Bachelor of Musicke in both the Vniuersities."

[197] *Grace Book B,* I, 229, 233; II, 4.

[198] No copy of the original is extant. See Boyd, *Elizabethan Music and Musical Criticism,* 154.

[199] John Venn and J. A. Venn, *Alumni cantabrigienses* (Cambridge, 1922–44), Part I, I, 15.

[200] Boyd, *Elizabethan Music,* 155.

[201] Venn and Venn, *Alumni cantabrigienses,* Part I, II, 387.

[202] This name occurs several times in the matriculation rolls: *ibid.,* III, 473–74.

Thomas Campion, distinguished poet and composer of the Jacobean period, was for some time a scholar at Peterhouse, Cambridge. He left the university, however, in 1584, without having taken a degree, possibly for further study upon the continent.[203] Among his many literary and musical compositions is a treatise on music: *A New Way of making Fowre Parts in Counter-point*, 1613.[204] In his dedication of this work to "Charles, Prince of Great Brittaine," Campion connects music and medicine—he was himself a physician —and then says that he will redeem "the skill of musicke . . . from such darknesse, wherein enuious antiquitie of purpose did inuolve it." Although this treatise is a practical work for beginners in counterpoint, it is not completely lacking in speculative ideas: the four voices used in music, for instance, the Base, Tenor, Meane, and Treble, are shown to resemble the four elements. Interesting here, too, is Campion's tribute of high praise to Sethus Calvisius, music director in Leipzig, whose treatise he has followed and who is also mentioned in certain Oxford treatises.[205]

In 1612 appeared a most unusual musical treatise, *A Briefe Discourse of the true (but neglected) use of Charact'ring the Degrees by their Perfection, Imperfection, and diminution in Measurable Musicke, against the Common Practise and Customs of these Times*, by Thomas Ravenscroft (born 1593), who received the bachelor's degree at Cambridge at the age of fourteen.[206] The treatise proper is remarkable for attempting to reintroduce the old mensural proportions of the late Middle Ages with the medieval time signatures, drawing upon Tunstede's *Quatuor principalia* for theory (although Ravenscroft continually refers to John Dunstable as the author of this important work on *musica mensurabilis*) and mentioning other medieval writers. In his opening "Apologia," Ravenscroft makes a plea for the restoration of music as a science and art,

---

[203] Miles Merwin Kastendieck, *England's Musical Poet, Thomas Campion* (New York, 1938), 47, and Percival Vivian (ed.), *Campion's Works* (Oxford, 1909), xl.

[204] *Ibid.*, 189–226.

[205] *Ibid.*, 219: "Of all the latter writers in Musicke, whome I haue knowne, the best and most learned, is *Zethus Caluisius* a Germane."

[206] Davey, *History of English Music*, 211. There is a copy of the treatise in the Huntington Library.

with much praise for John Case and Thomas Morley; and the work is embellished by commendatory poems from the hands of such distinguished musicians as Nathaniel Giles, Campion, Dowland, and others. As examples to prove his theory, Ravenscroft cites madrigals of his own composition as well as some by other men—some in dialect.

And finally, Henry Peacham (B.A., Cambridge, 1595, M.A., 1598)[207] included a chapter on music in his *Compleat Gentleman,* comparing music with poetry and medicine, telling its good effects, and describing the music of many composers of his time, both English and continental. His treatise is an interesting example of the use of the hortatory treatise, derived from the *protreptikos,* during the Renaissance: not to encourage the student to philosophy by way of music but to encourage the art of music as a gentlemanly accomplishment.

iv. SPAIN: SALAMANCA

SALAMANCA, one of the four most important *studia* in Europe at the beginning of the university period, continued to be a seat of culture and learning throughout the Renaissance, generally known for its humanistic spirit, toleration, and progressiveness. Music, it appears, was no small part of this culture—in academic affairs, in the lecture room, and in student activities. A chair of music, we recall, had been established at Salamanca in the thirteenth century by Alfonso, *"el Rey Sabio,"* the first such chair in any European university; and this chair continued to be a part of the university organization throughout the Renaissance and, indeed, into the nineteenth century. Statutes promulgated in the sixteenth century were very definite in regard to musical requirements. According to statutes of 1538, the first ever issued to the university by royal decree, music, along with astrology and *gramatica de menores,* might be taught in the native tongue.[1] The duties of the

207 Venn and Venn, *Alumni cantabrigienses,* Part I, III, 325.

music professor, who immediately precedes the professor of mathematics in these statutes, were carefully outlined: this professor was to lecture on speculative music for half the hour and to conduct his students in singing for the remaining period; plain song, mensural music, and counterpoint were to be taught, this last by the professor or his substitute.[2]

The *catredatico de musica* figures several times again in these statutes. For instance, even though he were a master and actually present at medical disputations, he was to be paid no fee.[3] Furthermore, those students who voted for a candidate to fill a vacant chair of music—at this university, organized along such democratic lines that even women might attend, students elected professors to vacant chairs[4]—must have spent a certain amount of time at the university.[5]

Statutes of 1561 made no real changes with regard to music. As in the preceding statutes, the professor of music was to "read" for half the hour in *musica speculativa,* for the other half in *musica practica;* and, again, music lectures did not have to be given in

---

[1] Esperabé y Arteaga, Enrique, *Historia pragmática é interna de la Universidad de Salamanca* (Salamanca, 1914–17), I, 148:

> Item estatuimos y ordenamos que los lectores sean obligados a leer en latin y no hablen en las catredas en romance excepto refiriendo alguna ley del rey no oponiendo enxemplo mas esto no se entienda en los lectores de gramatica de menores y astrologia y musica.

[2] *Ibid.,* I, 158:

> El catredatico de musica leera vna parte de su ora de la especulacion de la musica y otra pte exercite los oventes en cãtar: y hasta el mes de marzo muestre cãto llano y de alii a la fiesta de sant Juan canto de organo y de alii a vacaciones: el o su sostituto les muestre contrajunto.

Since the academic year was quite long, professors were allowed after eight months of continuous lecturing to read through substitutes for the rest of the year. See Caro Lynn, *A College Professor of the Renaissance: Lucio Marineo Siculo among the Spanish Humanists* (Chicago, 1937), 70.

[3] Esperabé y Arteaga, *Historia,* I, 162: "*En las disputas en medicina no ganen los catredaticos de retorica musica ni gramatica avnque sean maestros y se hallẽ presentes.*"

[4] See Aubrey F. G. Bell, *Luis de Léon* (Oxford, 1925), 79.

[5] Esperabé y Arteaga, *Historia,* I, 182: "*En la catreda de musica sean votos los que vuieren oydo en la dicha catreda seys meses desde cinco años atras ãtes de la vacadura y q esto se entiendi generalmete y que no sean otros votos.*"

Latin.[6] In these statutes, however, the part of the music lecturer in medical disputations was given more importance; for *tres reales* were to be paid the *"cathedraticos de Gramatica y Rhetorica, Musica y Astrologia, con tal que arguyan en el acto."*[7] The requirements for voting to elect a professor of music remained the same as in the statutes of 1538.[8] According to statutes promulgated for the Irish College in the University of Salamanca the year William Bathe of Oxford joined the staff (1604), we recall, each student in the college was required to study music and Greek literature.

Not only in the classroom but in academic ceremonies and student activities, music held a high place at Salamanca. The Spanish custom of serenading one's chosen lady was an established tradition with university students, whether rich or so poor as to be able to gather together only three singers and a guitar for the serenade.[9] Very poor students sometimes supported themselves by giving singing lessons[10]—a means of earning a livelihood we shall find at other universities, especially the German ones.

Students sang in the university choir, too, since the cathedral was very closely associated with the university and since the cathedral choirmaster was sometimes professor of music in the university. Statutes of 1561 specify Masses to be sung in the chapel on certain feastdays and also as part of the funeral ceremonies for members of the university, under the direction of the *maestro de canto*.[11] Individual colleges had their own choirs, which participated in various religious ceremonies—festivals and funerals—all very elaborate, if we may believe a Renaissance historian.[12] On religious

---

[6] *Ibid.*, I, 262, 266:

> El cathedratico de Canto ha de leer media hora de musica speculativa, y otra media hora de practica. . . . Yten estatuimos y ordenamos que todos los lectores de la vniuersidad . . . sean obligados a leer en latin. . . . Pero lo susodicho no se entienda en los lectores de Musica y Astrologia ni con los que leen Gramatica de menores.

[7] *Ibid.*, I, 275.

[8] *Ibid.*, I, 303.

[9] Gustave Reynier, *La Vie universitaire dans l'ancienne Espagne* (Paris, Toulouse, 1902), 55.

[10] See Bell, *Luis de León*, 67n.

[11] Esperabé y Arteaga, *Historia*, I, 323.

holidays, students and townspeople alike celebrated with colorful processions, singing, dancing, and playing instruments.[13]

After the election of a candidate to a professorship, singing and instrumental concerts were a part of the triumphant celebration, ending, perhaps, with a masquerade in which music was, of course, essential.[14] As in other universities, musical instruments were used to heighten the ceremonies connected with the doctoral act, which, like all celebrations at Salamanca, was an elaborate and expensive affair.[15] Possibly in an effort to reduce expenses contingent upon this act, statutes of 1538 ordered that only *"seys trompetas y tres pares de atabales y no mas so la dicha pena"* might be used in the doctoral act.[16] Before the ceremony a student mounted on horseback and preceded by trumpets and drums distributed to all the doctors who were to participate in the ceremony a list of theses to be sustained; and shortly thereafter the university personnel gathered together for a solemn procession through the town, headed by musicians[17]—all very similar to academic pageantry in the Italian universities. Oboes, trumpets, and drums were used to herald the candidate's doctoral address. And trumpets were used to announce the bullfight by which the entire academic body was entertained after the successful candidate had been invested with his degree.

The names of most of the men who held the chair of music in the University of Salamanca during the Renaissance are known to us through documentary evidence. In the fifteenth century, Bar-

[12] Pedro Chacon, *"Historia de la Universidad de Salamanca," Semanario erudito,* Vol. XVIII (Madrid, 1789), 35:

Pagase tambien de ésta lo que se gasta en la Capilla de Escuelas, que tiene muchos Capellanes, y Cantores para la fiestas, y para las honras de los Maestros y Doctores quando mueren, que en ella se hacen con mucha plata, y richos ornamentos, y cera que todo junto hace gran suma.

[13] Reynier, *La Vie universitaire,* 72–74.

[14] *Ibid.,* 79–80, 80n.

[15] Although the bachelor's degree involved comparatively little expense, the taking of the licentiate (consecration of the master's degree) or doctorate was such an expensive matter that few men proceeded to these degrees. See Bell, *Luis de Léon,* 73.

[16] Esperabé y Arteaga, *Historia,* I, 166–67.

[17] See Reynier, *La Vie universitaire,* 82–89, for a description of these ceremonies.

tolomé Ramos Pereira held this position for several years beginning in 1452 (terminal year unknown), Fernando Gómez de Salamanca for an undetermined period of time, ending in 1465, and Martín Gómez de Cantalapiedra from 1465 to 1479.[18] Ramos de Pereja, we recall, was summoned to Italy by Nicolas V and was teaching music in Bologna in 1482, according to his own words, as a public lecturer in the university. Fernando Gómez (died 1465) was cathedral *cantor* as well as professor of music in the university; but nothing is known of Martín Gómez except that he held the master's degree.[19] This, however, was one step more than the requirement; for professors of music, along with professors of astronomy, rhetoric, and languages, might be bachelors, whereas other professors were expected to hold the master's or doctor's degree.[20]

Because records are missing, there is a gap in the list of men who taught music at Salamanca in the closing decades of the fifteenth century and early years of the sixteenth; but from 1522 the list of sixteenth-century professors of music is complete:

> (?)–1522: Diego de Fermoselle.
> 1522–1542: Lucas Fernández.
> 1542–1566: Juan de Oviedo.
> 1567–1590: Francisco Salinas.
> 1590–1593: Roque de Salamanca.
> 1593–1603: Bernardo Clavijo.[21]

According to one source, Fermoselle, master and licentiate, probably began teaching in 1506, but a more recent authority says that Diego de Fermoselle was professor of music from 1503 until 1522.[22] Diego was the brother of Spain's distinguished poet-musician Juan del Encina, "the seventh son of a shoemaker named Fermoselle," who afterwards changed his name.[23] Juan de Fermoselle was a

---

[18] Esperabé y Arteaga, *Historia,* II, part 1, 249.

[19] *Ibid.,* II, part 1, 262.

[20] Lynn, *A College Professor of the Renaissance,* 22.

[21] Esperabé y Arteaga, *Historia,* II, part 1, 316.

[22] *Ibid.,* II, part 1, 347, and Gilbert Chase, "The Origins of the Lyric Theatre in Spain," *Musical Quarterly,* Vol. XXV (1939), 294.

[23] Gilbert Chase, *The Music of Spain* (New York, 1941), 37.

chorister in Salamanca's cathedral in 1484 and *capellan de coro* in 1490,[24] and studied law, philosophy, and theology at the university. Juan was not only the best composer of the time of Ferdinand and Isabella—some of his music is preserved in the *Cancionero de Palacio*, a huge collection of *villancicos* and *romances* published by Barbieri in 1890—but he was also an important literary figure; indeed, his pastoral *representaciones* written for his patron, the Duke of Alba, and incorporating his own music, form an important part of the beginnings of secular drama in Spain.[25] According to the historian Vidal y Diaz, Juan del Encina held the chair of music at the University of Salamanca for some years, although documents relating to this period (last years of the fifteenth century and early part of the sixteenth) have disappeared.[26] In all likelihood this is a mistake for Diego de Fermoselle, and the highly gifted poet Encina, although trained in the university and associated with the choir, was not a professor of music at Salamanca.

Diego's successor in the chair of music, Lucas Fernández (born 1474), *magister* and *licentiatus,* was also a poet-musician, some of whose work, like Encina's, may be found in the Madrid *Cancionero de Palacio.* In 1514, Fernández published a collection of poetry and drama, among which was a *Dialogo para cantar* (a dialogue between two shepherds), the first Spanish play to be sung throughout.[27] The next man to hold the chair of music, Oviedo, who referred to himself as *cantor,* was apparently a bachelor until 1555 when he was incorporated master; in 1551 he became a prebendary *(racionero)* in the cathedral and in 1553 he was called *Maestro de Capilla de la Iglesia de Salamanca.*[28]

[24] Chase, "The Origins of the Lyric Theatre in Spain," *Musical Quarterly,* Vol. XXV (1939), 294.

[25] Chase, *Music of Spain,* 37–38, and J. B. Trend, "Christobal Morales," *Music and Letters,* Vol. VI (1925), 20.

[26] Rafael Mitjana, *Estudios sobre algunos musicos espagnoles del siglo XVI* (Madrid, 1918), 14.

[27] Chase, "The Origins of the Lyric Theatre in Spain," *Musical Quarterly,* Vol. XXV (1939), 297.

[28] Esperabé y Arteaga, *Historia,* II, part 1, 381. Oviedo seems to have been confused with a composer who lived about one hundred years earlier, Juan de Ubredo (Urede). According to the *Memoria historica* of Don Alejandro Vidal y Diaz, quoted by Francisco Asenjo Barbieri *Cancionero musical español de los siglos XV y XVI* (Buenos Aires, 1945),

More famous than any of these was the musician and theorist Francisco Salinas (died 1590). Blind from childhood, Salinas studied at the University of Salamanca and afterwards attended the Duke of Alba, Spanish Viceroy in Naples, as organist. In 1567 he was called to fill the chair of music at Salamanca, and he received the master's degree there in 1568.[29] Salinas was apparently a great friend of the Spanish humanist and poet Luis de Léon, with whom he was sometimes associated in academic activities.[30] In 1582, for example, both men were members of a committee to decide whether the professor of grammar should be allowed to use his own textbook. Salinas testified for Luis in the latter's trials during the Inquisition, and the poet addressed one of his most beautiful odes to Salinas.

Roque de Salamanca was the only Renaissance music lecturer to hold the licentiate and doctorate, having earlier been prebendary in the cathedral and having substituted for Salinas before his own appointment to the chair of music at the latter's death.[31] Clavijo, too, was a *racionero* in the cathedral and apparently remained a bachelor, for his name is not found among *licentiati,* masters, or doctors.[32] A practical musician of the first order, Clavijo left his position in the university to become organist and afterwards *maestro de la real capilla* and clavichordist of the *real cámara* at Madrid.[33]

53: *"El Maestro Juan de Ubredo fué Catedrático de Música en la Universidad salmantina y compositor que floreció en la segunda mitad del siglo XVI."* Ramos has a reference to Urede in his *Musica practica* of 1482, 85: *"Johannes Urede, carissimus noster regis Hispaniae capellae magister."* Barbiero (*Cancionero,* 53) thought Ubredo or Urrede was a Flemish musician who settled in Spain, and J. B. Trend, *The Music of Spanish History* (Oxford, 1926), 100, agrees to his Flemish origin and his status in the early sixteenth century. Several of Urede's compositions are preserved in the Madrid *Cancionero,* and one of them appears in Petrucci's collection, the *Odhecaton* (1501). Obviously, Vidal y Diaz confused the fifteenth-century Urede with Oviedo, who was royal choirmaster and professor of music at Salamanca near the middle of the sixteenth century.

29 Esperabé y Arteaga, *Historia,* II, part 1, 391, and J. B. Trend, "Salinas, a 16th-Century Collector of Folk Songs," *Music and Letters,* Vol. VIII (1927), 14–16.

30 Bell, *Luis de Léon,* 181, and Trend, "Salinas, a 16th-Century Collector of Folk Songs," *Music and Letters,* Vol. VIII (1927), 16–18.

31 Esperabé y Arteaga, *Historia,* II, part 1, 390. Professors in the university could retire on a full salary after twenty years of service and pay their own substitute. See Bell, *Luis de Léon,* 76.

32 Esperabé y Arteaga, *Historia,* II, part 1, 340.

Of the many theoretical writings on music published in Spain during the Renaissance,[34] a number may be related to the University of Salamanca, and from these we may gain more insight into the teaching of music there. One of these is the *Musica practica* of Bartholomé Ramos, published in Bologna (1482). Having studied music with Johannes de Monte *("magister meus IOHANNES DE MONTE, qui fuit primus qui me musices imbuit rudimentis"),* Ramos later taught music (Boethius) at Salamanca *("dum Boetium in musica legeremus").*[35] Apparently Ramos had earlier written ten a treatise in the Spanish language summarizing Boethian theory[36]—which fits in with the fact that music lectures might be presented in the native tongue at Salamanca rather than in Latin. He was also the author of an *Introductio* or *Isagoge;* and in the best Spanish tradition, he was a composer as well as theorist, referring in his *Musica practica* to compositions he had written.[37] As its title suggests, the *Musica practica* deals with elements of plain song and mensural music, approached, however, from the mathematical point of view. The book is especially interesting for the progressive theory it expounds in solving acoustical problems, theories which, we recall, caused a great battle of words between Ramos and his pupil Spataro as exponents of newer doctrines and

[33] Mariano Soriano Fuertes, *Historia de la música española* (Madrid y Barcelona, 1855–59), II, 188–89.

[34] For a list and description of many of these, see Juan Facundo Riaño, *Critical and Bibliographical Notes on Early Spanish Music* (London, 1887), 70–82; Fuertes, *Historia,* II; and Henri Collet, *Le Mysticisme musical espagnol au XVIe siècle* (Paris, 1913), 162–246.

[35] *Musica practica,* 88, 91.

[36] *Ibid.,* 42–43:

> Hoc autem iam, cum in studio legeremus Salmantino, praesente et coram eo redarguimus et in tractatu, quem ibi in hac facultate lingua materna composuimus, ipsi in omnibus contradiximus adeo, ut ipse viso et examinato tractatu meo hoc dixerit: Non sum ego adeo Boetio familiaris sicut iste.

[37] *Ibid.,* 104:

> Sed qui veram et perfacilem huius disciplinae viam sine argumentorum obscuritate, sine probationum improbationumque longis ambagibus percipere desiderat, libellum nostrum musices, quem Introductorium seu Isagogicon appellavimus, inquirat.

Aron refers to this treatise: see *ibid., xii.* For mention of compositions, see *ibid.,* 91: *"Diximus etiam in missa, quam Salmantiae composuimus, dum Boetium in musica legeremus. . . . Sed in moteto Tu lumen . . . quod Bononiae, dum publice legeremus, composui."*

Nicolas Burtius and Gafori as upholders of the conservative point of view. For Ramos turned from the old hexachordal system and introduced a solmization system built upon the octave. Even more important was his construction of a scale, using simple proportions for intervals of the third and sixth (the "natural ratios" of 4:5 and 5:6 for thirds, 3:5 and 5:8 for sixths), doing away with the syntonic comma of the Pythagorean system, and laying the foundation for equal temperament. His experiments were, thus, of great importance in practical application, and his doctrines influenced Zarlino in establishing his harmonic system based on the natural third, a system still generally basic to our music.

Domingo Durán, student of the liberal arts and philosophy at Salamanca in the fifteenth century, left two treatises on music. His *Lux bella* (1492) is a nontechnical work on the chant, drawing upon the usual ancient authorities and some more modern ones (Gafori chief among them), giving the Boethian divisions of music, and characterizing the modes according to emotional effects rather than structure.[38] A commentary on this work by the author appeared in 1498, an erudite treatise in the Castilian language, in which Durán, evidently influenced by musical introductions of the *protreptikos* type, discoursed at length on the divisions, uses, and effects of music, the relationship between words and music in the chant, and music's mystical relationship to the number three.[39] Like many medieval writers interested in reforming the chant, Durán polemicized vigorously against corrupt performances of liturgical music.

Similar to Durán's treatise in certain respects—in advocating reforms in church music, in dwelling upon music's relationship to numbers—is the work of one of the most famous Spanish mathematicians of the sixteenth century, Pedro Ciruelo. Having studied at Salamanca, Ciruelo was called to Paris to teach music, and later became professor of mathematics at the University of Alcalá, where music was regularly taught. Afterwards he taught mathematics at Salamanca, and he published in 1516 his great work, *Cursus quat-*

[38] Collet, *Mysticisme musical espagnol,* 198–99.
[39] Collet, *ibid.,* 199–202, gives a translation of much of the text.

tuor mathematicarum artium liberalium. This work included a musical dissertation on the mathematical basis of music, largely drawn from Boethius, *Questiuncula previa in Musicam speculativam divi Severini Boetii;* and published in the *Cursus* was another popular mathematico-musical work, the *Elementa musicae* of Jacques Lefèvre d'Etaples, reproduced in full.[40] Nor is this the only Spanish treatise that shows the influence of the Paris mathematician Lefèvre. The anonymous author of a sixteenth-century treatise on *canto de organo* (polyphony) refers to *jacobus fabor stapulensis* in discussing Boethius on consonance, as the author explains elements of musical composition on mathematical grounds.[41] Bermudo in his *Declaracion* and a certain Bachelier Tapia in his *Vérgel de Música* also refer to Lefèvre.[42] Neither of these men was a product of Salamanca, but Bermudo studied at Alcalá where Ciruelo taught.

The most polemical of all Spanish theorists, Juan Espinosa, was also a graduate of the University of Salamanca. Typifying the attitude of Spanish musical savants toward the mere practitioner of music, Espinosa directed several musical treatises against Gonzalo Martínez de Bizcargui, who had written a treatise on plain chant and mensural music, introducing Ramos' theories of equal temperament of the octave.[43] In his *Tractado de principios de musica practica e theorica* (1517), Espinosa, a close adherent of Boethian learning, was bitter in denouncing Bizcargui and others who based their reasoning on judgments of the ear. Espinosa published another musical treatise in 1520—not all his treatises are known—in which, after giving an *apologia* for music, relating it to various aspects of human life, he again discussed Boethian theory; this work also contained his *Retractiones de los errores y falsedades escribió Gonzalo Martínez de Bizcargui,* a polemical work against Bizcargui published separately in 1514.[44] Espinosa was a composer

---

[40] *Ibid.,* 177, 207–209.
[41] Henri Collet, *Un Tratado de canto de órgano, siglo XVI* (Madrid, 1913), 63.
[42] Collet, *Mysticisme musical espagnol,* 181–82, 192, 196.
[43] *Ibid.,* 178, and Barbieri, *Cancionero,* 37.
[44] *Cancionero,* 38, and Collet, *Mysticisme musical espagnol,* 178, 210. Collet (178–81) translates a part of the treatise.

as well as a theorist, and some of his works were thought worthy of inclusion in the *Cancionero de Palacio*.

None of the Spanish theorists drew so heavily upon Greek theorists as Francisco Salinas, whose *De musica libri septem* was published in 1577 and 1592. Salinas, whose biography is given in the preface to this work,[45] was blind from the age of ten. He began the study of music early in life, and later went to the University of Salamanca where he studied Greek, philosophy, and the arts. Accompanying the Archbishop of Campostella to Italy and also serving the Duke of Alba (Viceroy of Naples) as organist, Salinas had access to many volumes on Greek musical theory in the Vatican Library and other places in Italy. Copies of such works were made for him, and these he studied assiduously. More than twenty years after leaving Salamanca, he was recalled to teach music in the university, and his *De musica libri septem* was the product of this period of his life. In this erudite, speculative treatise reflecting Salinas' great interest in ancient theory, the author draws freely upon Greek theorists, especially Ptolomaeus, as he explains at great length and with illustrative diagrams the proportions of intervals, the three *genera,* and divisions of the monochord. Salinas also discussed temperament of the organ and other instruments, but his divisions were not suitable for practical application.[46] More interesting for us today is a large section of the treatise on *rhythmus*—poetic meters—with frequent quotations from St. Augustine, whose musical treatise was predominantly a discussion of this same subject. In illustrating various types of meters, Salinas used folksongs of his own day, and his treatise contains a unique collection of these songs.[47]

Certain other theoretical works can be related to musical studies at Salamanca. Alonso del Castillo, who held a doctorate from Salamanca and directed the choir in Zamora, published in 1504 a now

[45] For an English translation of the entire preface and much of the treatise, see Hawkins, *History of Music,* III, 123–60.

[46] See Otto Kinkeldey, *Orgel und Klavier in der Musik des 16 Jahrhunderts* (Leipzig, 1910), 78.

[47] Trend, "Salinas, a 16th-Century Collector of Folk Songs," *Music and Letters,* Vol. VIII (1927), 19–24.

lost book on plain song.[48] The same year there was published in Salamanca a *Portus musice* by Diego del Puerto (Didacus a Portu), *"cantor Capellanum collegii novi divi Bartholomei,"* a treatise on plain song and polyphonic music: *Ars cantus plani Portus musice vocata sive organici;* written in the Spanish tongue, this work was an instruction book for *cantores* rather than a learned work for *musici.*[49] Toward the end of the century a somewhat unusual work appeared from the hands of Martin del Rio, who received the doctorate at Salamanca in 1574: the *Disquisitiorum magicarum libri sex,* one section of which has a title which makes one wish it were available—*De música mágica.*[50]

Juan Bermudo, author of several treatises on music, studied mathematics at the University of Alcalá. In 1550 he published *El Arte Tripharia,* a book dealing with plain song, mensural music, and keyboard performance.[51] His great contribution, however, is his *Declaracion de instrumentos musicales* (Osuna, 1555). Strongly supported by ancient and medieval theorists in *musica speculativa,* Bermudo in this comprehensive treatise explains elements of *musica practica,* composition, and performance—especially the art of playing the organ, lute, and harp.[52]

Most of the theorists who studied or taught at Salamanca, we have noticed, were composers or distinguished performers as well. In addition to these, a few men may be mentioned who, having studied in the university, followed careers as professional musicians.[53] One such was Martin de la Fuente, *cantor* of the Cathedral of Cordova in 1505. About the same time, Bartolomé Escobedo, formerly a student at Salamanca, became music director for the cathedral there; later he went to Rome, where his Masses and motets were performed in the pontifical chapel. Bartolomé del Rey, too, Salamancan student and *cantor* in the cathedral there, went

[48] Collet, *Mysticisme musical espagnol,* 205.

[49] *Ibid.,* 204.

[50] Fuertes, *Historia,* II, 158.

[51] Kinkeldey, *Orgel und Klavier,* 9.

[52] *Ibid.,* 11; see also Collet, *Mysticisme musical espagnol,* 216–23.

[53] Fuertes, *Historia,* II, 119–20, 154.

to Rome to direct the choir at St. John Lateran, where he was famous as composer as well as director.

At Salamanca, then, music was regularly taught, investigated, and cultivated throughout the period of the Renaissance. As in England during the same period, music held a high position in social and cultural life in general; and it was lavishly patronized by Charles V—said to have studied music in Flanders[54]—and his successors, who employed the best musicians of the day at court. The attractiveness of the salary and the permanence of the position, along with the freedom of thought and tolerant atmosphere which characterized the University of Salamanca,[55] drew men of great musical ability and general intelligence to the chair of music.

v. BOHEMIA: PRAGUE

AT THE UNIVERSITY OF PRAGUE, noted for its emphasis upon mathematics, the *Musica* of Jean de Muris had an assured place among the books to be heard in "ordinary" lectures from around 1367; and statutes of 1390, we recall, prescribed *aliquid in Musica* for the master's degree. A fifteenth-century manuscript in the university library containing three of the treatises of Johannes de Muris—two on music and one on arithmetic—reflects this teaching.[1] When the statutes were revised in 1528, these musical requirements remained in effect,[2] although later in the century, with the penetration of humanistic studies into the curriculum, music may have dropped out—certainly the *Musica* of Muris disappeared. We know, however, that astronomy was a leading subject for study at Prague during the sixteenth century and that distinguished mathematicians and astronomers taught in the university's Caroline College.[3] Tycho Brahe was called to teach at Prague, and Jo-

[54] *Ibid.*, II, 111.

[55] Even the Inquisition touched very lightly upon progressive thinkers in Spain, although liberal Spaniards suffered for their beliefs in other countries. See Bell, *Luis de León*, 55–59.

[1] Truhlář, *Catalogus*, II, 387: (*Joannis de Muris*) *Arismetica*, (*Eiusdem*) *Tractatus de proportionibus, Eiusdem musica.*

[2] *Monumenta Universitatis Pragensis*, I, *Liber Decanorum*, 126, 130.

hannes Kepler, imperial mathematician at Prague, lived for a time (1605) in the *Wenzelcollegium* there. Kepler's application of the laws of musical proportions to astronomical movements is an important aspect of the history of baroque music.

Known to us are the names of several musicians who studied at Prague during the Renaissance. Johannes de Glatovia, *cantor,* received the bachelor's degree in 1459, the master's degree in 1462, and the licentiate that same year.[4] Vitus Zittaviensis was trained in the Hofkapelle at Prague, studying in the university there; in a sixteenth-century history he is referred to as *"vir gravis, praestans, senator ac Musicus insignis."*[5] Wenceslaus Nicolaides Vodnianus, bachelor of arts (1542) and master of arts (1545), brought out an edition of *Cantiones evangelicae,* published by Rhaw in Wittenberg (1554), with a foreword by Philip Melanchthon. Although these are described by the Bohemian historian of music Batka as "translations of Czech sacred songs into Latin," Wenceslaus' preface indicates that they were more original than that; for not only did he arrange *aliquot cantilenas* for all holy days, but, as he says, *"Composui itaque aliquot odas. . . . Adhibui autem harmonias etiam pueris apud nos notas."*[6] In addition to Protestant hymns, then, he seems to have written songs in the homophonic ode style cultivated by humanistic composers associated with other European universities, especially the German ones.

One music treatise springing from studies at Prague during the period of the Renaissance is available to us in published form —the section on music in the *Liber XX artium* by Paulus Paulirinus de Praga. Having studied philosophy at Vienna and medicine at Padua and Bologna, Paulus taught at Prague in 1443 and matriculated at Cracow in 1451; his encyclopedia was written between 1459 and 1463 after his return to Bohemia.[7] The section on

---

[3] Wenzel Wladijow Tomek, *Geschichte der Präger Universität* (Prag, 1849), 197–200.

[4] *Liber Decanorum,* I, ii, 66f., 78, 81.

[5] Pietzsch, *"Musik an den Universitäten im Osten,"* AfMf, Vol. I, 279 (from M. Procop Lupacius, *Rerum Boemicarum Ephemeris,* Pragae, 1584).

[6] *Ibid.,* I, 280.

[7] Josef Reiss, *"Pauli Paulirini de Praga Tractatus de musica (etwa 1460),"* ZfMw, Vol. VII (1924), 259–60; text *"De musica,"* 260–64.

music continues the line of medieval works treating music as part of the quadrivium, embracing both *musica speculativa* and *musica practica*: after the usual scholastic introduction together with an explanation of plain song, there is a section on the elements of mensural music, with descriptions of various forms of polyphonic music—*motetus, rondellus, facetum, trumpetum, rotulum, balida, stampanis,* and *cantilena;* and the last section, a fragment, describes a number of musical instruments, including the *dulce melos* which turns up again in our study of Cracow. This section shows perhaps an influence of Bartholomaeus Anglicus' encyclopedia of the twenty arts, *De proprietatibus rerum,* a work much in vogue in medieval times, which also had a final section on musical instruments.

vi. GERMANY: VIENNA, HEIDELBERG, COLOGNE, LEIPZIG, AND WITTENBERG

Vienna

A STATUTE of the University of Vienna (1449) was characteristically specific in stating the musical requirement as part of the ordinary course of lectures for students in the arts faculty—four weeks, sixteen lectures. Since music is not mentioned in subsequent statutes for almost a century, we may assume that this requirement held for many years. In the reform statutes given to the university in 1537 by Ferdinand I, mathematics, always highly favored at Vienna, received special emphasis; and two of the twelve professorships established in the arts faculty at this time were for the teaching of mathematics. One of the two professors of mathematics was to "read" the *Musica* of Ptolomaeus, Boethius, or Jean de Muris.[1]

[1] Rudolph Kink, *Geschichte der Kaiserlichen Universität zu Wien* (Wien, 1854), II, *"Statutenbuch,"* 357:

Der acht Collegiat. so da sein Würdet Primus Mathematicus so lesen Anfennckhlich Arithmeticam Boetij uel Jordani, darnach Promotiora Elementa Euclidis. Zum anndern Prospectiuam Comunem vel alharun vel Vitellionis. Zum vierten Musicam Ptolomei oder wo die nit vorhannden. Musicam Boetij. Aut

Several treatises written by men who taught mathematics at the university show this continuing connection between music and mathematics. A manuscript in the Munich Library contains a commentary on the *Musica Muris* by Andreas Perlachius, student of the mathematician Tannstetter at Vienna, doctor of medicine in 1530, and professor of mathematics and medicine in the university.[2] The *Musica speculativa* of Erasmus Heritius, a clarification of Boethius' *Musica,* is also found in this manuscript.[3] Heritius, who matriculated at several universities, including Cracow, enrolled at Vienna in 1501 as *mathematicus* and taught mathematics (and therefore possibly music) there.[4] Henricus Schreiber, student at Cracow and Vienna, taught at Vienna early in the sixteenth century and published at Cracow (1514) his work on arithmetic and music, *Algorithmus proportionum una cum monochordi generis dyatonici compositione.*[5] Among the numerous writings of Guillaume Postell (a Frenchman who traveled and studied in many places in Europe, who was professor of mathematics at Paris in 1551, and who became professor of classical languages and mathematics at the University of Vienna in 1554) are several treatises on the disciplines of the quadrivium, including a work with musical implications published in Paris (1552), *Tabulae in astronomiam, in arithmeticam theoricam et in musicam theoricam.*[6]

> Joanns Muris. er sol sein Lection nach dem morgen mal. etwo auf ain gelegne stundt. furnemen vnnd verrichten. dardurch sein vnnd der Lectores In der Ertzney letzen. nit auf ain stund zusamen khumen.

The last sentence here recalls an earlier possible connection between music and the medical faculty, for a fifteenth-century witness stated that *Musica Euclidis* was required for the doctorate in medicine. See Chapter II, Vienna.

[2] *Annotationes in Musicen magistri Joannis de muris per magistrum Andream Perlachium accuratae traditae:* see Theodore Kroyer, "Die Musica speculativa des Magister *Erasmus Eritius,*" *Sandberger Festschrift* (München, 1918), 65, 70. See also Joseph Aschbach, *Geschichte der Wiener Universität* (Wien, 1865–88), II, 339–43.

[3] Kroyer, *Sandberger Festschrift,* 65.

[4] According to Tannstetter (whose Latinized name was Collimitius), "*Joannes Epperies et Erasmus Ericius, viri praestantissimi, hac etiam tempestate mathematicam cum multorum admiratione docuerunt*": see Pietzsch, "*Music an den Universitäten im Osten,*" *AfMf,* Vol. I, 433.

[5] Lynn Thorndike, *History of Magic and Experimental Science* (New York, 1923–41), V, 173–74.

[6] Aschbach, *Geschichte der Wiener Universität,* III, 243–47, 251n.

If in the university proper the age-old connection between music and other branches of mathematics was maintained well into the sixteenth century, the practical side of music under university auspices was cultivated just as strongly. Students in St. Stephen's *Bürgerschule* were given such instruction, choristers furnishing music for the cathedral under the supervision of the cathedral *cantor*. According to regulations for the school drawn up in 1460, the singing-master was to have a *Subcantor, "der eine gute Stimm hab,"* and two assistants, all of whom were to teach the boys Gregorian chant along with polyphonic music.[7] Naturally, many of these boys later entered the university proper. And many distinguished members of the university held the position of *Domkantor,* overseeing the cathedral music and musical instruction for the choristers. In 1493, for example, one Brictius Praepost de Cilia held several important posts in the university: canon and *cantor* of St. Stephen's, he was also vice-chancellor of the university and dean of the theological faculty.[8] Throughout the fifteenth and sixteenth centuries the position of *cantor* at St. Stephen's was filled by men who had studied and who taught law or theology in the university.[9]

Instruction in practical music seems to have been given occasionally by members of the university, probably privately, and some of the men who gave such instruction left treatises on various artistic aspects of music. Soon after the middle of the century Thomas Oedenhofer, *baccalaureus* in 1449 and regent (teaching master) in 1452, taught composition, as his letters to a former student show.[10] Josef Grünpeck, mathematician, historian, and member of the humanistic circle around Celtes, gave instruction in organ, possibly in Vienna, as a letter dated 1499 from the humanist Valentinus Kraus to Celtes shows; referring to a new organ in Kronstadt, Kraus praises the young organist, who had been a pupil of Grünpeck.[11] The Duke of Milan, Francesco Sforza, who enrolled

[7] Kink, *Universität Wien,* I, 87n.
[8] *Ibid.,* I, *"Urkundliche Beilagen,"* 25.
[9] See Pietzsch, *"Musik an den Universitäten im Osten," AfMf,* Vol. I, 284–92.
[10] *Ibid.,* I, 289–90.
[11] *Ibid.,* I, 286: *"Organista juvenis quidem aetate discipulus Gruenpekis sed suo magistro arte non inferior."*

in the university in 1509, brought with him the Netherlander Simon de Quercu (Van Eyken), Sforza's private teacher and *maestro di capella;* the latter published at Vienna in 1509 an instruction book dealing with plain song, mensural music, and counterpoint.[12] In this same year Wolfgang Greffinger, described in the university rolls as *componista excellens,* matriculated: pupil of Paul Hofhaimer (court organist in Vienna) and later organist at St. Stephen's, Greffinger composed sacred works in the style of the Horation odes cultivated by the Celtes circle.[13] A pupil of Greffinger was Ottomarus Luscinius (Nachtigall), who matriculated in 1505 and who, at various times, was a member of other universities—Heidelberg, Louvain, Padua, Paris, Freiburg im Breisgau—as well as organist for several years at St. Thomas' in Strasburg.[14] In Vienna Luscinius lectured on music. His two musical treatises were published in Strasburg in 1515 and 1536: *Musicae institutiones* and *Musurgia seu praxis Musicae.* Of the latter, the first section is a Latin translation and amplification of Sebastian Virdung's *Musica getutscht* and the second section an original work on composition. Among the works of another student who enrolled in the university in 1518, Wolfgang Khainer, is a treatise in manuscript, *Musica choralis.*[15] Stephen Monetarius, teacher of music at the University of Vienna early in the sixteenth century,[16] left a work, *Epithoma utriusque musicae practicae,* published in Cracow around 1519, which draws chiefly upon Gafori in explaining the elements of polyphonic composition.

Several of these musicians were associated with the humanistic group around Conrad Celtes at the beginning of the sixteenth century. Within this circle, under the patronage of Maximilian I, music was studiously cultivated in connection with ancient poetic meters and the performance of plays based upon classical models.

[12] *Opusculum Musices de Gregoriana et figurata atque contrapuncto simplici tractans:* see Aschbach, *Geschichte der Wiener Universität,* II, 81, 81n.

[13] *Ibid.,* II, 80n.; and see Hans Joachim Moser, *Paul Hofhaimer* (Stuttgart und Berlin, 1929), 24–25.

[14] *Ibid.,* 183 n.

[15] Pietzsch, "*Musik an den Universitäten im Osten,*" *AfMf,* Vol. I, 287.

[16] August Wilhelm Ambros, *Geschichte der Musik* (3d ed., ed. by Otto Kade) (Leipzig, 1891), III, 156.

The emperor, indeed, was noted for his musical interests and kept a flourishing Kapelle which drew many distinguished musicians to the court.[17] Georg Slatkonia, bachelor of arts, Vienna, 1477, later Bishop of Vienna (and called *Archimusicus* in the epitaph on his tombstone), was active in organizing the emperor's private chapel.[18] In 1501, Maximilian established in the arts faculty of the university a *Collegium poëtarum et mathematicorum,* a seminar for the study of the humanities, appointing *ad ipsum collegium* two teachers learned in poetry and oratory and two learned in the mathematical disciplines.[19]

The soul of this organization was Conrad Celtes, poet laureate and professor of poetry and rhetoric at Vienna (1497–1508), whose special interests were ancient poetry and German history.[20] A passionate lover of music who believed that a poet must know the practical as well as the theoretical side of music, Celtes, while teaching at Ingolstadt before coming to Vienna, had his students sing Horatian odes in four-part settings made by Petrus Tritonius, a *magister artium* who had studied the humanities at Padua and perhaps Bologna (where he may have heard Ramos lecture on music) and who had, in all likelihood, met Celtes in Padua.[21] When Celtes came to Vienna, Tritonius accompanied him and worked with him in the *Collegium poëtarum,* giving instruction in music.[22] The type of ode setting inaugurated by Tritonius—four-part, *nota contra notam,* in isometrical structure according to the quantitative meter of the text, as opposed to the more independent, imi-

---

[17] Cuspinian in his *Vita Maximiliani* speaks of him as *Musices singularis amator,* and adds, "*Quod vel hinc maxime patet, quod nostra aetate musicorum principes omnes, in omni genere musices omnibusque instrumentis in ejus curia, veluti in fertilissimo agro succreverant.*" See Aschbach, *Geschichte der Wiener Universität,* II, 80n.

[18] *Ibid.,* II, 81: and see Hugo Riemann, *Musik-Lexikon* (11th ed., ed. by Alfred Einstein) (Berlin, 1929), II, 1714.

[19] Kink, *Universität Wien,* II, 306.

[20] See Aschbach, *Geschichte der Wiener Universität,* II, 216ff.

[21] *Ibid.,* II, 79. See also R. von Liliencron, "*Die Horazischen Metren in deutschen Kompositionem des 16. Jahrhunderts,*" VfMw, Vol. III (1887), 26–27, and Fr. Waldner, "*Petrus Tritonius und das älteste gedruckte katholische Gesangbuch,*" MfMg, Vol. XXVII (1895), 14.

[22] Waldner, "*Petrus Tritonius und das älteste gedruckte katholische Gesangbuch,*" MfMg, Vol. XXVII (1895), 15.

tative lines of Netherlandish polyphony—was taken up by other composers after the publication in 1507 (with several later editions) of Tritonius' compositions as *Melopoeia sive harmoniae tetracenticae.* In addition to being the first publication of humanistic ode settings, Tritonius' *Melopoeia* has the honor of being the first book of mensural music printed in Germany.[23] Heinrich Isaac, Ludwig Senfl, and Paul Hofhaimer wrote compositions in this style, as did many other composers throughout Germany, usually at the request of teachers of classical poetry, or in connection with their own activities as teachers.[24]

Another outgrowth of humanistic studies cultivated at Vienna was the composition and presentation of plays in imitation of classical models, using musical choruses and solos, plays generally produced in secondary schools related to the universities through their teaching personnel. And here again a luminary is Conrad Celtes. His *Ludus Dianae,* performed before Maximilian at Linz in 1501, was the next such play after Wimpheling's *Stylpho* (the first of its kind) and Reuchlin's *Scenica progymnasmata,* both performed at Heidelberg (1480 and 1497). Written for the crowning of Longinus as poet laureate, the play called for twenty-four characters— singers, dancers, and instrumentalists.[25] The choral music was probably composed by Tritonius and was again an attempt to reproduce in the musical setting the quantities of the text.[26] Two other plays by Celtes were subsequently presented before the emperor: a *Rhapsodia* in 1504 (to celebrate Maximilian's victorious campaign in Bohemia), with students from among the young nobility singing the *Stasima;* and a *ludus* (of which only the title page remains) performed in 1506 to welcome the emperor to Vienna.[27] Benedict Chelidonius, abbot of the Scottish convent in Vienna, was also active in producing *Schuldramen;* his *Singspiel, Virtutis cum vo-*

[23] Anton Schmid, *Ottaviano dei Petrucci* (Wien, 1845), 158–60.

[24] See Hans Joachim Moser, *Geschichte der deutschen Musik* (Stuttgart und Berlin, 1930), I, 379–89.

[25] Aschbach, *Geschichte der Wiener Universität,* II, 241.

[26] R. von Liliencron, *"Die Chorgesänge des lateinisch-deutschen Schuldramas im XVI. Jahrhundert,"* VfMw, Vol. VI (1890), 350. Three of the compositions from the *Ludus Dianae* are printed here (p. 359).

[27] Moser, *Paul Hofhaimer,* 25.

luptate disceptatio, with music by the Viennese Jacob Diamond, was presented by his students before the *Fürstenkongress* in Vienna in 1515.[28]

The choral ode settings cultivated by humanists at Vienna are extremely significant in showing the effect of university studies upon the art of music, for this aspect of musical development was a direct outgrowth of philological studies in the university and in other such institutions at the same time and later. Vienna was most productive in this type of composition, however, owing to the enthusiasm of Celtes and his circle and to musicians connected with the imperial court who came under the influence of the Viennese humanists. Emphasizing as it did the harmonic element in music, since all voices moved simultaneously according to the meter of the text, the choral ode setting coincided in style with the homophonic *frottola* music in Italy. And although its sphere of influence was not great enough to change the course of German music—which adhered largely to the polyphonic style of the Netherlanders—music in the style of the Viennese ode settings enjoyed a considerable vogue and called forth many imitators, contributing in no small way to the gradual ascendancy of homophonic music.[29]

Heidelberg

Music apparently maintained the usual close connection with other branches of mathematics well into the Renaissance at the University of Heidelberg. This may be seen in statutes promulgated for the College of St. Dionysius (1452) which included music among "extraordinary" lectures to be read by regent masters in addition to the "ordinary" lectures, along with the other mathematical studies.[30] The traditional place of music in the quadrivium

[28] Aschbach, *Geschichte der Wiener Universität,* II, 81–82. The title of this play appears elsewhere as *Voluptatis cum virtute disceptatio:* see Liliencron, "*Die Chorgesange des lateinisch-deutschen Schuldramas im XVI. Jahrhundert,*" *VfMw,* Vol. VI (1890), 360–61, where the music is printed; and see Guido Adler (ed.), *Handbuch der Musikgeschichte* (2nd rev. ed., Wien, 1930), II, 669.

[29] For a detailed discussion of the composition and publication of ode settings, see Moser, *Geschichte der deutschen Musik,* I, 379ff.

is reflected in a passage from a *Scherzrede—Monopolium des Licht-schiffs*—given by Iodocus Gallicus as a part of the Quodlibet act of 1488: among those who guide the ship are musicians, along with others *totum docentes quadrivium.*[31]

Sometime during the second half of the fifteenth century Conrad von Zabern (died after 1471), student in the university between 1408 and 1412, taught music at Heidelberg.[32] Conrad's treatise on the monochord—the only existing copy of this, owned by the University of Basel, lacks a title—published at Mainz around 1474 or earlier, was probably the first theoretical work on music printed in Germany.[33] It differs from more conventional treatments of the monochord in giving, not mathematical divisions of the mono-chord, but a number of reasons why the monochord should be revived and used in teaching the ecclesiastical chant. A second incunabulum, published at Mainz in 1474, is Conrad's *De modo*

[30] Eduard Winkelmann (ed.), *Urkundenbuch der Universität Heidelberg* (Heidelberg, 1886), I, 168:

> Si aliquis eorum [magistrorum] ad subterfugiendum labores in facultate artium parvum elegerit ordinarium, utputa tractatum proportionum latitudinum formarum alienacionum vel restrictionum etc., quod idem magister posterius leget Boecium de consolacione ph[ilosophie], theoricam planetarum, Euclidem aut alium librum in [ari]smetrica musica geometria vel astronomia pregnantem et artium facultati placentem pro gloria facultatis et etiam universitatis honore.

Only two other references to music occur in the university statutes—both dealing with student activities. From 1454 a statute forbidding students to wander about at night *per plateas sine lumine* was interpreted by the rector a few months later to mean wandering about at night with lutes and other musical instruments:

> Ab hoc statuto nequaquam excipiuntur hii, ei qui sunt ut dicitur studentes et nostre incorporati universitati, qui de nocte aut potius circa aut ultra medium quandoque noctis hovisare dicuntur aliis masculini ac verius feminei sexus hominibus cum lutinis aliisve organis et musicis instrumentis (*ibid.*, I, 174).

From 1591, a statute for the College of Casimir decreed that a meal might end with music (*"Prandium vel coena cantu et musicis peritis finitur"*). See Johann Friedrich Hautz, *Geschichte der Universität Heidelberg* (Mannheim, 1862–64), II, 438.

[31] See Friedrich Zarncke, *Die deutschen Universitäten im Mittelalter* (Leipzig, 1857), 55: *"nec latera possunt astronomi geomatici chiromantici necromantici arismetrici computistae incantatores musici et totum docentes quadrivium."*

[32] Moser, *Geschichte der deutschen Musik*, I, 121.

[33] For a description and translation of parts of Conrad's two treatises, see Julius Richter, *"Zwei Schriften von Conrad von Zabern,"* MfMg, Vol. XX (1888), 41–48, 95–106. See also F. W. E. Roth, *"Nachtrag zu: Zwei Schriften von Conrad von Zabern,"* MfMg, Vol. XX (1888), 153.

bene cantandi choralem cantum, which again differs from conventional treatises in introducing plain song aesthetically, with directions for ideal performance of the chant. This *Ars bene cantandi* enjoyed a second printing in 1509, *"nunc revisa per florentium diel Spirensem"* (Gabriel Diel or Biel). Like other Heidelberg musicians—for example, Johannes ex Susato—Conrad was also a poet, writing verse in the German language.

References to mathematics in Heidelberg documents from the sixteenth century undoubtedly imply the study of music. In 1522 when Jacob Sturm of Strassburg expressed his opinion, at the request of Kürfurst Ludwig V, on the reformation of the university, he strongly emphasized the necessity for the study of mathematics and all the liberal arts.[34] Jacob Wimpheling, who also wrote the chancellor at the elector's request, was more specific in his ideas for improving the course of studies in the university, mentioning definite books and authors, including the famous encyclopedia in dialogue form, the *Margarita philosophica,* compiled by Gregorius Reisch.[35] Wimpheling certainly included music within the framework of philosophy here, for the *Margarita philosophica,* the first such encyclopedia produced in Germany (first published in Heidelberg in 1496) contains a section on music. The first seven books of this *epitoma omnis Philosophiae,* in fact, are devoted to the seven liberal arts, Book V consisting of a *tractatus* on *musica speculativa* (with reference to Boethius, Plato, and—somewhat unusual for this time—Ficino) and a *tractatus* on *musica practica.*[36] With the edition of 1512, this encyclopedia incorporated the *Musica figurata* of Malcior von Worms, which had first appeared in Wollick's *Opus aureum* in 1501—significant of the growing interest in

[34] Winkelmann, *Urkundenbuch,* I, 215:

Ante omnia maxime necessarium puto, ut et constituatur, qui in mathematicis erudiat; nam qui se septem artium magistros profitentur, vix tamen una aut altera instituti reliquorum omnino rudes et expertes sunt, digni, qui ab omnibus rideantur, artes nihilominus profitentes, quarum ne prima rudimenta gustarunt.

[35] *Ibid.,* I, 216: *"Utinam essent, qui in reformando dialectice et relique philosophie studio modum prescriberent. . . . Similiter margarita philosophica Gregorii Carthusiensis et dialectica Philippi Melanctonis et Iacobi Fabri."*
[36] See the copy owned by the Huntington Library, edition of 1503 (Freiburg).

the composition of polyphonic music among university teachers. Reisch, prior of a Carthusian monastery in Freiburg, had been a student at the University of Freiburg, 1487–89, where he became a *magister artium*.[37] Ornithoparchus, wandering scholar who visited many universities, gave instruction in music at the University of Heidelberg. In his *Micrologus* he states (author's epistle to the "Governovrs of the State of Lynebvrg") that his book "had been first brought forth at Rostock, that famous Vniuersity of the Baltick coast, and since amended by the censure of the Elders, and publicly read in three famous Vniuersities of *Germanie,* the Vniuersitie of *Tubyng, Heydelberg,* and *Maguntium.*" The dedication of Book III stresses the importance of music in Heidelberg, for this book (again in Dowland's translation) is dedicated to "Philip Svrvs of Miltenbvrgh a sharp-witted man, Master of Art, and a most cunning Musitian, Chappel-Master to the Count *Palatine* the Duke of *Bauaria.*" And after remarking upon Philip's great distinction and talent in music, Ornithoparchus concludes, "Whence it is come to passe, that all the Masters of the *Budorine* vniuersity, which they call *Heydelberg,* do singularly loue, honour, and respect you."

At the same time that Sturm and Wimpheling were discussing a revision of the university curriculum (1522), Jacob Spiegel advocated certain reforms, stressing the importance of a knowledge of the quadrivium of the seven arts and mentioning the two mathematics lectureships at Vienna which had contributed so much to the fame of the latter *studium*.[38] It was the duty of one of the Viennese professors, we recall, to instruct in music. As a result of these humanistic opinions and investigations, celebrated humanists (Oecolampadius for Hebrew, Grynaeus for Greek) were called to Heidelberg; and a chair of mathematics was established there in 1547.

[37] Gerhard Pietzsch, *"Zur Pflege der Musik an den deutschen Universitäten bis zur Mitte des 16. Jahrhunderts: Freiburg i. Br.,"* AfMf, Vol. VI (1941), 42.

[38] Winkelmann, *Urkundenbuch,* I, 218:

Oportet tamen adesse quadruvii cognicionem et numerorum, cum ridicula sit res, clarum dici quempiam et insignem titulo septem arcium liberalium et hunc ipsum quadruvii principia non degustasse. Scio ego, quantum fame Viennensi studio pepererit duarum lecturarum in mathematica a Maximiliano institucio.

Reformation statutes given to the university under Kürfurst Otto Heinrich in 1558 provided for a mathematics lecturer who was to include music in his teaching.[39] And we know that certain humanists who taught at Heidelberg included music with classical philology when they were associated with other universities— among them Celtes, Agricola, and Grynaeus; we may reasonably assume that they did the same at Heidelberg. Classical studies, in fact, were responsible for the production and performance of humanistic school dramas using choral music. The first of these, antedating even the Viennese *ludi,* was Jacob Wimpheling's *Stylpho,* presented by university students at a Heidelberg doctoral act in 1480 and published in 1494.[40] In 1497, Reuchlin's *Scenica progymnasmata* (or *Henno,* as it is better known) was performed at Heidelberg, with such distinguished men as the Bishop of Heidelberg and Jacob Wimpheling taking part. This drama made use of a chorus at the end of each act, singing lines set in the humanistic ode style; this one-voice music was published in semibreves on a five-line staff.[41]

As in other German cities, instruction in music was given in the preparatory schools of the university and of the Church of the Holy Spirit.[42] The oldest of these, the *Neckarschule,* furnished choristers

---

[39] A. Thorbecke, *Statuten und Reformationen der Universität Heidelberg vom 16.–18. Jahrhundert* (1891), cited by Gerhard Pietzsch, *"Zur Pflege der Musik an den deutschen Universitäten bis zur Mitte des 16. Jahrhunderts:* Heidelberg—Köln," *AfMf,* Vol. V (1940), 66:

> Die vierdt lection under den fünf gemeinen lectionen soll nachmittag von dreien uhren biss uff vier in der artisten schulen offentlich in mathematicis gehalten werden, und soll dieser lector die arithmetic, geometri und astronomi ein tag oder ein halb iar umb das ander lesen, nemlich zum ersten die arithmetic volgends sphaeram Procli oder Joannis de Sacro Busto, dess andern iars gleichermassen primum Euclidis oder elementale Joannis Vogellini und die theoricas planetarum, damit ein jeder, so ad magisterium complirt, innerhalb zweier iaren ieder der mathematik kunst ein stuck zu hören und zu erlernen habe, so diser professor sich die arbeit nit wolt dhauern lassen, möchte er auch obiter neben der arithmetic *von der music, sovil derselben theorickh und die proportiones harmonicas belangt, etwas anzeigen.*

[40] Moser, *Geschichte der deutschen Musik,* I, 386.

[41] See the edition of 1508 owned by the Huntington Library.

[42] See Fritz Stein, *Zur Geschichte der Musik in Heidelberg* (Heidelberg, 1912), 89ff., for information about these schools.

for services at the city churches and sometimes for festivities at the electoral court; and the *Kantor* of the *Heilige-Geistkirche* was probably singing-master in the *Neckarschule*. This same official, who was also city music director, had charge of the musical instruction given in the Pedagogium, a preparatory school for the arts faculty established in 1546, in which music held a respectable position. An order for the Pedagogium from 1556 states that each day at one o'clock in the afternoon music practice would be held for all boys (*"Teglich soll man die erste stund nachmittag alle knaben in der Musica üben"*). And an order for the *Neckarschule* from 1582 states that no boy would be accepted in this school without being examined by the rector of the Pedagogium in arts and by the *cantor* in music.[43] With the reorganization of this school in 1587 through the efforts of Johannes Casimir, specific rules for musical study and practice were laid down. These consisted of two hourly sessions a week of instruction in singing by the *cantor* of the Pedagogium, singing in four parts *"morgens, mittags und abends vor dem Gebet,"* and the singing of a piece from partbooks before and after meals.[44]

Not only did students from these schools later enroll in the university, but members of the university also held teaching positions in the schools. An important name here is Andreas Raselius, whose treatise on music throws much light on what was taught in these secondary schools. Raselius matriculated at the university in 1581, became bachelor of arts in 1582, and began to teach in the Pedagogium the next year.[45] In 1584, Raselius received the master's degree, and soon afterwards he became *cantor* of the *Gymnasium poëticum* at Regensburg, returning to Heidelberg in 1600 as *Kapellmeister* at the court of Friedrich IV. Although Johann Mattheson credits Raselius with a number of theoretical works

[43] Johann Friedrich Hautz, *Urkundliche Geschichte der Stipendien und Stiftungen an dem Grossherzoglichen Lyceum zu Heidelberg* (Heidelberg, 1856–57), I, 5: *"dass kein Knab furchin of diese schuelen angenommen werden solle, er were dan zuuor durch den Rectorem Paedagogii in artibus, und Cantoren [sic] in Musicis examinirt."*

[44] Stein, *Musik in Heidelberg*, 89–90.

[45] For information about Raselius and his treatise, see J. Auer, *"M. Andreas Raselius Ambergensis, sein Leben und seine Werke,"* Beilage zu den Monatsheften für Musikgeschichte, Vol. XXIV (Leipzig, 1892), 5ff.

(*Grundlage einer Ehren-Pforte,* 1740), the *Hexachordum seu Quaestiones Musicae Practicae* (Nürnberg, 1589) is the only one which has come down to us. This work, written for Raselius' students in Regensburg, is a handbook on the elements of music, dealing with notes, lines, and scales, the hexachord and its mutations, intervals, time values, and the modes—an instruction book in practical music for singers, illustrated with examples from contemporary composers, especially Lassus.

This type of musical instruction in the secondary schools was stressed even more strongly after the advent of Lutheranism, with its strong ideas concerning the value of music in the Church and in daily life. Perhaps even more important than the *Schulkantorei,* however, for the teaching and cultivation of music in Heidelberg was the *Hofkantorei* supported by the Elector of the Palatinate. As in earlier times, this choir continued to draw singers from among students in the university, and several men afterwards celebrated as composers of music received their training in the princely Kapelle, at the same time graduating in the arts and other faculties of the university. In 1479 the arts faculty refused a request from the former elector's sister that singers in the choir be allowed to hear the necessary *lectiones* privately rather than in the public *lectorium*.[46] In 1472, Johannes von Soest (ex Susato) became master of the chapel, having studied music, according to his autobiography, with some English musicians in Flanders and having held various positions before coming to the electoral chapel.[47] In 1476 he entered the university, and later he became a doctor of medicine. His activities in Heidelberg coincided with those of Heidelberg's early humanistic group, all of whom were interested in music and some of whom were composers; Dalberg, Agricola, Celtes, and

---

[46] Winkelmann, *Urkundenbuch,* II, 53:

Artistenfak. schlägt das im namen des kurf. eingebrachte gesuch der herzogin von Oesterreich [Mechtild, schwester des kurf. Ludwig IV, wittwe Albrechts VI. von Oesterreich] ab, dass den kurf. kantoren gestattet werde, die zu erlangung eines grades nöthigen lectiones formales nicht im öffentlichen lectorium, sondern in ihren eigenen häusern oder bei einem magister der fak. zu hören.

[47] Stein, *Musik in Heidelberg,* 13–15.

Reuchlin. Johannes, who was a poet writing in the German language as well as musician and doctor of medicine, apparently wrote a treatise called *Musica subalterna,* which he mentions in the commentary to a poem.[48] His musical erudition must have been considerable, for Schlick, in his organ treatise, refers to Johannes along with other leading musical authorities.

Two of Johannes' pupils left treatises on music, both springing from *musica practica.* One of these was Sebastian Virdung, whose *Musica getutscht* was published in Basel (1511). In describing certain instruments, Virdung refers to his master as having written a book on instruments.[49] But the book is no longer in existence, and Virdung's own book is not only the oldest extant work on instruments and instrumental music, but it is the first work to have established a theory of tablature. The *Musica getutscht* was amplified, translated into Latin, and published in Strassburg (1536) as part of the *Musurgia seu praxis Musicae* by Ottmar Luscinius, who had matriculated at Heidelberg in 1494 and had become a bachelor of arts there in 1496.[50]

Virdung's treatise contains a polemical discussion of a problem of chromaticism against Arnold Schlick, a contemporary of Virdung in the elector's choir and also a pupil of Susato.[51] Schlick, blind court organist, published his *Spiegel der Orgelmacher und Organisten* in Mainz in 1511. This work, the first of its kind, is a practical description of various parts of the organ, but its preface reflects old speculative ideas on the uses and effects of music and music's high place in princely courts. Like many another writer on music, Schlick connects music with bodily health, telling how Tales drove the pestilence from Crete by the strains of his music;

---

[48] *Ibid.,* 20n.: *"Sed de hoc satis dixi quando musicam subalternam gratia dei confeci."*

[49] Sebastian Virdung, *Musica getutscht* (Basel, 1511), (facsimile, ed. by Leo Schrade, Kassel, 1931) folio Cii verso: *"Ich hab der selben instrument Ouch etlich gemalet vñ bescriben gesehē durch mynē meister seligen Johānē de züsato Doctor der artzney in einem grossen bergamenen buch das er selb coponiert vñ gescriben hat."*

[50] Pietzsch, *"Musik an den Universitäten im Osten, AfMf,* Vol. I, 289.

[51] See Virdung, *Musica getutscht, fol.* E[iiij] and F, and Bertha Wallner, *"Sebastian Virdung von Amberg," KmJb,* Vol. XXIV (1911), 86.

and he discusses Aristotle on musical effects.[52] Schlick's knowledge of *musica speculativa* is seen again in his *Tablaturen etlicher lobgesang vnd lider vff die Orgel vnd Lauten* (1512), in the preface of which he supports his views against Virdung on the *genus chromaticum* by such *hochgelerten auctores* as "Johannes de muris, Johannes de felle (?), Johannes de Susato, Franchinus Gafferus, etc."[53]

In the first half of the sixteenth century various other musicians connected with the university belonged to the *Hofkapelle* of Ludwig V (1508–1544). Lorenz Lemlin matriculated in 1513 and became a bachelor of arts the next year; entering the choir as a singer about this time, he later became master of the chapel and teacher of Forster, Jobst von Brant, Caspar Othmayr, and Stefan Zierler—all members of the *Sängerei*, students in the university, and, eventually, composers.[54] Georg Forster, like Johannes ex Susato, studied medicine at Heidelberg, later practicing in Wittenberg.[55] His collection of 380 German songs, published between 1539 and 1556, is important not only for the contemporary music it contains but for the preservation of numerous old German folk songs, used as the tenors in these compositions.

The prefaces to the five parts of this collection give us information about various friends of Forster at Heidelberg. One of these prefaces tells us that Forster studied with Lemlin, the elector's *Kapellmeister*. The third book is dedicated to Jobst von Brandt, one

[52] Arnold Schlick, *Spiegel der Orgelmacher und Organisten* (Mainz, 1511) (ed. by Paul Smets, Mainz, 1937), 11:

> Ist gut den jungen scherpfft und macht geschickt die ingenia heilt und artzneyt die gebresten des leips. Als Tales Cretensij durch die süsse der harpffen die pestilentz vertriben und die wuteten menschen zü rügen bracht hott. Arestotiles sagt die music macht wolgeschickt ein landschafft bringt wider die gefallen und verzweyfelten sterckt die wegfertigen macht werloss die mörder und miltert den schloff.

[53] The *Tabulaturen* has been printed by Robert Eitner, "*Georg Forster, der Arzt und Georg Forster, der Kapellmeister*," *MfMg*, Vol. I (1869), 115–25.

[54] Unless otherwise noted, see Stein, *Musik in Heidelberg*, 34ff., for information about these musicians.

[55] Eitner, "*Georg Forster, der Arzt und Georg Forster, der Kapellmeister*," *MfMg*, Vol. I (1869), 6.

of Forster's *Tisch- und Schulgesellen,* student in the university in 1529, member of the *Kantorei* with Forster, and composer of songs included in the collection. This same preface speaks of Othmayr and Zierler as Forster's *"alten Heydelberger tisch- und behtgesellen"* and includes works by both. Othmayr, who published a number of instrumental works, received the master's degree in 1534 at Heidelberg, singing in the *Kantorei* and studying with Lemlin during his university years; and Zierler—to whom the fourth part is dedicated—matriculated in 1537, sang in the choir with Forster, and later became *Kammersecretarius* to the elector.

Two *cantores principis* matriculated at the university in 1535: Wolfgang Echter and Johannes Kluesbeck, the latter becoming a bachelor that same year. And the sons of several of our Heidelberg musicians enrolled in the university also. Arnold Schlick the Younger matriculated in 1511, later working as a musician in Heidelberg. For a long time a music treatise, *Explicatio compensiosa* (now considered anonymous), was attributed to him. Joseph Schlick, probably an elder brother of Arnold, became bachelor and master of arts in 1508 and 1510. Two sons of Sebastian Ochsenkhun, lutenist to the elector and compiler of a tablature book published in 1558, matriculated at the university in 1572 and 1588, one of them, Christopher, becoming a bachelor in 1589. Like many other students who earned their board by acting as servants in collegiate foundations, a son of Raselius was enrolled gratis as a *famulus Casimiriani* in 1613 after his father's death.

A papal bull of 1550 provided for the incorporation of certain confiscated convents and monasteries in the university, proceeds from them going toward the foundation of an arts college (the *Sapienhaus*) *"pro sexaginta vel octoginta pauperibus ad litteras idoneis"* and to support six priests and twelve singers along with other ministers to celebrate divine office.[56] This is the bull in which Ruprecht's choir is said to be the first in all Germany *("quod antiqua etiam dotatio capellae in arce eiusdem civitatis per eosdem fundatae, quae fertur prima in tota Germania extitisse");* and we know that in 1550 the electoral choir comprised twelve singers.[57]

[56] Winkelmann, *Urkundenbuch,* I, 251.   [57] *Ibid.,* I, 250.

The location of the electoral court at Heidelberg, then, had important bearing on the cultivation of music in the university. Students in the university supported themselves by singing in the princely chapel, and those especially interested received musical instruction from the masters of the choir. Heidelberg treatises and Forster's collection of songs were inspired by both these spheres of musical influence—university learning and activities in the choir. The fact that choirmasters, composers, and theorists active in the electoral chapel were graduated in arts or medicine at the university shows the high degree of erudition which characterized the German Renaissance musician.

Cologne

The University of Cologne is especially important in a study of music in the universities because it served as the model for subsequent institutions in whose curricula little is known about the place of music owing to insufficient documentation—Glasgow, Louvain, and Upsala, among others. At Cologne, a stronghold of traditionalism, music long held its conventional place in the mathematical quadrivium: from the founding of the *studium* in 1388 for nearly two hundred years *musica speculativa* was a requirement for the *magisterium in artibus*. According to statutes of 1398, bachelors seeking this degree had to hear *aliquem librum in musica* along with other specified books, in addition to those already heard previous to the baccalaureate; and apparently this requirement remained in effect until after the middle of the century.[58] Among the books printed in Cologne before 1500 were the *Etymologiae* of Isidorus and Aristotle's *Problemata* and *Politica;* and among books owned by the arts faculty between 1474 and 1497 were the *Liber de proprietatibus rerum, Musica Boecii,* and Isidorus'

---

[58] New statutes drawn up for the faculty of arts in 1457—"*Statuta reformata Facultatis Artium*"—contained no reference to the course of study: see Franz Joseph von Bianco, *Die alte Universität Köln und die spätern Gelehrten-Schulen dieser Stadt* (Köln, 1856), Anlagen, VIII, 74–77.

Etymologiae[59]—all significant of the traditional place of music as a mathematical discipline in the quadrivium.

Other documents tell us that music was still being taught as one of the disciplines of the quadrivium in the early sixteenth century. One of these, a *"Conceptus super ordinatione Lectionum in Facultate Artium"* (1525), specifying days and hours for each subject taught, stated that "the books on mathematics, that is geometry, arithmetic, music and astronomy," should be publicly "read" in the school on religious holidays—and at other times when there were no important lectures—indicating a continuance of the medieval tradition which placed the mathematical disciplines among the "extraordinary" lectures.[60] A letter from the faculty of arts to its dean (1525) assured him of the satisfactory teaching of the seven liberal arts—each of them specifically named, and *Physica cum Logica* added.[61] A writer describing the *studium* in 1572 stated that in the *schola artium* not only the *tres linguae sacrae* but also the mathematical disciplines were cultivated.[62]

In 1573 a period of reform for the university began, after which music's place in the curriculum probably underwent a change. The mathematical studies were retained in the *schola artium,* but in the

<hr>

[59] See Ernst Voullième, *Der Buchdruck Kölns bis zum Ende des fünfzehnten Jahrhunderts* (Bonn, 1903), 58, 63–66, 317 (I have been unable to find a similar study for the sixteenth century), and Pietzsch, *"Musik an den deutschen Universitäten: Köln," AfMf,* Vol. V, (1940), 78.

[60] Bianco, *Die alte Universität Köln, Nachtrag zu den Anlagen,* 327:

> Up den heiligen Tagen, so man gemeinlich fehret, und ob den Dienstag, wan dan Mittag just keine Lectien pflegen zu syn, soll man in der Schullen vor den Predigeren [Street of the Dominicans] offenbahr vor alle Bursen lesen die Bucher in der Mathematik, zu wissen in *Geometria, Arithmetica, Musica et Astronomia.*

[61] *Ibid.,* 409:

> Hoc primum cum satis constet nos promoveri in magistros septem AA. LL. ut etiam satisfaciamus titulo nostro, contendimus quod nobis praelegantur in scholis AA. LL. Dialectica, Rhetorica, Musica, Arithmetica, Astronomia, Geometria, his adiungatur Physica cum Logica; et haec omnia a probatissimis composita, atque ab eruditissimis translata sunt.

[62] *Ibid.,* 82n. (Middendort, *De academiis Orbis,* Col. 1572):

> Praeterea splendidissima Coloniae Publica Schola trilinguis est, quae vulgo artium appellatur; ubi tres linguae sacrae, hebrae, graeca, et latina, ingenuae artes et eloquentia mathematicaeque disciplinae a doctissimis hominibus traduntur.

statutes drawn up for the arts faculty following the reform of the university in 1574, works in *Physica* comprise the old mathematical studies.[63] A paragraph from the *"Ordo Lectionum in Gymnasiis"* (1573) defines very clearly the teaching of music and grammar in secondary schools.[64]

Instruction in music was given in ecclesiastical schools in Cologne from early times. Following the synod of 1549 under Archbishop Adolf III, a convocation much concerned with the reform of the university and the schools connected with it, musical instruction was clearly specified for these schools. A *Directorium* of 1597 which mentioned the investigations of Adolf III decreed the teaching of the Gregorian chant and other types of music in colleges and parochial schools for one hour each day.[65] And in one of the university colleges, instruction in the *ars musica* was highly emphasized—the *Musikanten-Haus* of the Jesuit College. Famous for its choir, the Jesuit school taught not only singing and the elements of polyphonic music but instrumental techniques as well; and talented young students were accepted for musical training along with other academic studies.[66]

[63] *Ibid.,* 357 (letter from the university to the papal representative dealing with the proposed reforms and discussing *"Publicos Professores linguarum, historicarum et mathematicarum disciplinarium in publico Artium Gymnasio"*), and 370 (statutes of the arts faculty, 1574, stating that works *in Physica* comprise the old mathematical studies and their texts, old and new, *"ut sphera Joannis de sacro Bosco; Cosmographia Henrici Glareani, vel Cosmographia Pomponii Melae; vel computo Ecclesiastico, Arithmetica Elementis Euclidis, Geometria Appiani"*).

[64] *Ibid.,* 345:

> Caeterum ut pueri discant cantum, et occasionem nullam conquerendi de Gymnasiis habeant Collegiatarum et Parochialium Ecclesiarum Ludimagistri, putaremus duas illis Classes Grammaticas relinquendas, in quibus cum litteras nosse et colligere pueri discant, et Declinationes, Comparationes, Coniungationes atque similia memoriae mandent, tum etiam initia Grammaticae, quae continebit Definitiones, Divisiones et faciliores regulas Generum, Praeteritorum, Syntaxis, fideliter percipiant.

[65] *Ibid.,* 488n. (*Directorium ecclesiasticae disciplinae Coloniensi praesertim Ecclesiae accommodatum*):

> ac Collegiatis et parochialibus ecclesiis integer puerorum sit numerus, qui chorum facere possint et divinum officium ac laudem Dei ex perpetua ecclesiae consuetudine magna cum populi aedificatione decantare. . . . In scholis Collegiatarum et Parochialium ecclesiarum quotidie una hora doceatur cantus Gregorianus etc.

Many of the university students, indeed, were performers of music; like students everywhere, they owned lutes and violins upon which they played as they wandered through the streets at night.[67] And music contributed to the colorful academic ceremonies of the university. In the procession which opened the juristic doctoral promotion, we are told, candidates and doctors, mounted on horseback, were preceded by trumpets and drums.[68] The *Doktorats-Festessen,* lavish doctoral banquet held in Cologne's *Quattermarkt* at great expense to the new doctors, also had its musical embellishment. An account of the expenses connected with a doctorate in theology (1591) contains a number of musical items, most of which refer to the musicians hired for the occasion—payments for four instrumentalists, a white pitcher of wine which these boisterous entertainers made away with, an organist, three people to transport the musical instruments, and two *Discanten* who aided in the singing (although the choirmaster at St. Mergen received nothing for his part).[69] For a similar ceremony in 1600 there are records of payment in food and drink to four *Herren Spilleuth.*[70] And a *"Modus Procendi in Facultate Theologica cum iis qui sunt futuri Coloniae Doctores"*

[66] *Ibid.,* 351–52.

[67] See Hermann Keussen, *"Die alte Universität Köln," Universität Köln* (Köln, 1929), 22, 33.

[68] *Ibid.,* 43.

[69] Bianco, *Die alte Universität Köln,* 89–90, 100:

Spielleuten: Item den vier unseren Herren Spielleuten aus Beuelch jederem 1 Golgulten—6 Thlr. 8 Alb.

Volgt was an obgemeltem Werck zerbrochen: Item für ein weisse Krug, so die Spilleuth hinweggenohmen, für 8 alb.

Item den Spilleuten die Kost geben, wie den Gasselbotten. NB. haben am vorigen Tag ein weisse Krug sampt dem Wein gefordert und hinweg genohmen, *nobis invitis* sagten, es wer der Brauch also, sein über 4 Q. Wein.

Organist W. Kubertus. Item hat W. Kubertus vor sein Theil nichts haben wollen, sonder vor seine zween Jungen gefordert 1 Reichsthlr. Item noch vor drey Personnen, so die Instrumenta musicalia hin und wider getragen, und einem so geblasen, zusammen 18 Alb. thut so W. Kubertus empfangen—1 Thlr. 22 Alb.

Capellen-Meister in Capitolio.

Item Herr Wilhelm der Capellen-Meister zu S. Mergen für sein Theil auch nichts haben wollen, hat für zween Discanten, so helfen singen, gefordert für jeden 1 Reichsthaler, thut so er empfangen—1 Thlr. 22 Alb.

[70] *Ibid.,* 104.

(collected in 1647 but written sometime earlier) refers to the use of music for entertainment at the banquets concluding the theological doctorate.[71]

Ortwin Gratius, who studied at Cologne and later became a professor in the *Bursa Cucana,* has gone down in history as the "hero" of the *Epistolae obscurorum virorum* against the theological faculty at Cologne (1515)—the man to whom these letters were chiefly addressed—and as the author of a refutation to the letters, *Lamentationes obscurorum virorum* (1518). The *Epistolae* contain some references to music and musicians.[72] More to the point for us, however, is the record of Ortwin's oration in the *disputatio de quolibet* (1507), an address *De philosophie laudibus* (published the next year). In debating the necessity for the study of philosophy, Ortwin discussed music along with other disciplines of the quadrivium —a discussion published the following year (1508): *Ortwini Gratii Daventreni oratio habita Colonie eodem tempore de laudibus musice discipline.*[73] In 1524 one of the subjects debated again dealt with the liberal arts, raising a question, medieval in tone, regarding whether the seven liberal arts were useful in explaining sacred writings[74]—significant, probably, of secular humanistic studies upon the liberal arts as the traditional basis for theological studies.

Among the men who contributed to the cultivation of music and musical theory are several who studied or taught at the University of Cologne—including Rudolf Agricola and Erasmus Heritius, who matriculated in 1462 and 1488 respectively.[75] Conrad Celtes studied in the university's *Bursa Montana,* leaving in 1484

[71] *Ibid.,* 84: *Tempore mensae saepius musica intercinit, saepius stultus exhilarat, saepius Doctores promoti circumeunt et monent ut hospites sint hilares. . . . Quando draco, quando sturius, aut pavo circumgertur, aut lusores civitatis aut musica comitatur.*

[72] See the Huntington Library copy, *Epistolae Obscurorum Virorum ad Dn. M. Ortuinum Gratium* (Francofurti Ad Maenum, 1643), 54, for the letter from Johannes Lucibularius to Ortwin thanking him for what he has taught him, including the satirical remark: *"Etiam sum Cantor, & scio Musicam choralem & figuralem, & cum his habeo vocem bassam, & possum cantare unam notam infra Gammaut."*

[73] *Ibid.,* 701; and see Georg Kaufmann, *Geschichte der deutschen Universitäten* (Stuttgart, 1888–96), II, 399.

[74] See *"Im Quodlibet behandelte Themata,"* Hermann Keussen, *Die alte Universität Köln* (Köln, 1934), 581.

[75] Pietzsch, *"Musik an den deutschen Universitäten: Köln,"* *AfMf,* Vol. V (1940), 78, 80.

to study with Agricola at Heidelberg.[76] While teaching at Louvain before proceeding to Heidelberg, the latter was known for his musical activities, both as teacher and as composer. Nicolas Wollick, bachelor and master of arts at Cologne in 1499 and 1501, includes in his *Opus aureum* (1501) a letter to Adam von Boppard, his former teacher, in which he tells how he heard daily lectures not only in the liberal arts but in music and poetry as well—a combination approved by him because it was approved by Aristotle.[77] In the *Opus aureum* Wollick treats of plain song, with the usual origins and descriptions of music, and he includes a section on mensural music (*musica figurata*) by Malcior von Worms, which was also incorporated into the 1512 edition of Reischius' *Margarita philosophica*. And we recall that in 1512, while lecturing at Paris, Wollick (who in the explicit calls himself *Nicolas gallus*) published an amplification of this work as *Enchiridion musices*, bringing his discussion of polyphonic music up to date with the doctrines of Gafori and Tinctoris.

Henricus Loritus, known as Glareanus (1488–1563), first studied at a private school in Bern, where he learned Latin and music; coming to Cologne in 1506, he became a bachelor of arts in 1507 and master of theology in 1510.[78] During these years he probably studied music with Johannes Cochlaeus, of whom he speaks in the *Dodecachordum* as *"olim in Musicis praeceptor noster."*[79] In 1512, when Maximilian came to Cologne, Glareanus composed for him a *Lobgedicht* which he sang to a Dorian melody. It was on this occasion that the emperor crowned him poet laureate. Gathering a

---

[76] Bianco, *Die alte Universität Köln*, 667.

[77] See copy in the Munich Stadtsbibliothek, and see the letter quoted and translated into German by Peter Bohn, *"Nicolaus Wollick aus Serovilla,"* MfMg, Vol. IX (1877), 56:

> Et certe hoc ejus philosophiae [Cleanthis] tam pertinax studium ita me animavit, ut non solum in artibus (quod vulgo dicitur) sed etiam in musica et in poetica lectiones quotidie audirem. Nec in eo reprehendendus mihi videor, quando Aristoteles philosophus facile omnium princeps, ut testatur Plutarchus, gravioribus illis disciplinis etiam poeseos perfectam quandam cogitationem adjungebat, et historiae tam curiosus erat, ut neque coelo neque terra neque mari quidque relinquere vellet incognitum.

[78] Bianco, *Die alte Universität Köln*, 696.

[79] *Glareani Dodekachordon* (Basiliae, 1547) (copy in the Yale Music Library), 196.

circle of young men about him, Glareanus taught at Cologne until 1514, when, the battle between Pfefferkorn and Reuchlin being at its height, he left for Basel. His teaching was of a private nature, like that of medieval regents, for although it is often said that he taught at the *Bursa Montana,* his name does not appear in the list of professors in the arts faculty of this college nor for any other *bursa* in the university. Glareanus' *Cosmographia* was specified as a textbook in the university, according to statutes of 1574.[80] His musical works more properly belong to our discussion of the University of Basel.

The teacher of Glareanus, Johannes Cochlaeus, became a *magister artium* at Cologne around 1507.[81] Later Cochlaeus received a degree in theology at Ferrara and became rector of the school of St. Lorenz at Nuremberg. Best known for his theological and historical writings, Cochlaeus also wrote two musical treatises. The first of these, a compendium called *Musica,* was published twice anonymously before it appeared at Cologne in 1507 under the author's name; and one of these editions was published by Riemann as *Anonymi Introductorium Musicae.*[82] An introduction to practical aspects of music, the book comprises the three sections on music customary in Renaissance treatises—*musica plana, musica mensurabilis,* and *contrapunctum simplex.* Scholastic in his logical order and the fine divisions of each point he makes, Cochlaeus shows his humanistic interests in quoting Vergil in his definition of music. An even stronger humanistic tendency combined with scholasticism characterized his expansion of this work called *Tetrachordum musices*—a title paralleled by Glarean, who called his book on the twelve modes *Dodecachordon*—first published in Nuremberg in 1511. Here there are many more classical allusions, especially in the first of the four tracts making up the *Tetrachordum,* as well as directions for composing music in conformance to classic meters in the last tract (which contains an example in four-part writing of *Melos Elegiacum,* with verses from Ovid; *Melos Jam-*

80 See note 63, this section.

81 Hugo Riemann, *Musik-Lexikon* (11th ed., Berlin, 1929) (ed. by Alfred Einstein), I, 329.

82 *MfMg,* Vol. XXIX (1897), 147–54, 157–64, and Vol. XXX (1898), 1–8, 11–19.

bicum, with stanzas from hymns; *Melos Sapphicum,* with the words, *"Ut queant laxis";* and *Melos Choriaambicum,* with examples from Horace).[83] Designed for the use of students in the St. Lorenz school, of which Cochlaeus was rector (his words on the title page read *"pro iuuentutis Laurentiane eruditione imprimis"*), the *Tetrachordum* takes the form of an expanded catechism, each paragraph opening with a question followed by a brief answer and longer explanation.

Bernhard Bogentanz (born around 1494) was a professor of music at Cologne early in the sixteenth century. There he published in 1515 his instruction book on plain song and mensural music, *Collectanea utriusque cantus,* which appeared in 1535 as *Rudimenta utriusque cantus.*[84] And a musical treatise written by Jean Taisnier of Hainault seems to have sprung from studies in the University of Cologne. According to biographical information in his *Opus mathematicum* (Cologne, 1562), Taisnier, like many other Renaissance scholars, was doctor of canon and civil law, poet laureate, musician, mathematician, doctor of medicine, and philosopher, having studied and taught in a number of Italian universities, including Padua and Ferrara.[85] His name appears on the matriculation roll of the University of Cologne in 1558, about which time he became *Kapellmeister* to the Archbishop of Cologne and a teacher of chiromancy in the university.[86] In a dedicatory letter to the archbishop which prefaces the *Astrologiae iudicariae ysagogica* (Cologne, 1559), he speaks of having written *nostrum librum Musicae.* And according to Taisnier's description, this work begins with various classifications of music and goes into the mathematical derivation of the scale, with *commata* or *dieses,* points closely connected with *musica*

[83] See copy of the second printing in the library of the Yale School of Music, *Tetrachordum Musices Johannis Coclei Norici, Artiū Magistri* (Nurnberge, 1512).

[84] See Robert Eitner, *Biographisch-bibliographisches Quellen-Lexikon der Musiker und Musikgelehrten* (Leipzig, 1900–1904), II, 92. For chapter headings of the Rudimenta, see F. W. E. Roth, *"Zur Bibliographie der Musikdrucke des XV. bis XVII. Jahrhunderts in der Darmstädter Hofbibliothek," MfMg,* Vol. XX (1888), 123–24.

[85] Lynn Thorndike, *History of Magic and Experimental Science* (New York, 1923–41), V, 581.

[86] Pietzsch, *"Musik an den deutschen Universitäten: Köln," AfMf,* Vol. V (1940), 82, and Thorndike, *History of Magic,* V, 582.

reservata and the use of chromaticism; this is followed by a section on specific problems of rhythm and notation, concluding with a section on composition. The lost music treatise appears to have included a section on musical instruments also, for in the dedicatory letter Taisnier lists a great many astronomical and musical instruments, saying that others "almost innumerable" have been mentioned "in our book on music."[87]

Another scientist and philosopher interested in the various facets of astrology was Henricus Cornelius Agrippa. Born in Cologne in 1486, he was probably educated at the university—which may explain his bias toward scholastic theology.[88] His *Three Books of Occult Philosophy* is very much in the neo-Platonic tradition and contains many chapters on music—on the magical powers of numbers, the mystical effects of harmony (with a huge compilation of myths and legends recounting the effects of music upon man and beast), the harmony of the planets (each with its musical interval), the harmony in man's body, and the harmony in man's soul.[89]

It appears, then, that various types of musical studies flourished at the University of Cologne all during the Renaissance, inspiring some of the most distinguished humanists and being offered in

---

[87] Thorndike, *History of Magic*, V, 584. Taisnier's description of his *liber Musicae* contains a reference to *musica reservata* generally overlooked by historians of music (*ibid.*, V, 583n.):

> Musica theorica practica et poetica mundana humana et instrumentalis choralis et figurata antiqua et moderna ab aliquibus nova dicta sive reservata qui arbitrabantur impositionem unius aut alterius dioesis aut diaschismatis in cantilena aut motteto diatonicum Musices genus in chromaticum verti differentiam Diatonici a Chromatico et Enarimonico penitus ignorantes quorum difficultatem in nostro libro Musicae satis exposui. Novumque quid ubi excogitare nituntur suarum cantilennarum tonos quae in Musicae principiis sistunt praetermittentes magnum errorem committunt notarum ligaturas valores in modo tempore et prolatione negligentes contrapuncta ut aiunt . . . harmoniosa fluentia currentia per minimam ad semi-minimam ad fugam reiterata in modo perfecto et imperfecto per hemiola maius et minus per sesqualtera sesquitertia sesquiquarta etc. Item contrapunctum 3.4.5.6.7. partium extemporaneum a diversis Cantoribus modulandum pro praedecessorum documentis in mentem revocent demum fiant cantores poetae opus absolutum praedecessorum exemplo provocati in sui memoriam et posteritatis usum linquentes.

[88] See Lewis Spence, *Cornelius Agrippa* (London, 1921), 11.
[89] Henry Cornelius Agrippa, *Three Books of Occult Philosophy* (London, 1651).

turn by them to students in colleges of the university. In line with the general conservatism in this university, *musica speculativa* was taught as a mathematical discipline from the founding of the *studium* until late in the sixteenth century, after which, if still taught with mathematics, it was included among the studies *in Physica.* But all the various aspects of *musica practica* were continuously available in schools connected with the university and at the hands of capable musicians under university auspices.

Leipzig

The history of musical studies at Leipzig during the Renaissance is especially clear, owing to the many published documents and records of the early days of this university. From the very beginning of its history, the arts faculty of the University of Leipzig (whose oldest statutes date from 1410) included the *Musica speculativa* of Jean de Muris among the studies required for the *magisterium;* a maximum of one month or minimum of three weeks was to be spent on these music lectures, with payment of two *Groschen* for each lecture. No change occurred in the musical requirements (restated in statutes of 1437 and 1440) until 1471, when the fee was reduced to one and one-half *Groschen.*[90] The last musical requirements during the Renaissance appear in various statutes written down between 1499 and 1522. Here the time and fee for lectures in *Musica Muris* are the same as in the statutes of 1471, and *Musica Muris* is found again among books to be studied *pro magisterio.*[91] In 1507 *musica Muris* was again included among books required for the master's degree, apparently "read" alternately with astronomy and arithmetic; and a paragraph *"Qui libri possunt pro concurrenti audiri"* explains that a student must hear three regular lectures daily and may choose a fourth from certain *libri concur-*

---

[90] Friedrich Zarncke, *Die Statutenbücher der Universität Leipzig aus der ersten 150 Jahren ihres Bestehens* (Leipzig, 1861), 398: *Pro de sensu et sensato maximum unum mensem; minimum tres septimanae . . . similiter pro musica Muris: pro quolibet illorum 1½ gr.*

[91] *Ibid.,* 462, 465.

rentes, of which music is one.[92] In the statute *"De disputatione ordinaria magistrorum"* (1507), masters are encouraged to hold disputations in mathematics and related subjects.[93] With the introduction of a new humanistic arrangement of studies by statutes of 1558, however, music is not specifically mentioned, although it continued to be taught, in all likelihood, as a part of physics (with the other mathematical disciplines) and as a part of classical literature.[94]

Many of the *magistri regentes* who taught music at Leipzig are known to us by name. Among those active in the fifteenth century were Nikolaus Gerstmann and Martin Furmann, who lectured on the *Musica* of Muris, according to the testimony of certain of their students, Gerstmann between 1458 and 1462, Furmann between 1483 and 1487.[95] From the first half of the sixteenth century certain

[92] *Ibid.,* 490: *"Libri ad gradum magisterii audiendi sunt isti. . . . musica Muris, theoricae planetarum, arithmetica communis et quaelibet harum trium est concurrens."* From *"Qui libri possunt pro concurrenti audiri"* (p. 491):

> Sed complens pro magisterio non poterit de die sub distinctis horis nisi tres audire lectiones, demptis tamen concurrentibus, puta veteri arte et topicorum, theoricis planetarum, arithmetica communi, musica Muris et rethorica Tullii aut Aristotelis, quarum quamlibet pro quarta per unam mutationem iuxta tabulae completionis signaturam audire poterit.

[93] *Ibid.,* 507:

> Item si quis magistrorum mathematicae scientiae diu operam dederit et ordinarie in ea disputare voluerit, non obstante priori ordinatione titulorum formandorum, ad disputandum in mathematica seu consimili laudabili arte, ut puta rethorica, non debt prohiberi.

[94] *Ibid.,* 533–34:

> Hi doctrinae publicae operas suo cursui propositas esse sciant sitas: primum grammaticae graecae et latinae, secundo dialecticae, tertio poeticae, quarto elementorum rhetoricae, quinto elementorum mathematicae. Cum autem spatium trium semestrium ad hanc petitionem praefinitum sit, placuit edici, ut primo semestri frequentaretur doctrina publica grammaticae graecae et latinae, dialecticae et poeticae, secundo semestri rursum grammaticae utriusque, dialecticae et simul rhetoricae praecepta, tertio rursum poeticae et rhetoricae, et praeterea physicae et mathematum elementa audirentur.
>
> Quo quidem tempore omni audient hi professorem philosophiae illum eximium, itemque professorem utriusque linguae et Fabii explicatorem, primo autem semestri et secundo insuper physica et ethica Aristotelis, tertio et quarto praeter haec etiam mathematicis disciplinis diligentem et praecipuam operam dabunt.

teachers of music are mentioned in university records. In a list of masters and their subjects (1502), Conradus Dockler de Nurnberga is named as the lecturer in music; and in 1504 and 1505 Conradus taught geometry, astronomy, and Euclid.[96] In 1505, Sebastianus Müchelen was the *lector musice et aritmetice*.[97] In the winter term, 1511, *"ad lectionem theorice pla[netarum] et musice etc. deputatus est magister Bartholomeus Negelein, qui substituit magistrum Dillingen."*[98] Simon Eysselin de Dillingen was the lecturer in various mathematical studies until 1519, and Sebastian Muchel taught mathematics in 1522, *libros phisicorum* in 1537.[99] In 1516 "Andreas Ornitoparchus Meyninigensis, mgr. Tubingensis" was incorporated at Leipzig, a note on the register referring to his distinction in music, *"Argutissimus artis modulatoriae fuit professor."*[100]

Certain other men are listed as musicians in the matriculation rolls. These include *"Ludolffus Organista de Moguncia,"* 1457, *"Johannes Organista de Melrase,"* 1479, Henricus Finck *bonus cantor,* 1482, and *"Johannes Organista de Turonia,"* 1500.[101] Two of those who graduated bachelors in arts are registered as *cantores*: Lodwicus Gotcz de Werdis, 1475, and Michael Schewss de Helpurck, 1482.[102] Many others who matriculated or received degrees at the University of Leipzig became *Kantors* or organists in important places afterwards.[103]

In addition to the study of music as a mathematical discipline in the university proper, many records point to the cultivation of practical music in the university, especially those dealing with the celebration of Masses. The *Libellus formularis* (written down by Johannes Fabri de Werdea in 1495) contains a decree by the dean

[95] Gerhard Pietzsch, *"Zur Pflege der Musik an den deutschen Universitäten bis zur Mitte des 16. Jahrhunderts: Leipzig,"* AfMf, Vol. III (1938), 316.

[96] Georg Erler, *Die Matrikel der Universität Leipzig* (Leipzig, 1895–1902), II, 389, 402, 409.

[97] *Ibid.,* II, 415.

[98] *Ibid.,* II, 468.

[99] *Ibid.,* II, 468–543, *passim,* 574, 639.

[100] *Ibid.,* I, 551, 551n.

[101] *Ibid.,* I, 205, 316, 330, 436.

[102] *Ibid.,* II, 248, 279.

[103] See the list of students and teachers compiled by Pietzsch, *"Musik an den deutschen Universitäten: Leipzig,"* AfMf, Vol. III, 310–30.

of the arts faculty requiring attendance of the entire faculty at St. Nicolas' at noon on the day preceding the Quodlibet for sung masses.[104] And each year at the same church (*ca.* 1488) an anniversary was to be celebrated *pro magistro Johanne Lirike* by the *Collegium maius*: for serving, five *Groschen* were to be paid *"rectori scholarium et succentori eius,"* two *Groschen "pro vigiliis et missa defunctorum per scholares decantandis, plebano,"* and seven *denarii "scholaribus cantantibus lectiones in vigiliis."*[105] A statute of 1511 tells how another memorial Mass was to be celebrated by this college at St. Paul's *cum cantu ad turbam.*[106] Anniversaries observed by the *Collegium minor* also included music, as is seen by the payment of one *Groschen duobus choralibus* in an expense account for this group.[107] A record of payments to musicians *in missa de spiritu sancto,* 1509, contained fees for the *cantor,* singers, bellows-blower, and organist.[108] And in a note written in 1541/2 the rector of the university, Casper Bornerus, attempted to set up standard fees for the bell-ringer, bellows-blower, *cantor,* and organist— the last of whom was to be invited to the "feast of Aristotle," a banquet held by the arts faculty during the doctoral ceremonies.[109]

In fact, music was an important part of festivities connected

[104] See Friedrich Zarncke, *Die deutschen Universitäten im Mittelalter* (Leipzig, 1857), 163: *"Mandatum decani pro interessendo missae ante quodlibeti inceptionem decantandae":*

Mandat Decanus facultatis artium omnibus et singulis suppositis huius studii, in artibus promotis aut promoveri affectantibus, Quatenus cras hora .n. in ecclesia Sancti .N. decenter habituati conveniant et missae inibi ad laudem et honorem omnipotentis Dei sollemniter decantandae et sermoni protunc fiendo intersint.

[105] Zarncke, *Statutenbücher,* 202.

[106] *Ibid.,* 208–209.

[107] *Ibid.,* 248.

[108] Erler, *Matrikel,* II, 447: 3 gr. cantori, 1 gr. pro canentibus [?] in missa et lectorio, 8 d. calcanti, 1 gr. organiste.

[109] Friedrich Zarncke, *Acta Rectorum Universitatis Studii Lipsiensis, 1523–1558* (Lipsiae, 1859), 167:

Impense in hanc fluctuauerunt in hac temporum nouitate. Verum à me sic est res stabilita, ne grauetur posthac fiscus: vt concionatori, sicut pridem, dentur quatuor grossi, campanario S. Nicolai duo grossi ad vnam (sunt igitur huic per annum grossi octo non amplius) vnus grossus cantori (id quod mihi C. B. semper ridiculum fuit et inuidie plenum), vnus grossus offertorium rectori, octo nummi ambolus famulis, octo nummi calcanti, vnus grossus organiste nec amplius, sic tamen vt facultas artium per famulum publicum aut honestum aliquem studiosum eum inuitet ad prandium Aristotelis.

with the awarding of degrees at Leipzig, as at other European universities, although most of the musicians who performed on these occasions appear to have been city or church musicians hired by the university. On the eve of the day of promotion, trumpeters of St. Nicolas announced the event to the whole city.[110] City pipers *(Stadtpfeifer)* played a musical interlude at the *Promotionsakt* after the vice-chancellor had empowered the dean to accept the successful candidates into the *magisterium,* and these musicians, together with the trumpeters, provided music for the procession of the newly created masters and other officials of the *Collegium majus* after the ceremonies. The rector and *cantor* of Leipzig's famous Thomasschule were among the officials invited to the great banquet given for the graduates, as was the organist of St. Paul's, as we have seen. At this feast—the *Prandium Aristotelis,* held on the eve of promotion—the city pipers again performed, and *cantores Thomiani* sang at the banquet and also at the *Promotionsakt* the following day. On the day after the promotion ceremonies, the *Prandium Platonis* took place. Again the city musicians and singers from St. Thomas' offered music for the occasion, and the dean had to see that an organist was present with his instrument. An interesting notice occurs in the *Acta rectorum*—1524—when the St. Nicolas organist, not invited to the Aristotelian banquet, refused to play on his instrument without extra payment, and a disagreement ensued—settled, eventually, by a compromise.[111]

Various decrees forbidding music are rather more numerous in Leipzig documents than in those of other universities—indicative as always of student activities which were disturbing to the serious officials in charge. Several such decrees are found in the *Liber formularis,* generally forbidding *"clamores horribiles aut cantus clam-*

---

[110] For an account of these ceremonies, see Georg Erler, *Leipziger Magisterschmäuse* (Leipzig, 1905), 150ff.

[111] Zarncke, *Acta rectorum,* 2:

> Organicen apud divum Nicolaum, in prandio Aristotelis neglectus, recusavit amplius ludere in instrumento musico, nisi tres grossi, sicut in aliis votiuis solitum est fieri, numerentur. Concilii decreto iussus sum ad parrochum rem deferre; detuli, respondit edituos curaturos, ne quid in ea re innouetur; nec ita multo post venit atque vno *gr.* contentus abiuit.

orosos et insolitos," "studentem vel studentes ... *clamores horribiles excitare seu cantilenas inhonestas per vicos et plateas vagando decantare," "clamores horribiles aut cantus insolitos in plateis aut collegiis"* along with other disturbances.[112] In the statutes of the *Collegium minus* compiled by Johannes Fabri de Werdea sometime during the sixteenth century, there is a notice forbidding students to carry lutes or other musical instruments into their rooms.[113] And the *"Nova Statuta Collegiarum Collegii Maioris"* (1565) declares that neither vocal nor instrumental music is to be countenanced when it is a nuisance to students and other people.[114] The attitude of the authorities seems to have changed somewhat, however, when statutes were given in 1628 to the *Collegium Beatae Mariae Virginis,* for songs were allowed, provided they were musical.[115]

Musical instruments and books owned by students occasionally figure in official documents. In an attack by students upon a *lehrmann* in 1533, for instance, the attackers went *"durch die studenten gassenn mit trommen vnd pfeyffen";* and an inventory of the belongings of two students (1536) listed *ein lauthenbuch gedruckt* and 2 *lauthen.*[116] The fact that one of two *magistri* involved in a dispute in 1547 refused to give up an *organicum positivum* shows the value placed upon the instrument.[117] And the record of another dispute (1548) contains a reference to partbooks of polyphonic music.[118]

A series of letters recording the private musical studies of a Leipzig student, Christof Kress, illuminates for us such studies and indicates their place in the overall picture of university life.

---

[112] Zarncke, *Deutschen Universitäten im Mittelalter,* 164, 175, 178, 186.

[113] Zarncke, *Statutenbücher,* 239: *"Neque arma seu lutinas vel quaecunque alia musicalia instrumenta aut etiam nivem hiemali tempore* ... *ad eandem stubam importet."*

[114] *Ibid.,* 220: *"Musici cantus tam vocis quam organorum usurpabuntur temporibus opportunis absque studiorum detrimento et aliorum offensione."*

[115] *Ibid.,* 286: *"Musicos cantus qualescunque nemini interdicimus, dummodo musici illi sint, i.e. studio bonarum artium et humanitatis digni."*

[116] Zarncke, *Acta rectorum,* 60, 85.

[117] *Ibid.,* 316: *"remittebat M. Iosephus Lupulo duos thaleros sed organicum positiuum, vt vocant, M. Iosephus retinuit.*

[118] *Ibid.,* 340: *"Desiderius Hedlerus furti accusabat Iohannem Zeicheum, vt qui ej partes cantilenarum quarundam amouisset; sed accusatus ostendit, se ab alio illas commodato accepisse, sicque iussus est eas restituere."*

A letter from the boy's father to Joachim Camerarius, the master with whom Christof lived from 1556 to 1559, tells that the lad had studied in Nürnberg with the organist Paul Lautensack and that he wished *"ein virginal oder dergleichen instrument zuhaben . . . (doch ohne verhinderung seines studio)"* upon which to practice.[119] Camerarius agreed to this: *"Des instruments und musika halber meldung, ist mir gantz gefellig, und sollte E.E. sune in seiner bei mir wonung auch darzu angehalten werden, dann ich solche Uebung für guth, nütze und ehrlich halte."* An instrument was purchased, after which Christof begged his father to write his master (Camerarius) that he might take lessons in playing the instrument; and later the lad requested that his father ask Lautensack for some compositions: *"Grus mir auch den Paulus Lautensack vnd bit in von meinetwegen, das er ein, zwei stucklein auf das instrument schick, die ich ein weil lern, bis ich hie unfung, vnd das er mirs deutlich aufsetz, damit ich alsdebesser lernen kann."* He received the pieces from his old teacher, and requested and received more. Christof also asked his father to get some *gute saiten* for his instrument from Lautensack, and when the strings arrived, he wrote that he had shared them with the organist who was his present teacher *("habe dieselben mit dem organisten meinem lermeister getheilt vnd sagen dir dafür grossen dankh")*. In another letter, Christof told his father that he must pay his teacher one *Taler* a month *"Wiewol es vil gelts ist, aber jedoch muss ich bekennen, das er mich fleissig vnd treulich darfür gelernet vnd vnterwisen hat, versich mich auch gentzlich, es sol nicht vbel angelegt sein."* And finally, the lad described in great detail his desire to learn singing and composition.[120]

[119] Excerpts from the Kress correspondence are quoted by Kinkeldey, *Orgel und Klavier in der Musik des 16. Jahrhunderts*, 90–94, and Pietzsch, *Musik an den deutschen Universitäten: Leipzig," AfMf*, Vol. III, 308–10.

[120] Pietzsch, *ibid.*, 310:

Ich bin auch von einem studenten oder 2, die organisten sindt, die mich haben hören schlagen, vnd gesagt, das mir nichts fel weder das ich nicht singen kun, vermant worden dass ich dasselbig lernen wöll, welchs mir zu grossem nutz geraichen werdt, hab derhalben mit einem wolgelerten studenten, der auch wol singen kan . . . geret, welcher mir solchs zulernen gesagt vnd verhoff auch dasselbig mit Gottes hilf, an meiner verhindernuss, in 6 oder 8 wochen zulernen (dan

Christof's correspondence indicates that instruction in practical music was sought and obtained by Leipzig students, but was evidently a private matter and was not to interfere with more important studies in the university proper. Many students, however, were trained in the elements of practical music in the schools connected with Leipzig churches before entering the university. A document from Leipzig's *Liber conclusorum* in which the Saxon Nation expressed its approval of the erection of a school in connection with the Church of St. Nicolas (1511) shows that it was customary for students trained in that school to enter the university later.[121]

A number of men who studied at the University of Leipzig became professional musicians afterwards. Some of them held the important post of *Kantor* at St. Thomas', having charge of the musical instruction of the choristers of the *Thomasschule* as well as the music performed at the churches of St. Thomas and St. Nicolas. Since the entire foundation of St. Thomas—monastery, church, and school—passed into the hands of the Town Council at the time of the Reformation, the *cantor* was also a city official and had to supervise the music for many civic ceremonies.[122] Some of the *Thomaskantors* were students in the university at the time of their directorship. Johannes Scharnagel, for example, master of arts, 1507, was *cantor* from 1505 until 1511; and Georg Rhaw, who matriculated bachelor from Wittenberg in 1518, became *cantor* of St. Thomas' that same year, writing his humanistic *Enchiridion musicae* for the

---

es nichts sonderlichs schwer ist). Vnd will absdan, so ich singen kan, den Paulus Lautensack zuhilff nemen, ime darum schreiben vnd selber lernen aussetzen vnd schlagen, was mir gefelt.

121 Friedrich Zarncke, *Die urkundliche Quellen zur Geschichte der Universität Leipzig in den ersten 150 Jahren ihres Bestehens* (Leipzig, 1857), 647:

De domo nova aedificanda per senatores huius civitatis, quia, ut dicitur, talis domus debet aedificari in honore dei et pro instituendis pueris in rudimentis grammaticae et musicalibus, ideo placet nationi Saxonum quod permittatur structura domus et in ea instituantur pueri, qui sunt filii huius civitatis et non extranei et domos privatas inhabitantes, ut est praefatum. Sed volentes complere, cum ad annos discretionis pervenerint, accedant lectiones publicas cum ceteris complentibus.

122 See Rudolf Wustmann, *Musikgeschichte Leipzigs* (Leipzig, 1909), I, 76ff., for a description of some of these activities.

students there.[123] Johannes Hermann matriculated at the university in 1534 during the time he held the Thomas directorship; his successor, Wolfgang Jünger, matriculated the year he became *cantor* 1536.[124] Ulrich Lange received the bachelor's degree in 1541 and was made *Thomaskantor* soon afterwards, later distinguishing himself as a composer.[125]

Better known than any of these, however, was Wolfgang Figulus, who matriculated in 1547 and held the cantorship from 1549 until 1551. His name first occurs in the *Acta rectorum*, 1549/50, when it was decided that each of his nine pupils owed him four *Groschen*, three *Pfennig*.[126] From Leipzig, Figulus went to Meissen to become *cantor* at the *Fürstenschule* there; and in addition to a large output of sacred compositions, some of them written especially *"ad voces pueriles pares in usum scholarum,"* Figulus wrote two theoretical works directly related to his activities as teacher of music at Meissen.[127] His *De musica practica liber primus ("ex ludo illustri Lisenae,"* Nürnberg, 1565) is an instruction book in music containing a catechism on the divisions of the monochord; and his *Libri primi musicae practicae elementa brevissima, in usum puerorum conscripta* appeared the same year in Nürnberg.

One of the nine pupils who owed fees to Figulus for music lessons as recorded in the *Acta rectorum* was Valentin Otto. Having matriculated in 1548, Otto was obviously studying music with Figulus while a student in the university, just as Christof Kress studied with his organist-teacher. From 1564 until 1594, Otto held the

---

[123] *Ibid.*, I, 20, 44.

[124] Pietzsch, *Musik an den deutschen Universitäten: Leipzig, AfMf,* Vol. III, 318–19.

[125] Wustmann, *Musikgeschichte Leipzigs,* I, 55–58.

[126] Zarncke, *Acta rectorum,* 370:

Vuolfgangus Figulus, cantor inter scholares Thomianos, coram rectore contentus abijt de precio semilectae musicae, soluto à sequentibus, nomine: Hieronymus Muller, Paulus Reimschussel, Christoferus Vulpius, Ioannes Maccelius, Elias Hermannus, Valentinus Thenner, Laurentius Simonis, Simon Gemmitschn, Valentinus Otto, Sebastianus Aeolus. Hi octo rectori, recto rursus cantori numerarunt semipretium. Nonus uero, Vitus Widenhopff, quod abijsset ex vniuersitate, illi adhuc 4 gr. 3 d., quantum et singuli dedere, debet.

[127] Robert Eitner, "Wolfgang Figulus," *MfMg,* Vol. IX (1877), 126ff.

Thomas directorship, and he is remembered for having organized the second chorus of the *Kantorei*.[128]

Otto was succeeded by Sethus Calvisius, of all *Thomaskantors* in the sixteenth century the most learned and distinguished. A student in the university in 1580, *cantor* at *Schul-Pforta,* 1582, where he taught science along with music, Calvisius was chosen *Thomaskantor* in 1594, holding this position until his death in 1615.[129] In 1611 he refused the offer of a professorship in mathematics at Wittenberg. Besides a large number of sacred compositions which he either composed or edited, Calvisius wrote several theoretical works combining speculative and practical aspects of music[130]—and we recall that Morley, in his *Plaine and Easie Introduction,* praised Calvisius above all theorists whom he had found useful. These works comprise the *Melopoeia sive melodiae condendae ratio,* 1592 and 1630, setting forth a theory of composition based upon the harmonic system of Zarlino: the *Compendium musicae pro incipientibus conscriptum,* 1594 and 1602, the third edition of which appeared as *Musicae artis praecepta* (Jena, 1611), teaching the elements of mensural music, rhythm, and notation; the *Exercitationes musicae duae,* 1600, of which the first part deals with the modes and the second gives an historical survey of music; and a debate, the *Exercitatio musica tertia,* 1611. The *Musicae artis praecepta* is unusual in recommending a new system of solmization—*bocédisation* —using the syllables *bo, ce, di, ga, lo, ma,* and *ni.* But not only as composer, theorist, and mathematician is Calvisius important in the annals of music. His essay *"De origine et progressu musices,"* the second part of the *Exercitationes duae,* is one of the early general surveys of music presenting an account of musical progress made by various "inventors" from Jubal and Apollo to Josquin and Lassus.[131] In this history, Calvisius, following accounts given

[128] Wustmann, *Musikgeschichte Leipzigs,* I, 185.

[129] *Ibid.,* I, 190–91.

[130] See Kurt Benndorf, *"Sethus Calvisius als Musiktheoretiker,"* *VjMw,* Vol. X (1894), 413ff.; for information about the treatises, see also F. J. Fétis, *Biographie universelle des musiciens et bibliographie générale de la musique* (2nd ed., Paris., 1873–83), II, 158.

[131] Warren D. Allen, "Baroque Histories of Music," *Musical Quarterly,* Vol. XXV (1939), 198.

by earlier theorists (especially Tinctoris, who had written a separate treatise on this subject, only a few sections of which now
exist), applied chronological method and historical discrimination
to a conventional topic heading found regularly in medieval literature—the section usually called *"De inventione et usu musicae."*

Treatises written by men who studied or taught in the University of Leipzig in the late fifteenth and early sixteenth centuries
reflect the old scholastic approach to music, based largely upon
the *Musica speculativa* of Jean de Muris. Ambrosius Lacher, bachelor of arts, 1490, left an *Epytoma Johannes de Muris in musicam
Boecii* (manuscript in the Prussian *Staatsbibliothek*); and Michael
Schmelzer (matriculated 1483) edited the *Isagoge in musicam* of
St. Bernard (Leipzig, 1517), a copy of which is in the university
library at Leipzig.[132] And Conrad Tockler, teacher of music and
mathematics at Leipzig early in the sixteenth century, left a commentary upon Jean de Muris, several copies of which exist in various libraries and one version of which appears in the Gerbert
Scriptores.[133]

Later Leipzig scholars reflect the new humanistic trends based
upon freedom and independence from tradition, drawing freely
upon Greek and Roman classics, and using elegant, polished Latin
along with various classical poetic forms; instead of Jean de Muris,
these theorists base their doctrines largely upon Gafori and Tinctoris. Elrich Burckhardus, *magister regens* in the Leipzig arts faculty and a member of the humanistic circle around Georg Rhaw,
wrote his *Hortulus musices* in 1514 (published in 1517), giving an
historical background from Linus to the church fathers and following this with brief and clear instructions in psalmody.[134] Ornithoparchus, whose *Musice active micrologus* (first published in
1517) found widespread use in secondary schools of Germany during the sixteenth century, matriculated at Leipzig in 1516 as *magis-*

[132] See Erler, *Matrikel*, II, 315, and I, 338; and Pietzsch, *"Musik an den deutschen
Universitäten: Leipzig,"* *AfMf*, Vol. III, 320, 326.

[133] GS, III, 256–83. Conrad later (1509) became bachelor and doctor of medicine
(Erler, *Matrikel*, II, 73) and was rector in 1512 (*ibid.*, I, 516).

[134] Wustmann, *Musikgeschichte Leipzigs*, I, 41–42.

ter artium from Tubingen; this *humanistischer Wandervogel* quotes the older authorities as well as Tinctoris and Gafori in his book comprising sections on plain song, mensural music, the ecclesiastical accents (chanting), and counterpoint. In the author's dedicatory letter (Dowland's translation), Ornithoparchus states that his book was "first brought forth at Rostock ... and publikely read in three famous Vniuersities of *Germanie,* the Vniuersitie of *Tubyng, Heydelberg,* and *Maguntium.*" Several editions of this work appeared in Leipzig, and as late as 1609 John Dowland, "Bachelor of Musicke in both the Universities," thought it worthy of translation into English. The *Enchiridion musices* (1518) of Georg Rhaw is an instruction book in music designed for students in the *Thomasschule,* dealing with elements of plain song and mensural music.

The composer Johannes Galliculus (matriculated 1505) wrote an instruction book on polyphonic composition dedicated to Rhaw —the *Isagoge de compositione cantus* (1520).[135] Lucas Hordisch (bachelor of arts, 1525, doctor of law, 1534, afterwards *supremus* at the *Thomasschule*) and Sebastian Forster (bachelor of arts, 1526) published in 1533 a collection of songs to be used in the secondary schools, with verses taken chiefly from Prudentius set to music in the humanistic ode style.[136] And Gregorius Faber, bachelor and master of arts at Leipzig in 1546 and 1547, left an instruction book on music, the *Musices practicae erotematum libri II* (published at Basel in 1553), written in 1552 when Faber was professor of music at Tubingen *("in Academia Tubingensi, musices professore ordinario").*[137]

Wittenberg

At the beginning of the sixteenth century (1502) a university was established by Frederick the Wise, Duke of Saxony, at the electoral seat, Wittenberg. According to statutes of 1514, *Musica Muris* was included along with Euclid and *arithmetica communis*

135 *Ibid.,* I, 44, and Erler, *Matrikel,* I, 469.
136 Wustmann, *Musikgeschichte Leipzigs,* I, 46–47.
137 Erler, *Matrikel,* II, 686, 702, and Eitner, *Quellen-Lexikon,* III, 370.

as requirements for the *magisterium*.[138] In the Reformation statutes given the university in 1545 during the leadership of Philip Melanchthon, a humanistic curriculum was set up, providing for two professors of mathematics in the philosophical faculty who were to divide the usual phases of this discipline between them;[139] and although music is not specifically mentioned in these statutes, it was probably included with the teaching of classical literature by Wittenberg humanists. Certainly such theorists as Faber, Spangenberg, and Listenius who came under Melanchthon's influence reflected his ideas in their own works. That there was no actual chair of music in the university (Salamanca, we recall, was unique in having an endowed chair of music as early as this) is clear from a letter written in 1546 by the elector to Adrianus Petit Coclico, who had requested that he be installed in such a position. Refusing this request, the elector wrote that there had never been a professor of music in the university.[140]

At Wittenberg the *Schlosskirche* was also the university chapel, and officials in the university often held offices in the church.[141] Singers from both the ducal *Kapelle* and the university choir furnished music for the services there. Six singers, students in the university, were on the university payroll, together with an organist and bellowsblower: both Johann Weinmann and Hermann Finck filled the position of organist in the first half of the sixteenth century. In 1535, *Sigismundus harthofer organicen* matriculated, according to a note added by Melanchthon, *coecus* (blind).[142] An

138 Walter Friedensburg, *Geschichte der Universität Wittenberg* (Halle, 1917), 24–25.

139 These statutes are printed (n.d.) at the end of the volume *Scripta publice proposita a Professoribus in Academia Vuitebergensi ab anno 1540 usque ad annum 1553* (Witebergae, 1553).

140 M. van Crevel, *Adrianus Petit Coclico* (Haag, 1940), 374:

> Weil aber unser gelegenheit nicht sein will, und es auch bis anher in unser universitet der brauch nicht gewesen, das zu dieser *lection* [Musica] ein sonderlich *stipendium* verordent oder ein sonderer professor derselben underhalten worden were; So haben wir ime [Coclico] . . . ein trangkgeld geben . . . und inen damit abgertigen lassen.

141See Johann Christian August Grohmann, *Annalen der Universität zu Wittenberg* (Meissen, 1801–1802), I, 48.

142 C. E. Foerstemann (ed.), *Album Academiae Vitebergensis* (Lipsiae, 1841), I, 155.

interesting notice in the matriculation roll from 1509 reads, *"Subsequentes XIIII sunt gratis intitulati ob reuerenciam ducis Friderici, quia eius cantores,"* and there follow the names of the fourteen singers of the ducal *Kapelle*.[143] Several ducal ordinances issued at various times mention *stipendia* in the university for the six ducal *Chorales* in the choir,[144] for it was evidently the elector's custom to furnish *stipendia* in the university to members of his choir. We know, moreover, that when the electoral choir was dissolved at the death of Frederick in 1525, the choristers did not receive the *stipendia* for study in the university, a situation similar to that which took place when the imperial choir was dispersed in Vienna at the death of Maximilian I.[145]

The inauguration of Georgius Maior as rector (1561) was marked by religious services using the music of Josquin des Prés, with choir and organ alternating.[146] In fact, a great musical collection owned by Frederick the Wise includes seventeen choir books in manuscript, showing the repertory used in the electoral chapel and in Masses and other services celebrated by the university— largely polyphonic music in the traditional tenor-*cantus firmus* style; and many printed part books in the electoral-university library show a repertory comprising works of three generations of Netherlandish composers and German musicians.[147] The students

[143] *Ibid.*, I, 26.

[144] Grohmann, *Annalen*, I, 62–67.

[145] Wilibald Gurlitt, *"Johannes Walter und die Musik der Reformationszeit,"* *Luther-Jahrbuch*, Vol. XV (1933), 34.

[146] *Album Academie Vitebergensis*, II, 19:

> Interea dum professores conveniunt, psaltae decantent psalmum unum ordiente liturgiam organicine et postea ad singulas cantiones alternatim intercinente.
> Psalmo subiungant psaltae precationem directam ad spiritum sanctum 'Veni sancte' harmonicis melodiis a Iosquino descriptam. . . .
> Interea alternatim organicine per vices intercinente psaltae decantent orationem dominicam harmonicis melodiis a Iosquino descriptam et, si deliberationes productae, fuerint, alia loco tempori isti et huic actui convenientia. . . . Qua peracta theologi cum rectore procumbant in genua et orantes expectent, donec psaltae decantarint gratiarum actionem comprehensam in cantione 'Te deum laudamus.'

[147] Gurlitt, *"Walter,"* *Luther-Jahrbuch*, Vol. XV, 20ff.

who performed these compositions undoubtedly received excellent training in music during their period of service.

Luther's views on the use of music as a force for uniting the worshipping congregation are well known. Educated in the choir school in Eisenach and grounded in the elements of musical theory, Luther strongly advocated the study of music in the schools of Germany—music as a mathematical discipline and as a practical art. This instruction was under the direction of the *Stadtkantor*, who was also *Schulkantor*. And for use in these schools, many theoretical instruction books as well as collections of songs were published, especially by Georg Rhaw, who established a printing press at Wittenberg in 1525. Rhaw studied at Erfurt and Wittenberg, where he became steeped in the educational ideas of Luther and Melanchthon; his own *Enchiridion musices* was one of the most popular instruction books used in the secondary schools of Lutheran Germany and was published in many editions.[148] The first great collection of songs (sacred) for use in the schools also came from Rhaw's press (1544): *Newe deudsche geistliche Gesenge für die gemeinen Schulen,* edited by Johann Walter, Luther's musical adviser.[149] *Kapellmeister* to Frederick the Wise until the dispersal of the choir upon the elector's death, Walter was subsequently called by Luther and Melanchthon to be *Schulkantor* in Wittenberg.[150] The close connection between electoral choir and university is seen again in an address by the rector, Caspar Cruciger, in 1548, extolling the virtues of music and calling upon any students who were willing and able to sing to join the electoral choir directed by Rhaw in Torgau, not far from Wittenberg.[151] And at the death of Rhaw the same year, Cruciger praised him in an oration, mentioning his educational works (*"Edidit enim et Theologica scripta multa, et Arithmetica, et Musicos libros"*) and urging the members of the university to attend his funeral.[152]

[148] For editions of this and other textbooks of Rhaw, see Robert Eitner, "Georg Rhau," *MfMg,* Vol. X (1878), 123–28.

[149] Edited by Johannes Wolf and published as Band 34, *Denkmäler deutschen Tonkunst* (Leipzig, 1908).

[150] Gurlitt, *"Walter," Luther-Jahrbuch,* Vol. XV, 34–39.

[151] *Scripta publica proposita,* fol. e⁵ verso and e⁶ recto.

[152] *Ibid.,* fol. e² verso–e³ verso.

Through its personnel and their interests and activities, thus, Wittenberg was directly connected with the great cultivation of sacred music in the schools of Protestant Germany, schools whose programs included a great deal of musical training. Such training in Wittenberg, however, was by no means limited to choristers and professional singers. Fortunately, we are fairly well informed about a number of musicians who were incorporated in the university and who gave instruction in music there until past the middle of the century. Like Luscinius at Vienna and Glareanus at Basel, these men, eminent as theorists or composers or both, were not public professors but were encouraged by the university to teach students privately.

First among these was Adam von Fulda, *Kapellmeister* to Frederick the Wise, whose name appears in the matriculation roll of 1502 and who taught music in the university that year.[153] A member of the humanistic circle for which Wittenberg was famous, Adam was active as composer, theorist, poet, and historian. Along with Heinrich Isaac, Adam was eulogized by the Wittenberg court poet Georg Sibutus for his musical activities.[154] In his treatise *Musica*,[155] written in 1490 before he came to Wittenberg, Adam showed his musical erudition along both medieval and humanistic lines. This lengthy work is like the learned medieval treatise in presenting the usual scholastic introduction (with definition, divisions, effects, uses, and inventors of music) followed by a treatise on the Gregorian chant (with elements of the modes) and a section on mensural music, together with a fourth book on *musica speculativa*—chiefly musical proportions (drawn largely from Boethius) and their application in rhythmic problems of mensural music.

---

[153] *Album Academiae Vitebergensis,* I, 2, and Moser, *Geschichte der deutschen Musik,* I, 413.

[154] Gurlitt, "Walter," *Luther-Jahrbuch,* XV, 7–8 and note 1:

> *Tunc* Adamus *adest de volda qui fuit olim*
> *Principe sub nostro magno provisus in auro*
> *Aut* Isaacus *adest divus quem Maximilianus*
> *Ad decus et clarum toties conduxit honorem*
> *Ut suus in totum cantus concresceret orbem.*

[155] GS, III, 329–81.

Humanistic influences appear in many allusions to and quotations from classical authors.

Adam's successor at the electoral *capella* was Johannes Weinmann, who had studied at Erfurt and Leipzig and who was active in Wittenberg from 1506 as composer, organist, and historian.[156] Weinmann's setting of the Lord's Prayer (*"Vater unser in Himmelreich"*) was included by Walter in his *Newe deudsche geistliche Gesenge* of 1544.[157] That he was closely connected with the university and highly thought of by its members appears from an oration at his death in 1542 by the dean of the arts faculty, who praised Weinmann, *"qui seruiuit Ecclesiae nostrae, et multos in musica erudijt."*[158]

The distinguished theorist Andreas Ornithoparchus (Vogelsang), associated, as we have seen, with several universities, may have taught music at Wittenberg. At any rate, he was incorporated there in 1516; a note on the margin of the register says, *"Fuit musicus insignis, Cuius Musica typis excusa est."*[159] The *Musica* is, of course, his *Musicae activae Micrologus,* first published at Leipzig in 1517, translated into English in 1609, and widely used as a textbook.

Nicolas Listenius, who matriculated at Wittenberg in 1529,[160] saw his *Rudimenta musicae* published in 1533 by Georg Rhaw, at Wittenberg. Later, when he had become music master of the *Stadtschule* in Salzwedel, he expanded this into a larger work, *Musica* (1537). This was one of the two most popular instruction books in Germany during the sixteenth century, running to many edi-

---

[156] Gurlitt, "Walter," *Luther-Jahrbuch,* XV, 11.

[157] *Denkmäler deutscher Tonkunst,* XXXIV, 82.

[158] *Scripta publice proposita,* fol. H⁶ verso and H⁷ recto:

> Erat artifex non contemnendus, et Musicam ad eum finem conferebat, propter quem data est generi humano, uidelicet ad celebrandas cantiones in templis. Ideo enim praecipue Musica diuinitus hominibus data est, ut seruiat propagationi Religionis. Est enim et iucunda, et diuturna memoria suauium et bonarum cantilenarum.

> Adiunxerat autem ad suam artem et cognitionem Germanicarum historiarum tantam, quam uix in alio uidimus.

[159] *Album Academiae Vitebergensis,* I, 64.

[160] *Ibid.,* I, 136.

tions and being specifically required in numerous *Schulordnungen* for various cities when schools were reorganized under the influence of the Reformation.[161] In these schools, Listenius' *Musica* was generally required for use in the upper classes, whereas Heinrich Faber's shorter *Compendiolum musicae* was used by the lower classes. Listenius' *Musica,* as we shall see, was also used as the text for music lectures at the University of Cracow in 1562. Highly practical in purpose and designed to be placed in the hands of students rather than to be used as a guide by the instructor alone, this work lacks the conventional speculative introduction, giving only Listenius' divisions of music—*theorica, practica (choralis* and *figuralis), and poetica* (composition). The influence of the medieval *introductio* is seen, however, in the dedicatory letter to Johann Georg (son of Joachim II, Elector of Brandenburg), an *apologia* for music describing its uses and effects. Clear and lucid in his explanations and lavish with musical examples, Listenius discusses elements of *musica plana* and *musica mensurabilis.* Poems are included, in humanistic fashion, before and after the treatise. And at the end of the treatise we find another medieval influence: *"Ne vacua maneret pagina, addimus carmen vetus,"* says Listenius, and he gives an ancient mnemonic song for learning intervals found in the treatise of Jerome of Moravia.

Michael Kosswick, who had studied at the University of Frankfort-am-Oder and who had published in Leipzig (1514 and 1516) his *Compendaria musicae artis editio,* matriculated at Wittenberg in 1525.[162] The *Compendaria,* obviously designed for pedagogical purposes *("Ego non laudis studio sed ut communi studiosorum utilitati inservierem"),* deals with plain song and draws upon Gafurius in teaching the elements of mensural music.[163]

The Swiss humanist Sixt Dietrich, famous for his psalm-set-

---

[161] *Musica Nicolai Listenii,* Norimbergae, MDLXIX (facsimile ed., ed. by Georg Schünemann, Berlin, 1927), pp. XVI–XVIII.

[162] *Album Academiae Vitebergensis,* I, 127; and see Pietzsch, *Zur Pflege der Musik an den Universitäten bis zur Mitte des 16. Jahrhunderts: Leipzig," AfMf,* Vol. III (1938), 320.

[163] See Georg Schünemann, *Geschichte der deutschen Schulmusik* (Leipzig, 1929), 61, 65n.

tings, matriculated *gratis* in 1540.[164] From letters he wrote to Amerbach in Basel, it is known that he was well received by Wittenberg humanists, who tried to get him a public lectureship in music.[165] Dietrich, however, did not receive the professorship, owing to his wife's refusal to leave Constanz for Wittenberg and the elector's lack of enthusiasm for the scheme. In 1541 he left Wittenberg, returning in 1544, when he was again *hospes humanissime acceptus,* according to the preface of his hymn collection of 1544, and where he again taught music. It was from Dietrich's lectures, in all likelihood, that Georg Donat (who matriculated at Wittenberg in 1542)[166] compiled a musical notebook, now owned by the *Staatsarchiv* in Weimar, important in giving us insight on the teaching of music in the university. These lecture notes, dealing with practical aspects of music, draw upon Martin Agricola (*Ein kurtz deudsche Musica,* 1528), Spangenberg (*Quaestiones musicae,* 1536), and Listenius (*Rudimenta musicae,* 1533).[167] Unlike most contemporary theoretical books the notebook does not contain a systematic presentation of the elements of plain song and of mensural music; possibly because students had already received such instruction in preparatory schools, the university teacher evidently discussed and stressed the most important problems, going immediately *medias in res,* with emphasis upon various aspects of composition: canons, polyphonic pieces in mensural notation, melodies based on the dif-

[164] *Album Academiae Vitebergensis,* I, 186: "*Sixtus Dieterich Musicus Constantiensis.*"

[165] Crevel, *Coclico,* 165:

Item im 40 Jar [1540] bin ich gen Wittenburg gezogen, da mich dan vill iar belangt hatt zu sechen gelertte leütt, ist mir auch gelungen; dan ich warlich gancz *humaniter* empfangen und erlich tractiert bey den höchsten *doctorn,* die mich all vil und offt geladen und zu gast gehaltten, Mich auch erbetten dass ich *Musicam* auch doselbst *publice* gelesen hab, und, wie sy sagen, nit on frucht der schuler und zuhörenden. Siend mir häfftig angehangen und gebetten, dass ich gar bey innen belyb. Woltten mir ain jar [jährlich] geben von der Lectur der Music 100 guldin, Aussgenommen wass ich *extra ordinarie* gewun, welchs warlich viel mer wurde sein.

[166] *Album Academiae Vitebergensis,* I, 201.

[167] For information about Donat and his treatise, see Adolf Aber, "*Das musikalische Studienheft des Wittenberger Studenten Georg Donat (um 1543),*" SIMG, Vol. XV (1913), 69ff.

ferent hexachords, and ligatures (with an example of a tricinium whose tenor is noted in ligatures).

Soon after Dietrich left Wittenberg, there arrived a Flemish musician—theorist and composer—important in the history of late Netherlandish music: *Hadrianus Petit flemingus Musicus,* as he registered in 1545.[168] Well received by Melanchthon and his circle, Adrianus Petit Coclico, as he is usually called, soon gathered a group of students about him, one of whom, Michael Vogt, later became Walter's successor as *Stadtkantor* in Torgau.[169] Obviously Coclico was highly successful as a teacher, for twenty of his students signed a petition (1545/6) asking the elector (Johann Friedrich) to endow a professorship for Adrianus, who taught them music.[170] University officials, who had earlier asked in vain for a teacher of music (Dietrich), supported this request, asking the elector to create a *stipendium* for Coclico, since such a lectureship would be a good thing for the students, most of whom were *arme gesellen.*[171] The elector, however, saw no need for a chair of music, refused to grant the necessary funds, and sent Coclico away with a *Trangkgeld.*

Coclico's *Compendium musices* was published in Nuremberg in 1552, some years after his departure from Wittenberg. Dealing with problems of practical music—performance and composition —the work comprises three sections: *"De moto ornato canendi,"* *"De regula contrapuncti,"* and *"De compositione."*[172] Throughout this treatise, which epitomizes the style and teaching of Coclico's

---

[168] *Album Academiae Vitebergensis,* I, 228.
[169] Crevel, *Coclico,* 145.
[170] *Ibid.,* 365–68 (*"Versatus est igitur in hac civitate aliquot jam hebdomadis summo cum fructu omnium qui eo in arte musica institutore usi sunt"*).
[171] *Ibid.,* 369:

Wann aber bei uns nicht stehet newe *lection* augzurichten, zudem dass kein uber-schluss vorhanden, sondern das geordente gelt und einkommen der Universitet disser zeit schwerlich raicht, domit die fundirte und vorhin geordente *lectiones* dovon mogen vorsoldet werden, so haben wir uns solcher *lection musices* halben in nichtes einzulassen wissen. . . . Und ist nicht an [nicht zu leugnen], dass solche *lectio* vor die jugent—der eine grosse mennige alhie seint—wol nutze und notig were.

[172] Hawkins, *History of Music,* III, 88.

distinguished teacher, Josquin, Coclico is seen as an exponent of the humanistic ideal in composition—the production of music closely allied to poetry, music following the rhythm and expressing the meaning of the text; music, in a word, expressing the emotions (*affectus exprimere*).[173] It it here that the much discussed concept of *musica reservata*[174] arises for the first time, a phrase used as the title of Coclico's collection of motets, published the same year as the *Compendium*.

Our list of illustrious musicians who registered at Wittenberg in the sixteenth century as private teachers of music closes with Heinrich Faber and Hermann Finck. Faber was a *magister artium*, probably from Wittenberg, known to have lectured on music in Wittenberg in 1551.[175] His *Compendiolum musicae pro incipientibus*, first published in 1548 with many subsequent editions, is an instruction book in the fundamentals of singing (with explanations of keys, syllables, mutations, and signs of notation, all illustrated with musical examples).[176] Written in questions and answers, this little book is a model of clarity and was much drawn upon

173 Coclico's ideals with regard to music are especially clear, too, from his division of musicians into four classes: first, the inventors of music—Orpheus, Boethius, Guido, Okeghem, Obrecht, and Agricola—*"Hi autem tantum Theoretici fuerunt"*; secondly, those who became involved in difficulties of rhythmic problems related to *musica speculativa* and so *"nunquam ad veram canendi rationem perveniunt"*—such as Tinctoris, Gafurius, Dufay, Binchois, and Busnois; thirdly, the real kings of music, who have best combined speculation with art—*"peritissimi musici et artificiosissimi symphonistae"*—such as Petrus de la Rue, Brumel, Morales, Isaac, and Senfl, but *"Inter hoc facile princeps fuit Josquinus de Pres"*; and finally, those who *"verum huius artis finem consecuti sunt"* —learned *musici* of the third class, who direct the precepts of their art toward composing and extemporizing in performance so artistically as to delight and enchant the listener. Opinions vary regarding who are meant to be included in the fourth class: see Crevel, *Coclico*, 51ff.

174 For the meaning of *musica reservata*, see in addition to Crevel's discussion (*ibid.*, 56ff. and 293ff.), Edward Lowinsky, *Secret Chromatic Art in the Netherlandish Motet* (New York, 1926), 87–110, as well as reviews of this work by Leo Schrade, "A Secret Chromatic Art," *Journal of Renaissance and Baroque Music*, Vol. I (1945–47), 165, and M. van Crevel, "Secret Chromatic Art in the Netherlands Motet?" *Tijdschrift der Vereeniging voor Nederl. Musiekgeschiendenis*, Vol. XVI (1946), 289–92. See also the summary in Reese, *Music in the Renaissance*, 511ff. And see Bernhard Meier, "The Musica Reservata of Adrianus Petit Coclico and Its Relationship to Josquin," *Musica Disciplina*, Vol. X (1956), 67–105.

175 *Album Academiae Vitebergensis*, I, 195, and Riemann, *Lexikon*, I, 483.

176 See Robert Eitner, "*Magister* Heinrich Faber," *MfMg*, Vol. II (1870), 25–30, for information about Faber and his works.

by Faber's contemporaries—even used as a model, as we shall see, for several Swedish treatises. The *Compendiolum* was part of a larger work, first published in 1550 and also running to many editions, *Ad musicam practicam introductio*. In the first section of this work, after a brief historical background explaining Greek musical terminology, Faber treats the various elements of plain song and polyphony; in the second part he deals with rhythmic-notational problems of mensural music (saying that his work is based not upon theoretical writings but upon actual musical practice, supported by the works of leading composers, notably Josquin and Isaac).

From 1554 to 1558 Hermann Finck, who had matriculated at Wittenberg in 1545 (a later note on the register adds *Musicus mort*),[177] gave instruction in music there. There is extant a *Musicae commendatio* given by the rector in June, 1554, stating that Finck was to teach the young people in the university *Gesang und Instrumentalmusik*, praising music for its softening effects, and ending with a quotation from Euripides; and in 1558 the rector publicly commended Finck and mourned his death, telling of some of his activities as teacher, composer, and choirmaster.[178] Finck's treatise, *Practica musica*, was published in Wittenberg in 1556, during the time of his residence there. Designed to teach the art of singing, this work is especially interesting for details about ornamentation, a subject also discussed by Coclico—the embellishment of a melodic line with figurated passages: the fifth book of the *Practica musica* is a systematic presentation of the subject.[179]

During the Renaissance, then, Wittenberg did not lack for eminent teachers of music, who practiced their profession in town and electoral choir as well as in the university in the capacity of private teachers. Music performed in Wittenberg was apparently quite up-to-date (pre-eminent was that of Josquin), and most Wittenberg theorists were especially interested in the most modern theories of composition. This great interest in music in town and university

[177] *Album Academiae Vitebergensis*, I, 227.

[178] From another collection, *Scripta publice proposita*, 1562 and 1569, cited by Robert Eitner, "Hermann Finck," *MfMg*, Vol. XI (1879), 11.

[179] For a German translation of the fifth book, see Raymund Schlecht, "Hermann Finck *"über die Kunst des Singens, 1556,"* MfMg*, Vol. XI (1879), 130–33, 135–41.

twice resulted in requests for an endowed chair of music in the university, and the failure of this to come to fruition appears in no way to have been the fault of the university.

vii. POLAND: CRACOW

FROM 1406 when the *musica muris* appeared on the statutes among books to be heard *ante magisterium* (with lectures lasting one month and costing *duos grossos*) until the mid-eighteenth century, the *Musica speculativa* of Jean de Muris had a regular place in the curriculum of the University of Cracow.[1] A statute of 1538 raised the fee for lectures in music and arithmetic to four *groschen;* a statute of 1550 again specified that music be studied for the master's degree; and in 1601 a statute *De examine magistrandorum* required the *Musica* of Muris, with a notice unique in our study that the candidate for the degree be able to give a practical performance on the monochord (clavichord) if the examiners wished it.[2] In 1601 when the dean addressed the arts faculty on the subject of filling vacant lectures, he included music.[3] In statutes of 1603 *"Arithmetica cum Musica speculativa Joannis de Muris una commutatione"* was specified *"pro gradu vero magisterii."*[4] The same year saw inaugurated a preliminary course of study to equip Polish youth for study

[1] An *"Index lectionum in Facultate philosophica,"* 1745, includes among the *"Lectiones matutinae pro gradu"* the *"Musica speculativa cum Arithmetica Joannis de Muris pro 2ᵈᵒ gradu."* See Josephus Muczkowski (ed.), *Statuta necnon Liber Promotionum philosophorum ordinis in universitate studiorum jagellonica ab anno 1420 ad annum 1849* (Cracoviae, 1849), clxvi.

[2] *Ibid.*, p. lvii (1538): *"Aritmethica [sic] cum Musica . . . soluant lectori quatuor grossos."* P. lxv (1550): *"Pro gradu vero magisterii . . . Arithmetica cum Musica."* P. cxxix (1601): *"De examine magistrandorum": "Arithmetica et Musica simul, auctoris Joannis de Muris. Ad extremum singuli candidati in monocordo aliquam melodiam effingent, examinatoribus jubentibus."*

[3] *Ibid.*, p. lxxxvi, from a manuscript *Observationes decani artisticae facultatis*, 1601, *"Convocatio pro vacantibus lectionibus":*

Adsit Humanitas Tua hodierno die in hypocausto communi majoris Collegii, dum signum campana datum fuerit, hora 19, ad accipiendas lectiones vacantes, v.g. Metaphysicam, Perspectivam, Musicam, etc., et alias, si quas vacare contigerit; tum ad permutandas horas cum lectoriis, si vi debitur.

[4] *Ibid.*, p. clv.

in the university proper, this curriculum consisting of four *scholae* —of grammar, poetry, dialectic, and rhetoric: in this preparatory school, music was taught with poetry.[5] Long before the appearance of this statute, however, music had been associated with poetry in the university. George Liban, professor of Greek, wrote several musical treatises, and in 1539 a certain *poeticae collegiaturae lector* was involved (as we shall see) in a suit over the teaching of music.

Other university documents refer to the use of the *Musica speculativa* of Jean de Muris as textbook at Cracow well into the Renaissance. According to the *Liber diligentiarum* of the university, giving the *"Registrum Leccionum et Lectorem"* for each term from 1487 to 1563, music was scheduled almost continuously until 1546. But from the latter year until 1562, with the single exception of 1555, when Stanislaus Ponijkijewskij lectured, the lectureship in music was vacant. During all these years, music was closely associated with mathematics, for *Arithmetica cum musica* is the usual subject of the lectures. But occasionally the regents taught such combinations as *Arismetricam, musicam et Speram materialem, Astronomiam, Arismetricam et musicam,* and in one case—significant of the relating of music to classical philology—*Arismetricam cum musica et Homerum.*[6] In 1492 the subject of the music lecture was to have been the Gregorian chant, but was changed to the usual arithmetic and music.[7] Another innovation occurred in 1562 when

---

[5] *Ibid.,* pp. *cxlvi–cxlvii*:

Quia major pars juventutis ad Universitatem nostram venit, quae privata eaque arctiori institutione indiget, magno consilio et longa deliberatione conclusum fuit anno 1588, ut scholae privatae propter hanc rudiorem juventutem in alma Universitate nostra instituerentur, in quibus prima septem Artium liberalium ac utriusque linguae initia et elementa via et ordine traderentur. Quas ad laudem et honorem Dei Omnipotentis utilitatemque publicam restituendas ac reformandas decernimus. Harum autem scholarum talis erit ordinatio:

    I. *Schola Grammaticae.*
    II. *Schola Poëticae.*
    III. *Schola Dialecticae.*
    IV. *Schola Rhetoricae.*

And see p. *cxlvii: "Antefestis diebus Musica una hora antemeridiana"* was to be given in the *Schola Poëtica.*

[6] Wladislaus Wislocki (ed.), *Liber diligentiarum facultatis artisticae Universitatis Cracoviensis, Pars I, 1487–1563* (Cracoviae, 1886), 40, 45, 66.

Magister Joannes Piotrcovita taught *Musicam Lastenii* (the treatise by Listenius); and in 1563 Martinus Nervitius Clodaviensis was the lecturer when *Musicae speculativae Joannes de Muris libri II* were read.[8] Items in the *Liber diligentiarum* make it clear that lecturers in music taught other subjects required by the arts faculty, not music and arithmetic alone.

In addition to the notice *Vacantes lectiones: Arithmetica cum musica* which occurs rather frequently between 1546 and 1562, several earlier items point to the occasional neglect of music on the part of the regent masters.[9] And in 1537 a *magister regens* was fined by the rector for failing to give his course in music.[10] Such notices as these only serve to point up the regularity with which musical studies were ordinarily carried on.

While *musica speculativa* was taught in the arts faculty of the university proper, *musica activa* was encouraged and cultivated in song schools and churches connected with the university and among the university students. Beginning with a notice from 1469

[7] *Ibid.*, 20: "*Stanislaus Obolecz Musicam choralem, non legit. . . . Martinus Schomotuli Arismetricam et musicam.*"

[8] *Ibid.*, 347, and see Pietzsch, "*Musik an den Universitäten im Osten*," *AfMf*, Vol. I, 425–27, citing Wislocki's *Catalogus* of manuscripts in the library:

> Musicae speculatiuae Joannis de Muris libri II, quorum alter tradit numerum sonorum et proportionem eorundem, correspondetque musice speculatiue, alter agit de instrumentis, tradens praxim eorum, que in primo libro docentur, correspondetque musice practice, scripti a.d. 1563 commutatione hiemali per mgrum Martinum Neruitium Clodauiensem, per eundemque lecti hora 20 L.S. [Hall of Socrates].

A note on the manuscript tells of Martinus' distinguished career: "*Iste Martinus Meruitius Clodauiensis tenuit scholam Curzelouiensem, postea vero fuit concionattor facundus Sigismundi Augusti, regis.*"

[9] *Liber diligentiarum*, 16, 86, 98, 208, 274: in 1490, "*mgr. Bartholomeus de Opoczno Arismetricam et musicam, non legit*"; in 1508, "*dr. Martinus Belze incepit post Epiphanie Arismetricam, Musicam non incepit*"; in 1511, "*mgr. Ioannes de Vyslicia Arithmeticam cum musica, tarde incepit et raro legit*"; in 1532, "*mgr. Simon de Cracovia Arithmeticam cum musica, incepit in crastino Simonis, raro legit nec finiuit*"; and in 1546, "*Andreas de Raua Arithmeticam cum musica, secundo die incepit, sed frequentissime non legit.*"

[10] Wladislaus Wislocki and Stanislaus Estreicher (eds.), *Acta rectoralia almae Universitatis studii Cracoviensis* (Cracoviae, 1893–1909), II, 17:

> Magister Martinus de Cerdonia, canonicus sancti Floriani, vocatus ad iudicium, cui obiectum est, quod dedit recognitionem Arithmeticae cum Musica, quam nunquam legisse inuenitur in registro decani leccionum. . . . Et condempnatus est in decem octo grossis.

in which a suit involving *"Discretum dnum Iohannem Viojczijk, cantorem chorj ecclesie maioris Cracouiensis"* came before the rector's court,[11] many persons whose names are recorded in the *Acta rectoralia* are listed as *cantores*—singers or choirmasters. According to one item, a witness *in causa percussionis* (1489) accused a *cantor* of somewhat harsh disciplinary actions.[12] There are many references to song schools in these records also—St. Anne's, St. Stephen's, and those in Bochnia, Elkusz, and Chaczijnij—obviously attended by small boys, one of whom was abducted by members of the university in 1494.[13] The heads of these schools figured several times in suits before the rector's court.[14] And graduates of the university sometimes held the *officium cantoriatus* in the schools.[15] In a case concerning Magister Stephanus Pestinensis (*"delatus a dnum rectorem pro introductione cujusdam mulieris in habitationem suam tempore senioratus sui"*), a witness testified that he was unable to tell whether the accuser had left the church or not— presumably to follow Stephen—*"quia testis cantabat et regnabat alys in choro."*[16] In 1612 a synod of the diocese of Cracow set up a *"modus instruendae juventutis in scholis parochialibus"* which emphasized music.[17]

In one instance, the abduction of a *discantista* resulted in trial before the rector, with Simon de Cracovia playing a principal role

---

[11] *Ibid.*, I, 11.

[12] *Ibid.*, I, 268: the witness testified that the accused *"ipsum cum stilo seu corulo ad modum stili cantorie leuiter tetigit . . . sed nescit, an ad caput uel alias ipsum percusserit."*

[13] *Ibid.*, I, 364–65: certain members of the university abducted *"iuuenem quendam, Antonium de Bochnya, etatis vndecim annorum vel citra."*

[14] *Ibid.*, I, 71, 587.

[15] *Ibid.*, I, 73, for example: *"Agnes, vidua, petit a dno baccalario Ambrosio de Rosumberk j marcam sine 4 grossis, quam debebat filio suo Iohanni racione seruicij cantoratus in Elkusz."*

[16] *Ibid.*, I, 559, 1083.

[17] *Liber promotionum*, p. cxlviii: *"Ut studia, ministerio Ecclesiae seruientia, neglecta, scilicet: Musica, Arithmetica, aliaeque artes liberales, postliminio ad scholas redeant et pubes recte instituatur."* And p. clii: *"Musices quoque studium, hactenus neglectum et ab Ecclesia semper desideratum, sit in posterum et diligens et fervens. . . . Praedictorum lectionum hic erit ordo. Matutino tempore.*

    I. *Examen memoriae ex Grammatica, Cicerone, Computo vel Musica.*

    IV. *Computi et Musicae, alternis diebus."*

—probably the same Simon who lectured sporadically on music in 1532[18]—significantly described here as an organist. Again, the connection between church and university is seen in the theft of a graduale and in the inventory of books taken from a student's room in 1534, including a collection *Hijmnij et sequencie de tempore et de sanctis.*[19] And on the historic occasion in 1549 when certain students were killed, music was a part of the last services before a large part of the student body dispersed.[20]

There are very definite indications that instruction in the elements of plain song and polyphonic music was given at Cracow, privately and publicly. From 1523 we have the record of a dispute over the teaching of music in which Simon de Lask petitioned that Andrea de Poltowuko, bachelor of arts, be held to his contract for teaching Simon music: Andrea, however, deposed that Simon was unacceptable as a student because of propensities toward fighting and dicing, and the rector decided in favor of Andrea.[21] George

---

[18] *Acta rectoralia*, II, 27:

Reverendi Ioannis de Jactarow, arcium baccalarii, ad propositionem occasione abduccionis et prodicionis Pauli de Byycz, discantistae ludi sanctae Mariae virginis, magister Simon de Cracovia, ludi litterarii sancti Spiritus, animo et intencione litem legitime contestandi, negavit narrata, prout narrantur, et nihilominus confessus est, se aestiva die fuisse ad Istulam extra portam novam, ibidem in obvium habuisse Paulum de Byecz, discantistam. Quem allocutus est: "tu ne es ille, qui pridie cecinit in organo"; illo respondente: "ego sum," mox dixit; "ecce tibi de sertum, ut in capite ponderes recipiendo a suo servitore" et mox subiunxit: ne iret ad Istulam, ne submergeretur, rogans Paulum ut sertum deferret sub gratia eius.

[19] *Ibid.*, I, 790, 819–20, 825.
[20] *Ibid.*, II, 154: *"Propter quam caedam et non administratam iusticiam"* on the part of the king and university officials, the students, along with the mendicant orders,

egressi sunt cum gravi iactura ita, quod duntaxat presbiteri solimet per aestatem decantabant processiones et missas, funesti et deplorati. . . . Ubi cantata missa in ecclesia sancti Floriani in Kleparz de Spiritu Sancto, post hoc occinendo responsum illud laudabile, nempe: Ite in orbem, ilico cathervatim foras omnes plorantes abierunt.

[21] *Ibid.*, I, 634: *"Simon de Lask, ad Omnes ss. Cracovie in schola degens,"* petitioned that Andrea de Poltowsko, bachelor of arts, *"cogi ad tenendum contractum secum de seruitio cantorie inito."* The latter replied that *"insolentiarum et ludum taxillorum et contencionum ipsius causam esse, quominus nollet eundem Simonem secum recipere ad supradictum seruitium, petentisque, se ab impeticione eiusdem absoluj. Et dnus rector quantum ad contractum super seruitio illum rescindit."*

Liban, bachelor and master of arts who had studied at Cologne late in the fifteenth century, was a teacher of music at Cracow, and his little treatise (published in 1540 *"ad Christi gloriam et studiosorum utilitatem"*), *De musicae laudibus oratio seu adhortatio quaedam ad musicae studiosos,* was first read as a lecture at Cracow in 1528.[22] Two official documents, moreover, point to occasional public lectures on the chant.[23] One of these was the will of Stanislaus Johannis Borek (1565), which specified that a *baccalaureus* should read publicly *diebus canicularibus et tempore Quadrigesimae* in the *Collegium majus* on one of a long list of subjects, including *Musicam et Arithmeticam* and *De accentibus ecclesiasticis* (performance of the Gregorian chant). The will of Stanislaus Rzeczyca (1572), leaving two thousand ducats to the *Collegium majus artistarum,* repeated this list in founding a course of lectures *utilitatis publicae huius regno gratio,* including *Musicam et Arithmeticam practicam* and also *de accentibus ecclesiastibus.*

We know, furthermore, that several eminent composers were members of the university at various times and that instruction in composition was given by men associated with the university. In the matriculation rolls of 1514, for instance, we read of an organist distinguished for his organ compositions, a man who died of the plague.[24] And a student was enrolled in 1526 as *magnus musicus Iusquin discipulus.*[25] In 1539 two men brought charges against Martinus de Crosno (called in a previous record *"doctorem Martinum de Chrosznya, poetica collegiaturae lectorem"*) because

---

[22] Pietzsch, *"Musik an den deutschen Universitäten: Köln,"* AfMf, Vol. V, 81. Albert Sowinski, *Les Musiciens polonais et slaves* (Paris, 1857), 368–69.

[23] *Codex diplomaticus Universitatis Cracoviensis* (Cracoviae, 1870–90), V, 58–59, 91.

[24] B. Ulanowski and A. Chmiel (eds.), *Album studiosorum Universitatis Cracoviensis* (Cracoviae, 1887–1904), II, 154: "Laurencius Martini Voyczik de Schadek, *organista mire fantasie in formandis organis—uxoratus organista Poznaniensis in Plessow obyt peste."* Many references to the plague and its effects appear in various records of the university.

The word *organa* is used in certain fourteenth- and fifteenth-century Silesian sources to mean compositions for the organ (in the style of the medieval organum). See Leo Schrade, "The Organ and Organ Music in the Mass of the 15th Century," *Musical Quarterly,* Vol. XXVIII (1942), 472ff.

[25] *Album studiosorum,* II, 231: *"Arnoldus Juliani Causin de Ath ex Hanoniensi Comitatu dioc. Cameracensis, magnus musicus Iusquin discipulus."*

he had not carried out his contract to teach them composition, the course to be based upon Ornithoparchus' *Micrologus*.[26] One of Poland's most eminent musicians was Sebastian Felstin, described by one writer as *"le doyen de l'enseignement musical en Pologne,"* who received the baccalaureate at Cracow in 1509 and later taught in the university; according to his biographer, Janocki, *"Primus omnium musicem docere Cracoviae coepit"* and *"in musica arte et doctrina, magnum adeptus est nominis celebritatem."*[27] The humanist Felstin, some of whose compositions are still in existence, is important in musical history in being one of the earliest Polish composers to write four-part polyphony and in having introduced Netherlandish influences to Polish music.[28]

One of Felstin's students in music at the University of Cracow was Martinus de Leopoli (Marcin Lwowczyk), a poet and composer who reached such heights of perfection that he surpassed those who had studied music at Rome.[29] Martinus wrote a cycle of music for the Church year which was adopted for liturgical usage throughout Catholic Poland, and he later became court organist to Sigismund Augustus, holding this position until the king's death in 1572. Another member of the king's household was the composer Waclaw Szamotulczyk—a student in the University of Cracow in 1538—whose compositions appeared in several collections of music outside Poland and who was the first to introduce music for double choirs to Poland.[30] In 1605 was registered Stanis-

---

[26] *Acta rectoralia*, II, 58–59:

Venerabilis domini doctoris Martini de Crosno ad proposicionem, occasione contractus docendi Musicam Ornithoparchi, a qua debuerunt solvere per viginti sex grossos. . . . Discreti Albertus, arcium baccalarius, de Bochnya ac Georgius de Oppatowyecz, agentes in schola sanctae Annae, animo et intencione litem contestandi negaverunt contractum sic initum, et adhuc per tredecim grosses sibi retinere ex ea causa, quia non perfecte eos composicionem et exempla docuit. Et dominus auditis partibus adhuc praefixit ad octavam, ut visitarent ad doctorem et ut eis necessaria demonstraret et ut ibidem componerent: in defectu [concordia] alias in octava comparebunt.

[27] Sowinski, *Musiciens polonais*, 185.

[28] Reese, *Music in the Renaissance*, 747.

[29] Sowinski, *Musiciens polonais*, 393–94. Several of Martinus' compositions are printed by Reese, *Music in the Renaissance*, 750–51.

[30] Reese, *Music in the Renaissance*, 748–49.

laus Nicolas Zielenski, a student who later (in 1611) wrote a great cycle of church music comprising 119 works; organist at Gniezo (*ca.* 1611), Zielenski was especially influenced by Giovanni Gabrieli and other Venetians, and his use of the organ with antiphonal choruses is significant of the emerging baroque style.[31]

Along with composition, instruction in the playing of instruments was available in the Cracovian university and sometimes even required by statute, as we have seen. As early as 1469, instruction *in cleuicordio* is associated with other *lecciones gradum baccalarii concernentes* in a suit brought before the rector's court by a mother who felt that her son was not being properly instructed: the defendant replied that he had indeed taught the young man *et in cleuicordio instruxerit.*[32] A case which came up in 1488 involved a debt for instruction *in artificio citharae.*[33] Several men called *organistae,* moreover, were involved in cases before the rector's court at various times, and one man left funds in his will *pro reparando organo* at St. Nicolas'.[34] In 1478 a student brought suit against his organ teacher, complaining that he had not been properly taught, although the organist maintained that he had taught the young man everything he need know about the organ.[35]

[31] *Album studiosorum,* III, 248; Zdzislaw Jachimecki, "Polish Music," *Musical Quarterly,* Vol. VI (1920), 559; Reese, *Music in the Renaissance,* 753.

[32] *Acta rectoralia,* I, 15–16:

> Barbara Casparowa de Cracovia proposuit contra Caspar de Apparias . . . ut filium eius nomine Stanislaum lecciones, gradum baccalarii concernentes, edoceret et propter huiusmodj informacionem expensas apud ipsam haberet, lapsis duabus septimanis, viso, quod dictus Caspar filium suum, ut debuit, non informat.

Caspar replied that he had taught the young man *"et in cleuicordio instruxerit, ac 'Tertium tractatum' Petri Hispani et 'Parva naturalia' integrum et totaliter presumpserit, in presencia dicte Barbare et Stanislao filio."*

[33] *Ibid.,* I, 247: *"Veniens Sebestianus de Cibinio, studens, recognouit se tenerj Honesto dno Hemenraus [sic] certi debiti quatuor florenos hungaricales et racione informacionis in artificio citare duos florenos."*

[34] *Ibid.,* I, 354, 530–32, 602; II, 213.

[35] *Ibid.,* I, 145:

> Honorabilis dnus Anthonius de Casszhowia, arcium liberalium baccalarius, proposuit contra et aduersus Valentinum de Pilszno, arcium bacc., qualiter recepisset et eundem conuenisset de informacione in organo tactum [tactuum] et insuper dedisset marcam vnam, deinde prefatus Anthonius asserebat, a prefato bacc. Valentino nichil informauisse. Ex aduerso Valentinus respondebat ad

In view of this emphasis upon organ music, it is not surprising to find that one of Poland's most important monuments of music is an organ tablature compiled between 1537 and 1548 by Johannes (Jan) de Lublin, one of the *canonici regulares* of the monastery in Krasnik, whose name appears in the *Liber promotionum* in 1508 and 1513.[36] The book, obviously written for teaching purposes, includes a theoretical section with rules for improvisation on the organ and many musical examples.

Several other records in the *Acta rectoralia* point to musical practices among members of the university. In 1470 a case involving a *tubam bubalinam* was brought to trial, the rightful owner of this trumpet asking that it be restored to him by the student who had taken it by force.[37] The instrument *dulce melos* (a stringed instrument similar to the English dulcimer) figures in two cases of theft which came before the rector for judgment, in 1486 and in 1491.[38] In 1491 there also occurred a dispute over possession of a *cithara*.[39]

proposicionem, quod eundem informauisset diligenter et aliquos tactus sciuisset in prefato organo tangere et omnia, que concernunt ad organum, ostendisset et insuper notauisset, et dixit, eundem bacc. operam ad prefatum ludum non habuisse neque fecisse.

[36] Adolf Chybinski, *"Polnische Musik und Musikkultur des 16. Jahrhunderts in ihren Beziehungen zu Deutschland,"* SIMG, Vol. XIII (1911), 478–79; and see the theoretical introduction to the collection of organ pieces, 486–90.

[37] *Acta rectoralia,* I, 33:
Blasius de Pobijedzyska contra Bartholomeum de Vijelun, studentem, verbo proposuit, quia anno presenti in quodam hospicio apud Stano, recipiens ab eodem Blasio vi tubam bubalinam valoris vnius floreni, sibj ad seruandum datam, restituere recusat, petens, ipsum compellj ad restitucionem huiusmodj tube, aut valoris eiusdem solucionem.

[38] *Ibid.,* I, 229, 328:
Stanislai de Voijslaw, baccalarij, et ex aduerso Nicolai, studentis de Carnijow, in causa ipse Nicolaus, reus, statuet euictorem infra hinc ad vnam septimanam ex decreto domini ipsi Stanislao, actori, accosione cuiusdam cithare alias dulce melos, ad ipso reo petite, et interim attemptabunt concordiam.

Iohannes de Liipniicza obligauit se soluere quinque grossos ex decreto domini . . . Stanislao, seruitori Vniuersitatis pro quodam instrumento musicali, dicto dulce mellos, sub censuris ecclesiasticis.

[39] *Ibid.,* I, 314:
Ad relationem Pauli, sapientie, et ad instantiam Michaelis, famuli sutorie artis,

The use of songs and instruments among the students was sometimes found objectionable—as in 1494 when certain students were brought before the rector's court for having created disturbances in an inn *in cantibus cithare tibiarumque.*[40] In 1550 a dispute took place among senior and junior members of the *Collegium minor* over unbecoming actions, including musical activities (*clamores, strepitus, cantus, pulsus et saltus*), on the part of the younger men: the court decided against allowing such activities in the future.[41] In 1556 a citizen brought suit against a certain bachelor of arts who headed a nearby school and his assistant teacher, complaining, among other things, that they disturbed the peace with singing: this was strongly denied when the case came to trial.[42]

Both the usual aspects of the teaching of music in the university —practice as well as theory—are reflected in manuscripts found in the university library.[43] Boethius and Isidorus have a place here, along with several anonymous tracts on *musica speculativa,* one of them opening with a quotation from Boethius. The *Tonarius* of Berno of Reichenau, with marginalia by A. (Albertus?) de Opatow (*ca.* 1450), bachelor and master of arts, doctor of medicine, and several times dean of the arts faculty, and the *Musica enchiriadis* (here attributed to Hucbald), annotated by Opatow, are also found among the manuscripts. Seven treatises attest to the popularity and predominance of Jean de Muris, most of them written anonymous-

---

citatus Thomas de Posnania, comparens, ad proposicionem actoris, quam fecit, quod citheram sibi Thome in diebus Carnispriuij in valore x grossorum accomodauerit, videlicet concessam ei citheram, negauit valorem.

[40] *Ibid.,* I, 377: the students were *"cittatj per Andream, cocum, et Annam, coniuges, aduersum quos deposuerunt de insolentys, quas assidue in cantibus cithare tibiarumque in eius domo faciebant."*

[41] *Ibid.,* II, 172–73.

[42] *Acta rectoralia,* II, 241: in the trial the bachelor (defendant)

cantilenas se decantasse negavit. . . . Et dominus auditis parcium proposicionibus et responsis, mandavit sub poena carceris graviterque edixit ac interminatus est praedicto Joanni baccalaureo ac ipsius hipodidascolo, ut omnino a praedictis minis, cantilenis ac suspicionibus quibusvis abstineant.

[43] Pietzsch, *"Musik an den Universitäten im Osten," AfMf,* Vol. I, 425–27, citing Wislocki's *Catalogus.*

ly. One of these was the book which Martinus Nervitius taught in 1563. A "modern" work found among these books is the *Liber XX artium* of Paulus Paulirinus of Prague, who was incorporated in 1451 at Cracow.[44] Paul's encyclopedia of the arts, written around 1460 after his departure from Cracow, describes an item of special interest here: the *dulce melos,* an instrument which we have seen was highly treasured by students in the University of Cracow at this period. Indeed, the high place of instrumental music among university studies possibly was responsible for the last section of Paul's treatise, a discussion of a number of instruments.

In addition to those whose treatises exist in the library in manuscript, at least two men associated with the university produced treatises on *musica speculativa.* One of these was Erasmus Heritius, who had studied at several universities and who matriculated at Cracow in 1494 from Cologne.[45] His *Musica speculativa,* largely an explanation of Boethian theory, was written in 1498 and thus may have been influenced by his stay at Cracow. Henricus Schreiber, graduate of the University of Vienna, matriculated at Cracow in 1515 and became a teacher there: his mathematical treatise on music *(Algorismus proportionum una cum monochordi generis dyatonici compositione)* was published in Cracow in 1514.[46]

Besides these mathematical works, numerous works on the more practical aspects of music—the ecclesiastical chant or polyphony—appeared from the hands of men who studied or taught at Cracow. Among these was Sebastian de Felsztyn, who published several works dealing with practical music. One of these, the *Opusculum musice compilatum noviter per dominum Sebastianum presbyterum de Felstin* (Cracow, 1519) had as byline, *"Pro institutione adolescentium in Cantu simplici seu Gregoriano,"* significant of its pedagogical intent.[47] Felsztyn later edited *Aliquot Hymni ecclesiastici* (Cracow, 1522) and Augustine's treatise on music (*Divi*

44 *Album studiosorum,* I, 131: *"doctor arcium et medicine totum."*
45 *Ibid.,* II, 35.
46 Pietzsch, *"Musik an den Universitäten im Osten,"* AfMf, Vol. I, 444.
47 This byline evidently applied only to the first half of the book: the second half, *"Opusculum musicae mensurabilis,"* dealt with the usual problems of mensural music, with examples in three parts. See Sowinski, *Musiciens polonais,* 186–88.

Aurelii Augustini, de Musica, Dialogi VI, 1536),[48] showing his interest in music as related to poetic meters. The last published work of this Polish scholar (he may have been a priest in the diocese of Przemysl) was a musical one, his *Directiones musicae ad cathedralis Ecclesiae Premisliensis usum* (1544), the result of his desire to standardize and improve the performance of liturgical music.[49]

A second edition of Felsztyn's *Opusculum musicae* (1534) included at the end a tract, *Musica figurata,* by Martin Kromer, Polish historian, bishop, and statesman who had studied music as a choirboy in Biecz and who received the baccalaureate in 1530.[50] Kromer was the author of another treatise on polyphonic music, *De concentibus musices quos chorales appellamus.*

We have already noticed that George Liban, first professor of Greek in the university, wrote musical works, probably for the members of his choir. In 1539 his *De accentuum ecclesiasticorum exquisita ratione* was published.[51] Ornithoparchus' *Micrologus,* published in 1517 and known at Cracow, contained a section on the ecclesiastical accents, the proper method of chanting the lessons and psalms; and public lectures, as we have seen, were sometimes given at Cracow on the same subject. When Liban published in 1540 his *De musicae laudibus oratio,* first presented as a lecture in 1528, he added to it a discussion of Greek words (*multorum vocabulorum graecorum interpretatio*) used in musical terminology. Typically, Liban's work is characterized by a combination of the new humanism (praise of music in Greek, Latin, and Hebrew) with the medieval point of view; and he mingles traditional scholastic instruction with scraps of information from the new theorists, chiefly Gafurius.[52] Johannes Spangenberg, printer at Cracow and once a student at Erfurt, left two instruction books on music: *Quaestiones*

[48] *Ibid.,* 188. According to Eitner, *Quellen-Lexikon,* III, 410, Felsztyn's biographer, Janocki, mentions the edition of Augustine's *Musica,* but no copy is extant.

[49] Chybinski, *"Polnische Musik," SIMG,* Vol. XIII (1911), 473.

[50] Sowinski, *Musiciens polonais,* 347, and Pietzsch, *"Musik an den Universitäten in Osten," AfMf,* Vol. I, 438.

[51] Sowinski, *Musiciens polonais,* 369–70.

[52] Chybinski, *"Polnische Musik," SIMG,* Vol. XIII (1911), 472.

musicae in usum scholae Northusianae (1536) and *Musicae* [*sic*] *choralis in alma universitate Cracoviensi . . . ad ministerium in Eclesia Dei sive ad laureas in artibus,*[53] pointing again to the teaching of practical music in the university. A final work dealing with the chant is the *Commentarium in Ecclesiae Romanae Cantilenas,* by Michel Wroclawski (d. 1553), a professor at Cracow, scientist, and theologian, known especially for his research in the Roman liturgy.[54]

In the seventeenth century, treatises inspired by university learning continued to appear. Johannes Broscius (Broski, born 1581), for example, famous as a mathematician, philosopher, medical doctor, astronomer, musician, and poet, left two musical works: one, published in 1641, on the subject of equal temperament and the other, published several years later, on the ecclesiastical chant.[55]

Our picture of music at the university of Cracow during the Renaissance, with its strong emphasis upon instrumental music in addition to the usual facets of music as a discipline of higher learning, may be rounded out by mention of the treatises which were available to teachers and students in the sixteenth century. These published works owned by the university library included books by leading German and Italian theorists—Heyden, Ornithoparchus, Galliculus, Rhaw, Listenius, Spangenberg, Zarlino, Lossius, Heinrich Faber, Galilei, Calvisius, Johannes Nucius (*Musices poeticae sive de compositione cantus praeceptiones utillissimae,* 1613), and Heinrich Baryphonus (*Pleiades musicae,* 1615).[56] An inventory of the Cracow booksellers Scharffenberg and Ungler (1547–51) also reveals that German, Italian, and Cracovian musical works were for sale at this time.[57]

[53] Sowinski, *Musiciens polonais,* 516.

[54] *Ibid.,* 582.

[55] *Ibid.,* 103–104.

[56] Adolf Chybinski, "*Die Muskibestände der Krakauer Bibliotheken von 1500–1650,*" *SIMG,* Vol. XIII (1911), 383.

[57] Chybinski, "*Polnische Musik,*" *SIMG,* Vol. XIII (1911), 469–70. The list includes *Musica Lignicensis* (Liban's *De musicae laudibus oratio*), Agricola's *Rudimenta Musices, Musica Ornithoparchi, Musica Philomatis, Musica Spangenbergi, Musica Franquini* (the *Musica practica* of Gafori), *Defensio Musicae* (?), and *Musica Heyden* (Sebald Heyden's *Musicae, id est, artis canendi libri duo*).

viii. Scotland: St. Andrews, Glasgow, Aberdeen

St. Andrews

EARLY STATUTES for St. Andrews had decreed that the liberal arts were to be studied according to Parisian usage, from which we infer the study of music. Reform statutes of 1570 again stressed conformance to Parisian usage; but with the assignment of separate subjects to individual regents, music may well have become a part of physics.[1]

Various foundations incorporated in the university—the most important of which were the Colleges of St. Salvator (1450), St. Leonard (1512), and St. Mary (1538)—provided for the support of poor scholars and choristers, along with regents in arts and students of theology. Bishop Kennedy's charter for St. Salvator (the early statutes no longer exist) provided for six scholars in the arts faculty to act as choristers for the collegiate church, and contained specific instructions for singing Mass; by 1475 there were twelve *choristi* or vicars-choral to maintain services in the church, and by 1534 a song school connected with the college had been organized —for in that year Provost Hugh Spens left money to the master of the school "for instructing the young in music."[2] Statutes of St. Leonard (1512) specified that some of its twenty scholars were to be instructed in the Gregorian chant and, if possible, in polyphonic music.[3] Later statutes (1544) stated that the applicant for admis-

---

[1] Robert Kerr Hannay, *The Statutes of the Faculty of Arts and the Faculty of Theology at the Period of the Reformation* (St. Andrews, 1910), 87: "*Imprimis statuimus et ordinamus quod in hoc studio in facultate artium sint determinantes solito more instar studii Parisiensis.*" And see Ronald G. Cant, *The College of St. Salvator* (Edinburgh and London, 1950), 174, for the New Foundation under which physics and astronomy were to be taught to *magistrands* by a separate regent (although in practice, regents continued for some years to carry their students through the whole college curriculum).

[2] *Ibid.*, 10, 15, 26, 28; see Bishop Kennedy's charter, 54–60.

[3] John Herkless and Robert Kerr Hannay, *The College of St. Leonard* (Edinburgh and London), 1905, 129:

> viginti *scolares* omnes in grammaticalibus (et eorum aliqui ut apciores fiant ad nostrum principale sanctiandree collegium in divinis officiis sustendandum et

sion must be grounded in the chant (*"cantuque gregoriano sufficienter instructum"*) and gave many directions for singing in religious services—for example, that a sung Mass take place on feast days and that at Vespers every day members of the college were to perform the Gregorian chant "in devoutness, without cutting their words and without vain or impertinent converse."[4] Occasionally a *cantor* was enrolled in the university, as was Thomas Scrymgeuor in 1539: Thomas' name occurs again among the determinants from St. Salvator, 1540, and among the *licentiati, 1541.*[5]

Several musical monuments related to the University of St. Andrews witness the great interest in sacred music there, as well as high standards of performance in collegiate foundations. An inventory of the possessions of the College and Collegiate Church of St. Salvator made soon after its founding lists *"antiphonaris notyt,"* *"four greit gralis for the quer"* (graduulia), *"ten processionaris,"* and other musical works.[6] Especially interesting here is the item *"ane gret prykkyt sang buk and tua smallar of prekyt senggyn"*— one large and two smaller books of polyphonic music. The first of these is still in the possession of the St. Andrews Library; the two smaller volumes are in the collections of Notre Dame music now in the ducal library at Wolfenbüttel. One of these (Wolf. 677), as mentioned earlier, formerly belonged to the St. Andrews Priory, according to a note on the margin. This manuscript was

decorandum in cantu saltem gregoriano et si commode fieri possit eciam in discantu) sufficienter imbutos ad ceteras artes liberales capescendas.

[4] *Ibid.,* 146f.:

Hora nona in diebus festivis pro summa missa (quam hebdomadarius cantabit) pulsetur, et eam cantu gregoriano devote tractimque cantent: sed in diebus ferialibus quum una tantum missa habetur ex debito, summa missa hora sexta ab hebdomadario cantetur. . . . Hora tertia quolibet die pro vesperis pulsetur quas similiter cantu gregoriano devote non sincopando nec vana aut impertinentia colloquendo persolvant. Hora septima pro Salve pulsetur, quod una cum commemoratione sancti andree et beati leonardi omnes alta voce cantabunt.

[5] James Maitland Anderson, *Early Records of the University of St. Andrews* (Edinburgh, 1926), 296: *"Thomas Scrymgeuor nunc cantor Brechinensis, praestitit juramentum sub Magistro nostro Petro Capelano, Rectore."* See also 142 and 145.

[6] See "The bukis for the Quher" in Cant, *St. Salvator,* 158–59. And for information about the Wolfenbüttel manuscripts, see James H. Baxter, *An Old St. Andrews Music Book* (London and Paris, 1931), p. *v* ff.

probably written in England, whereas the second manuscript (Wolf. 1206) in all likelihood originated on the continent. Both codices form a large part of the Notre Dame music described by the English musician at Paris, Anonymus IV. During the Renaissance proper, St. Andrews continued to provide inspiration for musical composition. In 1524, for example, Patrick Hamilton composed a Mass for nine voices to be performed in St. Leonard's College; and the *St. Andrews Psalter,* compiled by Thomas Wood in 1566, is a large collection (pre-Reformation) of five-part music by several Scottish composers.[7]

As to private musical studies in the university, the remarks of James Melville are highly significant. Melville, who "cam to St. Andros . . . in the . . . yeir 1571 and enterit in the course of Philosophie," gives in his diary a year by year account of his studies. In the "thrid and fourt yeirs" of his course he says,

> Mairower in these yeirs I lerned my music, wherin I tuk graitter delyt, of an Alexander Smithe, servant to the Primarius of our collage, who haid bein treanned vpe amangs the mounks in the Abbay. I lerned of him the Gam, Plean song, and monie of the treables of the Psalmes, whereof sum I could weill sing in the kirk; bot my naturalitie and easie lerning by the ear maid me the mair unsolide and vnreadie to vse the forme of the art. I louit singing and playing on instruments passing weill, and wald gladlie spend tyme whar the exerceise whereof was within the collage, for twa or thrie of our condisciples played fellon weill on the Virginals, and another on the Lut and Githorn. Our Regent haid also the Pinalds in this chalmer, and lernit some thing and I efter him.[8]

[7] *Ibid.,* p. *vi,* and H. G. Farmer, "Music in Medieval Scotland," *Proceedings of the Musical Association,* Vol. LVI (1930), 82–83.

[8] *The Diary of Mr. James Melvill, 1556–1601* (Edinburgh, 1829), 23. *Pinalds* here means *spinet.* The diary continues with typical Calvinist emphasis:

> bot perceiving me ower mikle caried efter that, he dishairted and left of. It was the grait mercie of my God that keipit me from anie grait progress in singing and playing on instruments, for giff I haid atteined to anie reasonable missure therin I haid never don guid vtherwayes, in respect of my amorus disposition, wherby Sathan sought even then to deboiche me, bot my God gaiff me a piece

Thus, private instruction in practical music—in singing and instrumental performance—was certainly available to St. Andrews students, if we may judge by Melville's experience, even though music, except for psalm singing, was generally frowned upon by the Calvinists. The allusions to music in the works of Gavin Douglas (1475–1522), who graduated bachelor and master from St. Andrews[9] and who became Bishop of Dunkeld, probably reflect musical activities in his student days. In his allegorical poem, *The Palice of Honour* (1501), Gavin mentions various types of polyphonic music which he "hard" along with many musical instruments:

> *In modulatioun hard I play and sing*
> *Fabourdoun, pricksang, discant, countering,*
> *Cant organe, figuratioun, and gemmell,*
> *On croud, lute, harp, with mony gudlie spring,*
> *Schalmes, clariounis, portatiues, hard I ring,*
> *Monycord, organe, tympane, and cymbell.*
> *Sytholl, psalttrie, and voices sweit as bell,*
> *Soft releschingis in dulce deliuering,*
> *Fractionis diuide, at rest, or clois compell.*

In another stanza of the poem, Gavin shows his knowledge of *musica speculativa*—proportions and ideas of celestial harmony:

> *Fresche ladyis sang in voice virgineall*
> *Concordis sweit, diuers entoned reportis,*
> *Proportionis fine with sound celestiall,*
> *Duplat, triplat, diatesseriall,*
> *Sesqui altera, and decupla resortis,*
> *Diapason of mony sundrie sortis,*
> *War soung and playit be seir cunning menstrall*
> *On lufe ballatis with mony fair disportis.*

Douglas includes, too, several references to *musica mundana*, as,

of his fear, and grait naturall shamfastnes, quhilk by his grace war my preseruatiues.

[9] John Small (ed.), *The Poetical Works of Gavin Douglas* (Edinburgh, 1874), I, iv–v. Passages quoted from *The Palice of Honour* appear on pages 20–21.

How that thair musick tones war mair cleir,
And dulcer than the mouing of the spheir.

The one extant Scottish treatise on music from the sixteenth century is a compilation by an anonymous writer: *The Art of Mvsic collecit ovt of all Ancient Doctovris of Mvsic* (after 1517).[10] Dealing with problems of mensural music, this work is organized like many contemporary treatises related to university studies, and it draws upon the theorists whose doctrine generally formed the basis for university treatises on *musica practica*—Jean de Muris, Tinctoris, and the then living Gafori and Ornithoparchus. Among the many examples of counterpoint, there is a four-part motet by Robert Fairfax. In the light of its content, this treatise probably sprang from musical studies at St. Andrews or at one of the other Scottish universities.

Glasgow

The University of Glasgow, the second of the three Catholic universities in Scotland, was organized at the request of William Turnbull, Bishop of Glasgow; a bull from Nicolas V (1451) provided that a *studium generale* be erected at Glasgow for studies *"tam in theologia ac jure canonico et ciuile quam in artibus et quauis alia licita facultate."*[11] The first statutes for the arts faculty (1482) included several references to customs at Bologna, Paris, and Cologne.[12] Although music is not mentioned specifically in these statutes, one may reasonably infer that it had a place in the early curriculum as in that of these archetypal universities.

In Glasgow a grammar school was conducted with the permission and under the supervision of the chancellor of the university.[13] The cathedral school, too, was apparently under the juris-

---

10 Augustus Hughes-Hughes, *Catalogue of Manuscript Music in the British Museum* (London, 1909), III, 314.

11 *Munimenta Alme Universitatis Glasguensis* (Glasgow, 1854), I, 4.

12 For example, *ibid.*, II, 25, 36: *"Item quod forma docendi et audiendi ad instar studii Bononiensis aut Parisiensis non omittatur,"* and *"Item quod in omnibus actibus scole conforment se magistri ad antiquam consuetudinem studii Parisiensis aut Coloniensis."*

diction of the university, and rents from university property were used for its upkeep.[14] In 1476, *Hugo Broun magister scole cantorum* was incorporated in the university.[15]

Many documents testify to the use of music in ecclesiastical services in the university, especially Masses to be sung for founders of chantries and for people who left gifts to the institution. The word *cantare* is generally used in these notices, if sung Masses are specified; but *decantare,* signifying more elaborate polyphonic music, occurs occasionally.[16] Vicars of the choir are mentioned in several records of rents from land, and many *vicarii chori* are found among members of the university.[17] Foundations in the university evidently owned many musical service books, too. In the "inventar of the evidents lettres gudis and geir perteining to the college of Glasgow the VIII. day of November anno 1582," for instance, we find, "Item all the commoun buikis abuve writtin with xvj buikis or thareby of musik of sangis and messis."[18]

In several instances men trained in music held high office in the university. The first rector of the university had been *precentor* of the cathedral before his election to the rectorship.[19] Two quitclaims tell us that a former *cantor* of Aberdeen became rector of Glasgow: one (1556) in which the queen "dischargeis exoneris and quietclamis Maister Archibald Betone chantoure of Aberdene rectour for the time of the said Vniuersite," along with several others "for thare part" of a certain tax; the other a year later in which the queen again exonerates "Master Archibald Betoune chantoure

---

[13] A record of 1494 tells how a priest who decided to teach grammar without the chancellor's permission encountered serious difficulties with the university officials: see *ibid.,* I, 37–39. Until the Reformation, the Bishop of Glasgow was also chancellor of the university (*ibid.,* III, *xxiii–xxiv*).

[14] In an account of "The Rentale of the College Leving yeirlie" is an item, "Payit out of the samin tenement for the sangsters of the Queir x s"; and of three rentals listed "In Trongait," one is "The Song Scole, iiij s": *ibid.,* I, 174, 182.

[15] *Ibid.,* II, 86.

[16] For instance, in an article adopted by the arts faculty in 1481: *"Super decantacione huius antiphone beate Virginis Ave Gloriosa omni sabbato pro anima Jacobi Domini Hammyltone fundatoris dicti collegii arcium."* See *ibid.,* II, 235.

[17] *Ibid.,* I, 21, 28ff., 139–41; II, 81–86, 109, 137, 176.

[18] *Ibid.,* III, 518.

[19] *Ibid.,* I, 20: *"venerabilis et egregius vir Magister Dauid Cadyow quondam precentor ecclesie Glasguensis ac primus Rector Vniuersitatis eiusdem."*

of Aberdeine instant Rector of the said Vniuersite" from taxes.[20] The name *D. Archibaldus Dunbar Precentor* occurs in Bishop Gavin Dunbar's foundation of a college in Glasgow in 1537.[21]

More informative than these documents is a unique notice in the list of masters (1464) that one of these men, Dominus Johannes Hugonis, was excused from this regency because he had gone to Edinburgh for further musical studies.[22] Johannes' name occurs frequently in subsequent annals. In 1494 he was elected dean of the arts faculty, and in this office he apparently performed his duties well, for the next year he was unanimously elected to continue as dean *"propter eius ingentia merita circa edificacionem et reparacionem collegii facultatis arcium."*[23]

When Johannes Hugonis went to Edinburgh in 1464 to study music, however, he obviously did not proceed to the University of Edinburgh, for this was not organized until more than a century later (1583). Johannes probably became associated with the Royal Court at Stirling, a center of musical activities, for Scotland, like England during the Renaissance, was blessed with rulers who were both amateurs and performers of music. Music, vocal and instrumental, was cultivated at Stirling, and the names of many foreign as well as native musicians appear on the royal payrolls.[24] Among those whom James III (1460–88) brought to his court was the English doctor of music William Rogers (possibly a graduate of Cambridge), who opened a *schola* for the teaching of music at Stirling.[25] This must have been a genuine inspiration for musical studies in Scotland and a great attraction to students interested in music.

[20] *Ibid.*, I, 60–61.

[21] *Ibid.*, I, 494.

[22] *Ibid.*, II, 202: *"cum eo dispensandum est de lectura ad biennium pro eo quod accessit ad Eddinburgum pro musicalibus addiscendis statim post magisterium."*

[23] *Ibid.*, II, 264, 266.

[24] For the cultivation of music at the Scottish court, see Charles Rogers, *History of the Chapel Royal of Scotland* (Edinburgh, 1882), *i–xxx*.

[25] Farmer, "Music in Medieval Scotland," *Proceedings of the Musical Association*, Vol. LVI, 80–81. Under Roger's direction, James III planned to establish a college of music in connection with the Chapel Royal. Roger's assassination precluded the fulfillment of this plan, but James IV established a collegiate church at Stirling, with prebendaries and choirboys, for the teaching and cultivation of sacred music. See Rogers, *History of the Chapel Royal, xxx–xxxiii.*

Aberdeen

Several decades after the establishment of the University of Glasgow a university was established at Aberdeen in imitation of certain typical medieval *studia,* especially Paris, Bologna, and Orléans. The leading spirit in this enterprise was William Elphinstone—bachelor and master of the University of Paris, lecturer at Orléans, rector of Glasgow in 1474, and Bishop of Aberdeen in 1483—who wished to provide a center of learning for the people in the north of Scotland, separated by natural barriers from seats of culture; and the bull of 1494 from Alexander VI, granting the petition of James IV for a university in the northern part of his kingdom, established a *studium generale* with the usual faculties, including the liberal arts, as at Paris and Bologna.[26]

Nothing more definite than this is known of the early curriculum at Aberdeen. Nor was a definite course of studies outlined in the charter for Elphinstone's foundation in 1505 of King's College (probably not considered necessary, in view of the models upon which this new university was patterned), or in a later one given by Elphinstone's successor, Gavin Dunbar, confirming a new foundation in 1531.[27] The first mention of music, indeed, along with other mathematical sciences, occurs in the *"Leges veteres, de novo promulgatae,"* of 1641. Here the usual works in natural philosophy are required of fourth-year students, and to these are added a number of other subjects, of which music is one.[28] How long these *leges*

[26] Robert Sangster Rait, *The Universities of Aberdeen* (Aberdeen, 1895), 14–21, and Cosmo Innes, *Sketches of Early Scotch History* (Edinburgh, 1861), 254. See the bull in *Fasti Aberdonenses* (Aberdeen, 1854), 4: *"Studium generale et Universitas existat studii generalis tam in Theologia ac iure Canonico et Civili necnon Medicina et Artibus liberalibus quam quavis alia licita facultate . . . sicut in Parisiensi et Bononiensi."*

[27] *Ibid.,* 80–108. A *Nova fundatio* for Aberdeen (instituted at St. Andrews and Glasgow soon after the Reformation) was not sanctioned by the Scots Parliament until 1597 (see Rait, *Universities of Aberdeen,* 105ff.). One significant change which came from this reorganization was that each regent was to instruct in only one department instead of guiding the same students through the whole quadrennium, as in the medieval system.

[28] *Fasti,* 231: *"Quibus addentur vel opportune inserantur Elementa Astronomiae Sphericae et Theoricae, Geographiae, Opticae, et Musicae, ex Alstedii admirandis Mathematicis, necnon Metaphysicae ex Kerkermanno, etc."*

veteres had been in effect is not known; but *musica speculativa* was undoubtedly taught at Aberdeen in its early days, just as at Paris or Cologne.

Bishop Elphinstone, moreover, was famous for his musical interests. According to his biographer, Hector Boece (first principal of the bishop's own foundation, King's College), Elphinstone was responsible for the reform of the chant in Aberdeen, having appointed a skilled musician, John Malison, for this purpose; and whatever of good music and musicians there are in the north, Boece states, is owing to Elphinstone's teaching.[29] This interest in music is everywhere reflected in Elphinstone's charter for King's College (1505), with allusions too numerous to cite in full. Eight prebendaries skilled in the chant and, if possible, *in rebus factis* (polyphonic music) were to be on the staff, as well as four choirboys instructed in the chant, to carry out religious exercises in the college: of the eight prebendaries, one was to be *cantor,* supervising the singing in the church and the musical education of the choristers and of *alii bursarii;* and another of the prebendaries was to be organist and was to teach the playing of the "organs."[30]

[29] *Hectoris Boetii Murthlacensium et Aberdonensium Episcoporum Vitae* (ed. and tr. by James Moir) (Aberdeen, 1894), 79:

> Prisco atque patrum more cantu[m] ubilibet celebrare jubet. Ad sacra rite exequenda in basilica Aberdonensi, creat designatorum Joannem Malisonum, musica disciplina eruditum, moribus probatum, penes quem (quos scribi et concinnari fecerat) libri forent rituales. Huic vero debent Aberdonenses, musicam praesertim edocti, quam parenti filii caritatem: quicquid illic musices, quicquid exactae in Dei ecclesia boreali jubilationis, hujus viro justissimi debetur operae; raris enim conspicitur Aberdoniae cantandi artem excellenter doctus, qui eo non fuerit usus praeceptore.

[30] *Fasti,* 60–62:

> Insuper . . volumus et ordinamus quod sint in dicto collegio octo prebendarii in sacerdotio constituti in cantu Gregoriano rebus factis videlicet priksingin figuratione faburdon cum mensuris et discantu periti et instructi si commode haberi possunt alioquin in cantu Gregoriano rebus factis faburdon et figuratione ad minus bene instructi qui similiter etiam in aliqua predictarum facultatum studere debeant In quo etiam erunt quatuor juvenes seu pueri pauperes abiles tantum in cantu Gregoriano ad minus instructi Quorum omnium octo prebendariorum et quatuor juvenum officium erit dominicis et aliis festivis diebus . . . matutinis vesperis et ceteris horis canonicis . . . atque missis in cantu celebrandis . . . interesse volumus. . . .
>
> Inter quos octo prebendarios primus erit cantor cujus officium erit in elevatione

Throughout the charter the bishop's instructions for the performance of religious ceremonies are very detailed, specifying clothes
to be worn, hymns to be sung, occasions to be celebrated, and
the like.[31]

Dunbar's charter, executing Elphinstone's reorganization of
the college in 1531, was even more explicit in its musical directions.
The number of choristers was here increased to six. Again, if possible, the eight prebendaries were to be skilled *"in cantu Gregoriano
rebus factis viz. priksinging figuratione faburdon et aliis generibus
discantus."*[32] In addition to the duties of the *cantor* set forth in the
earlier document, this officer had also to note absences from divine
service and had charge of the songbooks; again, one of the prebendaries was to be organist, elected by the other officers, and he
was to receive *ultra suum salarium,* two marks for regularly playing upon and for looking after the organs.[33] As in Elphinstone's
earlier charter, specific instructions were here given for the celebration of Masses and other ceremonies.

The university library was coeval with the university, and among
its incunabula were several books containing information about
music—Bartholomaeus' *De proprietatibus rerum,* Martianus' *De
nuptiis,* Quintilian's *Institutiones oratoriae;* Elphinstone presented
a 1483 edition of Bartholomaeus' work to his college, and Boece
left the library a copy of Aristotle's *Politica,* among other works.[34]
In a *registrum* of the belongings of King's College (1542) appear

et depressione circa cantum cantores regere et chorum gubernare ac ministros
altaris in tabula ordinare scolas per se tenere et in eisdem hujusmodi quatuor
pueros et alios bursarios in cantu instruere et docere ac singulos in choro et scolis
transgressores et errores circa cantum et ceremonias punire corrigere et re-
formare. . . .

Quorum octo prebendariorum . . . volumus qui unum de predictis in ludo
organorum peritum instituere teneatur.

[31] The opening of the college, for example, was to be celebrated *"cum duodecim
magne campane per intervalla pulsibus . . . solempniter cum organis et cantu" (ibid.,* 63).

[32] *Ibid.,* 84.

[33] *Ibid.,* 90, 95.

[34] See *A List of Fifteenth Century Books in the University Library of Aberdeen*
(Aberdeen, 1925), 5–53; and W. Douglas Simpson, "Hector Boece," *University of Aberdeen Quatercentenary of the Death of Hector Boece* (Aberdeen, 1937), 22, 24.

many *libri chori et templi collegii (antiphonalia, psalteria,* and *gradalia,* including a *Liber ad organiste usum accommodatus)* as well as *organa ipsa.*[35]

The name of the first university *cantor* is not known. *"David Dischinton cantor de Abdn."* is one of the signatories to Bishop Dunbar's charter, and *"David Dischinton, precentor ecclesiae cathedralis"* was rector of the university in 1535.[36] The name Jacobus Awell (Awill or Abell) *cantor* occurs in many documents published in the *Fasti,* the first being a grant (1548) made to the prebendaries and chaplains of the choir by Alexander Kyd, described as *"succentor ecclesie cathedralis Aberdonensis"* in this and other records.[37] John Hay was also a *cantor* in the sixteenth century and a member of the visitation committee in 1549—a *visitatio* which left detailed instructions for religious observances with singing, with special instructions to the *cantor* for conducting sung services each day; and in 1593 William Meldrum, *"prefectus cantus ecclesiastice cathedralis Aberdonensis,"* gave a scholarship to educate four students in the university.[38] It is significant for the position of music in the university that it was the duty of the chief musician at King's College to instruct not only choristers but also other boarding students (*bursarii*) in the elements of music, plain song and polyphony. With the Reformation statutes, *Nova fundatio,* the office of *cantor* seems to have disappeared, although the Aberdeen Song School was apparently flourishing at the end of the century,[39] and music, as we have seen, continued to be taught along with other mathematical disciplines well into the seventeenth century.

[35] *Fasti,* 568–70.

[36] *Ibid., lxxvi,* 107.

[37] *Ibid.,* 114.

[38] *Ibid.,* 134, 137, 259–62.

[39] A record of 1597 states that the "sang School" is not "subalterne to the maister of the grammer school," and a document of 1605 provides a house for the "Sang School." See H. F. Morland Simpson (ed.), *Record and Reminiscences of Aberdeen Grammar School* (Edinburgh, 1906), 26, 39.

ix. THE NETHERLANDS: LOUVAIN

In 1425 a *studium generale* was erected by papal bull in Louvain, chief city of the Duchy of Brabant; its formal opening took place the next year. A response to intellectual and religious needs for a university in the Flemish countries like those in surrounding countries, Louvain was a flourishing humanistic center in the first half of the sixteenth century; but in the latter part of the century it underwent a period of decadence, owing to great religious and political struggles, to be revived only after the rigorous *visite* and reorganization by the Archdukes Albert and Isabelle early in the seventeenth century.[1]

Music evidently had a place in the earliest curriculum, for the antiquary Molanus (d. 1585) states in his *Historia Lovaniensium* that the *Musica* of Jean de Muris was required with other mathematical disciplines to be heard before determination, according to the *Statuta prima*.[2] Information about the place of music in the *Collegium Trilingue* established by Erasmus with funds supplied by Jérôme Busleiden (*ca.* 1517) is not available,[3] but we have seen its high position in the Collège de France at Paris modeled upon Erasmus' foundation. Molanus refers again to the teaching of music in the university in the sixteenth century. Rudolf Agricola, who contributed strongly to the spread of humanism in Germany, studied and taught at Louvain before going to Italy for further study and to Heidelberg as professor of philosophy in 1482. Agricola was a painter, poet, and musician as well as philosopher, a composer of polyphonic music and a lutenist; and among his writings are some notes on the *Musica* of Boethius.[4] According to Mo-

---

[1] L. C. Casartelli, "Oxford and Louvain," *Dublin Review*, Vol. XLVI (1903), 289, and Leon van der Essen (ed.), *L'Université de Louvain à travers cinq siècles* (Bruxelles, 1927), 12–13.

[2] *Joannis Molani . . . Historiae Lovaniensium Libri XIV* (ed. by P. F. X. de Ram) (Bruxelles, 1841), I, 588: "*In mathematicalibus [legentur] tractatus de sphaera, primus liber Euclidis, tractatus de arithmetica et Joannis Muris musica.*"

[3] See Félix Nève's account, *Le Collège des Trois-Langues à l'Université de Louvain* (Bruxelles, 1856).

[4] Fétis, *Biographie universelle*, I, 30.

lanus, Agricola taught the French language and literature as well as the elements of music in one of Louvain's colleges; and he was skilled in singing, playing the organ, and string playing.[5] Several called *cantor* were teachers in the arts faculty: a Gualterus Waterlet, singer and chaplain to the Duke of Burgundy (d. 1494), taught in the Pædagogium Falconis, and Franciscus de Thevis, *cantor* of the cathedral, was a teacher in the Pædagogium Porci; Christianus de Beka, in the emperor's choir, was a member of the theological college in the university.[6]

In Louvain, connections between the university and the Collegiate Church of St. Peter were very close. As was customary in university centers, the provost of the church was also chancellor of the university in its early days, and some of the canons were professors in the university.[7] Many university services were held in the church. From 1451 there is a record of payment to singers for a Mass sung as part of an academic celebration at St. Peter's.[8] Molanus describes the academic procession, ending with a sung Mass, held when Francis I was captured in 1525.[9] At *"le jubilé de 1526"* (centennial of the university's founding) a *messe jubilaire* took place, with prayers sung at St. Peter's.[10]

[5] Molanus, *Historia,* I, 599:

> Rodolphus Agricola primas magisterii artium obtinuit inter multos competitores in paedagogio Cacabi, qui nunc Falconis vocatur.
>
> In ipso paedagogio gallicam linguam ita didicit, ut Hannoniorum simplicem rusticitatem devitaret, aulicamque ejus, linguae elegantiam feliciter imitaretur. . . .

Musices fundamenta iisdem annis jecit. Canebat enim voce, flatu, pulsu. (The arts faculty comprised four *pædagogia: Lilium, Falco, Castrium,* and *Porcus.*

[6] *Fasti academici stvdii generalis lovaniensis* (ed. by Valerio Andrea) (Lovanii, 1635), 153, 157, 173, 178.

[7] Molanus, *Historia,* I, 109.

[8] E. Reusens and A. van Hove (eds.), *Actes ou proces-verbaux des séances tenues par le conseil de l'Université de Louvain* (Bruxelles, 1903–1917), II, 220: *"Item proposuit rector an placeret Universitati dare x stuferos cantoribus ecclesiae Sancti Petri de missa Universitatis ipso die Remigii per ipsos solempniter cantata. Commissa fuit deputatis."*

[9] Molanus, *Historia,* II, 872:

> Anno 1525, capto rege Franciae, per octo dies pulsatae sunt campanae, et dominica secunda quadragesimae fuit solemnis processio, cui intererant episcopus Cameracensis et abbates quinque; canonici et capellani ferebant candelas, nobiles et magistratus taedas. Et canonici matutinum inchoarunt hora quarta, ut primam missam cantarent de dominica, secundam de Spiritu Sancto.

Like the English universities, Louvain early inaugurated the college system, and several of its foundations were established specifically for boys who were or hàd been choristers—for example, Henry Houterle's foundation for boys of St. Peter's in 1469.[11] Nicolas Ruitere of Luxemburg, bishop of Arras, and provost and chancellor of Louvain, left in his will (1509) funds to establish a college for art students, among them choirboys from Cambrai, Arras, and other nearby towns.[12] From the *Liber actorum facultatis artium,* a contract (1446) between Adam van Helen and certain members of the university—among them Pieter Ysebeele, organist at St. Peter's—provides for a new organ *"in die sacristie der Clercken capellen"* (chapel of the theology students).[13]

Musical instruction was given the choristers in these foundations, many of them students in the university at the same time or later. Some students are described as *cantores*—singers or choirmasters—in early academic records, either before or after enrolling in the university. Most frequently is the *cantor* of St. Peter's mentioned, although sometimes the names of singers from other places occur.[14] Several times *"Dominus Johannes de Beka, canonicus et cantor Sancti Petri Lovaniensis"* (matriculated in 1437) had occasion to petition the academic council.[15] The organist of St. Peter's, too, appears in these records—Petrus de Vileer (alias Ysabelle), who matriculated in 1430.[16] In records of 1441 the name Antonius

[10] Henri de Vocht, *"Les Jubilés de l'université sous l'ancien régime," Louvain à travers cinq siècles,* 19.

[11] Molanus, *Historia,* I, 621: *"Henricus Houterle, scholasticus Lovaniensis et dominici Sepulcri peregrinus, anno 1469 instituit confraternitatem septem Innocentium puerorum S. Petri."*

[12] *Ibid.,* I, 641, and see the *Fasti,* 179–80.

[13] Floris van der Mueren, *Het Orgel in de Nederlanden* (Leuven, 1931), Bijlage, I, 247–48.

[14] For example, in 1434 (see Reusens, *Actes,* I, 183):

Supplicavit dominus *Ludovicus de Steyvoerden,* cantor ecclesie sancti Petri Lovaniensis, pro protectione cum inhibitione ac monitionibus cum citatione contra debitores suos, tam ratione beneficii sui predicti quam ex mutuo. Universitas annuit.

[15] *Ibid.,* I, 369, 433.

[16] *Ibid.,* I, 141, and Van Hove, *Actes,* II, 204, 233–34, 266, 315, 349.

de Phalisia occurs; matriculating in 1432, Antonius became organist at St. Peter's after Pierre de Vileer.[17]

On May 15, 1470, a certain *"Mag. Johannes Tinctoris Morinensis dyocesis"* matriculated at the University of Louvain,[18] generally thought to be the distinguished musical theorist Johannes Tinctoris. From his published treatises, we know that Tinctoris *(ca.* 1435–1511) studied music early in life and that at one time he was master of the choirboys at the cathedral of Chartres.[19] Several times in his writings he speaks of himself as *in legibus licentiatum;* one treatise bears the caption, *"a magistro Tinctoris legum artiumque professore";* and in another the author modestly refers to himself as *"inter legum ac artium mathematicarum studiosos minimus.*[20] Undoubtedly, then, Tinctoris was graduated in arts and law at some university. If he was born around 1435 as Trithemius states, he may have been a student in arts at Louvain or elsewhere before returning later (1471) for his legal studies. Some years afterwards (possibly *ca.* 1476, for he completed his work *De natura et proprietate tonorum* that year in Naples, as the explicit states), he went to Naples to serve in the royal chapel, probably as a singer rather than as *maestro di capella,* as has sometimes been said. Tinctoris' further interest in musical artistry is seen in his own excellent compositions, some of which have been published.[21]

The twelve treatises of Tinctoris cover many phases of musical

---

[17] Reusens, *Actes*, I, 408.

[18] *Matricule de l'Université de Louvain*, II (ed. by Joc. Wils) (Bruxelles, 1946), 234.

[19] CS, IV, 1–200, comprises ten treatises. E. de Coussemaker, *Joannis Tinctoris Tractatus de Musica* (Insulis, 1875), is a new edition of these ten with one additional work. Karl Weinman, *Johannes Tinctoris (1445–1511) und sein unbekannter Traktat "De inventione et usu musicae"* (Regensburg und Rom, 1917), adds a twelfth treatise. For Tinctoris' dictionary, see *Johannis Tinctoris Terminorum Musicae Diffinitorium* (c. 1475), ed. and tr. into French by Armand Machabey (Paris, 1951).

For Tinctoris' own statements, see Coussemaker, *Tinctoris Tractatus*, p. 504, and Weinmann, *Tinctoris*, p. 34: ". . . musicen cui me ab ineunte aetate dedidi studio" and ". . . insignis ecclesiae Carnotensis: cujus pueros musicam tunc docebam."

Details of Tinctoris' life have never been settled, owing to conflicting reports, all of which are summarized in the excellent article by Charles van den Borren in the Belgian *Biographie nationale* (Bruxelles, 1866–1944), XXV.

[20] Coussemaker, *Tinctoris Tractatus*, pp. 1, 39, 172.

[21] For a description of Tinctoris' composition with sources, see Van den Borren, *loc. cit.*

learning. Of these, the only one published in his lifetime was the *Diffinitorium musices* (*ca.* 1474), the first real music lexicon, foreshadowed only by the eleventh-century *Vocabularium* of Johannes Presbyter. The *Expositio manus* is an explanation of Guido's system of solmization; and the *Liber de natura et proprietate tonorum* (dedicated to Okeghem and Busnois) treats of plain song, preceded by an *apologia* for music with various classical allusions. There is also a group of treatises dealing with specific aspects of *musica practica* similar to medieval treatises springing from the *ars musica* and designed for the professional musician.[22] Models of clarity and precision in explaining the complexities of fifteenth-century mensural rhythm, notation, and composition, these treatises were constantly cited, along with the works of Gafori, by the great majority of theorists in Germany and other countries in the sixteenth century. The *Proportionale musices* is a mathematical work on proportions in mensural notation (treated earlier, we recall, by Jean de Muris and Prosdocimus de Beldemandis). The preface to this work is especially interesting, for in it Tinctoris mentions the most distinguished men who have written about music or practiced that art (*"summus ille musicus Jhesus Christus"* being the first of those who have contributed to a flourishing of music in the Church). It is here that Tinctoris ascribes the invention of "new music" to the English Dunstable, *novae artis fons et origo,* and speaks of his French contemporaries Dufay and Binchois, succeeded in turn by such "moderns" as Okeghem, Busnois, Regis, and Caron.

The *Complexus effectuum musices* is a systematic presentation of the effects of music upon man, supporting each of twenty statements with quotations from the Bible, the patrician writers, and classical Greek and Latin authors. What is possibly Tinctoris' last work is a treatise *De inventione et usus musice.* Unlike most of Tinctoris' short treatises clarifying points of rhythm and notation, this work is a historical discussion of certain aspects of music, chiefly instrumental—discussions of song and singers, of the flute,

---

[22] *A Tractatus de notis et pausis, Tractatus de regulari valore notarum, Liber imperfectionum notarum musicalium, Tractatus alterationum, Scriptum super punctis musicalibus,* and *Liber de arte contrapuncti.*

the lute, and other instruments. In no other work is Tinctoris' rich humanistic and theological background so heavily drawn upon as in this treatise—which opens with the well-known line from Horace, *"Cujus quidem tractatus quinque libros continentis: in quibus nimirum (quoad mei fieri potuit) dulci utile miscui";* and especially interesting here is a statement related to Tinctoris' idea of *Christus summus musicus: "Christum lyra personat: et in decacordo psalterio ab inferis excitat resurgentem."*[23] This treatise, like the one on musical effects, is actually an elaboration of one of the inevitable section headings in the medieval treatise—the invention of music and its uses.

x. Switzerland: Basel

The initial impulse for the founding of a university in the city of Basel probably came from intellectual currents fostered by the Council of Basel, 1431–48. At the petition of the Town Council to Pius II (Aeneas Silvius Piccolomini, who had lived in Basel during the Council), a foundation bull was granted, in 1459, with privileges similar to those of the University of Bologna; and the new university was officially opened the following year.[1] The first set of statutes, drawn up in 1465 and based largely upon those of the University of Erfurt, established a curriculum usual in *studia* at this time, chiefly the reading and explication of Aristotle. Among the *lectiones pro gradu magisterii* was mathematics and the possibility (*si legantur*) of music: *"Item musica si legantur."*[2] In new statutes promulgated in 1492, *"Musica ... I Solid."* is found among the required *lectiones pro magisterio.*[3]

With the reorganization of the university at the time of the Reformation, music continued to hold a regular place in the arts faculty. The *Iudicium de schola,* around 1529, of the great Basel

---

[23] Weinmann, *Tinctoris' Traktat,* pp. 27 and 43.

[1] Wilhelm Vischer, *Geschichte der Universität Basel von der Grundung 1460 bis zur Reformation 1529* (Basel, 1860), 28–32.

[2] *Ibid.,* 154.

[3] *Ibid.,* 179.

reformer Oekolampadius, specified three professors, one to teach dialectic and rhetoric, one natural history and physics, and one mathematics, including music.[4] New statutes of 1540 required mathematics for both the bachelor's and master's degree, and music may well have been included as a part of mathematics here.[5] Virtually these same requirements are found in statutes of 1544, when the arts faculty was divided into three sections, the lowest of which was the Pedagogium, and in statutes of 1551.[6] And when fixed salaries were established in 1544 for various professors, *"damit sie bleiben täten,"* in the arts faculty, *"für den Lehrer . . . der Musik 16 fl., des Gesanges 6 fl."* were among the stipends,[7] indicating that two teachers of music were supported by the university. Evidence for a public professor of music in the university also exists from 1577, a year of great need and distress, when the university senate added a certain amount of wheat and wine (*"8 Viertel Dinkel und 8 Saum Wein"*) to the music teacher's salary.[8] And in 1589 teachers of Hebrew and music were exempt from a decision on the part of the university to increase the stipends of "ordinary" professors by an additional allowance on four feastdays during the year.[9] We know, too, that early in the seventeenth century the university notary was also the teacher of music.[10]

Music, then, seems to have been consistently offered at Basel during the Renaissance. We know that an early teacher of music was a certain Andrechin, for Adam von Fulda, in his *Musica* (1490), mentions *Andrechinum quemdam Baseleensem* who

---

[4] Rudolf Thommen, *Geschichte der Universität Basel 1532–1632* (Basel, 1889), 307, Beilage I:

> Unus dialecti et rhetoricis precepta ac artem cum elegantiis Valle prelegat. Alter historias naturasque rerum ex Aristotele et ex physica doceat. Tertius mathematica, ut cosmographicam, arithmetica et geometrica, ac musice principia tradat.

[5] *Ibid.,* 339, Beilage VIII: *"Audient autem Dialecticam Rhetoricam Physicam Mathemata exastissime et si tempore angustia admittat aliquid in Ethicis."*

[6] *Ibid.,* 340–44.

[7] *Ibid.,* 49. These salaries are much lower than those of other professors.

[8] *Ibid.,* 51n.

[9] *Ibid.,* 56.

[10] *Ibid.,* 69.

taught music in the philosophical faculty.[11] After the Reformation and with the restoration of liturgical music in the service at Basel (music had been prohibited in the Church by Zwingli), the emphasis appears to have been upon practical music, in the Pedagogium, the Gymnasium (erected in 1589 and supplanting the old Pedagogium), and the university proper; and a public professor of music was maintained to give such instruction. When Felix Platter, great lover and performer of music, became rector in 1576, one of his first official acts involved music: the calling of Samuel Mareschall from Tournai in Flanders to be cathedral organist and *musicus ordinarius* in the university—with a salary of eighty-four pounds and chief duty (aside from acting as organist) of instructing students in the lower school in music.[12] It was Mareschall who, late in life, was also *notarius publicus* for the university.[13] Both Platter and Mareschall were members of a commission appointed in 1600 to investigate the state of music in the university and to see how this discipline could be taught and practiced with more success; the result of this investigation was a decision on the part of the administration that all university students—in the Gymnasium and in the colleges—be required to take part in weekly musical exercises under the tutelage of Mareschall.[14]

As might be expected from this strong emphasis upon choral music, such music formed a part of academic activities from the early days of the university. On the day of consecration of the new *studium* in 1461 a Mass was sung in the cathedral; and after the reading of the bulls of foundation, an antiphon was sung, later in the service, the *Te deum*.[15] According to statutes of 1477, all members of the university were to celebrate the election of each new rector with the singing of a *Te deum* at the cathedral.[16]

[11] GS, III, 347.

[12] Karl Nef, *"Die Musik an der Universität Basel,"* Festschrift zur Feier des 450 jährigen Bestehens der Universität Basel (Basel, 1910), 305.

[13] Karl Nef, *"Die Musik in Basel,"* SIMG, Vol. X (1908), 549.

[14] Nef, *Basel-Festschrift,* 306.

[15] Vischer, *Universität Basel,* 284–85, 287: *"in dicta Ecclesia Basiliensi et Choro eiusdem, Chorus cleri, videlicet tam Canonici quam Cappellani Missam de spiritu sancto Nota solempni decantavit. . . . Chorus dicte Ecclesie nota etiam sollempni canticum laudis Te deum laudamus decantavit."*

Basel, moreover, led all Switzerland in the printing of music, with a *Missale Basiliense* in 1480, another *missale* in 1481, a *Graduale Romanum* in 1488, and an *Antiphonarium Basiliense* about the same time;[17] and during the last years of the fifteenth century several treatises published at Basel witness the teaching of choral music in the university. The oldest of these is the *Lilium Musice plane* (1496) by Michael Keinspeck, a work on plain song with introductory material on the scales, modes, and intervals.[18] Nothing is known of Keinspeck except for a few personal remarks in the treatise, the *explicit* of which tells that he taught in the university.[19] This book was important enough to merit several impressions and a second edition in Strassburg in 1506.[20] A treatise on the chant written by Balthazar Praspergius for use in the university was published in 1601: *Clarissima plane atque choralis musice interpretatio . . . in Alma Basileorum Universitate exercitata, which, like* the earlier work of Keinspeck, gives a summary of the theory of plain song, with rules, definitions, and examples.[21] The *explicit* states that it was used in the university and published at the request of the auditors. Mareschall, too, left an instruction book on music, the product of his activities in the university—his *Porta musices,* published in Basel in 1589 and dedicated to the rector of the university; and his *Melodiae suaves et concinnae Psalmorum aliquot atque Hymnorum spiritualium* (1622) is a collection of psalms and hymns in four-part arrangement, composed for students in the Gymnasium.[22]

[16] *Ibid.,* 116.

[17] See Arnold Pfister, *"Vom frühsten Musikdruck in der Schweiz,"* Festschrift Gustav Binz (Basel, 1935), 160–71.

[18] Otto Kade, *"Noch einmal die musikalischen Schätze des 15. bis 17. Jahrhunderts,"* *MfMg,* Vol. VIII (1876), 20–21.

[19] Nef, *Basel-Festschrift,* 323n.: *"Explicit Lilium Musice plane Michaelis Keinspeck de Nurnberga musici Alexandrini bñmeriti. in inclita vniversitate Basiliensi p eundem resumpta."*

[20] *Ibid.,* 301.

[21] *Ibid.,* 323n.:

Finis musices ex Orphei lyra et Saphus cythara manate atque per venerabilem dominū Balthasser Praspergiū Merspergeñ. In nobili ac preclaro Basileorū studio proceltico diligentia exactissima examinate. Rogatu tandem auditorum per providū virū Michaelem Furter Ciuem Basilieñ impresse.

The *Porta musices* contains a short introduction to playing the violin, an instrument which was beginning to overtake the lute in popularity at that time. This book, then, is evidence of an interest in instrumental music in the university, and many documents testify to the participation of members of the university in instrumental as well as choral musical activities. Some of these academic records are of a negative character—for instance, a *"Concordata primo facta per universitatem et civitatem Basiliensem"* (1460) specifying that students were not to sing and dance with the townspeople unless *"specialiter invitati."*[23] And a statute of the arts faculty in 1465 (similar to decrees we have seen in the English and German colleges), prohibited the playing of instruments by students in the *bursae.*[24]

Instrumental music, like choral music, formed an important embellishment to academic ceremonies. As in other universities, the candidate for the doctoral examination was escorted to the cathedral by trumpeters and pipers.[25] And after the Reformation, the ceremony of promotion was still heightened with music. Platter's description of his promotion to the degree of doctor of medicine in 1557 mentions several times the *bleser* who performed in the cathedral before the ceremony and in the procession after the act.[26] In 1594, when a rise in prices caused severe economic difficulties among the foundationers in the university, the administration encouraged

[22] Nef, *"Die Musik in Basel,"* SIMG, Vol. X, 549–50.

[23] Vischer, *Universität Basel*, 306–307: *"Item quod studentes per Rectores Bursarum et alias inducantur ut non chorisent in choreis civium publice nisi ad illas specialiter fuerint invitati."*

[24] *Ibid.*, 152n.: *"Prohibet facultas fistulas lutinas ceteraque instrumenta clamorosa levitatem inducencia."*

[25] Nef, *Basel-Festschrift*, 302.

[26] Heinrich Boos, *Thomas und Felix Platter* (Leipzig, 1878), 309–310: *"ich stalt mich in die undere cathedram, D. Isaac in die obere und nach dem bleser, so do waren, ufgeblasen, hült D. Isaac die oration und proponiert mir die themata."* And when the act was over,

> doruf die vier bleser anfiengen blosen und zogen in der procession also uss dem sal zu der Cronen. do dass pancquet angestelt war und gieng mit mir der rector D. Wolfgangus Wissenburger, hernoch der alt herr doctor Amerbach und andre academici in zimlicher zal, der pedel vor mir und die bleser, so durch die gassen biss zur herberg bliesin.

students to earn money by performing on musical instruments, as well as by writing, teaching children, and working as field laborers.[27]

University students also participated in the many plays presented in Basel during the sixteenth century, plays not only involving a great deal of instrumental and choral music, but sometimes even presenting discourses on music.[28] The musical notebook of an alumnus, Christophorus Alutarius, contains choruses from the play *Daniel* by Sixt Dietrich (Birk), presented in Basel in 1535.[29]

The publication in Basel in 1511 of the *Musica getutscht* by the Heidelberg musician Sebastian Virdung, filling a need for instruction in instrumental music, is further evidence of the growing interest in this art. The university possesses a well-worn copy of the original, with only a few of its pages remaining.[30] Bonifacius Amerbach, a professor in the university, made a great collection of keyboard as well as choral music. The organists Kotter and Hans von Constanz wrote little tracts on organ-playing for Amerbach, who at his death possessed no less than ten musical instruments, woodwinds and strings.[31] Felix Platter's love of music is shown throughout his famous *Tagebuch*. He himself played the lute, harp, and spinet, and he mentions other students and teachers in the university who were enthusiastic lutenists; at his death in 1614 he left behind a huge collection of instruments of all kinds, including four spinets and four clavichords.[32] Still extant are two lutebooks copied in 1575 by a Basel student, Ludwig Iselin, grandson of Amerbach and later professor of law in the university. Five of the

---

[27] Thommen, *Universität Basel*, 78: "*die jungen Leuten zwang, sich mit Schreiben, Kindererziehen, Saitenspiel und selbst Feldarbeit den nötigen Lebensunterhalt zu beschaffen.*"

[28] See W. Nagel, "*Die Musik in den schweizerischen Dramen des 16. Jahrhunderts*," *MfMg*, Vol. XXII (1890), 67–83.

[29] Nef, "*Die Musik in Basel*," *SIMG*, Vol. X, 546.

[30] See Julius Richter, "*Katalog der Musik-Sammlung auf der Universitäts-Bibliothek*," *Beilage zu den Monatsheften für Musikgeschichte*, Vol. XXIII (Leipzig, 1892), 3.

[31] Nef, "*Die Musik in Basel*," *SIMG*, Vol. X, 541–42, and see Ludwig Sieber, "*Ein Tractat von Hans von Constanz*," *MfMg*, Vol. VIII (1876), 23–24.

[32] Nef, "*Die Musik in Basel*," *SIMG*, Vol. X, 543–44, and *Basel-Festschrift*, 305.

compositions in one book are called *Studententänze*, and one of the books contains a set of instructions on playing the lute.[33]

All these documents attest to a widespread cultivation of music at Basel during the Renaissance. *Musica speculativa*, required in Basel statutes until the middle of the century, must have received a particularly strong impulse with the coming of Glareanus (Henricus Loriti) to the university in 1514. A master of theology from Cologne (1510), where he had studied music with Cochlaeus, Glareanus, who opposed the all-powerful scholasticism at Cologne, was allowed the regency of a hall when he matriculated at Basel.[34] As a private tutor (not on the public payroll), Glareanus gave enthusiastic instruction in classical philology, mathematics, and music to the students in his *bursa,* instruction so much sought after that in one year he had thirty students in his house, a considerable number for that time. Leaving Basel in 1515, Glareanus lived in Italy for two years, after which he taught on a royal stipend at Paris. From 1522 to 1529 he was again at Basel, where he opened his own school and taught the humanities. In 1524 he was on the council of the arts faculty. From 1529 until his death in 1563 he was professor of poetry at Freiburg.[35]

Glareanus' scientific investigations, including his musical research, evidently sprang from his Basel years, and his three musical books were printed at Basel. The first of these, the *Isagoge in musicen* (1516), is the conventional introduction dealing with music's origins, *genera,* intervals, and modes. His next published musical work was an edition of Boethius' treatises *De arithmetica* and *De musica*, a part of the complete edition of Boethius published at Basel in 1546. The *Dodecachordon* (1547) is Glareanus' most important work and one of the most important theoretical works of the century. It begins with a two-fold division of music (theory and practice)[36] and embraces both these aspects of music in its

[33] *Ibid.,* 304, and Richter, *"Katalog,"* *Beilage zu den MfMg,* Vol. XXIII.
[34] For information about Glareanus, see Vischer, *Universität Basel,* 195ff.
[35] Peter Bohn (ed.), *Glareani Dodecachordon* (Leipzig, 1886), p. IV.
[36] *Glareani Dodecachordon* (Basileae, 1547), 1: "*Musica duplex est, Theorice ac practice. Theorice circa rerum musicarū contemplationē uersatur. . . . Practice circa executionem cantus consistit."*

three books. The first of these deals with the elements of music, information already presented in the *Isagoge;* the second book contains Glareanus' famous discussion of the modes, adding the Aeolian and Ionian, authentic and plagal, to the usual eight—hence the title of the book; and the third book is a discussion of rhythm and notation, with musical examples in each of the modes and quotations from actual compositions written by many of the Netherlanders (Josquin, Brumel, Okeghem, Obrecht, Mouton, and others) and by some Swiss and German composers (Isaac, Senfl, Sixt Dietrich, and Gregorius Meyer). In preserving these compositions, the *Dodecachordon* is of great historical importance. In its many citations from Greek and Latin poets, moreover, the book reflects everywhere the author's humanistic and philological interests. Glarean, indeed, praises the study of Greek in his preface.

At least one other humanist, Simon Grynaeus, called to teach Greek at Basel in 1529, was known for his erudition in Greek musical theory, according to several letters from Sixt Dietrich to Bonifacius Amerbach. In 1534, Dietrich wanted to study with Grynaeus, but the latter was away from Basel at the time; and a subsequent letter (December 5, 1535) shows Dietrich's overwhelming desire to become acquainted with ancient musical theory by studying with Grynaeus.[37] Such a desire was quite characteristic of humanistic and early Protestant composers, for whom music was closely tied up with traditional medieval ideas of ethos. Dietrich

[37] E. His, *"Briefe von Sixt Dietrich an Bonifacius Amerbach,"* MfMg, Vol. VII (1875), 125, 127:

> Ess ist mir angezaigt, wie der hochgelert Her, Simon Gryneus ain Greichischen Musicam hab lassen ausgan, wayss doch den Nammen dess Autoris nicht, desshalb ist mein allerfraintlichest bit an euch, Ir wöllent den obgemeltten Herren Gryneum gar trewlich bitten, ob er mir auch der selben Griechischen Music ainen zustellet, wil ich im mit grosser dancksagung bezalen. . . .
>
> Mein lieber vnd getrewer Her, thund dass best, dass mir die Griechisch Music werd, stat mir zu verdiennen, dan ir solt wissen, dass mir die Music ye lenger ye mer geliebt; componier oder liss stettigs, dan ich sonst nichs zu thun hab. Darum ist die Music mein grösste kurkweyl in diesen schantlichen vntrewen verwirrten vnd ellenden zeytten, vnd vorab geliebt mir yetzundt gar fast speculativa Musica zu der ich gross lust trag vnd mich faintlich bemü, fürcht, das ess sey vmsonst, dan ich kain preceptoren hab. Mich rewent [*sic*] meine jungen tag, die ich zu Freiburg so vnnützlich verzert hab, do möcht ich studiert haben. Doch kam kain

himself became one of the most important composers of the century, active in Constanz, we recall, and in the Wittenberg circle around Luther and Melanchthon.

Both the *Isagoge* and the *Dodecachordon* of Glareanus appear in the catalogue of the university library.[38] Other works listed here show what books may have been available to Basel students of music in the Renaissance—medieval manuscripts; printed editions of the works of Renaissance theorists (Gafori, Faber, and others); Greek works in modern editions; printed collections of vocal part-music and instrumental tablatures; lute books; and the organ tracts written for Amerbach by Kotter and Hans von Constanz. Amerbach's personal library contained copies of the treatises of Prasperg (*Clarissima plane atque choralis musice interpretatio,* 1507) and Mareschall; Glarean's *Boethius;* Gafori's *Musica practica;* Faber's *Compendiolum musicae;* Glarean's *Dodecachordon,* with a German translation of this work; Virdung's *Musica getutscht;* and some anonymous treatises.

xi. Sweden: Upsala

THE UNIVERSITY OF UPSALA was founded in 1477 by papal authority at the request of the Archbishop of Upsala, Jacob Ulfsson, who modeled his *studium* upon those at Paris, Leipzig, and Rostock.[1] Since the latter two, patterned after Prague, required music specifically with other phases of mathematics in the arts faculty, it is likely that Upsala did the same. Early statutes and records of the university do not exist. The university library, however, con-

---

gutter arbaytter zu spat. Summa ich muss Musicam speculativam auch kunden vnd solt ich Hundertmeyl wegs ziechen. Wan ich wisst, dass Gryneus dass best mit mir thun wolt, vnd im nit schwerlich wer, wolt ich ain fiertel Jar oder mer zu euch hinab gen Basel vnd mein gelt doselbst bey euch verzeren, dan ess stat sonst der narung halb von Gots gnaden vol vm mich.

38 Richter, *"Katalog," Beilage zu den MfMg,* Vol. XXIII, 1–2. For Amerbach's library, see Pietzsch, *"Musik an den deutschen Universitäten: Basel," AfMf,* Vol. VI, 37.

1See Claes Annerstedt, *Upsala Universitets Historia* (Upsala, 1877–1914), Bihang, I, 2, and Carl Allan Moberg, *"Musik und Musikwissenschaft an den schwedischen Universitäten," MIGM,* Vol. I (1929), 54–55.

tains in manuscript (1508) the *Epytema in musicum Boetii* of Jean de Muris;[2] and this would seem to indicate that lectures based on the *Musica* of Muris were given at Upsala in the latter part of the fifteenth century and early part of the sixteenth century, as in the German universities.

Before the founding of a Swedish university, many Swedish students studied in the continental universities. Musical influences from Paris, for example, are seen in songs brought back by students and in a copy of the *Musica mensuralis* of Petrus Picardus now in the Upsala library.[3] Late in the sixteenth century, two men important in reorganizing the university after its restoration by Gustav Adolf, Petrus Petrejus and Johannes Schroderus Nycopiensis, studied philosophy at Marburg with Goclenius, and while there, both apparently studied music with the other liberal arts. In 1592, Petrus gave a *disputatio mathematica* at Marburg in which he included a discussion of music, outlining its divisions and describing proportions and intervals according to Nichomachos.[4] Somewhat more radical was Schroderus in his Marburg dissertation (1598), for he disagreed with old definitions and divisions of music (Boethius, Euclid) and even criticized Glareanus' division, *musica theorica et practica*.[5]

Schroderus (called Skytte after having been made a nobleman), a strong adherent of the philosophy of Petrus Ramus and opposed to Aristotelian scholasticism, became chancellor of the university in 1622.[6] A year previous to his appointment, he had drawn up

[2] Tobias Norlind, *Bilder ur svenska musikens historia från Vasaregenterna till Karolinska tidens slut* (Stockholm, 1944), I, 48.

[3] Carl-Allan Moberg, *Uber die schwedischen Sequenzen* (Uppsala, 1927), I, 103n.

[4] Moberg, *"Musik an den Universitäten," MIGM*, Vol. I, 57–58. In one of his theses he discussed musical judgment—*"Musices Harmonia non solum ratione, sed etiam sensu revera percipitur"*—and in another the theory of composition—*"Omnis cantilena debet in consonantiam terminari perfectam."*

[5] *Ibid.*, I, 58:

> Henricus Loricus Glareanus in Dodekachordo suo Musices definitionem aliam fecit Theoricae, aliam Practicae propriam . . . nos vero ad Musices naturam intelligendam unam sufficere cum Logicorum Scholis recte existimamus . . . Idem (Glareanus) Musicam in Theoricen et Practicen distribuit; quod, quia accuratar distributionis legibus contrarium, laudare non possumus necque debemus.

[6] Annerstedt, *Historia*, I, 195.

new statutes for the university, and it is here that a musical requirement occurs for the first time. According to these statutes, there
were to be three professors of mathematics who would rotate in
teaching the various phases of this discipline: the second of these,
the *professor Archimedeus,* was to teach optics, music, and me-
chanics.[7] In the constitution for the university, drawn up by Skytte
at the king's order in 1625, music was again among the required
mathematical subjects.[8] And in the constitution given the next
year by Skytte and Axel Oxenstjerna, more specific directions
for the study of music were given—that the Archimedean professor was to teach music either according to Frigius or to some other
approved author.[9]

The *Musica Freigij* called for here is a section of an encyclopedic
work by Johann Thomas Frigius, *juris utriusque doctor,* published
in Basel in 1582: *Paedogogus. Hoc est, libellus ostendens qua ratione
prima artium initia pueris quam facillime tradi possint.* The fourth
section of this work is a simple discussion in dialogue form of the
elements of music, similar to Heinrich Faber's *Compendiolum.*[10]
A pupil of Glareanus and of Ramus, Frigius uses Glareanus' system of twelve modes as the basis of his instruction.

Such emphasis upon practical music in university studies is
further seen in the fact that several teachers of mathematics, and

[7] *Ibid., Beihang,* I, 166–67:

Mathematici skola wara tree.
Then förste skal wara Euclideus, then som läs Arithmeticam och Geometriam. . . .
Then andre, som är Archimedeus skal wara förplichtat at sådana authores, som
om Optica, Musica, Isorrhopica och Mechanica Handlat och skrifwit hafwa, kunna
blifwa ungdomenom korteligen förestälte. . . . Then tridie, som är Ptolomaious
och skal läsa Astronomiam, Geographiam och Architectonicam.

[8] *Ibid.,* I, 251:

Sic in philosophicis fere anni termino absolvuntur
Arithmetica et Geometria.
Optica, Musica, Mechanica.
Geographia cum Geodesia.
Sphaera sine demonstrationibus cum triangulorum doctrina.

[9] *Ibid.,* Bihang, I, 278: *"Secundus [professor] erit Archimedeus, qui docebit Musicam
vel Freigij vel alterius probati authoris."*
[10] For information about Frigius, see Robert Eitner, "Johann Thomas," *MfMg,* Vol.

presumably of music, were composers as well. At the time of Skytte's statutes, music was taught by Johan Franck (in 1624 extraordinary and in 1628 ordinary professor of anatomy and botany), who had studied at several German universities. Franck published in 1625 a lengthy *Huldingsgesang,* in motet-style, written for Gustav Adolf.[11] And Johannes Rüdbeck, professor of mathematics at Upsala (1604) and later Bishop of Västerås, published in 1632 a *Quadricinium triumphale* in praise of the king.[12]

In secondary schools, some of them under the supervision of the university and all of them supplying students to the university, training in music was given in accordance with Lutheran doctrines; for Sweden accepted Lutheranism as the national religion after the Reformation (1527) and inaugurated a system of schools similar to that established in Germany in the wake of the Reformation. The oldest extant school directive (1581) was quite definite in specifying that pupils of all grades sing for an hour after the midday meal, practicing both plain song and polyphonic music; and not only were the pupils to sing *ex usu* but they were to be drilled in the elements of musical theory.[13] In 1622 appeared the *Musicae rudimenta pro incipientibus necessaria* by Laurentius Laurinus, rector of a secondary school, an elementary instruction book which approached the octave system—although it did not quite get away from the older hexachordal system of scales—and which treated polyphonic music briefly.[14] Two Swedish treatises from the mid-seventeenth century were also related to musical instruction in the schools. One of these is an anonymous instruction book in plain song, a *Libellus . . . Tonorum;* the other, *Ratio canendi,* is an introduction to plain song and polyphonic music.[15] In the latter

II (1870), 55–56, and Carl-Allan Moberg, *Från Kyrko- och Hovmusik till offentlig Konsert* (Uppsala, 1945), 17.

[11] Norlind, *Bilder,* II, 39.

[12] *Ibid.,* II, 50–52, and Annerstedt, *Historia,* I, 104.

[13] Quoted by Norlind, *"Schwedische Schullieder in Mittelalter und in der Reformationszeit,"* SIMG, Vol. II (1900), 555.

[14] Norlind, *Bilder,* II, 28.

[15] *Libellus Musicus in quo praecipue Tonorum ratio proponitur videlicet Ambitus et Tropi Tonorum* and *Ratio canendi praescripta Rudbero Juniori Lyrestadiensi:* see Norlind, *"Schwedische Schullieder,"* SIMG, Vol. II, 558–62.

work two systems of solmization are used, Latin and Gallic, both based upon the octave rather than the hexachord and based upon the major and minor scales.

Like other universities, the University of Upsala apparently used music to embellish its academic ceremonies, although documents from the Renaissance period are missing. From 1617, however, comes a record of a doctoral promotion in theology in which music played a most important part: musicians with their instruments preceded the academic procession to the cathedral, students presented vocal music as part of the ceremony, and the services ended with the hymn *Veni sancte spiritus,* after which the musicians led out the procession.[16] Dramatic performances, too, were popular at the University of Upsala from the mid-sixteenth century, when the earliest of the Swedish school dramas, *Tobiae comedia,* was given (1550).[17] Presented by students, these dramas made use of music, choral and instrumental, as well as dancing; special music was often written for them in the style of the humanistic ode settings—used, as we have noted, for similar purposes in the German universities. In 1640, Peder Hansson Ungius arranged a four-part setting of a hymn tune for use between the acts in Frischlin's academic comedy, *Phasma;* earlier, Ungius had held an oration, *De encomio musices* (praising Gustav Adolf's interest in and patronage of music) at the university in 1637, publishing this in 1642.[18]

The king was indeed a great lover and patron of music and kept a flourishing chapel at court. When Skytte held a rigid visita-

[16] Annerstedt, *Historia,* Bihang, I, 139–40:

Dicta die et hora invitati conveniunt, ubi prandium paratur, et inde decudunt Candidatos in templum, eo ordine quo M. domino Cancellario convenientissimum videbitur; nempe (si placuerit) praecedunt Musici [cum] instrumentis et Musica, subsequuntur studiosi, his succedunt pastores et professores cum M. domino Rectore, quem immediate tamen praecedunt academiae Bidelli praeferentes sceptra argentea. . . . Cum templum ingrediuntur, scholares musica vocali eorum adventum excipiunt eamque continuant, donec quisque suo loco in templo constiterit. . . . Dispositis omnibus, hymno: Veni sancte spiritus. . . . Musici iterum quod suarum est partium persequuntur.

[17] Norlind, *Bilder,* I, 72.
[18] *Ibid.,* II, 49n., and Moberg, *"Musik an den Universitäten,"* SIMG, Vol. I, 64.

tion of the university in 1627, during which it was decided to stress practical as well as theoretical aspects of the mathematical disciplines, the king's royal choirmaster, Jonas Columbus, was sent to Upsala to teach students music and to correct their *inflexibilem vocem*.[19] Columbus had studied music privately in Copenhagen and had afterwards entered the University of Upsala, taking the master's degree in 1617 and proceeding to the city of Västerås, where he became lecturer in Greek at the Gymnasium; in 1628 he was appointed *professor poeteos et musices* at Upsala, the first professor of music in the university, teaching Greek and Latin poetry as well as music.[20] A student's notebook, compiled in 1635, contains a set of lectures on music given by Columbus. This *Synopsis* deals with the elements of polyphonic music; and Columbus shows his acquaintance with newer trends in musical theory in using a system of solmization and scales based upon seven rather than the old six *voces*.[21]

xii. MUSIC IN THE RENAISSANCE UNIVERSITIES

AT THE BEGINNING of the Renaissance, musical trends and activities in the universities continued along lines well established in medieval times; in general, that is, music as a mathematical science held its traditional place in the quadrivium, and music as a living art was cultivated in collegiate foundations and often in public lecture rooms in the universities—for example, at Salamanca, where the emphasis upon the *ars musica* was always especially strong. As time went on, some institutions maintained this medieval approach, but in most of the universities, the status of music underwent considerable change. Both conservative and progressive trends may be observed, often in the same institution. On the one hand, one sees the continued integration of music with other philosophical studies, and on the other, a new place for music on the basis of its

---

[19] Annerstedt, *Historia*, I, 232, and Norlind, *Bilder*, II, 40.

[20] Moberg, *"Musik an den Universitäten," SIMG*, Vol. I, 62–63.

[21] *Ibid.*, I, 63–64, and Norlind, *Bilder*, II, 40n.

artistic nature. Still another trend—completely new and indigenous only to the period of the Renaissance—is a linking of musical studies to humanistic studies—classical Latin and Greek literature—aided by discussions and translations of ancient theoretical works on music.

The Italian universities, in which mathematics became increasingly important during the sixteenth century, continued to teach music as a mathematical discipline and as a part of physics. Although there was no chair of music in an Italian university during the Renaissance (with the possible exception of Pavia, where Gafori taught),[1] distinguished musicians taught music privately at Bologna under university auspices, and a similar arrangement apparently prevailed at Padua. In other words, musical instruction was an informal and private matter, just as it is in most continental universities today. The great fame of Bologna as a musical center, moreover, attracted northern students—like Christof Kress, who went to Bologna for musical studies after leaving Leipzig.[2] Indeed, many of the men who introduced humanistic learning, including music, into Germany were trained in the humanities at Bologna or Padua before returning to teach in their native land—such people as Conrad Celtes, Henricus Agrippa, and Rudolf Agricola. And it is interesting to see *musica speculativa* put to the service of *musica practica* in the Italian universities—as in the controversy between conservatives (Burtius, Gafori) and liberals (Ramos, Spataro) over temperament and the institution of the octave scale system in place of the medieval hexachordal system.

Farther north, the University of Paris, progressive and receptive to new ideas in medieval times, was a stronghold of conservatism and scholastic philosophy and theology in the sixteenth century; and not until the end of the century was a humanistic course of studies introduced into the university as a whole. But again, music continued to be taught as a part of mathematics, and certain teachers of mathematics in Paris colleges wrote musical treatises

[1] See Paul Kristeller, "Music and Learning in the Early Italian Renaissance," *Journal of Renaissance and Baroque Music*, Vol. I (1946–47), 261–62.

[2] See Kinkeldey, *Orgel und Klavier in der Musik des 16. Jahrhunderts*, 93.

(Finé, Pena) and also translated ancient works on *musica specu-lativa* (Forcadel, Amyot). One of the most distinguished of all French Renaissance philosophers, Pierre de la Ramée (Ramus), specifically named music among the disciplines to be taught by the incumbent of the chair of mathematics he established. And individual humanists were nowhere more enthusiastic, if we may believe contemporary reports, than in some of the Paris colleges, where lectures on music in connection with classical philology meant not only the study of metrics and the singing of Greek poetry to the accompaniment of musical instruments but the in-vestigation of Greek speculative theories as well, especially the idea of ethos. This concept of attributing ethical powers to music was an idea of greatest importance to those poets and composers who desired to unite poetry and music—Baïf and Ronsard, Thibault and LeJeune. In fact, the cultivation of Hellenism in the colleges of Paris was highly influential in forming the ideas culminating in the great body of humanistic literature and music of the French Renaissance. And the shadow of the university was back of the hu-manists, although the Sorbonne opposed the opening of an actual school of poetry and music.

The position of music in the English universities, conservative in most respects, was different from that in any other university. For on the one hand there was an obvious attempt to maintain the traditional philosophical studies intact, with music based on Boe-thius—at Oxford certainly, and by analogy at Cambridge—required of students in the arts and taught by regents in arts or professors of mathematics—not bachelors of music. At Oxford the taking of a degree in music meant that bachelors of music were admitted to lecture in Boethius and at Cambridge on *scientia musicalis*.[3] Notices in the Oxford records of occasional omissions of the music lectures indicate that such lectures were ordinarily given. On the other hand, the study of music as *ars* received new implications, for the bacca-laureate and doctorate in music continued to be awarded during the Renaissance, and by the sixteenth century music ranked as a

[3] Edward J. Dent, "The Scientific Study of Music in England," *MIGM*, Vol. II (1930), 84.

separate faculty among the higher faculties at Oxford and Cambridge. Although this faculty did not support a teaching staff, degrees in music were awarded only after the fulfilling of certain requirements, standardized late in the sixteenth century. Cambridge seems to have awarded fewer musical degrees than Oxford in this century, and the requirements for the Cambridge degree seem, on the whole, to have been more stringent than similar requirements at Oxford.[4] The granting of honorary degrees was perhaps more characteristic of Oxford than Cambridge. At least, among Cambridge degrees we find no such honorary ones as those awarded Heather and Gibbons: even when an eminent musician like Christopher Tye received the Cambridge doctorate, he had to prove that he had spent many years studying and practicing music. To be a bachelor or doctor of music in one or both of the universities was a mark of great distinction, and was of great practical value in obtaining positions in the royal chapel or in cathedrals throughout the country. Emphasis upon the *ars musica* culminated in the establishment of a chair of music at Oxford in 1626 and at Cambridge later in the century (1684).[5] But during the Renaissance the real study of music was a matter of private instruction, either outside the university or with a college musician. Morley's *Plaine and Easie Introduction* was not a textbook for a class of schoolboys or for university students: it was designed for *Philomathes* ("lover of learning"), for the lover of music studying this art under the supervision of a private teacher with no other aim than to become proficient in music for recreational purposes and to hold his own in social activities—in which music played a large part—practical performance and speculative discussion alike. Indeed, the great flourishing of music in the English universities was simply the academic aspect of England's Golden Age of Music.

As in the Middle Ages, during the Renaissance Salamanca was

[4] It is impossible, however, to compare records in the Cambridge *Grace Books* with the remarks of Anthony à Wood, chief source of information about Oxford degrees in music.

[5] See Dent, *loc. cit.*, 84: the Cambridge professorship in music was instituted by Charles II, who commanded the university to appoint Nicolas Staggins, Master of the King's Music, and to confer the degree of doctor of music upon him in 1684. The professor of music received no stipend, however, until 1868.

unique in maintaining a chair of music, filled by leading theorists and composers. During our period, moreover, this chair acquired permanent tenure for its incumbent, obliged, according to the statutes, to teach both *musica speculativa* and *musica practica*. The connection between the science and practice of music, indeed, was kept especially close at Salamanca. Instruction in the former, based upon Boethius, was responsible not only for traditional and conservative writings on music by Salamanca men but also for highly progressive treatises—Ramos' *Musica practica,* for instance—which disagreed with traditional concepts; and distinguished artists in the field of music—composers and choir directors—studied and taught there. Such men as Bernardo Clavijo, for example, whose pupils became the leading composers of the time, contributed to this sphere of university influence. And along with the enthusiastic cultivation of humanistic learning, music was taught with classical literature. It is interesting to point out, too, that several poets, chief among them Juan del Encina, famed for musico-literary innovations from which Spanish drama and opera developed, held the professorship of music at Salamanca in the sixteenth century—a significant commentary on the wide range and influence of university studies.

In many of the German universities, the teaching of music followed traditional medieval lines until the time of the Reformation, after which music as a mathematical discipline was eliminated from the curriculum altogether or absorbed in the teaching of physics. In Prague the *Musica* of Jean de Muris was required for the last time in 1528. Vienna's professors of mathematics were required to lecture on music according to Ptolemy, Boethius, or Muris until the middle of the century. At Heidelberg *musica speculativa* was likewise taught as a part of mathematics until well past the middle of the century. Cologne, noted for its strong adherence to scholastic philosophy until near the end of the century, required music as a mathematical discipline continuously from its founding until 1574, after which it was probably taught as a part of physics. The *Musica* of Muris was offered at Leipzig in the first half of the sixteenth century, but with the humanistic curriculum inaugurated there in 1558, music was eliminated from the prescribed course of studies and absorbed by the natural sciences (physics). Wittenberg, too, prescribed the *Musica* of Muris in its early statutes, but with the advent of the Reformation, this subject was dropped from the curriculum.

If music as a mathematical discipline tended to recede in importance, however, music as a practical art received more and more emphasis in these universities throughout the Renaissance, generally through the private teaching of musicians and composers incorporated in the universities; and just as in the south, humanists often included music with the teaching of classical literature. Luscinius and Monetarius lectured on music at Vienna; and early in the sixteenth century music was included with poetry in the Viennese *Collegium poetarum et mathematicorum* founded by Maximilian and led by Conrad Celtes. At Heidelberg music was regularly taught in secondary church schools under university direction and in the Pedagogium of the university proper. The earliest published book treating musical theory was a product of this aspect of university instruction—Conrad von Zabern's exhortation for the use of the monochord in musical studies. At Heidelberg, too, music was very much a part of humanistic learning: in fact, the earliest of all the school dramas using music in the humanistic ode-style was performed here—Wimpheling's *Stylpho*. At Cologne instruction in music had been given in ecclesiastical schools from early times, and one recalls that a leading medieval theorist, interested in music as both science and art, is always described by the word *Coloniensis*—Franco. During the sixteenth century such instruction continued to be available in the music school of the Jesuits (one of the university *gymnasia*) and at the hands of eminent musicians who were private teachers in the university. The treatises of Glareanus, Wollick, Cochlaeus, Bogentanz, and Taisnier, all dealing with composition and other aspects of the *ars musica,* bear witness to the type of instruction offered to university students. And the treatises of Glareanus and Cochlaeus point again to the integration of music and classical literature in university studies. Glareanus, in fact, mentions the performance of a Latin ode in praise of Henricus Agrippa, sung in the university lecture room by the humanist Herman von dem Busche to lyre accompaniment.[6] At Leipzig instruction in instrumental music, singing, and composition was provided by private teachers in the university; and official records tell us that many men who followed careers as organists, choirmasters, theorists, and composers were graduates of this institution. Of the many theoretical works written by Leipzig men, only the earlier ones reflect the teaching of *musica speculativa;* the majority of these works deal with practical aspects of music—performance and composition—often in humanistic dress. Musical studies were strongly encouraged at Wittenberg in the sixteenth century by humanists and reformers who tried several times without success to establish a professorship of music in the university. The friendly and liberal attitude of Luther and his circle attracted to Wittenberg theorists and composers—some of them active in the electoral choir and some serving the university as organists—who offered private instruction in music to university students under university auspices.

Because of excellent documentation, the history of musical studies at the University of Cracow during the Renaissance is happily clearer than in many other places. *Musica speculativa* was consistently required by statutes throughout this period, based chiefly upon the *Musica* of Muris. This requirement was interpreted very loosely, however, for certain lecturers combined instruction in instrumental music with the teaching of *musica speculativa;* others combined music and poetry; and others introduced modern texts —Listenius and Ornithoparchus—emphasizing composition. Thus, along with *musica scientia,* the *ars musica* was cultivated in the public lecture hall as well as privately. By the end of the century, this university, which was one of the earliest to embrace humanistic studies, required the combination of music and poetry of all students in the arts faculty. In line with the continuously high place of musical studies at Cracow, many men who studied there followed musical careers afterwards, holding important posts as court musicians or choirmasters of churches and schools, or combining their

[6] *Dodecachordon,* 188.

musical activities, in true Renaissance fashion, with their work as poets, theologians, and historians.

In the Scottish universities at St. Andrews and Glasgow (modeled upon Cologne, which long required music as a liberal art) music was probably taught with other mathematical disciplines in the fifteenth and sixteenth centuries; but with the penetration of humanistic studies after the Reformation, there are no documents to give us information about the place of music. At Aberdeen *musica speculativa* appears to have held its place in the quadrivium through the period and beyond. In collegiate churches connected with these universities, *musica practica* found wide cultivation, and instruction in the chant and in polyphonic music was given to members of these foundations, choristers and university students alike. As in England, however, musical studies in Scotland were more a matter of private than university training, just as remains true today. The Scottish Court at Stirling, with its Chapel Royal which attracted the best musicians of the realm, was an ideal place for the study of music; and we know that an occasional university man went to the royal capital for additional studies in music.

Documentary sources for the study of music at Louvain are inadequate, as for other subjects. We know, however, that the *Musica* of Muris was prescribed in early statutes; that music, both theoretical and practical, was offered at times by eminent private teachers (Rudolf Agricola); and that a leading theorist of the period, Tinctoris, matriculated in the university. Much clearer is the picture at Basel, where instruction in music was offered continuously from the founding of the institution. At first required as a branch of mathematics, after the Reformation music was more strongly emphasized as a practical art. From its early years the university kept one or more paid musicians on its staff, and after the Reformation it supported a musician-in-ordinary whose duty it was to train students in singing and to act as university organist. Through the private instruction of such men as Grynaeus and Glareanus, who combined the teaching of music with Greek literature, music also had a place in humanistic studies. And the fact that Basel was one of the most important printing centers north of the Alps had direct bearing on the wide cultivation of music as a part of university life—in the lecture halls, in various academic ceremonies, in the performance of school dramas, in the homes of eminent professors, and in informal student activities. Many theoretical works on music were printed at Basel, as well as numerous collections of vocal and instrumental music.

Musical studies at the University of Upsala followed both medieval and humanistic trends well into the seventeenth century. Although documentary evidence no longer exists, *musica speculativa* based upon Muris' treatise was probably required in the sixteenth century, for the Swedish university was founded upon German models which prescribed this work. At the beginning of the seventeenth century, men trained in German universities drew up a code of statutes for Upsala which included music with other branches of mathematics. Conservative in this respect, Upsala at the same time showed progressive tendencies in adding to its staff a musician to teach singing to university students, later appointing him *professor poetcos et musices*. This emphasis upon the art of music was in part owing to royal patronage and the chancellor's personal interest in the art. It was the royal choirmaster who was sent in 1628 to become the first professor of music in the university, just two years after the first such appointment at Oxford.

As long as music maintained its old position as an integral part of the mathematical quadrivium, it was taught by *magistri regentes* who instructed in all the arts. Some of these men, however, like certain of the regents at Cracow, were evidently musicians in their own right. As in medieval times, there are indications that music was required for the medical degree at Vienna. With the founding of special chairs of mathematics in the sixteenth century, music was often in the hands of specialists appointed to these chairs. And, of course, practical instruction in music, a part of the regular training given in medieval times to young students in secondary ecclesiastical schools or collegiate foundations in the universities, continued to be given in these establishments during the Renaissance. In the universities proper, as we have seen, musical arts received new emphasis, especially after the Reformation. Sometimes this phase of instruction was in the care of the choirmaster of the university church (as the *Thomaskantor* at Leipzig), sometimes it was given by professional musicians on the university payroll (as the *musicus ordinarius* at Basel and at Upsala), and sometimes it was supplied by the public lecturer in music (as at Cracow). Generally, however, this type of instruction was left to private teachers of music incorporated in the university (men like Ramos and Spataro at Bologna, and the various musicians at Cologne, Wittenberg, and Basel), who followed the system of the medieval regents, collecting fees individually from their students.

As a part of philosophy subsidiary to the more distinguished faculties of law, medicine, and theology, music naturally ranked among the lower arts in the universities, and teachers of music, if publicly paid, received a salary lower than that of professors in higher faculties. We notice certain concessions made with regard to music also, probably because of its unique nature: music lectures could be given in the native tongue instead of in the usual Latin; the music master at Salamanca was required to be only a bachelor; and the faculties of music at Oxford and Cambridge had no distinguishing dress and often no resident member who belonged to them—all pointing to a lack of set form and tradition in respect to the only one of the seven liberal arts to become a separate faculty.

This tendency toward a new emphasis upon music by reason of its artistic nature was accompanied, as we have seen, by the idea of keeping closely connected the two traditional divisions of music—theoretical and practical. The public lectureship at Salamanca, we recall, embraced both these aspects, and holders of this chair were often not only theorists but professional musicians of high standing—composers, masters of cathedral music, and court musicians. The Oxford chair of music likewise imposed upon its incumbent responsibility for both divisions of music, for the holder of this chair was to lecture on *musica speculativa* and to conduct exercises in instrumental music. Similarly, the English degrees in music were awarded on the basis of study in both branches of music: according to Oxford's Laudian Code, candidates for the degree must have spent seven years *"in studio vel praxi Musices,"* and many of the Cambridge graces mention *"studium in musica speculativa simul et in practica"* as the basis for granting the degree. These candidates may have been required to earn degrees in the arts first; at any rate, at Cambridge many graduates in music had previously graduated in the arts. Scholars in the music faculty at Oxford were expected to know Boethius, and upon admission to a degree were permitted *"ad lecturam alicuius libri musices Boecii";* but at the same time, most of the degrees were awarded only after the candidate had shown his skill in the composition of a Mass or other polyphonic form. At the University of Bologna the relating of musical speculation to practical matters—that is, rational explanations of facts observed in musical practice—was so enthusiastically pursued that it brought on a great controversy among Italian theorists. And at Cracow examinations in *musica theoretica* might actually conclude with an instrumental performance, if the examiners wished it.

The awakening of interests in Hellenic studies also had important bearing on both divisions of the study of music. As to musical artistry, the old Greek idea of an intimate relationship between music and poetry was re-established, and certain universities followed this idea in organizing their curricula—Cracow and Upsala, for example. In other institutions this idea formed the basis for private instruction in the humanities: by Agricola at Louvain, Cochlaeus at Cologne, Grynaeus and Glareanus at Basel, Celtes at Vienna, Etheridge at Oxford, and Dorat and others in Paris. Even more important was the study of classical writers upon *musica speculativa,* for humanistic scholars turned their attention to the investigation of ancient treatises on music, incorporating this theory in their own writings, editing and publishing these treatises (as Glarean's edition of Boethius' *Arithmetica* and *Musica*), and often translating Greek manuscripts into Latin, or Latin and Greek works into the vernacular—as Gafori's translations of Aristoxenus, Baccheios, Aristides Quintilianus, and others; Amyot's translation into French of Plutarch's *Musica;* and Forcadel's translation of Euclid's treatise on music. Humanistic school plays, too, which came to be progressively important during the Renaissance, called for the use of music, songs, choruses, and dances.

Treatises inspired by university learning or designed for use in the universities reflect all these varied tendencies. Many of these works are introductions to *musica speculativa* or to *musica practica,* for these Aristotelian divisions held in musical literature throughout the Renaissance.[7] Thus, some of the treatises deal with the science of music as a part of mathematics—Lefèvre's *Musica demonstrata,* Gafori's *Theorica musicae,* Heritius' *Musica speculativa,* and most of Salinas' seven books *De musica.* Sometimes strictly mathematical works contained a section on music—as Ciruelo's *Cursus* (which incorporated Lefèvre's musical book) and Postell's *Tabulae in astronomiam.* Introductions to music as a practical art appeared in even greater numbers from the hands of university men—Luscinius' *Musurgia,* Wollick's *Enchiridion musices,* Cochlaeus' *Tetrachordum,* Ornithoparchus' *Micrologus,* Morley's *Plaine and Easie Introduction,* and others too numerous to mention.

The old medieval *speculum* disappeared during the Renaissance, but certain treatises from the late fifteenth century achieved the comprehensiveness of the *speculum* by treating thoroughly both aspects of music: such are the works of Ugolino, Gallicus, Hothby, and Adam von Fulda. Indeed, all the extensive and truly learned treatises written during our period dealt with elements of music as both science and art—for example, Tinctoris (his works taken as a whole) and Gafori, whose most important works are called *Theorica musicae* and *Practica musicae.* Even Thomas Morley, writing not for a learned audience but for amateurs of music, dealt critically with ancient and modern musical speculation in his *Plaine and Easie Introduction;* but with a bow to English taste, which took its scholarship lightly, he placed his learned theoretical discussion in an appendix.

[7] Zarlino (1558) gives a clear description of the Renaissance concept of each aspect of music, placing reason and judgment, based upon knowledge of *musica speculativa,* above *musica practica,* and distinguishing the *musicus* from the mere practitioner of music. See Gioseffo Zarlino, *Institutioni harmoniche* (Venetia, 1572), 25–26.

The most important treatises on the complexities of mensural music (such as the various short works of Tinctoris and the *Practica musicae* of Gafori) were firmly rooted in *musica speculativa,* both in attitude (effects) and in musical mathematics (Tinctoris' treatise on proportions, for example, describes the application of mathematical ratios to augmentation and diminution of musical rhythms). Similarly, the problem of *musica ficta*—the introduction of chromaticism into the scale—was closely connected with theories of the mathematical derivation of the scale, some writers (like Gafori) relying upon the old Boethian division in which *commata* were inevitable and which was therefore impractical for instrumental tuning, and others (like Ramos and Spataro) polemicizing for a more modern and practical system. Glarean in his *Dodecachordon* also applied speculation to practice, for his systematization of the modes and his exposition of four modes in addition to the old ecclesiastical cycle of eight was based upon contemporary compositions.

Traditions established in musical literature by the medieval *eisagogé* and *protreptikos* continued in effect during the Renaissance, for most of the Renaissance treatises were organized according to the conventional patterns of the medieval treatise. But whereas the medieval *eisagogé* was usually an introduction to the chant, later works deriving from this type generally placed more emphasis upon polyphonic music and composition (although sections on *cantus planus* were occasionally included in these writings). Glarean's *Isagogé in musicen,* for instance, followed the tradition in giving origins and divisions of music, mathematical proportions, and a discussion of the modes. And such an introduction formed the first section of the *Dodecachordon* thirty years later, followed by sections on the twelve modes and rhythmic problems in composition. Similarly, Ornithoparchus' *Micrologus* opened with the conventional *eisagogé,* followed by sections on mensural music, plain song, and composition.

The influence of the old hortatory introduction *(protreptikos)* is seen in much of the literature of the *encomium musicae* tradition —the Cracovian Liban's *De musicae laudibus oratio,* Tinctoris'

Complexus effectuum musices, John Case's *Praise of Musicke,* and the Swedish Ungius' *De encomio musices.* But an interesting change took place during the Renaissance: the discussion of music's uses and effects often became the dedicatory letter in Renaissance treatises, a preface dedicating the work to some royal personage and exhorting his patronage. In Listenius' *Musica,* for instance, dedicated to a Saxon prince, this apologia is the only truly speculative section in the whole book. Ronsard's *Préface* is the same type of discussion, as is the dedication to Prince Charles in Charles Butler's *Principles of Musik.* Interpolations on music in plays and non-musical literature also frequently took the form of an *apologia* for music, describing its uses and effects. The influence of the hortatory treatise is seen, too, in such books as Peacham's *Compleat Gentleman,* where the emphasis is upon the art of music as a leisurely accomplishment, very much related to the rise of the middle class and the desire to become cultivated almost overnight (ideas delightfully satirized in Ben Jonson's *Every Man in His Humour*).

Orations, prefaces, and other discussions of musical effects, in fact, exemplify another change which took place during the Renaissance: the use of one topic from the conventional *kephalia* as the theme for an entire work on music. This influence is especially noticeable in the writings of Tinctoris, who left a number of separate tracts on various subject headings from medieval literature: *"De inventione et usu musice," "De natura et proprietate tonorum,"* and the like. Tinctoris' *Diffinitorium* is a comprehensive treatment of a topic which often opened the medieval treatise—*"De definitione musice";* and Calvisius' historical survey is an elaboration of the traditional section on the origins and invention of music. Most popular of any of the separate topics, however, was the treatise on music's uses and effects.

If the medieval treatise continued to exert an influence during the Renaissance, at the same time a new type of specialized writing made its first appearance during this period—the musical work devoted to problems of instrumental music. In line with a new emphasis on the *ars musica,* and filling the need for a particular type of instruction book, the instrumental treatise is directly related to university studies through the university men who wrote such works and the cultivation of instrumental music among university students. These treatises, which first appeared in Germany, were written in the vernacular—a fact indicating that they were designed for a larger audience than the strictly academic, and indicating, too, their authors' interest in the native tongue, a trend quite strong with German humanists. The oldest *incunabulum* of this type, Virdung's *Musica getutscht,* was a product of university and court activities at Heidelberg. The first instruction book in organ playing was also the work of a Heidelberg musician, Arnold Schlick, and was followed by Schlick's tablature for organ, the first of a number of such books. Oronce Finé, professor of mathematics at Paris, produced the first instrumental treatise in France, a book on the lute, written first in French and then translated into Latin for a more learned audience. Much later, John Dowland wrote a treatise on lute playing in English; Bermudo at Alcalá dealt with the organ, lute, and harp in his *Declaracion de instrumentos musicales;* and the Basel music master Mareschall discussed the art of violin playing in his *Porta musices.*

Humanistic influences are noticeable in treatises of all types written during the Renaissance: in the incorporation of odes and in poems addressed to the reader, in the use of quotations from classical authors, in the explanation of Greek terminology used in music, in the emphasis upon musical ethos, and in the relating of musical metrics to poetic meters. This last point, an important aspect of composition in the sixteenth century, found expression in many treatises, sometimes using Augustine's discussion of rhythm as a starting point. Augustine's *Musica,* we recall, was edited by the humanist Liban at Cracow early in the century; and Salinas drew upon Augustinian theories in his treatment of meters basic to Spanish songs. In treatises dealing primarily with composition, the relation of music to text had a place of primary importance: Calvisius, for example, in his *Melopoeia,* discussed the close relationship between words and music in musical composition and mentioned poetic figures to be effectively set. And Joachim Burmeister, in his *Hypomnematum musicae poeticae* (1599, with additions in

1601), transferred the whole system of rhetorical figures used in poetry to a parallel system in music based upon certain definite harmonic and melodic devices.[8] Such a work as this is the humanistic treatise par excellence and could have arisen only from university learning based upon the study of classic writers.

Thus, the study of music in the European universities during the period of the Renaissance (1450–1600) was a complicated, variegated matter, with some medieval traditions obtaining and with many new ideas and practices introduced. Even in view of widespread attempts to maintain *musica speculativa* along with *musica practica,* university studies were surely not hidebound. New influences were constantly at work, and an exchange of theories, books, and ideas appears to have gone on continuously among university musical people. We have seen how an increasing interest and development in certain realms of musical art (instrumental performance and composition) was reflected in university studies. It remains now to point out the effects of the academic upon the art of music—effects varying considerably in different countries because of social, economic, and cultural differences.

[8] For a description of this treatise, see Heinz Brandes, *Studien zur musikalischen Figurenlehre im 16. Jahrhundert* (Berlin, 1935). Burmeister was indeed a university man, a *"moderator classicus scholae Rostochiensis, tunc maritus"* when admitted to the *magisterium* at Rostock in 1594: see Pietzsch, *"Musik an den deutschen Universitäten: Rostock," AfMf,* Vol. VI, 31.

IV. THE INFLUENCE

OF THE UNIVERSITIES

UPON THE CULTIVATION

OF MUSIC IN THE

CHIEF COUNTRIES OF EUROPE

i. FRANCE

ALMOST FROM ITS INCEPTION, the University of Paris exerted a very definite influence upon the development of the art of music. Through its close affiliation with the Cathedral of Notre Dame in medieval times, it not only played a leading role in the development of a new musical style, polyphony, but in the development as well of a corpus of musical theory to explain and interpret this multilinear music. Professional musicians working in the cathedral in the twelfth and thirteenth centuries, Léonin and Pérotin, were instrumental in inventing and cultivating organum duplex, triplex, and quadruplex—not as an outgrowth of the old practice of singing in parallel fourths and fifths but organum as an artistic form—as well as the polyphonic conductus and the motet. Charged with musical affairs in the cathedral, these composers were university officials as well, and in all likelihood they taught music, publicly or privately, to students in the university. We have seen that the *novitates parisienses* were known to students at the Sorbonne and commented upon by them both favorably (Johann von Jenzenstein) and adversely (Roger Bacon).

Many problems naturally arose in the wake of the new polyphony, and mathematicians in the university were not slow to attack and solve these problems: the need for a system of notation suited to music in several parts; the establishment of an independent system of rhythmic values not dependent upon the rhythmic modes; and the use of thirds and sixths as consonant intervals along with the mathematically consonant fourths, fifths, and octaves. The first attempts at solving these problems, indeed, came from men associated with the University of Paris, not only the center of the new musical development but the intellectual center of all Europe: Robert de Sabilone, John of Garland, Franco of Paris, Franco of Cologne, and various anonymous writers who studied or taught in the university. When Franco of Cologne established a rhythmic system based upon triple time, with relative values for longs and breves whether in ligature or not, he paved the way for mensural notation and for a new and different phase of polyphonic music. The ever widening influence of the Sorbonne appears again in the rapid transmission of this doctrine to peripheral countries, Italy and England, shown by a number of treatises from these countries referring to and commenting upon Franconian doctrine.

Never again, in fact, was a single university so intimately connected with a large phase of musical development in both the art and the science. The leading French composers of the fourteenth century, Philip de Vitry and Guillaume de Machaut, were not, so far as we know, products of a university but were poet-musicians steeped in a literary background acquired by private instruction and independent studies. Such a background, nonetheless, was unthinkable without the learning which emanated from the universities. Similarly, Pierre de la Croix—whose innovations (*ca.* 1300) in the use of short note values in motet composition resulted in a flowing lyrical declamation in the triplum, freed from the rigidity of the rhythmic modes—was not directly related, so far as is known, to the University of Paris. But in the fourteenth century as in earlier centuries this institution was largely responsible for guiding musical composition and theory, chiefly through the writings and teaching of the mathematician and astronomer, Jean de Muris, and of the many who came under his influence. Philip de Vitry was a friend of Muris, and the two undoubtedly influenced one another. Philip, indeed, exemplifies the scholar in all fields of learning, led to the study of philosophy by way of music.[1] It was he who introduced novelties which set the style in French music for the whole of the century—new musical and literary forms (the isorhythmic motet and the ballade) and new rhythmic devices which freed the motet from the rhythmic modes (the division of the minim into semiminims, the use of four prolations to put duple time upon an equal basis with the older triple time, and the use of red notes for syncopation). In addition to *musica speculativa* according to Boethius, Jean de Muris taught this doctrine of Philip's in the university and explained it in his treatises. The *ars nova* embraced both secular and sacred forms, for by this time music was no longer completely subservient to the Church, and secular composition, developing from the art of the *trouvères* and related to princely courts, received the attention of composers and theorists alike. (Johannes de Grocheo, Jean de Muris, Philip de Vitry, and Eustache Deschamps all discussed secular music in their treatises.) Sacred or secular, the *ars nova,* culminating in the highly complex isorhythmic motet, was an intellectual art organized by rigid mathematical laws obviously related to the teaching of music in the quadrivium. The classical perfection of this art, indeed, was largely owing to the harmonious balance between abstract musical theory and its practical application at the hands of talented and cultivated men. And the University of Paris, through the influence of Jean de Muris, was instrumental in disseminating this theory and developing this art.[2]

[1] His interest in *musica speculativa* is seen as late as 1343 when, at his request, the philosopher, medical doctor, and mathematician Leo Hebraeus wrote for him a *Tractatus de harmoniis numeris:* see CS, III, x. And see Eric Werner, "The Mathematical Foundation of Philippe de Vitry's *Ars nova,*" *JAMS,* Vol. IX (1956), 128–32.

[2] Jean's doctrine even penetrated the liturgical drama, for a mystery play exists (Rouen, 1474) in which one erudite shepherd instructs his less learned companion in music, citing passages from Jean's *Musica speculativa.* See Henri Lavoix, fils, *"La Musique au siècle de Saint Louis,"* *Recueil de motets français* (ed. by Gaston Raynaud) (Paris, 1883), II, 224–31.

As the years passed, the musical center of Europe gradually shifted to the Burgundian court and later to the Netherlands. Dufay, who with Binchois led the composers of the so-called Burgundian School (both, according to Tinctoris, following along paths already broken by the English Dunstable), was a *magister artium* and a bachelor of canon law, having studied at Orléans or Bologna if not at Paris. And although Dufay's musical training was acquired in the various *capellae* in which he served—for his musical activities stretched from a choir school in Cambrai to the papal chapel at Rome—university studies were also important in shaping his career; and the fact that this gifted composer pursued higher learning at some university points to the prestige of the university degree and shows the Renaissance musician a man of many accomplishments and intellectual powers. Ottmar Luscinius went to Paris to study Greek; Willaert was attracted to Paris to study law, and while there had private music lessons with Jean Mouton, composer and Master of the Chapel Royal under Louis XII and Francis I; and Glareanus, while connected with the Sorbonne, also came in contact with Mouton.[3] Thus, the University of Paris continued to exert an influence upon musical art by its part in forming the intellectual life of such men as these and others engaged in active musical pursuits.

The cultivation of humanistic studies in the various colleges of Paris in the sixteenth century had almost as great an influence upon musical style as did the Sorbonne in the thirteenth and fourteenth centuries. For the study of classical literature, carried on independently in certain colleges long before being accepted by the university as a whole, brought about an interest in many phases of Hellenism, including musical ideas—especially concepts of the inseparability of poetry and music and of the strong ethical effects of music. Attempts to write native poetry in quantitative meter (in imitation of classical meters) resulted in the *vers mesurés à l'antique* of Baïf and the members of his Academy of Poetry and Music, a direct result of humanistic studies. Baïf's theories probably sprang at least

[3] André Pirro, "L'Enseignement de la musique aux universités françaises," *MIGM*, Vol. II (1930), 48.

partly from his reading of Augustine's and Quintilian's discussions of metrics.[4] And the *vers mesurés* were meant to be sung. Composers who set them to music attempted to follow faithfully in musical rhythm the accentuation of the text, and the resulting musical style differed considerably from contemporaneous polyphonic music with its use of imitation in a texture of melodies and rhythms interwoven among the parts. In contrast to this Netherlandish style, the French *musique mesurée à l'antique* was strictly chordal, with each part bearing the same syllable at the same time —or with a solo voice and instrumental accompaniment—so that, above all, the meaning of the words would be perfectly clear.

Claude Le Jeune (1528–1602), a member of Baïf's Academy and perhaps the most important French composer of the late Renaissance period, wrote a great deal of metrical music in various forms, including a setting of the psalms in this style.[5] The *musique mesurée* effected no change with regard to Church music, however; the psalters of the period were designed primarily for use in the home. Many of the pieces comprised in Le Jeune's great cycle *Printemps* are in metrical style, but with imitative patterns and melismatic passages within his metrical system, and with a great deal of chromaticism, in keeping with the humanistic ideal of setting the text expressively. Jacques Mauduit (1557–1627), to name only one other composer in the group around Baif, also set to music many *chansonnettes mesurées*.[6] Le Jeune was highly esteemed by his contemporaries for the psychological effects of his music;[7] for

[4] See D. P. Walker, "Some Aspects and Problems of *Musique Mesurée à l'Antique*," *Musica Disciplina,* Vol. IV (1950), 167–68.

[5] *Pseaumes en verz mezurez, Les Maîtres musiciens de la Renaissance française* (ed. by Henry Expert) (Paris, 1894–1908), XX–XXII; *Printemps,* XII–XIV.

[6] *Ibid.,* X, 2–4, "*Vous me tuez si doucement*" is a good example.

[7] See the *Ode sur la musique mesurée de Claudin Le Jeune* by Odet de la Noue, *ibid.,* XII, also printed by D. P. Walker and François Lesure, "Claude Le Jeune and *Musique Mesurée,*" *Musica Disciplina,* Vol. III (1949), 166:

> *Maints Muziciens de ce temps ci par les acors grave-dous,*
> *Et le beau chant harmonieus ravissoyent l'ame de tous.*
> *Qui venoit ouyr telle chanson*
> *Il demeuroit tout en extaze à ce dous son. . . .*
>
> *Mais aussitost que ce CLAUDIN par mouvemens mesurés*
> *De ce beau chant harmonieus les acors eut honorés,*

along with other humanists, Le Jeune viewed musical ethos as a phenomenon capable of being revived in modern times. How well he succeeded is evident from a curious anecdote of an occurrence at the wedding festivities for the marriage of the duc de Joyeuse (1581): at the sound of a certain strain of Le Jeune's music, a gentleman rushed to arms (like Alexander hearing the music of Timotheus) and became calm again when the singer changed to another mode.[8]

At this same wedding was presented the first great *ballet de cour,* the *Balet de la Royne.* Humanistic learning was responsible for its appearance: for the French humanists, aiming at a realization of Greek ideals, not only desired the union of music with poetry but wished to unite music, poetry, and the dance into one powerful art form. In musical style as well as conception, the *Balet de la Royne* came under humanistic influence, for its musical settings followed generally the style of the *musique mesurée.*[9] This and other such spectacular performances, fostered by an interest in Hellenic studies, were forerunners of the Baroque opera, based upon monody rather than the old polyphony. It should be emphasized, in fact, that Baïf's Academy (1570) preceded the famous Camerata Fiorentina in producing musical settings governed by rules of speech.[10]

The *musique mesurée* undertaken by Baif and the poets and composers of his circle was, like the *ars nova* motet, an intellectual art, and as such was designed for a small and learned group of

---

> *Ce qui ravissoit coeur & espris,*
> *Pres de cela soudain on vid comme sans pris.*
> *Par les éfors de sa chanson l'ame il élance ou i'veut:*
> *Ores en deuil morte i' l'abat, à la joye or' il l'émeut.*
> *I'va ranimant le plu' bas cueur,*
> *Au furieus i'va rendant toute douceur.*

[8] *Ibid.,* 158. The story is told by Artus Thomas, sieur d'Embry, *Philostrate de la Vie d'Apollonius Thyaneen* (Paris, 1611).

[9] See D. P. Walker, "The Influence of the *Musique Mesurée à l'Antique,* particularly on the *Airs de Cour* of the Early Seventeenth Century," *Musica Disciplina,* Vol. II (1948), 144.

[10] See Roland Manuel, *"Introduzione alla storia del gusto musicale francese,"* *Rassegna musicale,* Vol. XXI (1951), 20.

listeners and performers, not for widespread and popular consumption. Indeed, the story of the Sorbonne's influence upon the course of musical art lies in developing music of a highly intellectual type, meant for a certain class of people only. Early in the fourteenth century, we recall, Johannes de Grocheo, professor in the university, reserved the motet for an audience of connoisseurs. The Academy of Baïf had much the same idea. Nonetheless, the *musique mesurée* enjoyed considerable vogue, and it forms a respectable part of the music of the French Renaissance. Moreover, its syllabic style, with emphasis upon a clear declamation of the text, contributed in no small measure to the final breakdown of the Netherlandish polyphonic (fugal) style. Not only was this music a strong influence in the development of the *air de cour* in the seventeenth century,[11] but it paved the way for the monody of the Baroque generally.

In the realm of instrumental music, too, humanism wielded a definite influence: it was responsible for the great vogue of the lute. In the first half of the sixteenth century the guitar was easily the most popular instrument, but under the aegis of French poets and humanists, the lute became the ideal instrument around the middle of the century.[12] The first instrumental book published in France was, in fact, Oronce Finé's instruction book on the lute (Attaingnant, 1529); and as the century advanced, there grew up a whole school of lutenists. Humanistic ideas, cultivated and fostered in the colleges of Paris, were responsible for this aspect of musical art no less than developments in the realm of vocal and choral music.

ii. England

UNLIKE THE UNIVERSITY OF PARIS, neither Oxford nor Cambridge was affiliated with a great cathedral or with any circle responsible for important musical development. And so the influence of uni-

[11] See Walker, "Influence of the *Musique Mesurée* on the *Airs de Cour*," *Musica Disciplina*, Vol. II, 141–63.

[12] François Lesure, *"La Guitare en France au XVIe siècle," Musica Disciplina*, Vol. IV (1950), 187ff.

versity studies upon the cultivation of music in England is somewhat different from that of the French university and colleges. It cannot be emphasized too much that the English universities were the only institutions to confer the baccalaureate and doctorate in music, the only universities in which the art of music achieved the dignity of a separate faculty. Theoretically, the universities conferred the right to teach (to lecture on Boethius at Oxford, on *scientia musicalis* at Cambridge) when they granted degrees in music, but they made little provision for specialization in that field. In England, longer than in other countries, musical training based upon medieval tradition remained the task of cathedral schools, which, with the founding of the universities, had lost the liberal arts aspect so far as music is concerned; the universities, on the other hand, forced the liberal arts aspect (with variations, as we have seen) upon the musician. Cambridge seems to have provided more formal instruction in music as a discipline of the quadrivium than Oxford, although we cannot be certain about this because of the uneven records. At any rate, a whole year was spent in the study of arithmetic and music at Cambridge prior to the *magisterium,* and these subjects were taught by a *"magister peritus in his artibus."*

It is remarkable that none of the great English musicians ever held a public lectureship in either of the universities; but many of them held positions as organists and choirmasters in colleges of the universities, and it was these men who contributed to the cultivation of music in England, training choristers who in turn became famous musicians and teaching privately. The music degrees, we recall, actually represented a dichotomy based upon the ever present Aristotelian division of music into theory and practice, signifying on the one hand the right to teach the science of music and on the other recognition of many years spent in the study and practice of music, a mark of distinction awarded to capable and often eminent musicians. The significance and prestige of the English degrees, in fact, lies in the importance of music in English cultural life as a whole; and the awarding of these degrees was the academic response to and encouragement of a great national flourishing of music.

For centuries instruction in music was offered in song schools established throughout England in monasteries, cathedrals, collegiate churches, chantries, guilds, and hospitals, generally open to all children, rich and poor alike. As early as 796, Alcuin wrote to Archbishop Eanbald advising him to separate the schools of grammar, song, and writing at York;[1] and afterwards separate schools were established in important centers where singing played a large part in religious matters, with special masters trained to teach music. At Durham, for instance, there were grammar and song schools under separate masters, both of them chaplains of a chantry in the cathedral church.[2] To cite only one example from a later period, in 1477 William Horwode was appointed at Lincoln Cathedral to teach the choristers "playnsonge, pryksonge, faburdon, Diskant, and cownter as well as in playing on the organ, and especially those whom he shall find apt to learn the clavycordes."[3] Monasteries, too, employed trained outsiders to instruct students in plain song, discant, and sometimes organ technique.[4] One of our graduates, Robert Fairfax (doctor of music, Cambridge, 1501/2), was organist at St. Alban's Abbey. And in our study of Oxford and Cambridge, we have cited many collegiate foundations which provided musical instruction for choristers in residence there. These foundations had a special part, too, in shaping university policy where music was involved. Anthony à Wood tells us, for example, that the Nominators and Visitors for Heather's Music Lecture were the Vice-chancellor and "the Governors of the four Colleges with Choirs"—Christ Church, New College, Magdalen, and St. John's.[5]

The English song schools, in fact, were the most important type of elementary school prior to the Reformation.[6] With the suppres-

[1] A. F. Leach, *Educational Charters and Documents 598 to 1909* (Cambridge, 1911), 18–19: *"Praevideat sancta sollertia tua magistros pueris et clero; separentur separatim orae illorum, qui libros legant, qui cantilenae inserviant, qui scribendi studio deputentur."*

[2] A. H. Thompson, *Song-Schools in the Middle Ages* (London, 1942), 6–7.

[3] R. E. G. Cole (ed.), *Chapter Acts of the Cathedral Church of St. Mary at Lincoln A.D. 1536–1547* (Horncastle, 1917), 31 n.

[4] See the examples cited by David G. T. Harris, "Musical Education in Tudor Times," *Proceedings of the Musical Association*, Vol. LXV (1939), 109–11.

[5] *History and Antiquities*, II, 888.

sion of the lesser monasteries in 1536 and the greater ones in 1539, some song schools disappeared.[7] In 1547, Edward's Act of Dissolution saw the closing of many other church schools, although collegiate foundations in the universities, the choir of St. George's Chapel at Windsor, and the colleges of Winchester and Eton were exempt from this ruling, as were cathedral schools in general, for the cathedrals became Protestant and music continued to play a large part in the liturgy. In 1549 injunctions were "laid on" Magdalen College, as Wood puts it, that "all those stipends and other profits whatsoever, with which the Chaplains, Clerks and Choristers are maintained, should be converted into other uses for the University"; the citizens of Oxford protested, however, and the king established a commission restoring some of the schools which had been closed.[8]

This same year saw the appearance of the first edition of a book with marked bearings on musical education, the metrical psalms by Sternhold with additions by Hopkins, published in installments. "A Short Introduction into the Science of Musicke" prefaced the edition of 1561 and several subsequent editions, explaining the solmization system, note values, rests, and the like.[9] The edition of 1570 replaced the introduction with a brief preface stating that each note in the psalm melodies had beside it its letter name in the *solfa* system: "Thus where you see any letter ioyned by the note, you may easilie call him by his right name." Both prefaces probably did much to help the "rude and ignorant in song," as the many editions using one or the other show. It has been suggested, in fact, that Sternhold and Hopkins' psalter replaced to a certain extent the Free Song School abolished by the act of Edward VI.[10]

After the Reformation, some of the Latin grammar schools pro-

[6] For information about this type of school, see Foster Watson, *The English Grammar Schools to 1660* (Cambridge, 1908).

[7] See documents in J. R. Tanner, *Tudor Constitutional Documents* (Cambridge, 1922), 58–68.

[8] *History and Antiquities*, II, 101–102.

[9] See Sir John Stainer, "On the Musical Introductions Found in Certain Metrical Psalters," *Proceedings of the Musical Association*. Vol. XXVII (1901), 3ff.

[10] Harris, "Musical Education in Tudor Times," *Proceedings of the Musical Association*, Vol. LXV, 136.

vided for the teaching of music: Christ's Hospital, for example, specified in its statutes (1552) a "Scoole maister for Musicke."[11] Other schools seem to have encouraged musical studies, although no formal provision was made for them in the statutes. The Merchant Taylor's School in London made no such provision, and yet we know of the musical interests of its famous headmaster (from 1561), Richard Mulcaster. One of Mulcaster's students, James Whitelocke, later an Oxford scholar and a distinguished jurist, said of his master, "His care was also to encreas my skill in musique, in whiche I was brought up by dayly exercise in it, as in singing and playing upon instruments."[12] Ben Jonson's alma mater, Westminster School, founded by Elizabeth in 1560, provided for ten choristers with a singing master and *precentor;* and the statutes expressly stated that bachelors and doctors of music were to be preferred in appointing the *magistrum choristarum*.[13] Some of the men who became bachelors or doctors of music in the English universities received their early training in choir schools,[14] and many English musicians held positions in choir schools after receiving musical degrees in the universities.[15] If one may believe Thomas Ravens-

---

[11] *Ibid.*, 121.

[12] Sir James Whitelocke, *Liber famelicus* (ed. by James Bruce) (London, 1858), 12.

[13] Leach, *Educational Charters and Documents*, 504: *"Cui muneri doctores et baccalaureos musices aliis praeferendos censemus."*

[14] Christopher Tye (mus. bac. Cant., 1536; mus. doc., 1545) was a chorister in King's College, Cambridge, in 1511; Orlando Gibbons (mus. bac. Cant., 1606) was also a chorister in this college under his brother Edward in 1596; John Shepherd (probably music. doc. Oxon., 1554) and Thomas Ravenscroft (mus. bac. Cant., 1607) were choristers at St. Paul's in London; and Nathaniel Giles (mus. bac. Oxon., 1585) was trained at Magdalen College, Oxford.

[15] Among these, John Gilbert (mus. bac. Oxon., 1510/1) was granted in 1524, "the office of player on the organs of the cathedral . . . for the term of his natural life" at Lincoln: see Cole, *Chapter Acts . . . 1520–1536* (Horncastle, 1915), 52. William Chell (mus. bac. Oxon., 1524) was *precentor* at Hereford Cathedral; Edward Gibbons (mus. bac. Cant., incorporated at Oxford, 1592) became organist and choirmaster at Bristol Cathedral and later at Exeter; Thomas Weelkes (mus. bac. Oxon., 1602) was organist at Chichester Cathedral in 1608; Christopher Tye held, among other positions, the post of organist and *magister choristarum* at Ely Cathedral in 1541; Robert White (mus. bac. Cant., 1561) succeeded Tye at Ely in 1562, later becoming organist and choirmaster at Westminster Abbey; Michael East (mus. bac. Cant., 1606) was appointed to the same position at Lichfield Cathedral in 1618; Orlando Gibbons (mus. bac. Cant., 1606, mus. doc. Oxon., 1622) became organist at Westminster Abbey in 1623; and John Tomkins, brother of Thomas (mus. bac. Cant., 1608) became organist of St. Paul's.

croft, moreover, the professor of music in Gresham College, London, must have been a good deal more than a figurehead. Ravenscroft dedicates his treatise (1614) to "the Right Worshipfull, most worthy Graue Senators, Guardians, of Gresham Colledge in London," with great appreciation for his own instruction there, especially in music:

> And herein I must, and doe acknowledge it as a singular helpe and benefit, that I haue receiu'd divers *Instructions, Resolutions,* and *Confirmations* of sundry *Points,* and *Præcepts* in our Art, from the *Musicke Readers* of that most famous *Colledge.* . . . What fruits my selfe in particular haue receiu'd by that one particular *Lecture* of *Musicke* (whereof I was an vnworthie *Auditor*) I dutifully acknowledge to haue proceeded from that *Colledge.*

The reference is possibly to John Bull, the first lecturer in music, in office from 1596 to 1607.

In addition to the cathedral and collegiate choir schools, private choirs kept by wealthy nobles, as well as the royal chapels in London and Windsor, furnished a training ground for English musicians, talented choir members proceeding to the universities. To mention only one of the private chapels, that of Henry Percy, Earl of Northumberland (whose family is well known to every reader of Shakespeare's history plays), was a large establishment, accounts of which date from 1512; the earl's chapel even boasted an organ, for provision was made "for keapinge weikly of the orgayns" by various gentlemen of the choir.[16] We have earlier noted that a certain Lessy of the chapel of the Duchess of York became a bachelor of music at Cambridge in 1470/1, and that John Firtun had spent eight years in the chapel of the Duke of Norfolk before he supplicated for the Cambridge degree in 1515/6.

Most of England's musical talent, however, was concentrated in the Royal Chapel in London. Founded in 1349 by Edward III, the Royal Chapel was much strengthened during the reign of

---

[16] Hawkins, *History of Music,* III, 68, 72.

Henry V, himself a musician of some standing, represented by several compositions in the Old Hall Manuscript.[17] The first account of this chapel is found in the *Liber Niger Domus Regis* with household expenses of Edward IV, which provides for eight children and their master. As regards these little singers, one passage from the *Liber Niger* is particularly interesting:

> And when any of these Children comene to xviij years of age, and their uoyces change, ne cannot be preferred in this Chapelle, the nombere being full, then yf they will assente the King assynethe them to a College of Oxford or Cambridge of his foundatione, there to be at fyndyng and studye bothe suffytyently, tylle the King may otherwise aduance them.[18]

As early as 1420, Henry V issued a commission to press into his chapel talented boys from anywhere in the kingdom, and Henry VI did the same in 1440; Richard III also granted powers for pressing exceptional singers, boys and men, from all over England, and Elizabeth granted similar powers.[19] Musical standards in the Royal Chapel were, then, especially high, and the excellence of performances there often caused comment.[20] The Tudor rulers were especially interested and skilled in music, and their household accounts show payments to numerous musicians (a few foreigners, but mostly native Englishmen) of all kinds—minstrels, instrumentalists, and gentlemen and children of the chapel.[21]

Since the musical center of England was the court, the highest achievement possible to English musicians of the Tudor Era was

17 See W. H. Grattan Flood, "The English Chapel Royal under Henry V and Henry VI," *SIMG*, Vol. X (1908), 563–65. Although the "Roy Henry" of the Old Hall Manuscript has long been considered to be Henry VI, recently discovered documents show that Henry V was the composer: see Manfred Bukofzer, "The Music of the Old Hall Manuscript," *Studies in Medieval and Renaissance Music* (New York, 1950), 78–80.

18 Charles Burney, *A General History of Music* (London, 1776–89), II, 433.

19 See W. H. Grattan Flood, "Gilbert Banaster, Master of the Children of the English Chapel Royal," *SIMG*, Vol. XV (1913), 65, and Davey, *History of English Music*, 75.

20 See, for example, comments of the Venetian ambassadors (1521) cited by Harris, "Musical Education in Tudor Times," *Proceedings of the Musical Association*, Vol. LXV, 122.

21 See "Lists of the King's Musicians, from the Audit Office Declared Accounts," *Musical Antiquary*, Vols. I–IV (1909–13),

a position in one of the royal chapels. Practically every important musician of the period was connected at some time with the Chapel Royal in London or St. George's at Windsor.[22] And just as a university degree of any sort was a tremendous mark of distinction, a degree in music from one or both universities was of great aid in obtaining these posts. The universities obviously encouraged the cultivation of music by awarding such degrees, sometimes conferring them, especially the doctorate, upon men who had spent many years in the practice of music and who had become eminent in the field.[23] In addition to their official duties, these men did a

[22] To name only a few Oxford graduates in music, Nathaniel Giles was organist and master of the children of St. George's, and in 1597 was appointed to the same position in the Royal Chapel, holding both posts until his death in 1633; John Munday became organist to Queen Elizabeth; Thomas Morley was a Gentleman of the Royal Chapel; George Waterhouse became organist of the Chapel Royal after leaving Lincoln Cathedral; Thomas Tomkins was a Gentleman of the Chapel Royal; and William Heather was organist to the queen. Of Cambridge men, the first recorded bachelor of music (1463), Henry Abyngton, served as Master of the Song of the Chapel Royal from 1465; Robert Fairfax was a Gentleman of the Chapel Royal under Henry VIII and head of the choir which performed at the Field of the Cloth of Gold in 1520; Christopher Tye was a Gentleman of the Chapel Royal and organist for this group; and William Blitheman became organist to Queen Elizabeth.

[23] John Gwyneth supplicated twice for the doctorate at Oxford, basing his plea on twenty years spent in the study and practice of music, together with many published compositions; in 1531 his supplication was granted upon payment of a fee (See Wood, *Fasti*, I, 680). John Merbecke was organist at St. George's Chapel, Windsor, in 1550 when he was created doctor of music at Oxford, and that same year he published *The Booke of Common Praier Noted* (*ibid.*, I, 704). John Munday received the bachelor's degree at Oxford after succeeding Merbecke as organist at Windsor in 1585; he received the doctorate in 1624 after he had published a book of polyphonic songs and psalms (Williams, *Degrees in Music*, 72). John Bull was awarded the doctorate at Cambridge and Oxford (1592) after he had become organist of the Chapel Royal. Orlando Gibbons was organist of this chapel two years before his baccalaureate in music (Cambridge, 1606); he had published compositions for strings as well as sacred songs before he accumulated the bachelor's and doctor's degrees at Oxford in 1622 (Wood, *Fasti*, I, 842). And Nathaniel Giles received the doctorate at Oxford in 1622 after having been Master of the Children of the Chapel Royal since 1597, holding the same position at Windsor.

Many of our graduates in music, moreover, had served as organists and choirmasters in non-royal foundations before proceeding to the degrees. To mention only a few Oxford men, John Mason was instructor of the choristers at Magdalen when he received his degree in 1508; Robert Porret was organist at Magdalen when he became doctor of music in 1515; John Bull was organist of Hereford Cathedral in 1582, receiving the bachelor's degree in 1586; Edward Gibbons was organist and choirmaster at Bristol when he received the bachelor's degree in 1592; Arthur Cocke was organist of Exeter Cathedral when he supplicated in 1593; Thomas Weelkes was Winchester College's organ-

large amount of private teaching, which left its mark upon English musical development. Doctor Fairfax, we know, was paid (1510) for instructing two choirboys over a period of time while he was a member of the Chapel Royal; John Bull was trained by the queen's organist, Blitheman; and Thomas Morley "had been bred up under the most famous Musitian Mr. *Will. Byrde,* one of the Organists belonging to queen *Elizab.*"[24] Christopher Tye was music tutor to Edward VI: in Samuel Rowley's chronicle play *When You See Me You Know Me* (1605), Prince Edward calls him "Doctor *Tye* Our Musicks Lecturer" and commends him as the best musician in England. Tye delivers a lengthy eulogy of music to the prince, based chiefly upon the effects of music and actually interspersed with both vocal and instrumental music: after this he dedicates his *Acts of the Apostles* to Edward, who promises to "haue them sung within my fathers Chappell."

The age, indeed, looked upon the study of music as a necessary part of the education of the scholar and gentleman, and as part of the accomplishments of the perfect courtier. John Skelton's poetry is filled with musical allusion, and one whole poem mocks and satirizes the upstart courtier in terms of music.[25] Literature dealing with the education of the nobility advocated music for recreational reasons but—following Aristotle's *Politics*—never to the point of virtuosity. In the first pedagogical treatise in the English language, *The Boke named the Gouernour* (1531), Thomas Elyot, discussing the ideal education of those who are going to govern under Henry VIII, devotes a whole chapter to music ("In what wise musike may be to a noble man necessarie"). Here Elyot commends music for recreational purposes, citing many Scriptural and legendary examples of its soothing powers; he mentions Nero, however, as an example of the virtuoso who knew too much about music and used

---

ist and had published three sets of madrigals before becoming a bachelor in 1602. And William Blitheman had been master of the choristers at Christ Church, Oxford, since 1564, when he became a bachelor of music at Cambridge in 1586.

[24] See Willibald Nagel, *"Annalen der englischen Hofmusik, 1509–1649,"* Beilage zu den MfMg, Vol. XX (1894), 9; Wood, *Fasti,* I, 756; *ibid.,* I, 760.

[25] See Nan Cooke Carpenter, "Skelton and Music: *Roty bully joys," Review of English Studies,* Vol. VI (1955), 279–84.

this knowledge unwisely. The tutor, Elyot continues, must show the child that music

> onely serueth for recreatiō after tedious or laborious affaires. And to shewe him that a gentilmã plainge or singing in a cōmune audience appaireth his estimation. The people forgettinge reuerence whan they beholde him in the similitude of a cōmon seruant or minstrell.

The future ruler, says Elyot, must understand music for a better understanding of the "Public Weal," and he should read Plato and Aristotle on this subject.

Roger Ascham, Cambridge scholar, tutor to the royal family, Latin secretary to Edward VI and Elizabeth, and Greek tutor to Elizabeth, discussed music in his treatise on archery, *Toxophilus* (1545), advocating music for the young (following Plato and Aristotle), especially Dorian music, "verie fyt for the studie of vertue & learning, because of a manlye, rough and stoute sound in it, whyche shulde encourage yong stomakes, to attempte manlye matters," although he himself did not understand the meaning of Dorian music:

> Nowe whether these balades & roundes, these galiardes, pauanes and daunces, so nicelye fingered, so swetely tuned, be lyker the Musike of the Lydians or the Dorians, you that be learned iudge.

Like Elyot, Ascham thought that too much playing of instruments was improper:

> ... lutinge and singinge take awaye a manlye stomake, whiche shulde enter & pearce depe and harde studye. ... But yet as I woulde haue this sorte of musicke decaye amonge scholers, euen so do I wysshe from the bottome of my heart, that the laudable custome of Englande to teach chyldren their plainesong and priksong, were not so decayed throughout all the realme as it is.[26]

Castiglione's *Courtyer,* which, "done into English" in 1561 by

[26] Roger Ascham, *English Works* (ed. by William Aldis Wright) (Cambridge, 1904), 12–14.

Sir Thomas Hoby, enjoyed widespread popularity, contains a great deal of musical allusion. In discussing the qualities of the perfect courtier, Castiglione advises that he be a "musitien," in addition to many other things, having "understanding and couning upon the booke" and also "skill in lyke maner on sundrye instruments." Toward the end of the first book, the Count of Canossa gives a long eulogy in praise of music, recounting old theories of music of the spheres and legends showing the effects of music.

In England during the Renaissance, then, the scholarly approach to music was not emphasized as it was, for instance, in Germany at the same time. The upper-class youth of England and members of the rising middle class who wished to become gentlemen studied music privately with a tutor so that they might take part gracefully in social activities involving music. And so it is not surprising to find few textbooks on music of any kind printed in England during the Renaissance, and none at all until late in the sixteenth century. The best and most comprehensive of them all, Morley's *Plaine and Easie Introduction* (1597), was designed, we recall, neither for choirboys nor for university students, but for the amateur of music studying with a private master. "Learned" material—a discussion of Greek theory—was included but was placed at the end of the book; so also with the "Annotations" in Charles Butler's *Principles of Musik* (1636). Each of these treatises, moreover (as well as most of the others written by Oxonians or Cantabrigians) would be unthinkable without the university background which shaped the mind of its author, stimulated in him a desire for learning and for private investigation (Morley and Butler, too, to limit ourselves to these two, refer constantly to other theorists, ancient and modern), and taught him Greek (the language and literature is frequently drawn upon). In this respect, university studies had a very real influence upon the writing of musical treatises.

Indeed, humanistic studies in the universities, although not so important in shaping the course of music in England as in France, were not without influence on the British musical world.[27] It is

---

[27] See especially the discussion of Sidney's references to music and ancient meters in Bruce Pattison, *Music and Poetry of the English Renaissance* (London, 1948), 61ff.

highly significant, for instance, that the first playwright (a musician himself, Gentleman of the Chapel Royal and later Master of the Children of the Chapel) to use music for really dramatic purposes—to heighten the drama with music—was an Oxford master of arts, Richard Edwards; two of his most successful plays were performed, we remember, at Christ Church, Oxford, one of them before the queen. Edwards' work is considered far in advance of that of his predecessors, chiefly because he used classical plays as his models—surely a university influence. No formal "academies" were established in England, but British poets were much under the influence of the Pléiade—especially Sidney and Spenser.[28] Perhaps Gabriel Harvey's Areopagus group at Cambridge, to which both these young poets belonged, was the nearest approach to the academy for the discussion of music and verse. One of the prime interests of the Areopagus writers was the ancient quantitative meters and the possibility of basing English verse upon these meters.[29]

Thomas Campion of Peterhouse, Cambridge, whose *New Way of making Foure Parts in Counterpoint* (1613) was for years a standard text, was also connected with the Areopagus group. Representing in himself a Greek ideal—the combination of poet and musician—Campion's *ars poetica* (*Observations in the Art of English Poesy*) shows his interest in the abolition of rhyme, the adaptation of classical meters to English poetry, and the close interdependence of text and musical setting. This last—for which he was highly acclaimed by his contemporaries—had much to do with the success of his own airs. As he himself says in the preface to a volume of his songs, "In these English Ayres I haue chiefly aymed to couple my Words and Notes louingly together."[30] Campion was also interested in the Italian experiments in achieving a closer bond between words and music, and was actually associated with the two

---

[28] See Carpenter, "Spenser and Timotheus," *PMLA*, Vol. LXXI, 1141–51.

[29] See the passage of letters between Harvey and Spenser (1579–80) in Edmund Spenser, *Poetical Works* (Oxford, 1912), 609ff.

[30] Percival Vivian (ed.), *Campion's Works* (Oxford, 1909), 115.

English composers who affected the *stilo recitativo*—Coperario and Ferrabosco.[31] University studies, then, were responsible for an interest in literary and musical innovations which came to fullest fruition in the development of the English air, chief lyric form of the seventeenth century.

As for instrumental music, if the universities were not directly responsible for the development of a school of lute playing, at least they contributed the most important men whose efforts made up this trend—especially Cambridge. As late as 1676, Thomas Mace, in the most comprehensive of all treatises on the lute, speaks of the popularity of the lute at Cambridge, mentioning "eminent *Performances* upon that *Instrument* by divers very *Worthy Persons;* several such at this present remaining in our University of *Cambridge,* who have not been at *It* from their first undertaking yet a full Year; and in one *Quarter of a Year* could play extremely well, even to *Admiration.*"[32] It was a Cambridge man, too, John Alford, who translated and published in 1568 Adrien Le Roy's *Instruction de partir toute musique des huit tons divers en tablature de luth* (1557). Both Anthony and William Holborne, whose *Cittarne School* appeared in 1597, were also Cantabrigians, as was Thomas Robinson, whose *Schoole of Musicke* (an instruction book on the lute) appeared in 1603 and *New Citharen Lessons* in 1609. And John Dowland's *Necessary Observations belonging to the Lute* (published with his son's instruction book on the lute) is a most interesting and successful effort at keeping theory and practice firmly knit. For although he deals with such practical matters as "Chusing of Lute-strings," fretting and tuning the lute, Dowland invariably connects these subjects with specialized discussions of intervals and the like. He says that everyone who aspires to play the lute must know music, and continues,

> Wherefore I exhort all Practitioners on this Instrument to the learning of their Pricke-song, also to vnderstand the Elements

---

[31] See Pattison, *Music and Poetry*, 74.
[32] Thomas Mace, *Musick's Monument* (London, 1676), 45.

and Principles of that Knowledge . . . for which purpose I did lately set forth the Worke of that most learned *Andreas Ornithoparchus* his *Micrologus,* in the English tongue.[33]

Humanistic studies in the universities thus played a quite definite if somewhat limited role in shaping the course of music in England during the Renaissance. And the university degrees were related, both as cause and as effect, to the high position of music in English culture. By conferring musical degrees upon men who had long been active in the field, the universities rewarded outstanding musical achievement. By setting up certain requirements to be met before a degree in music could be obtained and by refusing to admit some who supplicated, they maintained high standards with regard to music. By offering a classical education to musicians and by encouraging if not actually requiring the study of the arts prior to the study of music, they doubtlessly raised the intellectual level of the musician and helped to create in the Renaissance musician the scholar and man of many parts.

iii. ITALY

WITH REGARD to the influence of university studies upon the course of musical development in Italy during the Renaissance, the situation is somewhat analogous to that in England, where musical studies were chiefly a matter of private instruction and independent research. Unlike England, however, Italy produced numerous treatises during this period; for Italian *musici* developed a theory of music compatible with the latest developments in the art of music —if not indeed responsible for them—and this theory was disseminated throughout Europe, especially by German musicians who drew upon it in compiling their handbooks and introductions to music. Most important of all, through the cultivation of humanistic

[33] Robert Dowland, *Varietie of Lute-Lessons.* . . . *Also a short Treatise thereunto appertayning: By Iohn Douland Batcheler of Musicke* (London, 1610), E recto (copy in the Huntington Library).

studies the universities played an essential part in shaping the development of music both as *ars* and as *scientia* in Italy.

The University of Padua, like the *studium* at Paris, was instrumental in the development of mensural music through the efforts of Marchettus of Padua in the fourteenth century and of Prosdocimus de Beldemandis in the fifteenth. In the *Pomerium* (1318), Marchettus posited a rhythmic theory in which the breve might be divided into smaller values according to arithmetical relationships, being thus the first theorist to present duple rhythm on an equal basis with triple.[1] Although these *divisiones brevis* corresponded to Philip de Vitry's combination of *tempus* and *prolatio*, Marchettus' theory antedates both Philip's *Ars nova* (*ca.* 1325) and the explanation of this rhythmic doctrine by Jean de Muris (*Ars novae musicae,* 1319). Professor Apel sees the origin of these innovations in the system of Petrus de Cruce (who may have been an Italian who came to Paris and introduced certain Italian features into the French motet), with its grouping of several semibreves to the breve and the use of the *punctus divisionis* for separating these groups; and he even wonders if *trecento* polyphonic music may not have had its origin in musical theory.[2] In any case, the rhythmic innovations of Marchettus are characteristic features of the works of leading composers in the first half of the *trecento*—compositions of Giovanni da Cascia, Jacopo da Bologna, and Giovanni da Florentia, chiefly the *madrigal, ballata,* and *caccia,* using lively figuration in the upper parts.

Prosdocimus, professor of mathematics at Padua early in the fifteenth century, was also concerned with mensural notation, among other aspects of *musica mathematica*. Comparing French and Italian notation, we recall, Prosdocimus preferred the Italian type because it was consistent in using the *punctus* as the *punctus divisionis,* whereas the same mark in French usage was ambiguous

---

[1] For a translation of Marchettus on "imperfect time," see Strunk, *Source Readings,* 160–71. Although the facts of Marchettus' life are unknown and we are not certain that he actually taught in the university, his treatises follow the learned style of the typical university treatise and his mensural doctrine is based upon *musica speculativa* taught in the universities.

[2] Willi Apel, *Notation of Polyphonic Music,* 368–69.

with a variety of meanings. Prosdocimus, moreover, was one of the earliest theorists to use proportional signs to show diminution or augmentation of time values according to mathematical ratios —a technique much in favor with fifteenth-century composers in the notation of canons and of the tenor part, which was often a repetition of the same phrase several times with changes in rhythm. Both Marchettus and Prosdocimus, as well as Ugolino of Orvieto (a product of one or more of the Italian universities), discussed also *musica ficta* or *falsa,* the use of chromaticism, first widely introduced in fourteenth-century secular music; these theorists justified its introduction and explained its use upon mathematical grounds.

Toward the end of the fifteenth century, musical studies at the University of Bologna inaugurated a controversy which had important implications on the development of music and which has not yet ended. The Spaniard Ramos, who was called to teach at Bologna and who probably left Spain because the Inquisition was not sympathetic to progressive ideas like his views on music, paved the way for modern harmonic theory with the publication of his *Musica practica* in 1482. Ramos realized that the Pythagorean system did not fully meet the requirements of "modern" choral music, with its chromaticism, nor of instrumental tuning; and he foreshadowed the tempered scale in advocating the use of major and minor thirds as consonant intervals in the natural ratios (4:5 and 5:6), eliminating the syntonic comma (80:81) found in the Pythagorean system[3] and laying the ground-work for a harmonic system based on the third. Seeing the need for a simplification of the old system of mutation by way of hexachords, he advanced a theory of scales based on the octave, the foundation of our present system. It is especially interesting for our study that Ramos claims to owe his discovery of a new system of tuning to the study of ancient authors.[4]

---

[3] Riemann, *Geschichte der Musiktheorie*, 318–19. Riemann points out that Walter Odington had arrived at these conclusions two hundred years earlier.

[4] Strunk, *Source Readings*, includes a section of the *Musica practica*, 201:

Let no one think that we have found this with ordinary labor, we who have indeed discovered it reading the precepts of the ancients in many vigils and

It was only to be expected that such unorthodox theory as this would not pass unnoticed by the traditionalists, and Ramos, we recall, was bitterly attacked by Niccolo Burzio (Burtius) in his *Musices opusculum* (1487). Ramos' tenets, however, were upheld in the sixteenth century by his pupil and successor as lecturer in the university, Spataro, who polemicized against attackers of his teacher—Burzio and later Gafori (*Apologia,* 1620), both of whom favored the Pythagorean system of interval derivation (based on the perfect fifth with altered thirds) and of the Guidonian hexachordal system.

In spite of such opposition, Ramos' doctrine eventually won out, chiefly because of its influence on Gioseffe Zarlino, who used Ramos' definition of the major third as the point of departure for his harmonic system. With Zarlino began the dual system of harmony based on the major and minor third which superseded modal harmony and is still in use today. In the first two books of his *Istituzioni harmoniche,* first published in 1558, Zarlino set forth his system, finding the tones of the major triad in the proportions of string divisions—the *divisione armonice*—$1 : 1/2 : 1/3 : 1/4 : 1/5 : 1/6$ and the tones of the minor triad in the converse of this—the *divisione arithmetice*—$1:2:3:4:5:6$.[5] Thus, Zarlino was the first to use the triad as the basis of a harmonic system rather than individual intervals. Although he favored equal temperament in instrumental tuning (organ and lute), in choral music he advocated just intonation—the intense diatonic of Ptolemy—in which each tetrachord in the octave contains two whole tones (8:9 and 9:10) and one half-tone (15:16). For this he was taken to task by his erstwhile pupil Vincenzo Galileo (*Dialogo della musica antica e moderna,* 1581), who polemicized for the Pythagorean system. Zarlino's *Dimostrationi harmoniche,* published first in 1571, takes the form of conversations among several musicians—Willaert (Zarlino says that the group met at Willaert's house for musical discus-

avoiding the errors of the moderns with care. And anyone even moderately informed will be able to understand it.

[5] See Riemann, *Geschichte der Musiktheorie,* 369ff. for an explanation of Zarlino's theory. Strunk, *Source Readings,* 229–61, includes a part of the *Istituzioni armoniche.*

sions in 1562), Merulo, and Francesco Viola. The Ptolemaic diatonic is upheld in these discussions, as well as in Zarlino's last published treatise, *Sopplimenti musicali* (1588).

Zarlino's theory, then, is directly in line with, if not partly responsible for, the musical development which took place in Italy during the latter part of the sixteenth century: the transition from polyphonic to homophonic music, with emphasis upon harmonic as well as melodic aspects, chiefly upon the triad. An ideal example of the *musicus,* the combination of philosopher and practicing musician, Zarlino received his musical training with Adrian Willaert in Venice, and eventually became choirmaster at St. Mark's. And although he seems not to have been directly related to a university, Zarlino was well versed in the usual university studies—theology, philosophy, Greek, Latin, and mathematics—and his own private investigations would have been impossible without this background.

The musical erudition of the earlier theorists Tinctoris and Gafori may be quite definitely related to university studies. Tinctoris, thoroughly grounded in musical artistry in the various chapels in which he worked, was a licentiate in law (which presupposes graduation in the arts) from the University of Louvain. The humanistic spirit and deep theological insight which pervade Tinctoris' works, as well as his mathematical approach to problems of practical music, are indubitable marks of his university studies. Taken altogether, his writings sum up the whole development of the Netherlandish and Italian schools. His work on counterpoint is perhaps the first thorough treatment of the subject, and his *Diffinitorium* is the first real attempt to codify musical terminology.

With Tinctoris, Gafori was the theorist most consistently and admiringly drawn upon by other theorists in the sixteenth century; and Gafori's background was in large part owing to mathematical and musical studies at Padua—for he studied in his youth at the humanistic school founded in the Gonzaga home at Mantua by Vittorino da Feltre, once professor of mathematics at the University of Padua. His fellow-townsman and contemporary, Pantaleo Malegolo, mentioned Gafori's diligence in musical studies at Mantua in an account of his life which appeared in the treatise *De armonia musicorum instrumentorum* (1508).[6] Gafori's teacher was Johannes Bonadies (Gutentag), a pupil of Vittorino who probably had studied with Hothby also, for it is his copy of one of Hothby's treatises that Coussemaker published. It was at Mantua, in all likelihood, that Gafori became acquainted with Boethian theory—we know that Johannes Gallicus studied Boethius' *Musica* with Vittorino—which he later defended against Ramos. Gafori's interest in ancient theory is seen again in the translations he made, or caused to be made, of Aristides Quintilianus, Briennius, Bacchius, and Ptolomaeus,[7] all of whom he drew upon in discussing speculative and mathematical aspects of music in his *Theorica musicae*. In his *Practica musicae* of 1496, Gafori discussed the elements of polyphonic music, a quite natural interest since he was choirmaster and composer at Milan's cathedral. While holding this post, he also lectured on music at the *Accademia degli Sforza* and at the nearby University of Pavia.[8]

If the universities thus contributed to the progress of music by keeping alive an interest in ancient theory as well as by stimulating new musical doctrines, the situation with regard to the cultivation of music was at the same time similar to that in England in that church *capelle* and the royal courts provided fertile training grounds for young musicians. In addition, the various *accademie* (groups of amateurs and connoisseurs of music and poetry), private schools of music (like Tinctoris' school at Naples) and private schools for the study of arts and letters like Vittorino's at Mantua, were flourishing centers for musical studies backed by university learning.

---

[6] *Franchini Gafuri Theorica musicae* (facsimile ed. by Gaetano Cesari) (Roma, 1934), 16: *"ubi duorum annorum studio acri labore noctu interdiuque intento multa in artis speculatione et actione diligentissime conscripsit: et plura subtiliter excogitauit."*

[7] *Ibid.*, 16–17: *"Praetereo ueterum musicorum graeca opera: Aristide quintiliani: Manuelis Briennii: Bacchei senis Introductorium et Ptholomei harmonicon: quae omnia eius cura et impensa a diuersis interpretibus in latinum sunt conuersa."*

[8] A list of professors in the University of Pavia (1498) has under the heading *Ad lecturam musices*, *"D. Presb. Franchinus Gafurus, Mediol. legens"*: see G. Porro, *"Pianta delle spese per l'Università di Pavia nel 1498,"* Archivio storico lombardo, Vol. V (1878, part 2), 511. Emilio Motta, however, believed that this notice and other evidence indicated that Gafori actually lectured in Milan rather than in Pavia: see his *"Musici alla corte degli Sforza,"* Archivio storico lombardo, Vol. XIV (1887), 550n.

Vittorino da Feltre was completely humanistic in his attitude toward music, believing firmly in its effects (ethos), especially the efficacy of Dorian music: he introduced it at mealtimes and had his boys practiced in both song and instrumental music, while at the same time he taught them musical mathematics.[9]

A typical product of private instruction, stimulated by the higher learning fostered by the universities and using ancient theory as point of departure, was Ercole Bottrigari (born 1531), who left many treatises on musical subjects. Tutored in his youth by several men, most of them law students at the University of Bologna, and later instructed in music by Bartolomeo Spontone, Ercole received a thorough grounding in Greek and Latin literature as well as in theoretical music, singing, and the playing of stringed instruments.[10] As he became more and more interested in Greek musical theory, Ercole studied in his own home, often discussing mathematical theory with the Bolognese professor of mathematics, Nicolò Simi.[11] His first published work was a dialogue called *Il Patricio, overo de' Tetracordi armonici di Aristosseno* (1593). Here Bottrigari refuted Patrizi—an ardent opponent of Aristotelian philosophy who had written a book on Platonic philosophy, *Della poetica* (1586), attacking Aristoxenos' theories—and upheld the Aristoxenian division of the tone into two equal semitones. Bottrigari is, then, another example of the theorist so devoted to his subject that he engaged in controversies about it—and in 1599 he published under his own name *Il Desiderio, overo De Concerti di varij Strumenti Musicali,* a dialogue which had formerly been published under the name Alemanno Benelli, anagram for Annibale Melone, Bottrigari's student. In the preface to this treatise, Bottrigari tells the "benign and courteous reader" how Melone

[9] William H. Woodward, *Studies in Education during the Age of the Renaissance* (Cambridge, 1906), 19ff. Rabelais' description of the education of the young giant Gargantua (described in great detail in chapter 23 of *Gargantua*) is a beautiful exposition of the humanistic tutorial method as it came from Italy, and musical studies are at the very center of this: see Carpenter, *Rabelais and Music,* 72ff.

[10] For an account of Bottrigari and his treatises, see Gaetano Gaspari, *Dei Musicisti bolognesi al XVI secolo* (Bologna, 1876), 3ff., and see the account in Fétis, *Biographie universelle.*

[11] For Simi's career, see Mazzetti, *Repertorio di tutti professori,* 291–92.

could not have written the work and he mentions his own translations from the Greek—*"della quale Melone non conosceua pur il Jota."* Bottrigari published two other "musical discourses" called *Il Melone—primo* and *secundo*. In the latter he gives his own "considerations" upon a discourse of Gandolfo Sigonio (practising musician and theorist, brother of Carlo Sigonio who was professor of philosophy at the University of Bologna) and upon Vicentino's treatise, *Antica Musica ridutta alla moderna Prattica*. His dialogue *Il Trimerone de Fondamenti armonici* (1597) is a discussion of modes, ancient and modern. The interest of this prolific writer in ancient theoretical writings and in making such works available to an unlearned public—especially to Melone, who, like a more famous writer, apparently had at his command "small Latine and lesse Greeke"—is seen again in Bottrigari's translations of Greek and Latin theoretical sources. As he himself says in the interesting preface to *Il Desiderio,* these include the *Harmonics* of Aristoxenos and Ptolomaeus, Euclid's *Regola armonica,* a part of the *Problemata* attributed to Aristotle, the *Compendium musicale di Psello* (a Byzantine writer, *ca.* 1050), the *Musica* of Plutarch, Gaudentius, and Alipius. Of Latin writers, Bottrigari translated into Italian the works of Martianus Capella, Censorinus, Cassiodorus, Bede (Lambert, whose treatise was long assigned to the Venerable Bede?), and Boethius.

Musical studies in the *accademie* were reflected, we have seen, in such works as Zarlino's *Dimostrationi,* which recounts informal discussions of musical problems among a group of connoisseurs. This informal approach was also responsible for the fact that many of the Italian treatises, like most of the English ones, appeared in the vernacular; for ever since the time of Dante, Italian literati had struggled for the use of Italian as the language of poetry and scholarship. A parallel situation is seen in Spain, for although many learned treatises were written as a result of university studies—at Salamanca and Alcalá—some of the important Renaissance treatises were obviously the product of private training and work at some princely court or chapel. This is especially true with regard to instrumental treatises. Diego Ortiz, for instance, whose *Tratado de glosas sobre clausulas y otros generos de puntos en la musica de violones* was published at Rome in 1553, was a native of Toledo and served the Duke of Alba in Naples as *maestro di capella* and composer. His *Tratado,* not simply an instruction book in the technique of playing the viola da gamba, is the first systematic presentation of the art of diminution—variations on a given theme—and its second part describes this art combined with an accompanying instrument, the cembalo.[12] Antonio Cabezon, famous blind organist of the Royal Chapel and clavichordist to Philip II (he accompanied his royal master on trips to England, Italy, and the Netherlands), wrote a *Musica theorico-practica* dealing chiefly with the art of composing canons and reflecting Netherlandish influences.[13] His *Compendio de Musica el qual servia para tecla vihuela y arpa,* of which no copy exists, was used as the basis of a tablature book compiled by his son (1578), showing the art of improvising on a keyboard instrument; and a pupil of Cabezon and organist for the Dominicans in Madrid, Tomas de Santa Maria (d. 1570), left an *Arte de taner fantasia* (1565), teaching improvisation upon keyboard instruments.[14] Early German treatises on musical instruments were also written in the vernacular, generally by men interested in German poetry, and were the products of musical activities at court as well as university studies in music.

Higher studies in the Italian universities had far-reaching effects upon music as related to humanism. For it was in Italy that the impulse toward humanistic learning first made itself felt, and men educated in the universities and in the private humanistic schools were responsible for the spread of this culture to other parts of Europe. One need only read through the matriculation rolls of the Italian universities to see how many *ultramontani* were enrolled. Many of the men who introduced humanism into Germany, for example, first became interested in classical studies while studying in Italy. Rudolf Agricola, universally acclaimed as having been

---

[12] Max Schneider (ed.) (Kassel, 1936). See the editor's foreword.

[13] Fuertes, *Historia,* II, 129.

[14] Kinkeldey, *Orgel und Klavier,* 87; see also 25–55, where Tomas' treatise is described in great detail.

instrumental in spreading the New Learning in Germany (and well-known for his skill as a musician as well as his interest in musical theory), spent about ten years studying the classics in Italy—chiefly at the Universities of Pavia and Ferrara.[15] Italian humanists sometimes went to universities in the northern countries to teach: the Italian Vitelli, to name only one, was a private tutor teaching Greek in New College, Oxford, as early as 1470–75.[16] Further, Italy was the repository of manuscript copies of ancient treatises on music; and since an urge to study these sources was very much a part of interest in classical sources generally, Italian theorists rendered a great service to musical scholars throughout Europe when they made many of these works available in Latin or Italian translations. (Salinas, we recall, while ducal choirmaster at Naples, had copies made of many of these works in order to study them at his leisure.) Chief among these ancient sources was, of course, Plato, whose influence upon musical theorists assumed more and more importance during the Renaissance: Gafori's *Theorica musicae* as well as his *Practica musicae,* for example, are filled with Platonism.

Humanistic studies in Italy, finally, had a very direct bearing upon certain musical innovations which appeared during our period. First of all, it was no accident that the German ode settings, a type of homophonic composition which grew directly from university studies, corresponded in style to the Italian *frottola,* one of the chief musical forms of Italy's humanistic period. More important, perhaps, was the part played by humanistic studies in fostering the development of a new form which appeared at the end of the century—the opera. Whether its inventors attended the universities or not, university learning propagated by private investigation—in the academies as well as in the universities proper—led such people as Vincenzo Galilei (whose son, at any rate, was one of the great luminaries of the University of Padua) to experiment in a new musical style based upon his concept of Greek music, the *stile rappresentativo,* with its close affinity between words and mu-

---

[15] See the chapter on Agricola in Woodward, *Studies in Education,* 79ff.
[16] *Ibid.,* 107.

sic.[17] Peri and Caccini followed, and the "new" art form was under way, actually born of the investigation of "old" theory, the interest in Greek concepts of musical effects upon man, and the attempt to emulate the Greeks in making music add to the understanding of the words.

iv. GERMANY

HERMANN FINCK, in his *Practica musica* (Wittenberg, 1556), stressed a need on the part of German musicians for a closer acquaintance with the finer points of musical performance. Quoting an old and rather unflattering proverb, Finck describes the German propensity for making a thorough study of many branches of knowledge without concentrating upon one alone, as foreign musicians do, and he gives this as the reason for a lack of rapid advance on the part of German musicians.[1] The continuous study of music in the German universities during the Middle Ages and Renaissance was indicative of this scholarly interest in music along with other branches of higher learning, characteristic of the German mind. And although Germany contributed little that was new (until the great *Blütezeit* of the eighteenth century, indeed, Germany remained largely peripheral in musical culture), during the Renaissance, German theorists and composers—most of them scholars and graduates in one or more of the university faculties—had a large share in the cultivation and perpetuation of Netherlandish music throughout Western Europe by compiling and disseminating the latest Italian theory and by assimilating the leading style of the period and making it their own.

It was in the German universities, traditional and conservative, that the work of Jean de Muris was required by academic statutes as the basis for musical studies for several centuries and that music

[17] For a contemporary account of the first attempts in the "representative" style, see Pietro de' Bardi's letter of 1634 to G. B. Boni, translated by Strunk, *Source Readings*, 363–66.

[1] *"Die Deutschen brüllen, die Italiener blöcken, die Spanier heulen, die Gallier singen."* See the German translation of the fifth book of the *Musica practica* by Raymond Schlecht, *"Hermann Finck über die Kunst des Singens, 1556," MfMg.* Vol. XI (1879), 135ff.

was taught under traditional liberal arts aspects as a part of mathematics until past the middle of the sixteenth century (in certain cases, throughout the century). With the advent of humanistic studies to the German universities, music, although no longer required by statute, received a new and personal impetus in both speculative and practical aspects. For here, as in other continental universities, the investigation of classical literature and philosophy awakened a new interest in ancient musical theory, in *musica poetica* (the composition of music), and in vocal and instrumental performance—all reflected, as we have seen, in university studies. Leading musical theorists, most of them composers as well, were incorporated in the universities, where they lectured on music under university auspices if not on public stipends. That humanists at Wittenberg held music in great esteem is largely responsible for the fact that more distinguished musicians successively taught at Wittenberg in the sixteenth century than at any other single university; and university students were strongly encouraged by the academic authorities to avail themselves of the opportunity of studying with these men.

Those universities—of which Wittenberg was one, along with Heidelberg and Vienna and Cracow in Poland—which happened to be located near the seat of imperial or electoral courts were especially fortunate in drawing to them the best professional musicians of the time, men often active in both university and court *Kapellen.* The emphasis upon performance and composition of music at Vienna early in the sixteenth century was largely owing to imperial patronage of this art, just as the humanistic circle at Vienna was sponsored by Maximilian. The first treatises on musical instruments ever to be published (Sebastian Virdung's *Musica getutscht* and Arnold Schlick's *Spiegel der Orgelmacher und Organisten,* both published in 1511) were products of university studies and of participation in musical activities at the electoral court at Heidelberg. Schlick published an organ and lute tablature the following year, and subsequently other treatises on musical instruments appeared, we recall, from the hands of German and Swiss university men.

Musical studies pursued by the humanistic group at Vienna and elsewhere had, perhaps, the most original effect upon musical style. According to humanistic ideas, classical Latin, to be properly rendered, should be sung, the musical rhythm faithfully reproducing the quantities of the syllables. Such was Tritonius' aim in introducing the ode settings in four homogeneous parts, note against note. This resulted in a homophonic type of music quite different from the polyphonic music of the Netherlanders. This music actually bore great similarity to the Italian *frottola,* although its chordal structure resulted from the reproduction of the textual meter in all parts of the music simultaneously, whereas the *frottola* was based upon a more strictly harmonic concept. First published in 1507 as *Melopoeia,* Tritonius' innovations called forth many imitators.[2] Johannes Murmelius, for example, included several four-part odes in his *Protrepticus studiosorum poeticae* (Wittenberg, 1517); Cochlaeus included some in his *Tetrachordum musicae* (1511, with later editions); Senfl composed in this style; and Michael made ode settings for the use of Heidelberg students. In Leipzig (1533) appeared a collection of poems by Prudentius and Virgil set to music in the ode style by Hordisch and Sebastian Forster. Paul Hofhaimer's fifty-three settings of Latin poems were published posthumously in 1539 as *Harmoniae poeticae.* The Prague musician Wenceslaus Vodnianus also made settings of odes, and several Swedish musicians connected with the University of Upsala set odes for special occasions. Tangible evidence of the effect of university learning upon musical culture, these musical settings were actually used in the teaching of Latin literature in the schools and in school plays attempting to revive Hellenic drama. Although the sphere of influence of this style of music was relatively limited—for in general, German composers continued to cultivate the polyphony of the Netherlanders—the ode compositions were highly important in shaping the style of the Protestant congregational hymn (the so-called *Kantionalstil*), a homophonic structure with the melody no longer in the tenor but in the *discantus.*[3]

[2] See Moser, *Paul Hofhaimer,* 162–63; and see 112–28 for reproductions of Hofhaimer's *Harmoniae poëticae.*

[3] Friedrich Blume, *Die evangelische Kirchenmusik* (Potsdam, 1933), 44–45.

In their ode settings, composers were guided by an intimate relationship between music and poetry, achieved chiefly through rhythmic effects. Those who followed the Netherlandish style were more concerned with setting the text expressively, reflecting as far as possible in the music the meaning of the words.[4] This aim was achieved mainly by melodic techniques—the use of expressive and often chromatic motives, imitated in all the parts—rather than by isometric emphasis. Humanistic studies were no less responsible for the *musica reservata* than for the ode compositions, and German humanists wrote copiously on the composition and performance of music, their treatises enjoying wide circulation at home and abroad. Glareanus, in establishing his theory of the modes (*Dodecachordon*, 1547), drew largely upon Netherlandish composers, along with German and Swiss musicians who followed the Netherlandish style. Glarean, in fact, considered Josquin the fulfillment of a classical, humanistic ideal, whose music was an *"ars perfecta, cui ut nihil addi potest"*; and the basic element of this *ars perfecta* was its four-part structure, with each part equally important for the whole, a classic equilibrium between polyphonic-linear music and homophonic-chordal.[5] Coclico, too, epitomized the style and teaching of Josquin in explaining composition and expressive performance in his *Compendium musices* (1552), aiming for the closest possible relationship between text and music; and Hermann Finck, whose favorite composer was Gombert, set forth in his *Practica musica* (1556) a system of figural improvisation, coloratura to be used in all voices.

These books and others springing from humanistic ideals (the expression of the "affections" in music) were used in the teaching of music in schools and universities and did much to foster in Germany and neighboring countries the cultivation of polyphonic

---

[4] The often quoted words of Samuel Quickelberg describing the *musica reservata* epitomize this ideal, which consists in *"ad res et verba accommodando, singulorum affectuum vim exprimendo, rem quasi actam ante oculos ponendo"*: see Lowinsky, *Secret Chromatic Art*, 92.

[5] Josquin, as exemplifying the height of Renaissance classicism, is discussed by Herbert Birtner, *"Renaissance und Klassik in der Musik,"* *Theodor Kroyer-Festschrift* (Regensburg, 1933), 40–53.

music in the imitative style of the Netherlanders. A distinctive touch is seen in many of the polyphonic compositions of the period, however, in the use of old German folksongs as tenor *cantus firmi*. The *tenor-cantus firmus Lied,* indeed, had been developed by German composers independent of outside influences in the fourteenth and fifteenth centuries, and the fact that this type conformed structurally to the Netherlandish ideal was another reason why German musicians adhered to the style of the Netherlanders.[6] Coincidental with an interest in classical literature, during the Renaissance a strong nationalistic feeling and an interest in early German history arose: some of our treatise writers, we remember, also experimented in poetry and other works in the vernacular. Both of these interests helped make the *Lied* a favorite type with native composers. The five collections of songs (380 in all) published by Georg Forster, associated with the University of Heidelberg and with the electoral court there, is the most important repertory of these songs.

Closely integrated with humanistic studies and bearing even more strongly upon the assimilation of the Netherlandish style by native composers was another movement within the sphere of university influence: the Reformation. Under the leadership of Luther and Melanchthon, schools and universities were reorganized (Tübingen and Wittenberg among others) and new ones were established (Marburg, Königsberg, and others) for the study of classical letters and theology. The great task of Philip Melanchthon was the reconciliation of the literature of antiquity with Protestant ideals and national consciousness; and in the systematic organization of schools under his influence, evangelical religion became intimately associated with classical teaching.[7] Although the great *praeceptor germaniae* left no work on music among the instruction books he wrote for the youth of his country, he wrote prefaces to some of Rhaw's collections—among these the preface to the *Cantiones evangelicae* by the Prague professor Wenceslaus Vodnianus, pub-

---

[6] See Leo Schrade, "The Choral Music of the Lutheran 'Kantorei'," *The Musical Heritage of the Church* (ed. by Theodore Hoelty-Nickel) (Valparaiso, 1946), 77–78.

[7] Woodward, *Education During the Renaissance,* 124–25.

lished by Rhaw in 1554. The writings of his students also reflected Melanchthon's interest in this subject; Rhaw, Spangenberg, Heinrich Faber, Lossius, and Listenius, all of whom left textbooks on music, were taught by Melanchthon at Wittenberg. In secondary schools with programs instituted by Melanchthon, music had a place of paramount importance; often as much as one hour a day was devoted to it.[8]

In reorganizing the educational system of Germany, Melanchthon worked in close association with Luther, under whose influence he had fallen when, after study at Heidelberg and Tübingen, he came to Wittenberg as professor of Greek in 1518. Luther's love of music is well known. Familiar with music from his schooldays in Eisenach, Luther enjoyed playing the lute, and he set vocal compositions in lute tablature as a bachelor at Erfurt.[9] But for Luther music was more than a pleasant pastime: it was an art to be used for the glory of God, a strong force for uniting the congregation in the common act of worship. In contrast to other reformers—Zwingli, who prohibited the use of music altogether, and Calvin, who permitted only the singing of metrical psalms—Luther, in reorganizing the church, laid great stress upon music in the Protestant liturgy. Aided by Johann Walther and Conrad Hupff, he himself arranged a musical setting for the German text of the Protestant service; and complete musical settings were provided in the *Cantionales sacrae* of Spangenberg (1545), Lossius (1553), and others.[10] The great contrast between the many Lutheran choirbooks and the one similar product of the Church of England (Merbecke's little *Booke of Common Praier Noted*, 1550) is highly significant of the strong emphasis upon music in the Lutheran ser-

---

[8] In the school at Eisleben, generally considered the first product of Wittenberg's evangelical and humanistic influence (1525), music was taught for an hour a day; in his *Declamatio in laudem novae scholae*, presented in 1526 when a new school was opened in Nürnberg, Melanchthon included the daily teaching of music in his plans for organizing the schools of that city; and Melanchthon's *Schulordnung* for Saxony also specified daily instruction and practice in singing from the first year onward. See Woodward, *Education During the Renaissance*, 219ff., and Schünemann, *Geschichte der deutschen Schulmusik*, 82.

[9] Martin Luther, *Werke* (*Weimar*, 1883–1939), *Tischreden*, V, 6428.

[10] For information about the Lutheran service, see Luther D. Reed, *The Lutheran Liturgy* (Philadelphia, 1947), 82ff.

vice. Luther's great predilection for congregational singing, moreover, gave the vernacular hymn (of which he himself wrote nearly forty) an assured place in the service and made hymn singing a characteristic feature of Protestantism. Not only were the German chorales used for unison singing: they served also as the basis for polyphonic music—motets and, in the period of the Baroque, cantatas. Thus they gained an historical importance never attained by Calvinistic psalm settings or English hymns. Everyone knows how skillfully Bach exploited the chorale as *cantus firmus* for the cantata; and even today one need only quote Luther's great hymn, *"Ein feste Burg"* (as Mendelssohn and others have done), to arouse overtones of the German Reformation.

In organizing a new musical liturgy, Luther worked through the schools. His ideas on teaching music to the children of Germany actually embraced the age-old dichotomy of theory and practice, as his oft-quoted words of 1524 show: "I speak for myself, but if I had children of my own I should have them learn not only languages and history, but singing and music as a part of the full course of mathematics."[11] Luther's orders, however, were private; the actual reform of the church and schools was done under the authority of princes or free cities which appointed commissions of theologians and educators for this purpose.[12] Under the new rulings, all children were to be instructed in plain song, figural music, and the elements of musical theory.[13] From among all the children

[11] For instance, in Schünemann, *Geschichte der deutschen Schulmusik,* 78: *"Ich rede für mich: wenn ich Kinder hätte, und vermöchts, sie müssten mir nicht alleine die Sprachen und Historien hören, sondern auch singen und die* Musica *mit der ganzen Mathematica lernen."*

[12] See Reed, *The Lutheran Liturgy,* 87ff. In addition to Melanchthon, Johannes Bugenhagen was especially active, reorganizing the Church in Brunswick, Hamburg, Lübeck, and Pomerania, establishing the liturgy for the Church of Denmark, and having a large share in preparing the Wittenberg *Kirchenordnung of 1533.* Bugenhagen's orders, giving special attention to the schools, stressed the teaching of music. In his *Braunschweigische Kirchenordnung of 1528,* for instance, he specified

> dat se allen kynderen gröt vnde kleyne, gelert vnde vngelert, singen lernen (alse Philippus Melanchthon in dem genomeden boke bescreven hefft) gemeynen sanck düdesch vnde latinisch, dar to ock in figurativis, nicht alleyne na gewänheit, sonder ock mit der tidt kunstlich, dat de kyndere leren vorstan de Voces, Claves, vnde wat mehr höret to sulker Musica, dat se leren vaste singen vnde renlick etc.

in a school actively participating in music, excellent choirs comprising the best singers could be selected to perform in the church and also upon special occasions in the community—at weddings, funerals, and the like. Between this musical institution, the *Schulkantorei*, and the vocal polyphony of the Netherlanders there was the closest possible connection, for the *Kantorei*, with its rigid organization and strict discipline, became the ideal vehicle for the expression of Netherlandish music, the music of the Protestant repertory.[14]

With the inauguration of this system of musical instruction for all children of Germany—not alone, as in England, for those in choir schools—and the use of selected groups of these children to furnish music in the Protestant Church, the place of the *Kantor* became increasingly important, his position being second only to that of the rector. This position called forth highly educated men, well versed in Latin grammar and literature. Since the old medieval connection between mathematics and music was never broken, the teacher of music often taught mathematics as well—like Calvisius, active at Leipzig as mathematician, astronomer, and historian as well as musician. Both the rector and *Kantor* in the secondary schools (and the latter often acted as choirmaster and composer in some church as well) were men trained in the universities. (Most of the men fortunate enough to go through the universities chose careers as ministers or schoolmasters.) Cochlaeus,

---

[13] To cite only one other example, Bugenhagen's orders for reorganizing the Church in Lübeck (1531) contained similar requirements for the teaching of music, stressing its importance among the other liberal arts:

> Tho tweluen alle werckeldage schal de Cantor allen iungen groten vnd kleynen singen leren, nicht alleine vth waenheyt, ssünder ock myt der tidt künstlick nycht alleyne den langen sanck, sünder ock yn Figuratiuis etc. . . . Wente de Musica is eine kunst van den fryen künsten, de me dem kyndern van iöget vp fyn vnde vaste wol leren kan, vnde de me thom besten ock wol brüken kan, so wol alse andere künste. Wenn se öuerst alleyne leret werdt, vnd nycht andere kunst dar by, so maket se lössgengere vnd wylde lyde.

See Heinrich Heppe, *Das Schulwesen des Mittelalters und dessen Reform im sechzehn Jahrhundert* (Marburg, 1860), Beilage, 10.

[14] Schrade, *loc. cit.*, 73, 81.

Figulus, Listenius, and Ornithoparchus are only a few of the musicians and theorists who followed this sort of career.[15]

As is often true in Europe today, the upper classes in the best of these schools were not to be distinguished from the arts faculty in the universities: the same learned instruction was given in both.[16] Many of the German treatises we have mentioned were written for specific use in the schools, treatises which (like Cochlaeus' *Tetrachordum*) sprang from university studies and teaching. The *Musica* of Listenius (1537) and the *Compendiolum musicae* of Heinrich Faber (1548) surpassed all others in popularity here;[17] and Martin Agricola's *Ein Kurtz deudsche Musica* (1528) was also a favorite text. Especially suited to the needs of the schools, these works ran to many later editions and were required in *Schulordnungen* throughout Germany as basic texts. These and other such works are solid evidence of the typically German thoroughness of musical instruction in the schools, and also of the scholarly erudition of the men who provided this instruction. The great number of theoretical works on music produced in Germany, as compared with other countries, is directly proportional to the emphasis laid upon the study of music in Germany's schools and universities in the sixteenth century.

Since they were trained in the Netherlandish tradition and were also instruments for carrying on this tradition, these German theorists and composers contributed largely to the coincidence of Netherlandish vocal polyphony with Protestant music. And through this coincidence, German music during the sixteenth century showed a unity in sharp contrast to the confusion of the later Baroque epoch, with its conflict of secular Italian trends with tra-

[15] Johannes Cochlaeus (1479–1552), after teaching at Cologne, became rector of the St. Lorenz school in Nürnberg; Wolfgang Figulus was *Thomaskantor* while studying in the arts faculty at Leipzig, 1549–51, and from 1551 until his death in 1588 was *Kantor* of the school of St. Afra in Meissen; Nicolaus Listenius, bachelor and master of arts at Wittenberg where he matriculated in 1529, afterwards became *Kantor* in Salzwedel; and Ornithoparchus, who studied and lectured on music in several universities, became a schoolmaster in Münster, 1533. See Gerhard Pietzsch, *"Bildung und Aufgaben des Kantors im Mittelalter und Frühprotestantismus,"* Die Musikpflege, Vol. IV (1933), 230–31, and Moser, *Geschichte des deutschen Musik*, I, 388n.

[16] Schünemann, *Geschichte der deutschen Schulmusik*, 95.

[17] *Ibid.*, 100–102.

ditional German concepts. Sacred choral music was the ideal form of expression for the Renaissance German composers, some of whom, like the early Protestant composers, favored simple polyphonic settings based upon a folk-*Lied* as *cantus firmus,* with surrounding parts emphasizing and underlining this melody; and some of whom followed the more complicated imitative style of the humanistic composers, like Adrian Petit Coclico with his *Musica reservata* in the style of Josquin. Whatever the style, Protestant music was written specifically for use in the Protestant service (largely in the form of motets, polyphonic arrangements of chants from the Proper of the Mass) and performed by the specially selected *Schulkantoreien* with additions from civic musical organizations *(Gesellschaftkuntorcien):* thus Protestant music achieved its great glory in the sixteenth century through a common purpose basic to the composition of the music and the vehicle which expressed it.[18]

The influence of the universities in bringing about this musical flourishing was strong indeed, for the universities furnished spiritual leaders to direct the reorganization of the schools, placing music at the very center of the curriculum, making its study compulsory for all students, and building up for each student a wide background of musical experience and appreciation which remained throughout life. The universities offered musical instruction to students in the arts, generally through private teachers in the academic community and sometimes through public professors on the staff. And they sent forth men with high scholarly attainments to become *Kantors* and rectors in the schools, men who integrated their teaching of music with literature and mathematics and who also served as composers and theorists.

V. GENERAL CONCLUSIONS

UNIVERSITY STUDIES through the centuries have exerted a very strong influence upon the course of music from many different

[18] Schrade, *loc. cit.,* 70–81.

points of view. The very development of polyphony in the late Middle Ages was a process very much within the sphere of university influence, for the center of this art was the official church of the University of Paris, Notre Dame, and the process was implemented by officers and teachers in the Sorbonne. Not only in evolving the music but in developing a body of theory to explain, interpret, and note the music, musical philosophers (mathematicians) in the Sorbonne took the lead. In the fourteenth century, music and doctrine of the *ars nova* flourished again under university auspices, especially through the inventions of Philip de Vitry and the teaching of Jean de Muris. Owing to the ease of intercourse between the Sorbonne and British and continental universities, this doctrine quickly reached peripheral countries. In Italy, indeed, under the inspiration of Prosdocimus, there evolved a doctrine of rhythm and notation to fit the complicated polyphony of the time; and again, mathematics as a university study was an important factor in shaping this doctrine. The earliest interest in chromaticism from the speculative point of view, too, seems to have been the result of university studies, and the fact that musical theorists tried to reconcile it with the mathematically derived scale is significant again of the close connection between theory and practice. Especially during the late Middle Ages and most particularly during the fourteenth century, then, music was characterized by a marvelous balance between theory and practice, on a solidly mathematical basis.

If France led the way in the development of musical art and theory in the late Middle Ages, it was Italy that, at the time of the Renaissance, produced theorists—either native Italians or foreigners like Tinctoris and Ramos working under Italian influences —who followed development in the art of music with explanations of these phenomena in the light of *musica speculativa*. Licentiate in laws from Louvain, Tinctoris and Gafori, professor of music in the University of Pavia, summarized theory for the fifteenth century; their works, based upon musical practice of the Netherlandish school, were drawn upon over and over by other theorists. Gafori was also a vehement participant in the controversy between ancients and moderns toward the end of the century over certain theoretical questions which had a great deal of bearing upon the future course of music. Shadows of the universities of Salamanca (where Ramos began his professional career), Bologna (where Ramos was called to teach), and Padua (to which Gafori's ideas and background may be traced) hover over the whole controversy. Ramos polemicized for a new scale, mathematically derived, using only one type of major and one type of minor third (thus opening the way for a harmonic system based upon the triad) and advocating the use of the octave instead of the hexachordal system as the basis of the scale. Although strongly opposed by Burzio and Gafori, Ramos' theory won out when Zarlino evolved his harmonic system based on the triad. And so an intellectual debate begun centuries ago in the University of Bologna still has its repercussions today.

The treatises of Tinctoris and Gafori were most often drawn upon by German theorists who answered a direct need in the newly reformed schools of Luther's Germany for instruction books in music; and in propagating the doctrine of the Netherlandish School, these theorists played an important role in shaping the course of sixteenth-century music in Germany. Products of the Netherlandish style and also instruments for carrying on this musical tradition, German theorists and composers, through their teaching and writing, contributed strongly to the coincidence of Netherlandish vocal polyphony with Protestant music. Germany has long been aware of the efficacy of inculcating a particular ideology through the schools; and the succcess of the Reformation was in large part owing to its school program, with great stress upon music. The rectors of the schools as well as the singing masters were erudite men, products of the universities, a fact which led to high standards in the *Kantoreien* of school, town, and church.

There was no such demand for school textbooks in England during the Renaissance, and not until the end of the sixteenth century did this type of book appear, generally from the hands of men actively teaching music. Even then, the most important of all Renaissance treatises (Morley's) was meant for the intelligent amateur, not the schoolboy or the professional musician. The whole of England's Golden Age was a period of great musical flowering, and the high position of music in social life was responsible for its encouragement in such courtesy books as Peacham's *Gentleman*. Academic participation in this musical flourishing resulted in the awarding of degrees in music at Oxford and Cambridge. Eminent musicians who trained choristers and organists in cathedral schools, the royal chapels, and private chapels of the nobility fulfilled certain university requirements (in theory and practice) and became bachelors of music, doctors of music, or both, only to go out and work in these same chapels and schools, teaching, composing, and directing musical activities.

All over Europe, wherever humanism flourished—as it did in most universities long before the end of the century—academic studies included musical investigations and inspired the editing, translating, and publishing of ancient treatises on music. This was especially true in Italy and France; and coincident with the spread of Platonism generally, musical philosophers came to draw more and more upon Platonic ideas on music. A strong interest in classical poetry and in reviving musical ethos as an actual phenomenon, implemented by studies in certain French colleges, resulted in a corpus of music known as *musique mesurée à l'antique;* and humanistic ideas of *mousiké* in the larger sense—music, poetry, and the dance, the underlying ideal of Baïf's Academy—also played a part in the evolution of the opera in France by way of the great *ballets de cour,* contributing to the breakdown of the Netherlandish style and paving the way for the monody of the Baroque. In Germany this type of study inspired ode settings—based upon quantitative meters and directly motivated by Greek ideas of the close union of music and poetry—which likewise contributed to the breakdown of polyphony and the evolution of the homophonic, chordal Protestant hymn. In Italy, emulation of Greek practices led to the experiments of the Florentine Camerata and the invention of the opera. Even in England there was a small circle of poets and philosophers, chiefly at Cambridge, interested in experimenting with classical meters. Through Thomas Campion and others related to the group, the evolution of the English air was at least partly the result of this interest. Thus, unlike France, Germany, and Italy, England felt its most important academic musical influence in the seventeenth century with the air, chief lyrical form of the Baroque. And humanistic studies, finally, were coincident with the growing interest in musical instruments, especially the lute, thought to be the instrument most closely approximating the Grecian lyre.

By fostering humanistic studies, in a word, colleges and universities played an indispensable part in shaping the music of the period. Music historians generally agree that the great difference between Renaissance music and earlier music is the new relationship between words and musical setting which found expression with the Renaissance composers. Credit for this is due largely to the humanists. In the words of a recent critic, the "humanistic spirit, equally with the progressive 'harmonization' of music, was responsible for the vocalization of polyphony and for the emergence of the new choral art."[1] University men, as we have seen, led the way in both aspects of this development.

[1] I am glad to find my own conclusions supported in the excellent survey by Edward E. Lowinsky, "Music in Renaissance Culture," *Journal of the History of Ideas,* Vol. XV (1954), 509–53. See p. 552.

INDEX